# THE MAKING OF THE BRITISH MIDDLE CLASS?

## STUDIES OF REGIONAL AND CULTURAL DIVERSITY SINCE THE EIGHTEENTH CENTURY

EDITED BY

ALAN KIDD AND DAVID NICHOLLS

SUTTON PUBLISHING

First published in 1998 by
Sutton Publishing Limited · Phoenix Mill
Thrupp · Stroud · Gloucestershire · GL5 2BU

British Library Cataloguing in Publication Data
A catalogue record for this book is available from the British Library

ISBN 0 7509 1780 6 (hardback)
ISBN 0 7509 1781 4 (paperback)

*Cover photograph: Tea at Lane Foot, Kendal, 1905, Margaret Shaw, from* Family Album *by John Satchell, Sutton, 1996.*

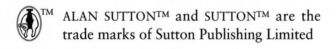
ᵀᴹ ALAN SUTTONᵀᴹ and SUTTONᵀᴹ are the trade marks of Sutton Publishing Limited

Typeset in 11/14pt Sabon.
Typesetting and origination by
Sutton Publishing Limited.
Printed in Great Britain by
MPG, Bodmin, Cornwall.

# CONTENTS

# CONTRIBUTORS

**John Belchem** is Professor of History at the University of Liverpool. He has published widely on nineteenth-century social and political history. His present interests include ethnicity and Irish migration, the cultural history of Liverpool and the modern history of the Isle of Man.

**Stephen Caunce** is Senior Lecturer in history at the University of Central Lancashire. Previous employment includes periods with the University of Leeds, and Kirklees Museums, based in Huddersfield, West Yorkshire. Previous work includes *Amongst Farm Horses: The Horselads of East Yorkshire* (1991) and *Oral History and the Local Historian* (1993). He is currently working on a study of the heavy woollen district of West Yorkshire from the sixteenth to the nineteenth centuries, from which this essay has sprung.

**Michael Dintenfass** teaches history at the University of Wisconsin-Milwaukee. He is currently completing a book about the discourse of individual excellence in the modern British coal industry and is at work on another about the autobiographical writings of historians.

**John Garrard** is Senior Lecturer in the Department of Politics and Contemporary History at the University of Salford. His research interests lie on the borders between social/urban history and political science. His books include *The English and Immigration: English Reactions to Jewish Immigration 1880–1910* (1970); *The Great Salford Gas Scandal of 1887* (1988), and *Leadership and Power in Nineteenth-century Industrial Towns* (1983). He is currently writing a book on *Democratization in Britain 1800–1939*.

**Robert Gray** is Professor of Social History at the University of Portsmouth. He recently published *The Factory Question and Industrial England, 1830–1860* (1996) and is now engaged on a study of middle-class autobiographies.

**Ruth Grayson** is an associate lecturer in history at the Open University. She formerly worked with Dr Alan White at the University of East London on a study of the industrial structure of nineteenth-century Sheffield.

**Nick Hardy** is a postgraduate in the Department of History at the University of Liverpool, researching the social and cultural history of the commercial and entrepreneurial class in nineteenth-century Liverpool.

**Bob Harris** is Senior Lecturer in the Department of Modern History at the University of Dundee. He is author of *A Patriot Press: National Politics and the London Press* (1993), *Politics and the Rise of the Press: Britain and France, 1620–1800* (1996) and of several articles on British politics in the mid-eighteenth-century. He is working on a study of mid-eighteenth-century British politics and political culture, as well as on Scottish radicalism and political communication in the 1790s.

**Alan Kidd** is Reader in History at Manchester Metropolitan University. His publications include: *Manchester* (2nd edn, 1996); *Gender, Civic Culture and Consumerism: Middle-class Identity in Britain, 1800–1940* edited with David Nicholls (forthcoming, 1999); *Cholera and Community: The Proceedings of the Manchester Board of Health 1831–2* edited with Terry Wyke (forthcoming, 1999); and *Self Help, Charity and the State: Poverty and Welfare in Nineteenth-century England* (forthcoming, 1999).

**Brian Lewis** is Assistant Professor of History at McGill University, Montreal. He was brought up in Blackburn and educated at Oxford, Cambridge and Harvard. He is currently working on a book on the middle classes and social stability in Blackburn, Bolton and Preston in the early industrial period.

**R.J. Morris** is Professor of Economic and Social History at Edinburgh University where he has taught since 1968. His published works include *Class, Sect and Party. The Making of the British Middle Class* (1990) and a chapter on 'Associations' in the *Cambridge Social History of Britain* (1990). He was joint editor of *The Victorian City, 1820–1914* (1993) and founding editor of the journal *History and Computing*.

**David Nicholls** is Professor of History and Head of the Department of History and Economic History at Manchester Metropolitan University. He is the author of *The Lost Prime Minister. A Life of Sir Charles Dilke* (1995) and co-editor, with Alan Kidd, of *Gender, Civic Culture and Consumerism: Middle-class Identity in Britain, 1800–1840* (forthcoming, 1999).

**Vivienne Parrott** completed a Ph.D. at the University of Salford in 1992. Her research interests lie in the history and development of lawyers as a professional group, and she is currently investigating the development of legal educational provision. She has delivered papers on this general theme to various academic conferences, and has also written Occasional Papers in the Politics and Contemporary History Series at the University of Salford. An honorary lecturer in the Faculty of Law, she is also Director of Validation Services at the University of Manchester.

**John M. Quail** has had a disorderly career which may be read as narrative, text or cautionary tale. Now fifty-four he has worked as a builder and a bureaucrat. Paladin published his history of the British anarchist movement, *The Slow Burning Fuse*, in 1978. In 1996 he completed a part-time Ph.D. at the University of Leeds on the development of organizational structures and control techniques in large British enterprises. He is currently writing a book on the subject.

**W.D. Rubinstein** is Professor of Modern History at the University of Wales, Aberystwyth. Prior to 1995 he was Professor of Social and Economic History at Deakin University in Victoria, Australia. His works on modern British history include *Capitalism, Culture and Decline in Britain, 1750–1990* (1993).

**Paul Thompson** is Research Professor at the University of Essex and Founder of the National Life Story Collection at the British Library. He is Director of Qualidata and Founder-Editor of *Oral History*. His books include *The Work of William Morris* (3rd edn, 1991), *The Edwardians* (2nd edn, 1992), and *The Voice of the Past* (1978).

**Richard Trainor** is Professor of Social History at the University of Glasgow, where he is also vice-principal and co-director of the Computers in Teaching Initiative Centre for History, Archaeology and Art History. The author of *Black Country Elites* (1993) and of a range of articles on the nineteenth- and twentieth-century aristocracy, middle class and urban élites, he is writing a social history of the British middle class, 1850–1950.

**Michael Winstanley** is Senior Lecturer in History at Lancaster University. He has a special interest in the urban and rural history of north-west England during the nineteenth century, and has published on radical politics, newspaper reporting, the textile factory workforce, housing, retailing and small-scale farming.

# ACKNOWLEDGEMENTS

The essays in this volume began their lives as short papers delivered at a conference on 'Aspects of the History of the British Middle Classes since 1750', held at Manchester Metropolitan University in September 1996. The conference attracted over forty speakers and more than 100 delegates, and the editors gratefully acknowledge the contribution which those who attended made both at the time and in bringing its deliberations to publication. We would like to take this opportunity to thank Keith Nield and Geoffrey Crossick for leading and stimulating debate at the opening and concluding plenaries. The papers selected for inclusion here have been reworked and extended by their authors to take account of the critical debates which they prompted at the conference and to elaborate upon common themes and issues.

A version of Professor Rubinstein's paper has since appeared in *Contemporary British History*. We are grateful to the editor and publishers of that journal for allowing us to reproduce it here.

# INTRODUCTION: THE MAKING OF THE BRITISH MIDDLE CLASS?

ALAN KIDD AND DAVID NICHOLLS

There has been a marked increase in interest in the history of the middle classes in recent years which to some extent mirrors the preoccupation with working-class history in the 1960s and 1970s. Much early historical writing on the middle class tended to follow one or other of two approaches. On the one hand, there was the hagiographical 'Great Man' school characterized by studies of the heroes of a modernizing society; on the other was a more rounded ('Manchester School') model which charted the inexorable rise and triumph of the middle class and whose central tropes were the progress of the state, of liberalism and of industry. Although in many ways quite distinct, the two approaches together constituted a type of celebratory history which, by creating a particular narrative of middle-class progress, itself contributed to that very making which it purported to describe. More recently, the emphasis upon industrial expansion and the triumph of an urban, provincial middle class has been challenged by an altogether different narrative of the trajectory of modern British capitalism, the *leitmotif* of which is the subordination of the industrial middle class to a metropolitan-centred, imperially oriented social formation ('gentlemanly capitalism') comprised of landed, commercial and financial élites. But this later narrative is also now in need of qualification and revision in the light of what we are learning from an increasing number of specialized studies of particular aspects of middle-class life such as wealth and consumption, beliefs and values, gender relations, structural and geographical differences and local peculiarities.[1]

The reappraisal of middle-class history was influenced by the study of the working class in whose wake it trailed, especially by the pioneering advances in class analysis made by the great British Marxist historians (Thompson, Hobsbawm, Hill) and the critical scrutiny to which their work was subjected. These debates within social history culminated in the 1990s in serious disagreements about the continuing utility of many of its hitherto sacrosanct concepts. While working-class history provided much of the terrain upon which these theoretical disputations were conducted, the tardier interest in the history of the middle class meant that it automatically became caught up in them. The present volume therefore appears at an important and exciting moment in the evolution of the historiography of the 'social' and is, indeed, symptomatic of it. This introductory essay will identify some of the key issues, approaches and themes which have arisen and will suggest how the contributions which follow address them in an attempt to move the argument forward. The central problems are encapsulated in the main title of the book and the uncertainties surrounding them by the question mark at its end. 'Making', 'British', 'Middle' and 'Class' each represent hotly contested sites and it is necessary to interrogate them in turn. Let us consider them in reverse order.

I

Social historians have been particularly troubled by whether the concept of class continues to have any heuristic value in understanding social structure. 'Class' has acquired loaded meanings over time that were not apparent in the eighteenth and early nineteenth centuries when the term was interchangeable with others like 'rank' and 'order' (and, to a lesser extent, 'sorts', 'parts', 'interests', 'degrees' and 'stations'), and, it has been argued, these later meanings should not be applied anachronistically to earlier periods. Class began to replace most of the other terms as the principal descriptor of social position from around the mid-eighteenth century and was firmly entrenched by the mid-nineteenth.[2] Over time, a whole collection of definitional and conceptual baggage has become attached to it. Is it best defined in terms of wealth, or occupation, or power, or lifestyle, or some combination of all of these things? And, how many classes can be identified once these variables have been established – two, three, or more? The meanings of class have become increasingly more difficult to unpack as the concept evolved from its primitive sense of classification, that is of an attempt to position individuals within a static social hierarchy, to one in which it signified complex social characteristics and dynamic social relationships. Part of this evolving complexity was the attempt to understand class not only as an objective phenomenon, measurable in terms of income or occupation or some other clearly definable index, but also as one with a subjective component – with consciousness, ideology and language. It is precisely in this latter realm that most of the difficulties have arisen and that the critics of class have moved to reject its conventional usage, which they regard as historicist.

Here, the charge has been led by historians influenced by postmodernism, especially its distrust of teleological grand narratives which employ all-embracing concepts like class, and by post-structuralism, with its attention to language and the nuances of discourse. In contrast to Marxists, who see class power as constituted by the organization and control of the means of production, and language as a site of conflict intricately linked in an interactive way to social structure, postmodernists are concerned with the production of meaning, that is with explaining how discursive categories like class come to be seen as the foundations of knowledge. Class, they suggest, collapses in the face of theoretical conceptions of the self and of identity, not least of gender identities, and of theorizations (the so-called 'linguistic turn') about the ways in which discourse establishes the boundaries of people's ideas and actions. Language is not a neutral medium which reveals some external social reality but is an arbitrary system of 'signs' whose meaning is shaped by power and cultural relationships. In this light, historical writing bears no necessary relation to that which it purports to describe, and is further mediated by the dependence of the historian on sources (usually textual) that are themselves cultural products. The result is a whole range of interpretations and perspectives, the validity of which derives not from the use of evidence but from the moral, aesthetic or political preferences that are invested in them. Discourse establishes the boundaries of ideology; conflict takes place within the limits established by discourse; and change is the product of the articulation of alternative meanings that displace the ascendancy of a hitherto dominant ideology. In sum, if language constitutes our knowledge of the world, then it follows that that knowledge is limited by the capacities of language to describe it. History is no more than a particular form of discourse, comparable to literature, with its own methodological practices and rhetorical devices. The 'truth' about the past is not recoverable. Historians instead engage in the production of a multiplicity of narratives about the past, each dependent upon the employment of a language that is unable to reveal the real world.

There is not space here to expand upon, or engage at length with, the theoretical literature on class, which is now quite extensive,[3] but a couple of caveats are called for regarding the extent to which it has been dislodged from its place in the pantheon of useful historical concepts by the recent interventions. The first concerns the discordance between theory and practice. In discourse analysis, no one, fictive, historical narrative is better than any other. This can lead to relativism and an acceptance of the futility of writing history, except perhaps as an exercise in subjectivism – writing self-referential history or uncovering the ideologies of individuals who produced texts or 'histories' (the power relations hidden beneath their use of knowledge) as a means to supporting or challenging beliefs about meaning. Historians (at least those who heeded E.H. Carr) have long recognized that historical writing cannot provide a 'true' or objective account of the past, only a reconstruction in the present by individuals constrained by the limitations of their own subjectivity and consciousness and by the 'contaminated' nature of the documents and source materials which they use.[4] However, they have usually defended their craft by emphasizing its regard for the empirical approach to evidence, which permits judgements to be made about the merits (for example, in terms of reliability and comprehensiveness) of the source materials used and of the respective narratives based on them. Because of this attention to factual accuracy and a methodological practice which allows for replication and verification, historical narratives are not the same as fictional narratives but have an approximate relationship to a reality which lies beyond the language in which they are couched. Of course, for postmodernists this conventional defence of historical practice will simply not do: it is a realist illusion. There is no truth out there by which to judge historical work, including their own. But, if this defence is unacceptable, what has postmodern theory to offer in its place, at least for the practice of history? How can postmodern historians escape the relativist paradox inherent in discourse theory, namely that they too must be producing fictive narratives which we are not obliged to believe?

The second caveat concerns the novelty of historical approaches inspired by postmodernism and the implications of these approaches for the writing of history generally. Cassandra-like warnings about the 'end of social history' have over-dramatized somewhat the significance of postmodernism for historical practice. Even before the 'linguistic turn', historical writing about class had shifted from what might broadly be termed a 'political-economy' perspective to a 'socio-cultural' one. Behind this was the understandable and laudable desire to avoid the economic determinism which characterized much early writing on class, especially in its cruder Marxist manifestations. Writings on class by British social historians were influenced by E.P. Thompson's seminal study of the English working class. Despite Thompson's claims to demonstrate co-determination in class formation (a class that made itself as much as it was made), the emphasis of his book was very much on the former not the latter, that is on questions of class consciousness rather than structure. British historiography on class was shaped by the questions which Thompson's work posed and has ever since been hinged around this culturalist type of social history. In this regard, then, the interest in language could be seen as following on from an already well-established approach to British social history and much of the so-called 'new cultural history' is rather less novel than its practitioners might sometimes have us believe.[5] Indeed, some of it has been remarkably conventional, if not old-fashioned, once theory gives way to practice. Certainly, this has been the case with some recent writing on nineteenth-century Britain which has turned it into a seamless web, with conflict evacuated from the picture by continuities, personalities restored to centre stage, and in which the 'master narrative' is shaped by politics and constitutionalism. This is 'back-to-the-future' history, its content rather less novel than its theoretical premises might lead one to expect.[6]

There is no need to go to the wall to defend 'class' and it should be abandoned if it no longer serves to illuminate historical inquiry. For the time being, however, the concept remains widely used by historians and will no doubt continue to be so until they come up with a satisfactory alternative. For the purpose of the conference (and this book) class was perceived not as some sort of conceptual straitjacket but as an organizing focus, permitting the several contributors to handle its premises in their own ways, from their disparate standpoints and with due regard for the many qualifications within which each of them might wish to see it hedged. Whatever might be said about the limitations of postmodern histories, the approach they represent affirms the importance of serious investigations of culture and ideas and has attuned historians to a more sensitive handling of language, texts, signs and symbols and to the role of cultural processes in the construction of identity. So, even though it did not of itself initiate it, the critique of class based upon discourse analysis encouraged further the exploration of the multiplicity of identities that shape individuals and their behaviour and thereby contributed to a more sophisticated understanding of ideology and consciousness, and this influence is evident throughout this volume.

The several historians represented here seek in their own ways to explore the significance for social and political behaviour of shared or conflicting forms of identity. These include various cultural practices – religion, voluntary and charitable activities, leisure pursuits, the cultivation of professional status, education, writing and so forth – and their organizational and institutional forms: churches, schools, newspapers, voluntary and charitable associations, socio-cultural networks and professional bodies. Local empirical studies are couched within and implicitly, if not in each case explicitly, acknowledge broader theoretical and historiographical debates about class and about the British middle class in particular. This is not to claim that the contributors reach a consensual position on these vexed issues. They have not been chosen as representatives of a particular approach and they are certainly not of one mind on what can only be described as controversial and perplexing questions. Indeed, their respective standpoints can be located at different points along a spectrum which has regional diversity and localism, occupational subtleties, conflicting identities, economic competition and individualism at one end and political solidarity, national interest, cultural and ideological convergence and class consciousness at the other. These problematic issues, however, are confronted and handled in controlled and informed ways which suggest that, if the recent disabling theoretic incursions into social history are to be surmounted, then social groups or classes must not be treated as fixed categories but as contextually created, constituted and reconstituted through historical eventuation. In other words, the challenge is to describe classes without reifying or hypostasizing them, for the historian has to deal with movement and contingency not abstraction. The close attention paid here to the significance for social and political behaviour of shared forms of identity and to the specificities of time and place are important refinements to our approach to the problem of social categorizations. However, that said, whether class has some sort of priority over the other types of identity or whether they are mutually constitutive, their precise interrelationships and meanings dependent upon chronology and context, or indeed, whether they represent discursive categories that are just as fragile as class, remain unresolved theoretical conundrums that are likely to occupy and divide social historians, including the present contributors, for some time yet.[7]

Too many historically based attacks on class have been constructed from a narrow national focus. In the case of Britain, the comparative quiescence in social relations has often been explained in terms of socio-cultural or idealist mechanisms which are not located within the political economy of British capitalism.[8] At one time, it would have been axiomatic to situate social relations within a broader economic context but, with the ascendancy of the culturalist approach to social history, to do so nowadays smacks of old-fashioned orthodoxy. The result has been the displacement of economic determinism by a form of cultural determinism of varying degrees of sophistication. It seems sometimes as if economic and social historians rarely speak to each other despite having been brought into proximity in (an albeit dwindling number of) university Social and Economic History Departments! Geoffrey Crossick, in his remarks to the conference's concluding plenary, drew attention to this over-concentration on 'cultural' to the neglect of structural issues and to the comparative paucity of empirical studies of property ownership, webs of money, finance and credit, the coercive aspects of class power, work experiences, and sectional links within the middle class. The 'material' and the 'cultural' are interlinked and interact in complex ways and no matter how difficult this relationship might be to theorize, to focus upon one and not the other is, as Perry Anderson once observed, about as satisfactory as one hand clapping.

This interdependence would have been taken for granted twenty years ago and establishing the precise relationships between the constituent elements of a social formation was the ambition of attempts to write 'total' history. The emphasis, in what was primarily a Marxist-inspired project, upon class as the dynamo of social change meant that much of this theorizing took place in the realm of political economy, and due weight was quite often not given to the 'cultural' which was perceived as superstructural or epiphenomenal. As we have seen, the efforts of Thompson and his followers to correct this influenced British social history towards an overly culturalist approach (even though Thompson himself wished to retain a notion of co-determination) to the point where nowadays the 'material' is frequently taken for granted or ignored. Because of this, and despite the postmodernist repudiation of 'structures', it is perhaps necessary to remind ourselves that class relations cannot be adequately understood by reference to domestic factors alone but must take account of changes in the international division of labour and the massive increase in global inequalities since the Industrial Revolution.[9] It is within the macro-economic context of an interdependent global economy that the whole debate about the evolving social structures within the developed capitalist countries must be set. Britain's imperial history has had profound social consequences, not least for the growth, consolidation and outlook of the middle class and for its relations with the working class. Britain has been a most inegalitarian society throughout modern history and British capitalism, far from reducing inequalities, has in fact increased them.[10]

None of this in any way 'proves' the existence of classes, only of economic and social inequalities. But the hard facts about the exigencies of daily material life for the majority of people have so often in recent times been the ghosts at the feast in the debates on class, heavily influenced as these have been in British historiography by a preoccupation with ideas, culture and, latterly, with discourse. Nor does it argue for a return to a reductive Leninist explanation in which superprofits from imperialism somehow act as a bribe to contain working-class militancy. Rather, it is intended to act as a reminder that social relations, however we describe them, cannot be properly understood by reference to social, cultural or political categories alone, but that due regard must be paid to disparities in life opportunities. It is essential to retain some conception of the 'material', and of what Thompson called 'experience', and to recognize that a society with fundamental economic inequalities has problems in reproducing itself. In this regard, questions of power are quintessential, and any concepts which help us to a better understanding of power relations (Marxist, Foucauldian or whatever) remain vital tools for historical investigation.

Indeed, precisely how to theorize the cultural dimensions of power in non-reductive ways is very much at the heart of the current debate on the future of social history. Some of the best of the new social history is making a valiant attempt to grapple with these issues and to avoid both an economic *and* a cultural determinism. For example, Dror Wahrman in his recent book *Imagining the Middle Class* has argued for the existence of a degree of freedom in the space between social reality and its representation. The growth of bourgeois economy and a bourgeois public sphere in the seventeenth and eighteenth centuries does not prevent this 'reality' from being represented in divergent, even incompatible, ways by contemporaries. According to Wahrman, social change predicated some transformation of social consciousness but did not determine it. Nor was it determined by discursive practice. Whether Wahrman's conclusion, that politics was the terrain where various choices between particular conceptualizations of society were contested and where both agency and contingency came into play, succeeds in squaring the theoretical circle is a matter for debate.[11] But his attempt to avoid unilinear narratives and to situate discursive practices in their social and economic context and to recognize the contingent and historic specificity of notions that appear to us to be naturalized and universal, is a tribute to the contribution that the best of the new social history can make to a more sophisticated understanding of the British past. His book is a good example of how recent writing on the middle class has opened up possibilities for social historians sensitive to the importance of discourse analysis but who reject the epistemological conclusions of postmodernism.

II

Defining the qualifying adjective 'middle' is as fraught as defining 'class'. 'Middling sort' and afterwards 'middling' and then middle class came increasingly into use from the mid-eighteenth century onwards to distinguish growing numbers of people from the aristocracy above and the workers below. But, this was an essentially negative usage from which it does not necessarily follow that those in the middle were in any way homogeneous.[12] Whereas the adjectives 'ruling' and 'working' denote functions, 'middle' describes no more than a static position – as John Seed perceptively puts it, 'not something that exists in its own right but a grouping that fails, or refuses, to fit the dominant social division between upper and lower, rich and poor, land and labour'.[13] The problems arise, as with class, when one tries to attach some sort of explanatory, dynamic or heuristic value to the term, that is to see the middle class as a historical agent. There have been social groups situated between the highest and lowest social ranks throughout history. Interest in these middling groups grew in line with their growth in size and in economic and social importance with the rise of capitalism and, especially, of industrial capitalism. By the early nineteenth century, the term was being used to identify the relationship of groups within the productive system.

The term increasingly, therefore, came to have a dynamic meaning within nineteenth-century political economy, not least, of course, in the theoretical work of Karl Marx. In Marx's theoretical schema, with its central emphasis upon the conflict between owners and non-owners of the means of production, the 'middle' at first sight appears to have been evacuated. The problem is partly a semantic one. Marx often used the term bourgeoisie to refer to the ruling class which owned and controlled capital. He recognized, however, that this class embraced older forms of capital such as commercial, mercantile and banking, as well as the newer industrial capital. Unfortunately, the ascription 'middle class' was also often given to urban capitalists, and this term implies subordination in a class hierarchy to an 'upper' class. So, while bourgeoisie – with its original etymological sense of people who live in boroughs[14] – was something of a misnomer for landed aristocrats, likewise 'middle class' was hardly an appropriate description for the banking, trading and industrial plutocrats who were making vast fortunes from the expansion of the new productive processes. It would seem sensible to use 'bourgeoisie' to describe the capitalists who controlled the means of production and captured political power and to reserve 'middle classes' for the intermediate groups spawned by economic growth, attached to and dependent upon capitalism, but at some distance from real power beyond the capacity to trade in ideas, their greatest source of influence. Unfortunately, the historical literature does not use the nomenclature in any such consistent way.

The conceptual problems do not end here. Marx recognized that industrialism created these intermediate 'middle' groups who were neither owners nor exploited workers, but he left unanswered the question as to their ultimate destiny. He sometimes wrote as if they would eventually sink into the proletariat. At other times, he acknowledged their persistent and partially autonomous place within the capitalist social structure. Elsewhere, in his discussion of the rate of profit, he introduced the notion of tendential laws – in this case the tendency of the rate of profit to fall – which can be offset by the strategies of capitalists. Perhaps class polarization should be seen as just such a tendential process – though Marx himself, to the best of our knowledge, was never explicit about this – in which conflict could be meliorated by the attachment in various ways of non-owners to the perpetuation and continued reproduction of capitalism, albeit fated one day to go down with the system as it collapsed under the weight of its ineluctable contradictions. In the absence of any clear direction from Marx on these matters, it was left to his epigones to embellish his theory to explain the persistence of the middle class.

The middle class, then, is stratified, with enormous differentials in power and influence, income and status, between the *haute bourgeoisie* at one extreme and the *petite bourgeoisie* at the other. These differences are compounded by religion, education and politics. Is it possible, therefore, to talk about a middle *class* at all, or should we not think, if we wish to continue to think in terms of class, of the middle class*es*? The picture is further complicated by the fact that individuals do not live out their lives within neat, homogeneous social categories. People move up and down the social ladder, and it is not unusual for individuals to have more than one occupation and source of income. In the seventeenth and eighteenth centuries, the sons of the country gentry came to London to make their fortunes and in time constituted a metropolitan aristocracy scarcely distinguishable from the urban bourgeoisie with whom they shared a metropolitan culture and intermarried.[15] The nineteenth century witnessed further diversification of investments and interpenetration of capital, and on an increasing scale. Landowners exploited the minerals on their estates or invested in the railways that traversed their properties; mill-owners bought country estates; the daughters of wealthy bankers married the sons of aristocrats. Nor was this diversification confined to big capital. Economic expansion impinged on all levels of society creating both upward and downward social mobility. As the middle classes grew in numbers – and Stana Nenadic's estimate for Glasgow of an increase from about 15 per cent of all families in the mid-eighteenth century, to 18 per cent early in the nineteenth, and around 23 per cent by 1861 provides a good indication of just how sizeable this growth was[16] – even the less wealthy might acquire property and status, and the common attachment to property and to the power and influence conveyed by its ownership was a crucial centripetal force, moderating the divisions within the bourgeoisie.

The growth and fluidity of nineteenth-century society must be borne in mind in respect of any attempt to categorize social strata and much ink has been spilt in attempts to analyse the various sub-groups of the middle class. One approach to the members of the middle class who were not big capitalists or significant property-owners (professionals, intellectuals, managers and so on) has been to describe them as representing the separation of 'thinking' work from the process of production, leaving manual workers to execute instructions given by others.[17] In this sense, these groups are understood in terms of the functions or services that they perform for capital and which give them a stake in its reproduction. Alternatively, they have been analysed in terms of their access to and control of cultural or organizational assets as opposed to economic capital.

The professions in particular have attracted a great deal of attention from historians in recent years. At one time they were seen very much as a creature of the industrial revolution and of the expansion of society in the nineteenth century. However, research on the seventeenth and eighteenth centuries has demonstrated their long and important history, not least in terms of their relationship to the state and its evolution, with the church, military and legal professions exerting considerable power and influence for centuries.[18] The rise of Britain as an imperial state was an important factor in the expansion of the professional middle class, though one which has still not been fully charted by historians.

By comparison with the professions, the history of managers has been neglected. The rise of managerial and technocratic élites has conventionally been explained as a necessary by-product of the growth in the scale of modern capitalism from the late nineteenth century onwards. As firms became larger and moved from family control to control by shareholders, as markets and product diversification increased, as the processes of production became more sophisticated, so the need for workers with organizational and technical skills increased. The extent to which these managers evolved into an adjunct of the professional middle class, with credentially controlled entry, or remained dependent upon their firm for their social position, has been a source of some disputation,[19] and the relationship of managers to the middle classes generally requires further study.

The extent of a sense of identity among the *petite bourgeoisie* has been similarly contested. Following the Marx of the *Communist Manifesto*, some historians have seen shopkeepers, artisans, small property-holders, private landlords and white-collar workers as unstable groups, more likely to descend into the ranks of the proletariat than to ascend into the settled middle class above them. Others, however, have been more alert to their coherence and identity and to their survival as a recognizable social stratum. By the 1870s, the term 'lower middle class' was being used frequently in Britain to describe these intermediate groups, whose livelihoods were derived from their employment of their own capital and their own labour, with the family as the centre of economic activity.[20]

At this point, some historians have been inclined to despair at reaching any satisfactory definition of the middle class.[21] How can millionaire financiers, millocrats, farmers, shopkeepers and the like possibly be lumped together in one social category? Is not the search for *a* middle class simply a waste of time and energy? However, while some historians have tended to accentuate differentiation within the middle class, others have preferred instead to emphasize common and unifying characteristics, not least an engagement in broadly the same enterprise, the capitalist enterprise of accumulation and improvement, and to foreground its dialectical relationship with other social classes.[22] Even more fruitful in this regard has been the investigation of social and cultural practices and mores as providing a bridge between the propertied capitalists (the 'bourgeoisie') and the intermediate groups of professionals and managers (the 'middle classes').

Indeed, the focus of attention in consideration of the 'middle' upon what might be called its location in respect of political economy cannot be readily divorced from more broadly social definitions. Even in its early use, 'bourgeoisie' carried derogatory connotations that derived from its employment as a term of contempt. (Lower middle class was used likewise.) This pejorative meaning was present in Marx, perhaps explaining why he settled on the word to describe all capitalists and not just town-dwellers, for it signalled a social and cultural outlook shared by capitalists of all stripes in their fetishism of commodities, and is echoed elsewhere among nineteenth-century intellectuals, for example in the *de haut en bas* strictures of Matthew Arnold on philistinism. The point made earlier about class in general applies with equal force to the middle class in particular – namely, that analysis of middle-class composition derived from apparently 'objective' data relating to wealth, property, income, occupation and so forth must needs be considered together with 'subjective' aspects of social life, such as culture, ideology and politics.

A number of social theorists, notably Pierre Bourdieu and Jürgen Habermas, have been particularly inspirational and influential in this regard. Bourdieu has identified the creation of what he calls 'cultural capital' through the contestation over cultural forms, the outcome of which contributes to the formation of antagonistic classes and to a relationship of dominance and subordination as the control of cultural capital is converted into social power. 'Cultural assets' have, in a sense, to be 'cashed in' in areas of economic life or organizational contexts to release social power. Bourdieu does not, therefore, divorce discourse and symbolic conflicts from struggles over economic and political power as in some cultural history. He retains a conventional Marxist interest in 'economic capital' based around ownership of the means of production, as a source of power and social division. The emergence of cultural capital helped both to distinguish the middle class from the aristocracy but at the same time to mediate their potential conflict, though cultural practices could be a source of division, for example over religion, as well as of cohesion. Most important of all is the way in which this new cultural capital was explicitly drawn upon by the professions – with the institution of formal credentials, the importance of liberal education and so on – to the point where professional middle-class reproduction began to take place via the education system, and was important also in both allowing and denying women (according to profession) access to positions of influence.[23]

Habermas's conceptualization of 'civil society' and the public sphere as a means to understanding how individuals came together to construct new kinds of organization and collective identity and action through discourse and practice has been remarkably influential in historical writing upon the bourgeoisie. It inspired an interest in the local power bases of the middle class. In an important study of the voluntary associations in Leeds, R.J. Morris argued that they were created by the emerging middle class as unitary foci to transcend the great sectional divisions which existed even at a local level and which were encouraged by the aristocracy's domination of church and state.[24] Other institutions which helped shape bourgeois identity in the public sphere were schools and universities, clubs and societies, and looser collectivities such as newspaper readerships. The role of a public sphere in the formation of middle-class identities cannot, however, be divorced from that of the private sphere (especially of the family) in this regard – as Davidoff and Hall's pioneering study of gender identities and the separation of male (public) and female (private) spheres showed.[25]

## III

Some of the recent theoretically informed cultural history has also contributed to a more refined understanding of the third of our titular terms: 'British'. As we have seen, the uncertainties surrounding the employment of grand organizing concepts like class have led to a preoccupation with other sources of consciousness and identity. From this perspective, class is only one of the ways by which a sense of personal and collective identity is arrived at. Other social constructs to which individuals are introduced through cultural practices include gender, generation, religion, race and nation. Two recent books have helped to further our understanding of the last of these, the forging of national identity. In *Britons*, Linda Colley describes the emergence of a distinctive British identity from a melting pot into which had been cast Protestantism, parliamentary democracy, commerce, war with France and empire, while in her study of post-Chartist radical politics, Margot Finn explores what she calls 'the protracted evolution of English national consciousness'. 'Nation' is given equal footing with 'class' in her account of the unravelling of radical politics. What it meant to be 'British' – or English, Welsh, Scottish or Irish – is undoubtedly a question that has been given too little attention, and histories like Colley's and Finn's are important beginnings. Governments certainly recognized the importance of 'nation' in the creation of a sense of identity and sought to mobilize nationalism or chauvinism or jingoism as occasion arose.[26]

However, measuring the success of this, and of the purchase which a feeling of nationhood had upon the individual, is an extremely difficult enterprise. Not only do different and potentially contradictory nationalisms (Welsh, Scottish, Irish, English, ethnic) have to be understood alongside what it meant 'to be British', but an individual's consciousness was affected as well by local and regional loyalties. The essays in this collection demonstrate only too well the complexity of social structures at the local level and the extent of regional and cultural diversity. But this begs the question: how do the variegated local, regional and cultural forms of identity relate to national ones? One conventional answer has been to suggest that the progress of British capitalism has, historically, been influenced by two quite different 'middle classes': a northern industrial middle class and a southern commercial and professional middle class (with affinities with landed capital). The debate on this issue has shaped much of the historiography on class formation, that is on the fourth of our quartet of problematic terms – 'making'.

## IV

Any complete account of the making of the British middle class would require an extremely broad canvas. The development of capitalist relations of production in Britain was a slow process, the origins of which can be traced back to at least the twelfth century. Any such account would have to pay attention to trade and commerce and mercantile accumulation, and to the commercialization of agriculture, and be sensitive to the slow, sporadic, uneven and contextualized nature of its development.[27] There has been an efflorescence of studies in recent years of the pre-industrial middle classes, partly encouraged by an interest in the language of class and early descriptions of social structure. Historians like, for example, Barry, Corfield and Earle have greatly increased our knowledge of the seventeenth- and eighteenth-century 'middling' classes and, by bringing a broader and more balanced perspective to the impact of industrialization on middle-class formation, have contributed enormously to our understanding of that process. Barry has traced the history of early forms of middle-class urban association, Corfield the early emergence and consolidation of the professions, and Earle the rise of the London middle class.[28] The 'peculiarities' of British capitalist development have long been accepted by historians as the product of the dependence of the first nation to industrialize upon the prior introduction of capitalist relations of production in the countryside, and the rapid and massive capital accumulation made possible by Britain's imperial successes in the seventeenth and eighteenth centuries. Where historians have parted company, however, is in assessing the implications of this unique economic trajectory for social and political power.

The traditional account of the rise of the middle classes, which foregrounded the importance of industry, has now, as we indicated earlier, been largely (though not entirely) superseded by an interpretation which sets the northern industrial towns and the rise of the industrial bourgeoisie in an uneasy and subordinate relationship to the commercial and financial centres of southern England, above all London, and which highlights the persistence there of a form of 'gentlemanly capitalism'. This later narrative has been extremely influential – not just in the writing of history, but in national politics where it has informed debate on national economic decline and on measures to encourage industrial recovery. In the emphasis which it places upon two very different middle classes, this interpretation subsumes within it a whole set of dichotomies: north/south; domestic/imperial; making goods/making money; self-made men/gentlemen; failure/triumph; modern/traditional; subordination/hegemony; grammar school/public school; nonconformist/Anglican; provincial/metropolitan.

But the history of middle-class formation is far more complex than such a binary model suggests. For example, it is a mistake to conceive of London as bereft of manufacturing industry. In 1861 almost one million manufacturing workers were employed there – 14.9 per cent of the total for England and Wales. It was an important centre for engineering and shipbuilding, and for numerous consumer industries, such as brewing, silk, printing, tanning and so on. The northern industrial towns for their part had their own commercial, financial and professional groups.[29] Moreover, indices of wealth and property-ownership are not an entirely reliable guide to the distribution of power within British capitalist society. Nor should the hegemony of a southern landed and commercial élite be simply 'read off' from its political control of Parliament. Due weight has to be given to the importance of the local state through municipal government in securing the power and influence of the industrial middle class. And economic, political and sociocultural differences were less pronounced with time as capital investments became more diversified, Parliament was reformed, and the middle class gained entry to the public schools.[30] The debate on the making of the British middle class around the 'two middle classes' thesis is continued in this volume, but several of the contributors here also attempt to move it into new areas. By focusing upon regional differentiation and cultural diversity, or, alternatively, by considering the dissemination of ideas, values and rational knowledge across regional and social boundaries, they seek to transcend the familiar binary model of the social structure and of the cultural history of the middle classes. Geography, economy and occupation recur as factors contributing to differentiation between middling social groups, but as much differences *within* economic and geographical regions as differences *between* them, as in the conventional north versus south paradigm. At the same time, professional men were developing national cultural networks that weakened regional differences, not least that between north and south, a fact which should further caution against an overly simple 'two middle classes' model.

The ambition of the 'making' of the title of this book is not to chart the long history of the British middle class but rather to focus upon that period which saw its most rapid expansion and to raise new questions and cast fresh light upon class formation by emphasizing the importance of specificity and contingency in that process. In sum, neither the editors nor the contributors wish to return to any teleological or unilinear reading of class formation but rather acknowledge the importance of contextualization as demonstrated in the best of the 'new cultural history'. Nor is the concern with regional difference, or with the broad chronology, intended simply to provide the widest possible geographical and temporal coverage – though the editors are conscious of the importance of representing this variety and diversity – but rather to explore the extent to which cultural context is either a localized or a nationally integrated experience or a combination in varying degrees across time and space of both. The implications which a more highly refined sense of structural differentiation, regional diversity and cultural practice have for the conventional history of the middle classes – constructed as it so often has been around the polarities of 'triumph' and 'failure' – should therefore be readily appreciated by the readers of this book. Cultural and regional variety affected political behaviour – what has elsewhere been called, in the respective cases of the middle classes of Peterborough and Leicester, 'cultural receptiveness' versus 'cultural assertiveness'.[31] In the former case, the influence of the region remained pervasive whereas in the latter something like a national position was becoming evident. It is precisely this sort of relationship between the local, regional, specific and contingent on the one hand and the national and general on the other, that the essays in this book pose and explore.

## V

In the first of these essays, Bob Harris re-examines relationships between the eighteenth-century press and the middling sort and in doing so questions as oversimplistic the conventional emphasis upon the rise of the press as mirroring and contributing to the development of a middle class and a middle-class culture. British historiography on the press has been strongly influenced by political questions, but Harris shifts the agenda here to examine in a more systematic way the wider social and cultural significance of the early newspapers. By way of a detailed analysis of content, he is able to demonstrate the problems involved in treating the eighteenth-century press as a principal means by which middle-class social and collective identities were forged. There was, for example, the difficult fact that the middling sort was not exclusively urban (a point emphasized elsewhere in the essays by Caunce and Winstanley). Indeed, urban life was seen by some as a corrupting influence. Moreover, while newspapers did affirm community and collective values, their main concern before 1800 was to present national and international news. Finally, in an attempt to appeal to and secure a broad readership, they were inclined to eschew controversy, especially religious controversy. In sum, instead of shaping a distinctive middle-class identity, the press rather reflected the diversity of a society in great flux, and it was perhaps only in the nineteenth century that it came to play the more directive and less problematized role conventionally assigned to it in historical writing on the development of the British middle class.

The fluidity of eighteenth-century society is a theme also of Steven Caunce's essay. His focus and main source is the autobiography of Thomas Wright, a member of one of the leading entrepreneurial families in the expanding heavy woollen district of West Yorkshire. Wright wrote his *Memoirs* in 1797 and they were published posthumously in 1864. They provide an account of four generations of family life from the mid- to late eighteenth century and reveal the importance of kinship and of non-kinship links, such as community and religion. During his life, Wright was compelled to turn his hand to a multiplicity of occupations – including cloth manufacturer, speculative builder, liquor wholesaler and retailer, shopkeeper and mill accountant – and with variable fortune. Likewise, his kith and kin were largely preoccupied with surviving the exigencies of day-to-day life and, for all their enterprise, not one of them succeeded in founding a business dynasty. Their experiences, therefore, while suggesting a vibrant, local economy do not, in the quasi-urban environment of eighteenth-century West Yorkshire, support the conventional picture of proto-industrial economic development based on merchant enterprise and the exploitation of labour by capitalists. Perhaps better, Caunce concludes, to regard them as middle income rather than middle class. Of course, West Yorkshire may not have been typical of other industrializing regions, but Caunce, like Harris, points to the difficulties of generalizing about the eighteenth-century middling sort or to constructing dogmatic formulas about early class formation.

Nor were the complexities of social structure and class relations confined to the more rural areas of Yorkshire. In the case of Sheffield, for example, the conventional emphasis upon the close and socially stabilizing relationship between masters and men in an industrial structure of small workshops is here questioned by Ruth Grayson. There were significant differences in the size of firms in nineteenth-century Sheffield and class relationships were complicated by the increase in the number of small factors and merchants who established an extensive control over capital and credit networks in the city and who, by the end of the depression of 1837–43, were coming to exercise considerable influence in local economic and political affairs. Sheffield's 'little masters', far from being a rising middle class were, in general, outworkers dependent upon these factors for finance. The system of small workshops, therefore, was fostering exploitation of the former by the latter, rather than the close relationship of masters and men of the conventional picture. Because outwork and not the factory system was more typical of nineteenth-century industrial Britain, Grayson's observations have a relevance for understanding class relationships beyond their direct applicability to Sheffield.

If a merchant and banking élite was particularly influential within the rising middle class of an industrial centre like Sheffield, then one would expect it to be even more so in a commercial port like Liverpool. In the nineteenth century Liverpool was England's second commercial city after London, and yet the story of its middle class has been comparatively neglected. John Belchem and Nick Hardy set about the task of remedying this deficiency in their account of the cultural formation of Liverpool's commercial élite – of how local identities and social networks were constructed to span political and religious divisions among its gentlemanly capitalists. In view of what has been said already about regional and cultural diversity, it perhaps hardly needs reiterating that generalizations about the Victorian middle class based on one locality are not easy, in the particular case of Liverpool because of the presence of a local Irish middle class, but also because of its commercial, non-industrial character and the desire of its élite to forge an identity that distinguished it from the industrial middle class of Manchester and the rival commercial class of London.

Brian Lewis too is concerned with the relationship between the Lancashire middle class and the old power structures centred on London but his focus is upon industry not commerce and, although he registers the importance of Dissenting religion in the forging of a collective identity among the north-west middle class, upon political, rather than cultural, languages and networks. In a close study of the radical bourgeoisie of Blackburn, Bolton and Preston from the late eighteenth to the mid-nineteenth century, he explores the ways in which it built a narrative which defined it in opposition to the old ruling bloc but which at the same time strove to preserve social stability. The adaptability of the state to bourgeois interests and relations between middle-class and popular radicalism are vital parts of this equation. Identities were shared across classes and divisions existed within classes. The bourgeoisie was not a unitary actor and its multiple voices came to form 'the most critical aspect of the formation of modern Britain'. It was this very diversity emanating from a disunited bourgeoisie that, paradoxically, accounts for its hegemony, which was not dependent upon united class action. The variety of organization and ideology was a sign of strength not weakness. Lewis therefore eschews a model of class domination and power. Instead, lack of class unity opened up the possibilities for consensus and accommodation and underpinned an hegemony that had to be perpetually renegotiated.

In the next essay, which completes a trio on early nineteenth-century Lancashire, Michael Winstanley examines the neglected question of just who owned urban property and explores the importance of property relations for middle-class social formation and political consciousness. He shows that the bulk of the burgeoning middle class of Lancashire in the first half of the nineteenth century were occupiers rather than owners of property, and that this was a major factor in influencing middle-class political behaviour. The importance of occupation could be seen, for example, in the terms of the 1832 Reform Act and in the qualifications for membership of local government bodies. To illustrate his general argument, Winstanley dissects the membership of Oldham's Police Commission between 1827 and 1848, using his analysis to draw conclusions about how local power was sustained and negotiated.

The disposition of property is central too to the next essay, although in R.J. Morris's case, the focus is upon the transfer of property at death as revealed by a sample of wills and intestate property of Leeds' middle class brought for probate in the early 1830s. He shows how the middle-class passing on of property was underpinned by the principle of 'gendered equity', though the manner in which equity was maintained differed, with men receiving their inheritance in the form of capital and women as income flow. This method of property transfer distinguished the middle class from the aristocracy (primogeniture and entail) and from will-makers on the margins of the middle class, including women, who were inclined to be more discriminating when it came to disposing of their property. Morris distinguishes three ways of conceptualizing property – as 'things', 'categories' or 'real property' – which, he shows, led to very different approaches to achieving equity. He introduces us as well to what he calls the 'urban peasant', a possibly even more oxymoronic conception than the 'rural bourgeoisie' encountered elsewhere in this collection and a further illustration of the fine distinctions that are called for when describing complex societies in transition and flux.

Of course, this is not to gainsay the importance of broad generalizations in social classifications; as Richard Trainor reminded us at the conference, historians tend to be either 'lumpers' or 'splitters', and in the case of the middle class it is perhaps easier to operate as a 'lumper' when writing about its more recent history. Certainly, historians have felt more comfortable in using broad-brush terminology once we pass into the latter half of the nineteenth century. They have been more inclined to accept that classes were made by this time and have accordingly turned their attention more to the relationships within or between them. There is less emphasis upon the local and provincial and the distinctiveness of urban élites and more interest in the development of patterns of national life and culture. The focus tends to shift from questions about whether or not a middle class existed and how best to describe the middling members of society, to a concern with its constituent parts and to the roles which these played in the economic, political, social, and cultural life of modern Britain. Historical interpretations have been inflected by the relative weight attached to the respective contributions made by the several sections of the middle class – professionals, managers, industrialists and financiers – in this story. As we saw earlier, the most influential of these interpretations argues that the industrial middle class has been subordinate to a coalition of 'gentlemanly capitalists' consisting of a southern financial élite aligned with professional and landed interests. The remaining essays explore some of the central themes of this particular narrative from new and different angles.

Regional identity could, as several of the contributions considered so far show, assist in the creation of class identity at the local level in the early nineteenth century but in doing so it might complicate any sense of national class identity. Robert Gray's essay on the industrial towns suggests how, as we move into the second half of the century, this important ways from the dailies or tri-weeklies, as did papers which devoted most attention to domestic, political and foreign news from those papers, such as John 'Inspector' Hill's mid-century the *London Advertiser, And Literary Gazetteer*, which attempted 'to bring Entertainment from the Parties of the Great, to People less exalted above the common level of Mankind'.[10] Similarly, provincial newspapers differed in several important ways from their metropolitan counterparts. There was also change in form and content over time, with, for example, reports of parliamentary debates rapidly assuming a very important position in the press from the early 1770s.[11] Fitting the proliferation of newsprint which the eighteenth century witnessed into a single overarching interpretative frame risks, therefore, distortion or oversimplification. On the other hand, there were important features common to most newspapers in this period, not least in respect of the sources and types of information and comment published. Newspapers of the eighteenth century were even more constituted as a common circuit of communication than they are today, and it is this, together with the absence of a similar survey, which provides the justification for the approach adopted here. Hopefully, it may also act as a spur to other scholars to undertake their own, more narrowly focused investigations.

The term 'middling sort' also requires some explanation. As already referred to, the nature and identity (or identities) of this group are currently the subject of much research and debate among students of this period. Here the term is used as an umbrella category to refer to the expanding but disparate range of people who occupied the spaces in society between the lower orders and the landed élites. This is admittedly a very loose usage, but it is one that reflects the ways in which the term was often deployed in the eighteenth century. Contemporaries knew there was a middling sort, but they struggled to give precise definition to it.[12] Some sought to define them by what they were not – the upper sort or the lower orders – but nearly always there was room for disagreement about whom this meant. Other commentators, often politically motivated, sought to define the middling sort in terms of a series of values or patterns of income and expenditure. 'Estimate' Brown, for example, defined the 'middle station of life' in terms of its security and the mass of private and public virtue present among its ranks.[13] As for the more well-known Dissenting radical Richard Price, for Brown the exemplary member of the middling sort was someone not infected by the corrupting influences of city life, a fact which should alert us to the dangers of making simplistic assumptions about radicals necessarily being spokesmen for a rising urban middle class in the later eighteenth century.[14] Yet, even this very brief summary is to exaggerate the coherence and clarity of contemporary comment. As Peter Earle has suggested, 'middling meant different things at different times to the writers who employed it and was probably understood in a variety of ways by contemporaries who read their books'.[15] In short, it was a group which was not exclusively urban – it also included farmers, an increasingly affluent and important section of eighteenth-century society – and the boundaries of which were imprecise, both at the lower and upper ends. How this section of society (or important groups therein) saw themselves, or were seen by others, is something which this chapter aims to explore from the perspective of the newspaper press.

The deep imprint that the middling sort left on newspapers can, as referred to at the outset, at one level be seen simply as another facet of the broad-based and increasingly cumulatively impressive contemporary economic progress. The growth of the press was, to a significant degree, dependent on the same gathering economic forces which were working to transform large areas of British economic, social and cultural life from the later seventeenth century, and of which members of the middling sort were some of the principal authors and beneficiaries. Recent general studies of the press have made much of this ground familiar, and it is unnecessary to re-examine it in detail here.[16] Several points do, nevertheless, deserve special emphasis. Firstly, it was the middling sort who represented the major source of growing demand for newsprint in eighteenth-century Britain. This is not to ignore the fact that members of the social and political élites continued to include some of the most avid of newspaper readers in this period, or the fact that skilled artisans and shopkeepers had increasing access to newspapers. But without the capacity and desire of growing numbers of the middling sort to read and to purchase newspapers, their eighteenth-century rise would have been less rapid and less impressive. This was a function of numbers, disposable incomes and the relative cost of eighteenth-century newspapers. It is also a reality which is underlined when we recall the types of products and services usually advertised in newspapers in this period – luxuries of various sorts, property, and relatively expensive entertainments and services – together with the steadily increasing importance of advertising to the press from the 1730s.[17]

Secondly, it was the commercial ambitions of men and a few women (usually widows) of middling rank that provided the major impetus behind the growth of the press. Before the 1790s, relatively few papers were established for primarily political reasons. As far as the metropolitan press is concerned, a small number of largely essay-style papers, for example, the *Craftsman* or John Wilkes's *North Briton*, were set up by politicians, and a larger number were subsidized by politicians at different times.[18] The former were often short-lived, especially when they achieved negligible commercial success or because of changed political circumstances. As far as the latter are concerned, by the later eighteenth century, it is questionable whether subsidies had the importance that some have attributed to them.[19] In the case of most papers, booksellers and printers and other men of middling status – for example, publishers, theatre managers and auctioneers – saw in these opportunities for profit, as well as ways of promoting their other businesses.[20] It was also profit and not subventions that determined the stance and contents of most London papers. Outside London, political motivations only became of primary importance in the founding of newspapers in the 1790s and then only in a minority of cases.[21]

The relationships between newspapers and the middling sort were, thus, close ones, at the points of supply and demand, and newspapers were for the most part products of the commercial ambition and energies of individuals from the middling sort. But what views of society and of the middling ranks did the press create? And how did newspapers serve, if at all, as instruments in the definition and articulation of new social identities?

As already emphasized, few attempts have been made to impose any pattern or meanings on the multitudinous social, economic, and cultural news and comment carried on the pages of eighteenth-century newspapers. A notable exception, however, is a collaborative article by Stephen Botein, J.R. Censer and Harriet Ritvo. These historians have compared a number of British newspapers from the central decades of the century with several of their French counterparts, seeking thereby to throw light on the different perspectives on society the respective presses offered.[22] They suggest that the contents of most British newspapers conveyed a view of society which emphasized the influence and importance of the middling sort, as well as one which strongly endorsed upwards mobility. A common thread binding many of the different elements of the contents together was commerce or a sensitivity towards the importance of commerce and commercial interests. For example, they point out that foreign news – a hugely important feature of news reporting throughout the eighteenth century – was often reported in terms of its consequences for trade and commercial interests. Unlike in French papers, individuals of middling rank were also frequently the subjects of praise in the British press, whereas the nobility were frequently criticized. In so far as the latter received a more favourable press, it was as patrons or supporters of charity or enterprises that were often controlled or created by men of middle rank or as the 'benevolent lords of the traditional countryside'. The heroes of the English press were local functionaries, members of the local civic élites, not the landed élites. As for the bulk of the population, the lower orders featured as criminals or as proper objects for the enlightened benevolence or intervention on the part of their betters. Summing up, they write:

> Despite discordant and threatening behaviour from members of other groups, the English-language press at the middle of the eighteenth century presented a positive image of an independent and thriving middle order of society – respected and respectable. It was an image that the publishers and editors themselves epitomized in their own entrepreneurial activity and that their readers could both recognize and emulate. . . .[23]

Aspects of this portrayal of the contents of the eighteenth-century press can be endorsed, accepting that what we are doing here is trying to fit a multiplicity of newspapers into a single, general frame. Just as newspapers were dependent on the gathering forces of economic progress for their growth, so they were, in various ways, chroniclers of these forces and their impact. The pervasiveness of commercial information in the provincial press has been emphasized separately by Jeremy Black and Geoffrey Cranfield.[24] Ship news, advertisements, data on prices at important markets – aspects of newspaper content which assumed ever greater prominence as the century progressed – all helped, as Kathleen Wilson has recently very powerfully argued, to create in the press a vision of Britain in which the national interest was identifiable with trade and in which commerce and goods served to link together, in increasingly visible and substantial ways, the different parts of Britain's expanding empire and various of the peoples who inhabited them.[25] It was especially true in respect of papers published in important port towns, for example Liverpool, Bristol or Glasgow. 'Commercial people', as the *Edinburgh Weekly Journal* once called them,[26] were seen as a very important element of newspaper readership throughout the press and papers responded accordingly. Reporting of legal cases in several papers was clearly influenced in part by their perceived interest for individuals involved in commerce or business.[27] Much domestic and foreign news, in addition to the data on trade, stock and product prices referred to above, was also included with an eye to the interests of merchants and traders.[28]

More generally, economic change provided the press with much copy. In this context, the press gave frequent expression to contemporary enthusiasm for 'improvement', or progress conceived of in social and cultural terms as well as economic and technological ones. The ideology and ethos of improvement were at various moments and in a wide cross-section of newspapers vigorously endorsed and promulgated. In 1790, an important voice of later eighteenth-century provincial radicalism, the *Sheffield Register*, declared that 'every article [in its pages] which relates to the improvement or advantage of Agriculture, cannot but prove highly serviceable to the community at large'.[29] The pages of the press also contained a substantial amount of material on important economic debates, on issues such as transportation, enclosure, the market in grain and foodstuffs and the effects of new technology.[30] The general impression created by such material is often one of endorsement of change and the potential for change, of a society being constantly reshaped, and, especially in the later eighteenth century, of ever quickening economic activity.[31]

The lower orders, as Botein, Censer and Ritvo suggest, appeared in newspapers in ways which served to distance them from the reader. Nicholas Rogers has recently emphasized that during the crime wave which coincided with the end of the War of the Austrian Succession, press reporting served to reinforce class perceptions of crime. 'If newspapers chose to focus on violent crime', he writes, 'they also chose to emphasize the vulnerability of the wealthy.'[32] As well as criminals (and threats to the wealth and security of the better off), the lower orders commonly appeared in the guises of the hapless victims of misadventure or the beneficiaries of the benevolence of their betters. They were also the source of a constant stream of 'amusing' or 'diverting' tales, often serving to affirm the rational and superior judgement of the reader. Typical was the following paragraph from the London press, reprinted in the *Ipswich Journal* on 16 February 1754:

> Last Thursday Morning a shoemaker in Tuttle Street, Westminster, coming down Stairs, told his Family that he had dreamed he had fallen into a Trance, in which he continued eight Days, and he recommended to his Wife, that if he should die first, she would take care to keep him eight Days unburied; and in ten minutes after dropt down dead, and his Relict is determined to observe his dying order.

Members of the lower orders were also usually represented as incapable of constructive independent action; the accent was always on dependency and subservience. Direct action on their part was viewed with disapproval if not downright hostility. It was also portrayed as ineffective or unnecessary (or both), even when, as in the case of many food riots, newspaper editors and readers shared their hostility towards the middlemen whose monopolizing activities were seen as the cause of much hardship and shortage.[33]

Hostility towards the nobility or aristocracy in the press usually took the form of criticism of the 'fashionable world', a sphere of metropolitan society that provided a huge volume of material for eighteenth-century press reportage and comment. It is worth emphasizing that not all (perhaps even most) of such comment was critical. As Roy Porter puts it, London, or 'town', represented 'an addictive imaginary space' for the Georgians.[34] Through its fashions, its excesses, its bewildering array of often exotic entertainments and diversions, and its many social successes and victims, it provided an unceasingly fascinating drama. Where the tone was critical or mocking, this was also far from solely directed at those members of the landed élites who chose to frequent the clubs, pleasure haunts and parties of the West End. Some of the most savage comment was reserved for members of the middling ranks who sought to emulate their social superiors. Such people could easily find themselves portrayed as grotesques, their overbearing physicality (or even bestiality), their smell and deformities, offering a tell-tale counterpoint to the fashions in which they sought to disguise their origins.[35] Yet from the 1750s, usually under the impact of failure or perceived failure in war – pre-eminently the War of American Independence –

many papers did print letters and comment, usually from London sources, attacking the excesses of 'the great' as part of a more wide-ranging critique of luxury and political corruption. As leaders of society and of fashion, it was easy to blame 'the great' for the perceived spread of enervating luxury and dissolute habits through the rest of society.[36] The implicit contrast, however, often seems to have been with an older set of values, those of hospitality and benevolent paternalism as much as with middling sobriety, responsibility or patriotism. As we will also see later, it is easy to find material in newspapers that endorsed the position of the landed classes as leaders of local communities and of society more generally and which provided reminders of their prestige and splendour.

How were the middling sort represented in newspapers? A recent claim that they were continuously the object of praise in the press exaggerates matters.[37] Nevertheless, they did regularly appear on its pages and in ways which indicated approval, and which emphasized their social standing. Notices of the deaths and marriages of individuals of the middling sort frequently appeared in newspapers of the period. In April 1782, the *Bath Chronicle* reported:

> Saturday last the remains of William Denison, esq, were carried from this city in great funeral pomp to be interred at Leeds, of which place he was one of the most considerable merchants, and is said to have died worth half a million of money, the greatest part of which is left to his brother.[38]

Less exalted (or at least less wealthy) members of the middling sort also made their way on to the pages of the press. Earlier in the same month, the list of local deaths in the *Bath Chronicle* included a gardener, a surgeon and apothecary, and the wife of a maltster.[39] The pattern in other provincial and London papers was similar. John Shebbeare, acerbic Tory-Patriot polemicist and writer, cast his not inconsiderable scorn on the phenomenon in his novel, *Matrimony*, published in 1755. An attack on the Marriage Act (1753), the novel gave Shebbeare another opportunity to rehearse various of the many hatreds he entertained. At one point early on in the novel, Shebbeare referred to a paragraph 'which had been printed in the Daily Papers, telling the world that important Piece of Intelligence, that Yesterday died Mr Thomas Stem, an eminent Tobacconist; which word eminent, in all such instances, means nothing but rich'.[40]

If the interests, marriages and deaths of many members of the middling sort made a large impression on the contents of newspapers, we are still some way from establishing how far the press served as an instrument for fixing a sense of collective identity among the middling ranks (or indeed any section of society) or the sorts of specific social identities which the press endorsed either explicitly or implicitly. Beginning with the first question – that of the influence of the press on the formation of social identities – there are a number of levels on which this can be approached. As Charles Clark has pointed out, the very techniques of putting together a newspaper in the eighteenth century, the abundant miscellany which characterized their content, may have increased their 'representative' function. Printers and editors made limited attempts, certainly before the end of the century, to define or prioritize between what was newsworthy. Concerned primarily to fill their papers and constrained by the rudimentary technology of the hand press, they adopted a posture of what we might term pragmatic eclecticism – they tended to use what came to hand in the order it came to hand. Because of this, better than any other element of the culture of print, newspapers represented communities – or at least sections of them – in all their variety. As Clark has written:

> For those who read them in their own time, they built community solidarity and affirmed common values by combining materials from all walks and levels of life and binding them with the ideology that was articulated only in the more formal essays and letters that took an easy place amongst the reports of ordinary affairs.[41]

Other printed media – books, broadsides, and pamphlets – with their necessarily selective and more narrow concerns, could not achieve this.

Because newspapers held out the possibility of regular communication with readers, their impact was also cumulative – again unlike other contemporary forms of print culture. Moreover, they also served to link reader to paper and reader to reader, as well as to a series of larger worlds – the world of national political debates and conflicts and, beyond that, the world of international rivalries and hostilities. The press may have played, in this way, an important and distinctive role in posing questions about loyalties and belonging.

The newspaper was both a facet and symbol of the increasing linkages in the eighteenth century, physical and imaginative, between individual localities and other parts of Britain and the world beyond.[42]

Before 1800 this was something that was mostly implicit in the function and contents of newspapers. The majority of papers, or their editors and compilers, made very limited efforts to define or clarify what constituted local interest or community. This feature of their contents represents an important difference between the provincial newspaper of the eighteenth century and some of their nineteenth-century successors, although it is a difference that often leads nineteenth-century historians to be unduly dismissive of the press of the previous century.[43] The 'provincialism' which John Cookson has seen as such an important strand in the liberal press of the early 1800s, and which is often regarded as an important aspect of a distinctively middle-class consciousness, is discernible in outline in some provincial papers at an earlier stage, but only in outline.[44] A number of historians have emphasized the role of the press in reflecting and creating a distinctive provincial public opinion in the later eighteenth century. Money, for example, has written of a number of papers taking 'an intelligent and active part in the development of the region', in this case the West Midlands.[45] Barker has more recently articulated a similar view, arguing that provincial newspapers relied on their ability to create distinctive 'local' selections of news to create sales and thus survive in an increasingly competitive environment.[46] Such emphases can partly be explained in terms of a reaction to earlier depictions of eighteenth-century provincial papers. Yet it is necessary to be careful about how we represent this and its significance. Crucial at this stage were the various ways in which newspapers connected localities to London and, through London, to national concerns. Any tendencies towards regionalism in the press were strongly restrained by the ways in which papers mirrored wider trends towards identification with metropolitan norms and values. A further point, perhaps an obvious one, although one that is often insufficiently emphasized in this context, is that printers and editors saw their task as first and foremost furnishing the most complete and up-do-date national and international news that they could. It was this that editors tended to emphasize when appealing for readers or condemning competitors.[47] In so far as innovation was an aspect of newspaper production in the later eighteenth century, it was in terms of the collection and presentation of news, which meant international and national news for the most part.[48] What constituted news might well be affected by local interests, or perceptions of these, and here newspaper editors or printers needed to select carefully and skilfully. Yet, even here, the impression which many papers leave is of a great demand for fast and accurate news of major national and international events – parliamentary debates, the course and conditions of war and diplomacy. It was a demand that was no less strong at the end of the century than at the beginning; if anything, under the impact of the French Revolution and the French Revolutionary Wars, it was more so.[49]

Most eighteenth-century provincial newspapers also circulated across a wide geographical area; some even did so on a national basis.[50] It was partly for this reason, that most printers or editors made few or no attempts to divide their readership. Rather they sought, as the editor of the *Edinburgh Evening Courant* put it in 1782, 'to please every class of reader'.[51] The *Observer*, boasted at its foundation in 1791 that 'to every rank and order will the OBSERVER have its separate recommendation'.[52] Little attempt was made to differentiate between the contents in terms of importance, although it is clear that domestic political and foreign news took precedence when they were available. During parliamentary sessions, major debates could easily take up over a quarter of total space available in a paper. The aim for editors and printers was to appeal to the widest possible readership. Many printers also seem to have acted as agents of what Jeremy Black has called 'consensualization'.[53] They sought, in many cases, to downplay important local disagreements and sources of controversy. This was not true of all papers, and partisan allegiance was a growing feature of the press in the later eighteenth century, but it continued to be true of a significant number. Moreover, even those papers that displayed a definite political alignment refused to print matter they deemed too controversial; they appear to have set quite tight limits within which partisan debate was acceptable. Religious controversy, for example, was frequently eschewed.[54] This further impeded any role for the press as an instrument for defining or reinforcing a sense of collective or group identity, narrowly construed.

The fact that many (perhaps most) newspapers were aimed at overlapping groups of readers clearly complicates any assessment of their function as carriers or creators of shared beliefs. It also underlines another important fact about the contents of papers in this period – their diversity and miscellaneous nature. The aim of many editors was precisely this: 'Miscellany' was, as one editor put it, 'the soul of a Newspaper.'[55] As a result newspapers gave full expression to the often conflicting and discordant voices and attitudes present in contemporary propertied and literate society. Because of this, they are a peculiarly faithful mirror of contemporary perceptions and debates at this level of society, as well as the ambivalence and ambiguity with which contemporaries often responded to contemporary social and economic change. Thus, while newspapers often printed, as we have seen, items which endorsed a world increasingly driven by commerce and innovation, it is important equally not to underestimate the amount or range of material in their pages which expressed concern about modernity and its unwanted social consequences, which could be construed as displaying admiration for rank and in particular the titled nobility, or which drew on overtly religious perceptions and values to question worldly or unduly materialist values. There is not space here to illustrate this in detail, but a few examples can be brought forward. With regard to the Edinburgh press, the array of attitudes and values expressed in the 1770s and '80s in one of its most enduring and important papers, the *Caledonian Mercury*, has been examined by John Dwyer. He has emphasized how patriotic improvers, such as John Knox, George Dempster and James Anderson, and projects of economic improvement, such as the Highland Society – which sought to establish manufactures and fishing villages in the Highlands – were celebrated in the pages of this paper, but equally writers who remained more anxious about less beneficial effects of modernity also found their place. He has also argued that never was there any suggestion that the national community was not led by the nobility.[56] The precocity of economic development in Glasgow and its environs by the 1780s, and the relatively less important role of members of the nobility and gentry in local affairs, could hardly fail to be reflected in the contents of that city's papers. For example the *Glasgow Courier*, founded in 1791, gave full expression to the burgeoning economic confidence of the city and its environs. Yet it too found time to praise various members of the landed élites for their conduct; nor did it articulate any hostility to land and rank.

In England, the Bath press and other papers closely linked to resort or county towns – which constitute a fair proportion of the total – as well as the London press, regularly chronicled the comings and goings, illnesses, births, deaths and lavish funerals of the notable. Often such reports constituted a high proportion of domestic news in the papers. In the early 1780s, the *Bath Chronicle* included a section entitled 'Recent Arrivals', which listed new visitors in order of social rank. Several London papers in the mid-eighteenth century contained lists of prominent guests at various resort towns and notables present at major race meetings.[57] Local celebrations of births and marriages in great families were frequently reported in considerable detail in provincial papers, as were major acts of philanthropy by their members. For example, the *Leicester and Nottingham Journal* reported on 11 October 1788:

> This day (Friday) will be celebrated at Stapleford, in this county, the birth-day of Lord Sherrard (the son and heir to the Right Honourable the Earl of Harborough), who will then attain the 21st year of his age. We also hear that the noble Earl has sent money and liquor in great plenty, to all the towns belonging to him; his indisposition (which the whole country must lament) preventing him from seeing so great a concourse of the populace as would otherwise have attended.

Such items provided constant reminders of the prestige and influence of the landed élites, and of the prestige their involvement and presence conferred on activities and places.

How far items about the titled and the 'bon ton' worked to 'distance' readers from their subjects or promote identification with them is difficult to say. Towards the end of the century, remarkably detailed descriptions of high society functions were carried in the press, including the balls at Court held annually on the King's and Queen's birthdays. (Earlier in the century, these events had attracted only very limited notice in the press.) Very widely reprinted in different newspapers, the reports chronicled attendance, the lavish surroundings, and even more lovingly the clothes worn at the pinnacle of polite society. Typical was one which appeared in the *Bath Chronicle* of 28 March 1782, and which described in considerable detail a reception given at Devonshire House for the Prince of Wales and Duke and Duchess of Cumberland. The report, which extended over almost two columns of the paper, included information on the contents of the picture-room and drawing-room and four other rooms laid out as supper-rooms. A short extract conveys the general tone:

> The appendages of the confectionary consisted of temples, Turkish pavilions, fountains, triumphal arches, and colonnades, in every magnificent stile. The windows of the different rooms were illuminated by lights, suspended on festoons of foliage; the avenues, with cut crystal girondeles and Or Molu branches.

Earlier in the century, the *Evening Advertiser*, a London tri-weekly, included the following item:

> We hear that some of the most eminent of the Italian Masters at Rome are at present employed by the Earl of Northumberland to copy five of those celebrated pictures of Raphael, in the Vatican, amongst which, one is the Assembly of the Gods, 30 feet by 12, which are to be placed in the great Room in Northumberland House, now finishing in the most superb and elegant Taste, which will, when compleated, vie with (if not excell) any Thing of that kind in Europe.[58]

Through the press, members of the social élite, like members of the middling ranks, were becoming more visible as a group and on a wider scale. From the contents of the press, it would be wrong to conclude that this was necessarily something that they should have feared, even had they been minded to, which is not to say that some contemporaries did not see their behaviour as requiring reform.[59]

Newspapers, Kathleen Wilson has recently written, 'were central instruments in the social production of information'.[60] They presented their readers with a huge amount of admittedly often very disparate information and comment about contemporary society. Much of this material was banal, even trivial. Oliver Goldsmith counselled the *Public Ledger*, a London paper founded in 1760, to include a survey of new publications since this would be much more interesting 'than a journal of battles or negociations, an elopement, or a broken leg, the marriage of a celebrated toast, or the adventures of a mad cow'.[61] Much of this material also resists easy categorization or characterization in social terms.

How this material was read and understood by contemporaries is also likely to prove elusive. Readership and the effects of readership are usually the missing element in discussions of newspaper content and for good reason. We simply lack much evidence about how contemporaries responded to most items in the press. Contemporary images of readership are various. Much reading took place in public places, taverns, coffee houses, clubs and shops; it was part of a spreading culture of discussion and argument. On the other hand, diaries, travel accounts and letters make clear that for some newspaper readership was an individual pleasure.[62] Whichever was the case, we have to acknowledge, along with Roger Chartier and others, that the consumption of print is active and not submissive and that different people are likely to have found different meanings in its contents.[63]

Yet despite this, newspapers did contain in this period a great amount of material that, either explicitly or implicitly, reflected and endorsed the broadening and stretching of propertied society that took place in the eighteenth century. New and diversifying forms of wealth and property made a strong impression on both the form and content of newspapers. At one level, this is unremarkable: newspapers were, as has been emphasized, part of the same complex of forces. Newspapers also conveyed an impression of a society increasingly driven or shaped by the values of the market or, more simply, sometimes by money. Advertisements for property and even for places in the Church of England carried in the pages of the papers might be seen as full of meaning in this context. So too might items like the following: 'This week a Waiter at a Coffee house near the Royal Exchange was married to a young lady of 7,000*l* fortune.'[64] Marriage, the press appeared to declare, represented a lottery in which great fortunes could be won. But perhaps more importantly, newspapers also reinforced conceptions of contemporary society that emphasized fluidity, movement and change. By reaching out to encompass different sections of propertied society, rural as much as urban, by not differentiating between them, they implicitly, as well as explicitly in some cases, endorsed middling ambitions and activities. They also probably helped to widen conceptions of gentility or even to shift in subtle but important ways the meanings of gentility. The newsworthy were more than the traditional élites.

The press occupied a cultural space where élite and non-élite cultures met and became hopelessly intertwined. It was partly for this reason, as well as because of the amount of social and sexual scandal that passed across its pages, that the press aroused the anger of contemporary moralists like Jonas Hanway or Vicesimus Knox. (Hanway lambasted the press in one pamphlet as a 'pamper'd child'.[65]) But at the same time, through its contents and its form, the press served to underline the chasm between the literate and judicious section of society that made up newspaper readers and the rest – the commonalty. For all these reasons, newspapers may have had a peculiar and distinctive significance for the middling sort in the eighteenth century, quite apart from the more prosaic and almost certainly more pressing motivations for reading them – the need for information and news.

It is, however, hard to see newspapers in this period, through their non-political contents at least, as having helped to foster a strong sense of collective identity among the middling sort or having facilitated the elaboration of a set of values that we can meaningfully call middle class. There is a danger, in this context, of extrapolating backwards from later developments. Some newspapers, particularly provincial papers, did emerge in the quarter century after 1800 as powerful vehicles for expressing a middle-class provincial opinion that was different in scale and nature from the provincial opinion which existed in the 1770s and '80s, let alone earlier in the century. The contours of early nineteenth-century provincial opinion, and the distribution of power and influence which it reflected, were, however, notably different from those which existed in the Britain of the last quarter of the eighteenth century.[66] The press which emerged alongside this changing opinion, or at least elements of it, was also changing in form and function – political motivations were more important in the establishment and running of papers – and in its relationship to local opinion, which was much more directly reflected in its pages.[67] The discontinuities in this context can easily be exaggerated, but that an important shift did take place is indisputable.

Looking at the eighteenth century as a whole, the social messages conveyed by most newspapers were, seen in very broad terms, about both inclusion and containment, and in this it seems plausible to suggest that they were reflecting rather accurately contemporary social realities. Old hierarchies were being challenged, and a more flexible and variegated social structure was emerging, particularly, but not exclusively, in urban society. Partly because of this transformation, social and indeed political boundaries became more blurred. Because it was a medium which served to narrow and dissolve boundaries between élite culture and the cultures of certain non-élite groups, the relatively widespread readership of newspapers added to perceptions of social fluidity. In sum, in so far as the press had a contribution to make to social and class formation in the eighteenth century, this should probably be seen in terms of reinforcing cohesion among the different and increasingly diverse elements of propertied society – a group which encompassed the élites as well as those in the lower echelons of the middling ranks – and of emphasizing areas and values on which these groups could agree and around which they could organize themselves. This does not necessarily preclude the development or existence of a sense of distinctive identity among the middling ranks in this period, but it does suggest that we may need to rethink how the press contributed to this. The norms and aspirations which the press gave expression to were embraced by more than the middling ranks; they were also complex, ambivalent and often contradictory.

CHAPTER

2

# NOT SPRUNG FROM PRINCES:

MIDDLING SOCIETY IN EIGHTEENTH-CENTURY
WEST YORKSHIRE

STEPHEN CAUNCE

During the eighteenth century, West Yorkshire[1] experienced unprecedented prosperity due to the success of its dynamic wool textile industry. A substantial and independent 'middling sort' did particularly well since production was based on small, often household-based, production units with a very high degree of real autonomy, all co-ordinated by an abnormally large number of merchants.[2] Many historians have identified this area as one of the crucial loci of class formation in England in the early and mid-nineteenth century, but during the previous period it had shown few signs that class conflict was developing.[3] Indeed, Smail has even argued that the Halifax middle class had already become a conscious entity by 1750, but he saw this as a relatively painless process of separation rather than one of forcible cleavage.[4] A potentially chaotic mass of manufacturers and merchants had thus evidently managed to generate a consensus that organic economic change was both necessary and beneficial for the whole community, something that is clearly of great interest to the historian, especially given the general perception that class conflict was soon to envelop the area. Understanding the nature of this consensus and how it was created and sustained, must depend to a great extent upon recovering the attitudes and expectations of the mass of middle-ranking clothiers and small merchants, and their relationships with other sections of society.

Statistical analysis of probate, bankruptcy and similar records is an essential part of this, but to understand motivation we have to get closer to the typical actors as individuals in their own social settings. Earle's work on London, for instance, aims to see the middling sort 'as complete human beings, rather than just cyphers with a certain economic function'.[5] Davidoff and Hall tried to get even closer to the ethos of the middle class in East Anglia and Birmingham through a greater reliance on personal documents.[6] Valuable work has been done on the West Yorkshire middle class, but with so decentralized an economy and a social structure with so low a centre of gravity, the typical actors were extremely unlikely to leave records that allow much intimacy.[7] However, one particular document, the 'Memoirs of Thomas Wright and his Family, interspersed with Remarks and Moral Reflections on Occurring Circumstances, &c., written by Himself for the Information, Instruction, and Amusement of his Children, 1797', forms a rare exception.[8] The author was born in 1736, described himself simply as a clothier when he married in 1766 and died of typhus in 1801, so he was entirely a man of the eighteenth century and wrote with no sense of the vast changes to come.[9] He seems to have been intelligent and perceptive and whereas most business autobiographies are celebratory, this is a justification for a life of self-confessed under-achievement.[10] Arguably Wright was a particularly perceptive commentator precisely because of a conscious intellectual detachment from the local obsession with business, to which he attributed his failures in large part.[11] He was also apparently noted locally for his memory and where it can be checked against other records, his accuracy is proven.[12] His account thus creates a small and rare loophole in Thompson's rule that 'only the successful . . . are remembered. The blind alleys, the lost causes, and the losers themselves are forgotten.'[13]

The narrative is discursive and mostly concerned with everyday life, and provides much unwitting testimony on the nature of local society. Around seventy relatives appear in some detail, most of them involved in business either personally or as part of a family unit. It is the four generations alive in the mid- to late eighteenth century which are the real focus, and unlike conventional family trees this one ramifies out through cousins and connections by marriage rather than back through time so that distant relatives with little connection with Wright receive substantial attention. The emphasis on kinship is appropriate for a face-to-face society where people naturally turned to relatives for help, but the account also shows the importance of non-kinship links, particularly those based on community and religion.[14] Informal networks were crucial for the business community because this was a predominantly rural area. Urban institutions such as guilds and corporations only existed in Leeds, and even there the normal institutional framework was mostly either lacking or ineffective.[15]

On its own no one person's account can be definitive, and any study of a small area has limitations, but this one complements existing studies which tend to focus on towns, on their wealthier inhabitants, and on radical changes in industrial activity and organization.[16] The rural manufacture of coarse woollens, which were the original product of West Yorkshire and the contiguous parts of east Lancashire, is a socio-economic matrix with few parallels in its ability to generate and support continuous change from within, and the woollen district Wright lived in represents the area where this original matrix seems to have persisted longest.[17] Traditional community structures were at their most robust and persistent here and its entrepreneurial group showed the greatest continuity of personnel and small-scale activity into the nineteenth and even twentieth centuries.[18] Birstall parish, where Wright spent most of his life, was also one of the main centres of West Yorkshire Luddism, and the famous siege of Rawfolds Mill in 1812 occurred only half a mile from his house.[19] Joseph Priestley was born and spent his formative years there, and Davidoff and Hall see him as a key figure in developing the new middle-class outlook they document.[20] Wright himself stood socially just above the point where a fracture would occur if a controlling middle class was to break with an exploited working class, so there is every reason to see the views and experiences contained within his account as of much more than local or personal significance.

This account is not suitable for rigorous statistical analysis, but when the information scattered through the narrative is brought together its relational and dynamic nature allows a nuanced examination of many lives over long periods.[21] Contrasting Wright's views with his own actions, and then with those of others, also provides a double guard against excessive subjectivity. However, even subjectivity has a value in that the radical changes West Yorkshire went through during this period stemmed in part at least from the mentalities of people like Thomas Wright, for the course taken by West Yorkshire was very different from that of the other traditional English wool textile areas even though they all traded in the same world markets.

## I

Wright was born at Mulcture Hall, near the parish church in Halifax. This was the home of his maternal grandfather, Thomas Cordingley, who had grown up in Bowling, near Bradford, and had inherited a small estate there, including at least three farmhouses and four cottages. Cordingley leased and operated several local fulling and corn mills, and as he prospered he acquired houses in Halifax and another estate at Little Bowling.[22] His family, who were Dissenters, thus came to be considered 'very creditable and substantial'.[23] He was elderly at the time of his daughter's marriage to Wright's father John, and soon handed over the business to his son-in-law. Thomas Wright was the only one of four children to survive infancy, and his early childhood was therefore geared to expectations of a fairly elevated station in life by local standards. In 1738, however, his mother, father and grandfather died in quick succession, leaving his grandmother in sole charge of both the business and a very young Thomas. She 'was obliged to rely on the faithfulness of different persons to transact her business for her, which she did till nearly stript of all her property', while the nurse she engaged appropriated many personal possessions.

Soon the mills and Mulcture Hall were given up, and they moved into 'one of our own houses at the bottom of the town'. One of the mills was taken over by another Thomas Cordingley, Wright's half-uncle, and the rest went to Richard Aked, who may have been a relation by marriage.[24] Wright's grandmother died soon after, bequeathing everything to him under the guardianship of his widowed great-aunt, her half-sister Lydia Ellison. She took Wright to live with her in Birkenshaw, which lies about six miles east of Halifax. It formed one of several hamlets within the township of Gomersal, which in turn was one of the eight townships in the ancient parish of Birstall. The Ellisons were a substantial and extensive Dissenting cloth-making clan that spread over several of the townships and also had links towards Bradford, about three and a half miles north-west. Over the next few years Lydia and Wright moved in with several of her children in turn. For a while he attended Bradford Grammar School to get a classically-based education suitable for the son of a man of substance, but it became clear that his dwindling inheritance would not support such a lifestyle as an adult. He was taught mathematics and accounting by Betty Ward, who gave classes at her home, and he did odd jobs for relatives, such as taking cloth to the mill for his uncle Samuel Wood. He also worked alongside another clothier uncle, Richard Ellison, in a desultory fashion as an informal apprentice. This was a common arrangement, and when Richard died in 1754 Wright remained with the widow until she remarried. He then bought the cloth-making equipment off her to set up on his own. Most, but not all, links with the Ellison clan were broken off acrimoniously when he came of age as he felt that they, and especially Samuel Wood, were simply appropriating his inheritance under the guise of recouping expenses.[25]

His training was very incomplete, especially on the marketing side, and he had little enthusiasm for the clothier's trade. However, he felt obliged to try life as a manufacturer, saying that 'my eagerness to remove the odium of following little or no trade out of the way of my being accepted as a husband, was my chief motive'. He borrowed £200 as a 'stock', or capital, on the security of his estate, though a good part of this went on expenses that had nothing to do with the business, and he formed a partnership with an experienced neighbour.[26] He sold his own cloth at the Briggate market in Leeds, using the Golden Lion Inn as his base, but he says little about his actual working arrangements while he was single, beyond the fact that he 'boarded out' and 'occupied a room or two' at Birkenshaw.[27] Thus, in West Yorkshire quite menial work could actually improve the social standing of someone who had a good education and owned property. In a more genteel area, a man such as Wright would undoubtedly have gravitated immediately towards a position in the government bureaucracy, or as a schoolmaster, and not towards manufacturing, if he could not have realized Wright's own favourite option of living as a rentier.[28]

His ideal type of a wife seems to have been embodied by a Miss C. H., 'a very handsome, genteel, young lady . . . whose father could give her some fortune, had given her a good education, and who was likely to make a very agreeable, managing wife'. After several amours, however, he married Lydia Birkhead, a clothier's daughter whose parents disapproved so completely that the couple had to elope to Scotland. Diligence at the loom now seemed doubly important if he was to build a good relationship with them, as well as earning a living.[29] He took Lower Blacup Farm, a typical dwelling, workshop, and farm combined, in Cleckheaton township (about two miles south of Birkenshaw) at a rent of £15 a year. He also 'bought a cloth-tenter as it stood in the tenter-croft, and a little old cart and its furniture, and other goods and implements for the house and barn, of William Cordingley [apparently no close relation], the late tenant, for which I paid him twenty pounds; but I afterwards thought this a dear bargain'.[30] He still had the loom and other necessities for manufacturing acquired from the Ellisons, and a pack of wool was sent over by his new father-in-law.

Starting up in business was thus relatively easy, and he was able to capitalize to a limited extent on the resources and experiences of relatives by both birth and marriage, and of an unrelated neighbour. Compared to many of his contemporaries, success must have seemed very likely but two elements were missing: firstly, he lacked real determination and commitment, and secondly, although his wife came from a prosperous family, she brought no portion because of her parents' disapproval of the marriage, and subsequent appeals that one should be provided retrospectively were never acceded to. The most he got was an interest-free loan of £50 after they were married, and a similar amount in 1773 when he was in difficulties but trade prospects seemed good. His children received another £300 or so.[31] This contrasts with the experience of William Birkby, who seems to have married a younger sister of Lydia with the Birkheads' approval, and who received an estimated £1,000 from them in their lifetime.[32] Wright's initial partnership with his neighbour turned out badly and was terminated after heavy losses, and he never earned enough to support his family without steadily eating into his capital. He was finally absorbed into the small bureaucracy of the area near the end of his life. By then he had sold the coal that lay beneath his land, and mortgaged and sold much of the land itself. He estimated that his estate would have been worth £2,000, if he had retained it into the 1790s, and he was still able to derive £30 per year from it even after the sales.[33]

His first wife died in 1777, leaving five surviving children from seven births, two of whom died in childhood at a later date. After four years as a widower he married Alicia Pinder, the fifteen-year-old daughter of a neighbouring farmer. She had a further six children, making a total of thirteen, and even though only seven survived to adulthood simple economic survival became an increasingly pressing concern. Wright had continued at the clothing trade throughout his first marriage, occasionally attempting other ventures as well, but then he gave it up in favour of another partnership with a neighbour, this time as a dealer.[34] At one time or another during his life he tried a bewildering variety of careers. He speculated through the building of a few cottages and became a sleeping partner of a friend who was a wool dealer. He tried his hand at wholesaling liquor, and then retailing it. He kept a shop and a school, and went on to do the accounts for a local ironworks as well as combining the roles of overseer and accountant in two separate cloth mills, finally finding a haven as a cloth searcher and tax receiver for the government.[35] He saw himself as the victim of many fraudsters for he felt that his partners regularly deceived and robbed him. The £100 invested in the wool trade received only simple interest instead of the expected share of the profits; as a shopkeeper 'we lost money by roguish customers'; and while he could get scholars for his school, nobody paid the fees.[36]

There was clearly no presumption locally that a man must be trained for a particular trade and remain within it for life. Despite being an inward-looking society in many ways, in this sense it was very open, something that is also reflected in the substantial journeys which he records. Most dramatic was his elopement to Scotland, but he also made social visits to York and Hull while on an extensive tour into Lincolnshire with a friend who went there to buy wool, and there was a ten-day trip to London with another friend. He was sent on a mission to Nottinghamshire as a commissioner in a Chancery case, but most extensive of all was a general tour through Wales and the Midlands helping to raise money to build a Methodist chapel. Regular trips to Manchester and Liverpool formed part of his venture into the wholesaling of alcoholic beverages, and as a youth he had pursued a girl he was courting (ultimately without success) on several trips to Bolton. He spent many seasons at the spa in Scarborough, and pleasure trips to Ripon and Harrogate are also recorded.[37]

Mere possession of assets did not ensure that Wright would participate in the good life such trips symbolize, and he felt that his education had actually harmed his prospects as a manufacturer. Yet his intellectual abilities gave him a position of respect in the community outside the economic sphere, and even towards the end of his life others approached him to offer him responsible positions precisely because of their good opinion of him, and because of his knowledge of accounts. When acting on his own behalf he admitted that he could not summon up the diligence necessary for success, or the ruthlessness that was sometimes appropriate, even though he could make saleable cloth.[38] West Yorkshire suited small businesses, but not because it was characterized by general benevolence or altruism, as his grandmother's experience in Halifax confirmed. Some of his relatives proved that there was plenty of money to be made in Birstall, but it was not made effortlessly. Rather, effective businessmen respected each other and saw no reason to drive each other to ruin, but those who could not look after their own affairs got little sympathy.[39] This was mutuality with a very hard edge, and a capitalist who was not personally able and willing to make his money work for him was almost certain to suffer the consequences. Yet the rewards for those who could do well were high, better than those that attached to drawing rents from an agrarian estate, so the area was not characterized by a desire to seek security through the purchase of land for its own sake.

This made for a meritocratic approach to life rather than egalitarianism and Wright allocated his relations and acquaintances to differing social strata very readily, mostly within the middling sort. Thus, while his maternal grandfather John Brooke, a Presbyterian and a cloth manufacturer, was 'among the better sort of the middling rank of people' because he had landed property, his father-in-law William Birkhead, who also made coarse white cloth, 'ranked as one of the lower order of tradesmen in the middle ranks of the people' in his early years because he did not. He did not regard the group as closed or privileged, and said of the Birkheads:

> their predecessors, themselves, their descendants, and the collateral branches of the families on each side . . . were not sprung from princes; . . . a few of them were in easy circumstances, but far the greater part in a low situation; . . . they themselves, (notwithstanding their accidental good fortune in accumulating a little wealth on some favourable occasions, which made them, in this respect, a *little* better than *some* of their neighbours) were of mean education and low attainments in knowledge. They bore, indeed, a pretty fair character for honesty in their dealings in common with many of their neighbours, and paid a strict attention to the formalities of their religion; but had no just ground, I conceive, for that mighty self-importance which they seemed desirous of assuming over their neighbours.[40]

Only two members of the upper classes receive even a mention. Cordingley's mills were all leased from Lord Irwin of Temple Newsam, Lord of the Manor of Halifax, while after some of the shooting sessions that regularly took him away from the loom as a youth, Wright spent some evenings in the home of Dr Richardson, the non-resident Lord of the Manor of Birkenshaw. His education and continued wide reading would presumably have made him a congenial companion compared to many of the other local men, especially given Dr Richardson's known scientific bent, but there is no certainty that the two actually even met.[41] Less rare, but still not common, are references to labourers, people he clearly pitied to some extent but was concerned to keep at arm's length. He refers to clothiers' establishments which included a good number of subordinate workers, but it is clear that many of them were boys and apprentices. He later records that his first wife, with whom he had a very troubled relationship, 'was so weak and imprudent . . . as to rail on me behind my back, to the vulgar fellows we had working in the fields, though they laughed her to scorn for her pains'.[42] This was a society where the long-term personal dependence implied in regular wage work was rare and was looked down upon by the entrepreneurial class, though it should be remembered that many of them would have been journeymen in their time. Some people obviously needed to work for wages regularly for at least part of their time, but even they generally worked on contract rather than for wages for one master. Wright rarely hired anyone to work for him except domestic servants, all of whom acted very independently and with little deference. His links with his ploughmen were not those of master and servants and they were clearly in no awe of him. Wright did not regard himself as a wage-earner when he was employed as an overlooker or a searcher, but his experience showed the vulnerability of anyone who relied on others for their income. He was enticed out of a secure situation into a new one, only to be summarily dismissed once his new employers felt they could manage without him.

Religious affiliation was very important and the rise of the Moravians, Inghamites and, above all, Methodists was reawakening a long and rich tradition of Dissent in Birstall parish after a rather sterile period.[43] Anglicanism was so weak in West Yorkshire in terms of committed adherents, places of worship and clerical personnel that it really already functioned as another sect, though obviously a privileged one.[44] Some of the very few churches were actually chapels of ease paid for by local congregations, who could appoint ministers to reflect their own views rather than those normally associated with the established Church.[45] Wright himself pursued a course of wry detachment, baptizing his children by his first marriage at a Calvinist chapel of the Old Dissent to please his in-laws, and those by his second marriage at the parish church. He was never personally a Calvinist, and this was the source of some of the bitterness between himself and his first wife's family.[46] He leaned instead towards the Methodists and though he never formally joined them he was willing to go to great lengths to raise funds and wrote several long poems attacking their critics, which they published. A malicious relative's accusation that Wright's eldest son was an atheist provoked him to public declarations of distaste for deism and abhorrence for atheism, showing that there were real limits to the acceptable.[47] This was definitely a tolerant society, but mostly because it was impossible to prevent a diversity of views flourishing.

## II

Turning now to the general experience as it is reflected in the kinship web (see below pp. 40–1), there are no dominant occupational patterns to be found there. Fifteen men were clothiers for at least part of their lives, and this was by far the largest block, but they were by no means a majority even when the solitary cloth dresser is added. The four millers were all probably involved in milling cloth as well as grain, but it is impossible to be precise. Landed property seemed the dominant element in the livelihoods of another six, though patterns of acquisition and inheritance are not those of a true landed class. There were three farmers (as opposed to clothiers with land), a cattle dealer and a butcher. The trades and professions were represented by two innkeepers, two hardware sellers, two apothecaries (one also a surgeon), one Dissenting minister, one retail tobacconist, one stationer/bookseller/printer, a saddler, two shoemakers, a blacksmith, two men involved in speculative building of houses for rent, one cabinet-maker and one joiner. At the bottom of the scale come one labouring mason, three labourers and three soldiers, while most women have no recorded occupation.[48] If we extend consideration to those who appear in the account only in passing, there are no radical changes to this picture, though cloth-making is even less dominant, and the professions (very loosely defined) are much better represented, with several ministers, schoolteachers and surgeons added.

Wright thus acknowledged a wide variety of connections, some with individuals well beneath his own status. He respected his uncle Julius Whitehead, 'a mason by trade, an inoffensive orderly man, who ranked among that class . . . who obtain their bread by their labour', but not most of the eleven children of Nathaniel Brooke. The eldest son fled the country to avoid his father's debts, two others became labourers, two enlisted as soldiers, and a sixth, Edmund, was thrown onto the parish because he had fits. Worst of all perhaps was their sister Lydia, 'who turned out bad, and followed the soldiers'.[49] Wright records no attempt to keep Edmund Brooke from needing parish relief, but Elizabeth Wright of Bradford, who was widowed twice, showed that a great deal of help could be obtained from relatives despite very aggravating behaviour. She disputed Wright's guardianship after his parents died and later interfered several times in his affairs, even having him arrested to recover her costs over these actions. He paid up despite his conviction that she was in the wrong and he assisted her on several other occasions explicitly because of their kinship, as did Joseph Hollings of Cottingley, a 'distant and substantial relation'. The existence of children may have been a factor here, but straightforward poverty was clearly more acceptable than apparent mental illness. Even so, with children by both husbands she was always 'very poor and distressed' and eventually 'died in straitened circumstances'.[50]

Movement up and down the social scale both within a lifetime and over the generations was the norm rather than the exception. However, there was no sense of one privileged group moving up as a group, or of a disadvantaged one moving down. Real success in business was not common, and depended upon more than mere application. Personal abilities seem to have been a deciding factor in many cases, and sheer luck should not be discounted, for the cloth trade was so prone to severe shifts of demand that simply being in the right product at the right time could make a man. Thus, Wright saw a boom in the Russian trade as the basis of the success of his father-in-law. Trading was potentially much more rewarding than manufacturing and John Hinchliffe, who had perhaps the most dramatic success, achieved it through cattle dealing. His parents were 'poor all their life', but he acquired considerable property, took a large farm near his parents, and provided for them in their old age. His only child, Joseph, was classed as a farmer by 1797, lived at Newell Hall, and was characterized as 'a man of good character, much business, and considerable property'.[51]

Sons of clothiers were the most likely to follow their fathers' occupations. The Ellisons stand out as a family dominated by the trade, and William Birkhead and his brother were also maintaining a family tradition when they first set up in business together. However, it is likely that cloth manufacturing was both more widespread and persistent than any other occupation simply because it offered such men the best all-round opportunities. If Wright represents the extreme case of flexible career structures, his grandfather's successful change from cloth-dressing to innkeeping was quite typical, and shows that men could better themselves by moving out of the cloth trade. Wright's father was apprenticed as a cabinet-maker, but became a miller on marriage. The only other formal apprenticeship was that of Wright's own son Thomas with a bookseller and printer at a premium of £20 (borrowed from the Birkheads), and this ultimately proved a good investment. Wright himself was not prevented from trading as a clothier though his customary apprenticeship was weak even by the standards prevalent in West Yorkshire. The partnership with an existing clothier may have been the key to this. There is no mention at all of farm service for boys, and surprisingly little detail on domestic service, though it is clear that many families did keep one maid and that service in itself was not degrading. Wright's own experience with servants he described as dire – a long succession of pilfering and poor work – and avoiding dependence on them seems to have been a significant motivation behind his second marriage.[52] However, he let two of his own daughters go as servants to their grandmother just for their keep, with him providing clothing, and they both went on to marry respectably.

Women were not expected to be passive, nor were they inherently inferior even though public life was undoubtedly led by men. Several women ran businesses, and Martha Horton/Haworth/Longbottom kept the Old Cock Inn, one of the best in Halifax, 'with great credit and reputation, above thirty years' despite a disastrous marriage to Nathaniel Longbottom, who deserted her to go to London where he married again (illegally) and plagued her with letters demanding money.[53] Other women are credited with guiding their family's affairs: Obadiah Brooke remained a bachelor to an advanced age, but after marrying Betty Wood, 'to her talents he is entirely indebted, under providence, for the present favourable state of his family'.[54] Conversely, Samuel Wood had been 'as careful, sober, and managing a man as any in the neighbourhood; but after the death of [his] first wife he became an extravagant, quarrelsome, drunken sot'.[55] Wright expected his first wife to control his family's finances even when she was slipping visibly into alcoholism and they were quarrelling repeatedly.[56]

Many people were married more than once. Wright's maternal grandfather had three wives, while we have just seen that fairly open bigamy was possible, and this example was not unique.[57] Marriages mostly took place within Birstall parish, but this was a very large and diverse area. They did not follow occupational lines at all, and frequently were apparent mismatches in status terms. Thus William Birkhead's sisters married a labouring mason, a shoemaker, and an ordinary labourer respectively rather than clothiers like their father and brothers.[58] Wright's second wife was the daughter of a neighbouring farmer, and her sister married a joiner. Again, though Nathaniel Brooke's many children mostly formed an embarrassing and potentially draining set of relations for any aspiring spouse, Mary married a Lancashire blacksmith and possibly returned to the status her father had known as a child, while Betty married Benjamin Fearnley, the only child of 'a man of considerable property in Cleckheaton, who is lately dead, and has left property to his son, it is said, of upwards of 2,400*l*'.[59]

Family sizes and the composition of households varied enormously, partly due to frequent deaths among both parents and children. The typical family is hard to settle upon, even though the nuclear unit was clearly the ideal form.[60] The three largest families (two of eleven and one of nine children) were all headed by fathers involved in the cloth trade, but as they all ruined the parents, large numbers of children clearly did not generate income for the middling sort through employment opportunities arising out of industrialization.[61] None of Thomas Wright's children apparently earned anything over and above their keep, and several of his friends and neighbours were amazed that he should marry a young girl likely to have many more children when he already had five living and no great income. Several were boarded out with relatives for long periods, and one son was virtually adopted by his hated in-laws.[62]

Transfers of wealth down the generations were largely a matter for personal decision, and the dispute that began in 1796 over William Birkhead's will, which forms the focus of the second part of the narrative, shows the bitterness this could generate. Wright's in-laws were embittered by his elopement, the failure of the marriage and their daughter's death from alcoholism, together with his inability to make a go of anything. The teenage escapades of his eldest son Thomas, who Wright felt had the strongest claim to inherit after William Birkhead's own son died, turned them against him too. William's wife Mary was then credited with devising a will which left Wright's son virtually disinherited. Although thirteen years younger, Mary predeceased her husband, and a struggle developed over their property that made William's last years very distressing. When Timothy Greenwood, Wright's son-in-law, moved into William's house to look after him and his farm, panic ensued among the others who hoped to inherit. They feared, with some justification, that Timothy would strip the estate and get the will rewritten in his favour. A legal inquiry as to whether the old man was a lunatic incapable of revising his will was held, and after his death there was an expensive court case to decide which of two extant wills should be implemented.[63] Joseph Greenwood, Timothy's cousin (and also married to one of Wright's daughters by his first wife) was Timothy's main opponent, and though he eventually secured victory in court he was declared bankrupt, partly due to neglecting his own affairs.[64]

Primogeniture, and the building of permanent estates as patrimonies, were principles largely ignored in Birstall, even where land was concerned. All children were usually provided for, though it was acceptable to pass over a natural heir where there was provocation. Thus, Samuel Brooke should have inherited a substantial family business after his elder brother died, but due to his choice of a wife he was provided with a house, a workshop, and some fields, and then 'in effect, disinherited, forsaken by the family, and treated ever afterwards as an alien to their blood'.[65] A sole heir, of course, received the best possible start to adult life, and as an only child of wealthy parents Joseph Hinchliffe probably inherited the most secure position of any of the members of his generation within the web. John and Betty Fearnley's son was similarly well-placed, while William Birkhead and his brother began their cloth-making partnership by pooling a joint inheritance. They separated their common stock on William's marriage, but when the brother died young he left all his property to William, to the disgust of their sisters.[66] There was thus a constant flux in holdings, rather than either the concentration of land into a few hands, or the creation of a mass of micro-holdings and a kind of industrial peasantry. Land ownership was desirable, but not for its own sake, and there was no use of entails and trusts as this would have prevented that active utilization of its value.[67] The Whiteheads passed land at Streetside, Tong, down to the eldest son through at least three generations, but it was primarily seen as a bankable and saleable business asset. Land was easily and routinely mortgaged to avoid sterilizing capital, which was there to be used not hoarded. Borrowing from relatives and friends in the course of business was common, and despite the lack of cordiality between Wright and his in-laws money or goods regularly passed between them. Conversely, many relatives felt they had claims against each other, either through bequests or simple equity, and several running disputes over clothes and personal possessions are recorded.[68] Wright's comments show that he was aware of relatives of whom he knew little or nothing, but this patchiness and selectivity did not destroy the power of a web such as this to mobilize resources and care. It is also clear that kin groups did not constitute market-free relationships, for money intruded into many interactions even between quite close relatives.[69]

Despite these attitudes to land ownership, and despite the involvement in manufacturing for world markets, the basic structures of local identity remained immensely powerful both for individuals and communities. Families were not tied to particular places, but virtually all their surnames, such as Hinchliffe, Cordingley, Greenwood, and even Brooke, were very local in their origins and remain highly localized today, a characteristic of the West Riding.[70] Most recorded moves were over short distances, and women were much more likely than their brothers to marry out of their home areas. Heads of households were probably the least mobile but even they could relocate, and when William Birkhead's young wife brought a substantial small estate with her it became the centre of family activities. Hamlets rather than townships or parishes provided the real framework for people's lives and distance is not a good guide to the significance of any particular move. It is therefore hard to generalize about the effects of this localized, swirling mobility, which created new interactions and relationships as well as reinforcing old ones, and which encouraged the widest possible exchange of ideas, information and business opportunities. Most communications routes ran east–west, but if there is a dominant migration pattern it is a north–south interaction both within Birstall parish and on a slightly wider scale. The manufacturing fringes of Cleckheaton and Tong townships show a lot of interaction, perhaps because of the limited opportunity in such late-developing areas.[71]

Bradford and its surrounding townships occur frequently, partly because the Wrights had moved down to Birstall from Keighley via Bradford and Halifax over three generations. Leeds was the prime marketing centre for the whole clothing district but it is hardly mentioned except in connection with Wright's elopement and his cloth marketing. However, Joseph Greenwood did move there to set up a tobacconist's business and married Wright's daughter Betty in the parish church.

Nathaniel Longbottom went to London when he deserted his wife; Hannah Brooke went into service there, marrying and taking up residence as a result; and one clothier used it as a haven while he retrieved his financial affairs from bankruptcy.[72] John Brooke emigrated to Jamaica to escape the attention of his father's creditors, and his sister Mary went to Lancashire as a result of marriage, while their brothers Nathaniel and Benoni joined the army and Lydia became a camp follower. Their uncle Richard also became a soldier, and his family background may likewise have been difficult as he was the son of a first wife surrounded by the numerous children of a second marriage. Over a few generations movement could be cumulative, and the Wrights' progress continued when the author's eldest son moved to Shropshire with the bookseller he had been apprenticed to. However, such long-distance migration was rare, and the general tone of the narrative does not indicate that this was because anyone who left Birstall was lost to sight. Given the encouraging economic situation locally, it is more likely that long-distance migration simply seemed unnecessary.[73]

### III

Thomas Wright's Birstall emerges as a vibrant, diverse, and locally centred economy with little resemblance to conventional pictures of a proto-industrial economy founded on exploitation by merchants based in towns.[74] The focus of its whole middling sort was business, due to a combination of genuine opportunity, lack of alternative activities and strong community pressure not to be idle. Their incomes were widely perceived, especially among themselves, to be derived from personal effort rather than status, patronage or rents. Ability had space to flourish in a way that many agrarian or craft-based communities would have rejected, but there was still a strong sense of localities, of codes of behaviour, and of respect for neighbours and for community leaders. The economy was definitely market-driven and many of the markets served were distant, but not everything was for sale.[75] Communities were inward looking in everything except trade, with local dialects and traditions remaining vital forces for the overwhelming majority.[76] Wright's house at Lower Blacup is a perfect example of the traditional design and rural setting of most clothiers' activities, and even when vernacular building styles began to incorporate symmetry and other aspects of polite architecture in the eighteenth century, it was by blending them in with older, more traditional forms.[77]

It may be more useful to describe such a group as middle income rather than middle class. Modest but adequate incomes were neither enough to make them complacent and conservative nor too little to be able to try and do something with their lives. No one within this web founded a business dynasty and the effectiveness of the local economy was enhanced by this tendency to live in the present, constantly re-allocating resources according to current conditions.[78] Men without much education, whom Wright regarded as his intellectual inferiors and who probably would have agreed with him, could make a decent living through common sense and application. A continuum of experience and expectations still linked the journeyman, the hopeful young man starting up on credit, and established merchants, who often remained part of the local community and supplied specialist information about prices and markets without seeking to create personal dependency. Many traded only in a small way and were involved in manufacturing as well, such as John Taylor, the owner and builder of Hunsworth Mill, who employed Wright as an overseer there. It is worth noting that this mill never became a textile factory.[79]

There are no recognizable factory owners in Wright's narrative, in fact, and talk of progress and of change in manufacturing techniques is conspicuous only by its absence, though Birstall closely resembled the modern conception of the dynamic industrial district.[80] Clothiers were not isolated competitors, but complementary actors who were effectively all part of an organization, even if that organization was never formalized as either an old-fashioned corporation or a new-style company. Fierce personal rivalry was common, but entry costs were low and equipment could always be sold on. In addition, the combination of opportunity and social pressure ensured the maximum mobilization of available resources for use in business. Clothiers' small farms cushioned them effectively against times when trade was bad, and their extensive kin and religious networks gave access to capital and opportunity. Success did not mean severing contact with neighbours and relations, and the desired result was a comfortable living, respect in the community, with the ability to provide for all one's children. There was no drive to retreat into the countryside because most had never left it, and life in these hamlets and villages did not lend itself to solid social stratification.[81] Small patrimonies like Wright's only allowed the owner to live well when used as the basis for inherently risky business activity, especially as inheritance practices tended to divide them at death.

Moreover, even if families like the Birkheads had possessed the resources to ape the squirearchy, role models were lacking.[82] Substantial landlords were usually absentees with little meaningful contact with the active middle class, and the Anglican clergy were similarly too thin on the ground to matter. Without such men to encourage unbusinesslike ways of life through emulation, and with dissent and the low status of their occupation acting as barriers, the bulk of the middling sort remained firmly outside polite society.[83] Even Leeds in the early eighteenth century offered few attractions to the gentry, and a century later the smoke and dirt of industrialization halted gentrification almost before it had begun.[84] A kind of meritocratic deference filled the gap this left, often accorded to those playing the role of community leader. Social groupings were clearly recognizable and widely accepted, but they were not closed and they did not perpetuate themselves automatically down the generations, which reinforced the sense of both opportunity and rationality and made inequality more acceptable. Many clothiers were unequivocally artisans and all remained personally involved in manual work, which could be distinctly unpleasant, so their identification with the merchants as a sharply defined class was never certain.[85]

Religion provided no firm reinforcement for class formation either because as yet chapels brought people together more than they separated them off, and involvement was a personal affair. No one sect moulded the area's undoubted work ethic, but the sense of an individual's right, even duty, to build their own relationship with God was a force that both supported and constrained business activity. If we take religion as a social vision, this was an area where several versions competed on fairly equal terms and none could hope for hegemony. The networks based on chapels encouraged trust, capital pooling, and the sharing of business advice and opportunities. They can even be seen as precursors of Morris's voluntary societies of the next century, creating links across potential social rifts.[86]

Conflict with the gentry was actually quite unlikely as they profited from the ability to let very poor agricultural land at relatively high rents. Some actively developed their estates by creating the small farms the clothiers wanted, while the Ramsdens built up and promoted Huddersfield as a new and highly profitable urban centre while seeking to make the most of their manorial revenues at the same time.[87] Absentee status meant few landlords allowed ties of sentiment to block change, or had fears that development would affect their own lifestyle. In a period of substantial general economic growth there was no need to transfer resources from one group to another, and the success of the middling sort lay rather in their preservation of a large share of the new wealth. At the other end of the scale, widespread poverty was a feature of all early modern economies and it is no surprise that it existed in Birstall. This account throws no light on its extent, but it is clear that it was usually possible to earn some sort of living by labour. Being personally poor did not necessarily mean either exclusion from close connection with the middling sort or from the possibility of getting on, though for many, especially immigrants with no networks to support them, it would have been extremely difficult. The bulk of the clothiers were descended from clothiers, but they did not own the economy and Wright's own case shows that access to substantial capital did not guarantee even modest success.[88] He did not think like a businessman, he travelled purely for pleasure, he was prone to taking long spells away from work, and he had no eye for driving a bargain or reading the fine print. In contrast, when he asked a friend and member of a very successful local business family to act as his guide and companion on his elopement, the friend arranged enough work to do in Edinburgh to occupy him while the Wrights travelled for pleasure round the locality.[89] Wright's failure in business, moreover, made way for others who could make better use of opportunity, which promoted overall growth. He himself lost, but he did not sink into the ranks of the absolutely poor.

For all the overall success of the West Yorkshire system, individuals could have felt no sense of inevitability about becoming or remaining personally prosperous. The web illustrates many ways in which networks smoothed out the harshness of the untamed business cycle, and thereby made business life more tolerable. Within the web there were constant interactions arising out of kinship, common interests and activities, while kin relationships to those outside the group played an important part in preventing its social and economic closure.[90] If class differences are fracture-planes within society, lines where a break will readily occur if the whole is put under sufficient stress, then these were barely developed as yet and there is certainly no great divide opening between capitalists and proletarians in Wright's account. The overriding impression is that no simplistic analysis can adequately explain West Yorkshire society and its industrial creativity in the eighteenth and nineteenth centuries. Luddism showed that even this apparently quiescent locality was not simply passive: it could become a hornet's nest in a very short time if a threat was perceived.[91] Yet we know that those who smashed shearing frames came from many trades and from many parts of the middling sort. Luddism was self-aware, but only on the basis of a general sense of grievance against individuals who wished to bring in the factory system. If Luddism therefore looked forward to a class-based division, it did not reflect one which already existed in Wright's day. The middling sort individually and as a group were key actors, but it would be impossible to show that they saw their interests as inherently opposed to those of the rest of society. Class conflict in West Yorkshire seems to have come out of the collapse of its distinctive early-modern consensus, not as a legacy of a feudal society which had never really had much hold on the area. When contrasted with the west of England woollen industry, the conclusion seems to be that while clearly drawn class lines and proto-industrial organization may have been an effective mechanism for extending and perpetuating existing production systems, rather than supporting change they strongly inhibited it.

Indeed, the conventional language of class conflict can seriously mislead, for the group that Wright was a part of was in no sense a bourgeoisie before 1800. While Earle's context was thoroughly metropolitan, and while most other authors tie the development of a middle class to urbanization, here the vast majority of the middling sort lived, like Thomas Wright, on farms and in cottages scattered through an intensively settled but still rural landscape. Farmhouses stood only short distances apart, hamlets were turning into villages, and villages had populations comparable with small towns elsewhere, but they had not yet become towns. Marketing centres played a distinct and vital role in coordinating manufacturing activities, but even Leeds was relatively small and lacking in most distinctively urban institutions.[92] Many aspects of the activities and mentalities of the local middling sort are either the same as those found elsewhere, or are variations on a theme, but this must cast doubt on the stress that is often placed upon urban locations as an essential part of their evolution.[93] This was an area which had created a quasi-urban environment, with access to markets, banks and professional services, but which lacked the constraints and high costs often associated with either feudal villages or over-regulated towns. Even if this is simply put down as an oddity, it is one that lies at the heart of the industrialization process in the key area of Yorkshire and Lancashire and it therefore cannot be dismissed lightly.

# THOMAS WRIGHT'S KINSHIP WEB – SELECTED MEMBERS

Richard Horton.
No information.
=

**Martha Hopkinson/Horton/Wright.**
Paternal grandmother. Born Batley.
=

**Thomas Wright.**
Paternal grandfather.
Cloth dresser, Keighley. Occupation unknown, Wibsey. Innkeeper, Bradford.

?? first wife
=

**Thomas Cordingley.**
Maternal grandfather. Born Bowling, Bradford.
Inherits small estate. Leased four mills, Halifax.

**Martha Whitehead/Cordingley.**
Maternal grandmother. Born Streetside, Tong.
8 known siblings, no other information.

Samuel Whitehead.
Great-uncle. No information.

Abraham Whitehead.
Great-uncle. No information.

**Matthias Whitehead.**
Maternal great grandfather.
Clothier. Streetside, Tong.

Mary Whitehead/Richmond.
Great-aunt.
=
? Richmond.
Dissenting minister, Cleckheaton.

Lydia Whitehead/Ellison.
Great-aunt. TW's guardian.
Birkenshaw. Widowed.
=
Timothy Ellison.
Clothier, Birkenshaw. Died young.

?? first wife
=
? Webster/Brooke.
Maternal grandmother.
Morley.
=
John Brooke.
Maternal grandfather.
Considerable property, Cleckheaton.
=
?? third wife

John Wood.
Hardwareman, Bradford.

William Birkhead.
First wife's grandfather.
White clothier, Streetside, Tong.

---

Martha Horton/Haworth/Longbottom.
Half-aunt. Innkeeper, Halifax.

Abraham Horton.
Half-uncle. Shoemaker, Bradford.

Elizabeth Wright/Northrop/Craven.
Aunt. Poor, Bradford. Two husbands.

**John Wright.**
Father. Born Bradford. App. cabinet-maker, Halifax.
Miller, Halifax. Died 1738.

**Elizabeth Cordingley/Wright.**
Mother. Died 1738 in childbirth.

Thomas and Joshua Cordingley.
Half-uncles. Miller and butcher respectively.

**Thomas Pinder.**
Second father-in-law. Farmer, Cleckheaton.

Matthias Whitehead.
Uncle. Streetside, Tong. No occupation given.

Christopher Whitehead.
Uncle. Saddler, Wakefield.

Richard Ellison.
Uncle. White clothier, Birkenshaw. Died 1754.

Mary Ellison = William Brogden.
Aunt/uncle. Clothier, N. Bierley.

Hannah Ellison = Samuel Wood.
Aunt/uncle. Mixed clothier, Bradford
SW widowed and remarried.

John Ellison.
Uncle. Clothier, Birkenshaw. Died young.

Richard Brooke.
Uncle of first wife. B. Cleck'n. Soldier. Died young.

Samuel Brooke.
Uncle of first wife. Born Cleckheaton.
Disinherited for bad marriage. Clothier?

Obadiah Brooke.
Uncle of first wife. Inherits.
Born Cleckheaton. Clothier.
=
Betty Wood

Nathaniel Brooke.
Uncle of first wife. Born Cleckheaton.
Clothier? Little Gomersal.

**Mary Brooke/Birkhead**
Mother-in-law. Born Cleckheaton 1720. Died 1796.
=
**William Birkhead.**
Father-in-law. Born Streetside, Tong, 1697.
White clothier. Cleckheaton. Married at 50. Died 1797.

Thomas Birkhead.
Uncle. White clothier, S'side, Tong. Died young.

? Birkhead = Julius Whitehead.
Aunt/uncle. Labouring mason.

? Birkhead = Joseph Wooller.
Aunt/uncle. Shoemaker, Bradford.
JW widowed, remarried.

? Birkhead = John Hinchliffe.
Aunt/uncle. Poor, Bradford. JH widowed, remarried.

John Fearnley.
Propertied, Cleckheaton.

---

## NOTES:

Each column on this chart represents a generation in relation to Thomas Wright. As far as possible, sibling groups (indicated by a square bracket, broken where one parent is different) are organized in the order of birth, but information is often lacking, and where necessary the order has been changed to make the chart simpler in terms of inter-generational linkages.

Thomas Wright's parents, grandparents, and great grandfather are shown in bold, as are his son and grandson who he regarded as his direct heirs.

Not everyone dealt with in the autobiography is included (to save space), but no one is excluded who is mentioned in the essay or on whom there was significant information.

Thomas Greenwood.
Farmer, Cleckheaton.

Joseph Greenwood.
Son-in-law. Tobacconist, Leeds. Bankrupt 1797.
=

William Birkhead Greenwood.
Grandson. Born Leeds 1791. Died 1793.

Elizabeth Wright/Greenwood.
Daughter. Born Cleckheaton. Servant to
grandmother. Married 1797.

Thomas Greenwood.
Grandson. Born Leeds 1793.

? Birkhead = William Birkby.
No other information

Lydia Greenwood.
Granddaughter. Born Leeds 1795.

William Birkhead.
Brother-in-law. Presumed died young.

Mary Wright.
Daughter. Born Cleckheaton, 1769. Died 1770.

Mary Ann Greenwood.
Granddaughter. Born Leeds 1797.

LYDIA BIRKHEAD/WRIGHT.
Born Cleckheaton 1747. Died 1777.
=

Thomas Wright.
Son. Born Cleckheaton 1771. Apprentice
bookseller and stationer, Bradford 1787.
Stationer, Bradford and Shropshire.

Thomas Wright.
Grandson. MA and FRS. Lives in London.
Editor of autobiography.

THOMAS WRIGHT. Author.
=

ALICIA PINDER/WRIGHT
Born Cleckheaton 1766. Married 1781.

Sarah Wright/Greenwood.
Daughter. Born Cleckheaton 1773. Married 1793.
=

John Brooke Greenwood.
Grandson. Born 1794.

Ann Pinder/Brooke.
Sister-in-law. Born Cleckheaton.
=

Timothy Greenwood.
Son-in-law. Surgeon and apothecary, Cleckheaton.

Mary Ann Greenwood.
Grandaughter Born 1796.

Thomas Brooke.
Brother-in-law. Joiner, Birstall.

James Wright.
Son. Stillborn, Cleckheaton 1774.

Benjamin Greenwood.
Clothier. Cleckheaton.

John Wright.
Son. Born Cleckheaton 1775.
Died 1783, unknown illness.

Obadiah Brooke.
Cousin to first wife. Bachelor.
Surgeon and apothecary, Leeds.

William Wright.
Son. Born Cleckheaton 1777.
Died 1781, smallpox.

John Brooke.
Cousin to first wife. Born Cleckheaton.
Married Quaker. Kept hardware shop. Rich.

Martha Wright.
Daughter. Born Birkenshaw 1783.

11 children

Ann Wright.
Daughter. Born Birkenshaw 1785.

Obadiah Brooke.
Cousin to first wife. Born Cleckheaton. Died young.

Benjamin Wright.
Son. Born Birkenshaw 1787.

John Brooke.
Cousin to first wife. Fled to West Indies to
avoid father's creditors. Died Jamaica.

Hannah Wright.
Daughter. Born Birkenshaw 1790.

Thomas and Joshua Brooke.
Cousins to first wife. Born Cleckheaton.
Labourers.

John Wright.
Son. Born Birkenshaw 1793.

Nathaniel and Benoni Brooke.
Cousins to first wife. Born Cleckheaton. Soldiers.

Joseph Wright.
Son. Born Birkenshaw 1796.

Edmund Brooke.
Cousin to first wife. Born Cleckheaton. Pauper.

Hannah Brooke.
Cousin to first wife. Born Cleckheaton.
Servant in London, married and died there.

Lydia Brooke.
Cousin to first wife. Born Cleckheaton.
Camp follower.

Mary Brooke.
Cousin to first wife. Born Cleckheaton.
Married Lancashire blacksmith.

Betty Brooke.
Cousin to first wife. Born Cleckheaton.
=

Ben Fearnley.
Inherits property.

? Fearnley. Inherits all property.

John Ellison.
Cousin. Builds houses at Birkenshaw.

? Wooller = Samuel Webster.
Cousins. 'Man of property'.

John Hinchliffe.
Cousin. Cattle dealer. Acquires property.

Joseph Hinchliffe.
Resides 1797 near Wibsey.
Farmer, considerable property.

Numerous children

## CHAPTER 3

# WHO WAS MASTER?

## CLASS RELATIONSHIPS IN NINETEENTH-CENTURY SHEFFIELD[1]

RUTH GRAYSON

The traditional view that the factory replaced cottage industries and outwork during the industrial revolution has been challenged by a number of scholars in the past generation. In 1969 Phyllis Deane observed that until at least the mid-nineteenth century most industrial labourers worked in small workshops, or on a casual basis as unskilled labour. Until the 1840s, even in factory trades such as textiles, more people were engaged in outwork in their own homes than worked in the factories themselves.[2] Moreover, it was only in the late 1850s and 1860s that the textile factories began to convert to steam on a large scale, and as late as 1871 it is estimated that there were still two workers to every unit of steam power in the textile mills.[3]

Developing this theme several years later, Raphael Samuel noted the continued coexistence of workshops and factories, and of manual techniques within factories, until even later in the century. It was far more cost-effective for a manufacturer to employ cheap labour, of which there was a superabundance in Victorian Britain, than to install expensive machinery which took up space and required to be both minded and maintained. A response to growing demand, and a cheap alternative to mechanization, was 'the division of labour and the simplification of the individual task' which in the mid-Victorian era was as likely to result in the proliferation of small workshops and outwork as in the erection of large factories.[4] The rise of the factory, spectacular though it was, was much slower than is often portrayed and 'has cast a shadow over our understanding of industrial growth in nineteenth-century Britain that may be out of all proportion to its actual occurrence'.[5] But just as lack of change does not generally make news headlines, so it rarely makes the pages of the history texts.[6] Specifically, in economic history the very term *Industrial Revolution* diverts our attention away from continuity to change. It puts immediate and undue emphasis on novel and rapid development. In fact, for many people, the only changes the Industrial Revolution brought to their lives were an increase in their workload and a consequent worsening of their working and living conditions. For the majority, even their place of work did not change to the factory from the workshop, or from the home, for most of the nineteenth century.

Despite a widespread acceptance of Deane's hypothesis, there is still a shortage of literature to substantiate it. Case studies are gradually accumulating that illustrate the organization of labour within the industrial system. They stress the role played by capital, rather than the workplace *per se*, in this process and in the development of class relationships within it. Such studies include those by Hudson on the textile industry in the West Riding of Yorkshire, Lloyd-Jones and Lewis on the cotton industry in Manchester, and Behagg on the Birmingham metal trades.[7] Berg notes 'the shift to a slow evolutionary view of capital accumulation and technological changes in the process of industrialization, in which the emphasis is placed as much on changes in the culture and organization of labour as on mechanical innovation';[8] and elsewhere that although traditional craftsmanship and manual work continued, it was now organized within the framework of industrial capital.[9]

Among these references, the lack of a detailed study of the industrial organization of nineteenth-century Sheffield is perhaps remarkable.[10] For it is Sheffield, to a greater extent than any other city in England other than possibly Birmingham, which was characterized during the course of the Industrial Revolution by the persistence of small workshops, of 'little mesters' and of outworkers in its metal and ancillary trades.[11] If Deane is indeed correct, then Sheffield ceases to be an anomaly in the course of British industrialization – as it is so often regarded – and becomes instead a classic example of it.[12] It is also Sheffield that was used by the late nineteenth-century economist Alfred Marshall as a prime example of an 'industrial district',[13] and for both reasons it merits our further attention here.

# I

Given the preoccupation in the 1980s with consumption, as well as the concerns of economists about the saturation of mass markets and of environmentalists about the exhaustion of natural resources and about pollution, it was perhaps inevitable that the attention of historians would return to the role of small firms in industrialization.[14] While the term *industrial district* was first devised by Marshall to describe the structure of the light trades (cutlery and edge-tool manufacture) in the Sheffield area and the textile industry in south-east Lancashire as clusters of small firms normally working in cooperation rather than in competition with one another, it has recently come to be used more generally to describe identifiable geographical areas to which networks of small companies with similar interests are attracted. These localities are ideally suited for 'flexible specialization', as the companies within them exist in a mutually beneficial relationship based on both competition and cooperation. Outside the districts firms continue to compete with one another for markets. Within them innovative technologies and flexible production techniques flourish.[15]

The concept of 'flexible specialization', which has been developed by economists, geographers and political scientists as well as by sociologists and historians, was recently amplified in the work of Charles Sabel and Jonathan Zeitlin.[16] They argue that Fordist mass production technologies took over local forms of production which were perfectly viable in their own right, and that the post-Fordist emergence of 'new localized and flexible industries . . . is nothing other than the re-emergence of an old production technique in a new technological guise'.[17] They examine and compare the historical development of industrial districts both in mainland Europe and in Britain, of which Sheffield is one. They attribute the eventual demise of light industry in Sheffield to 'stalled innovation' and labour unrest in the face of change rather than to any inherent difficulties with the concept of industrial districts *per se*.

A further theme advanced by Marshall, and developed by a number of his disciples, is the potential for workers in industrial districts such as Sheffield to achieve a far greater degree of independence than is possible within the factory system. The common interests of, and thus the lack of distinction between, employers and workers is often emphasized in the literature. It has been suggested both by contemporaries and by historians that during the nineteenth century there was less poverty in Sheffield than in other industrial cities, a generalization that lends credence to the theory of upward social mobility and appears to strengthen the arguments in favour of industrial districts. Frank Hill, writing in 1860, observed that 'the distinction between the capitalist and workman is not so sharply marked in Sheffield as elsewhere. The artisan is to a certain extent a capitalist: he contributes not only his manual skill and strength, but, in many cases, pays wheel rent – the materials only being found by the employer.' He went on to note that the Sheffield artisan had a greater degree of independence than his counterparts elsewhere with regard to his working hours.[18]

One difficulty with this type of argument is that it may be taken out of context, as is illustrated by other contemporary interpretations of that same Sheffield scene. The government inspector Jelinger Symons, in a report that predated Hill's work but was based on similar observations, commented on the overworking of both adult and child labourers in Sheffield resulting from precisely the lack of regulation of hours and conditions in the cutlery trades that Hill applauded.[19] Another difficulty is illustrated by the credence given to the argument by those politicians and academics alike who, almost a century and a half later, seek to justify a return to Victorian principles of *laissez-faire* in both the economic and social spheres. For example, a group of Sheffield-based business historians has recently sought to contradict the theory that Britain's failure to adopt a 'big business' strategy left a disastrous legacy of underinvestment, inadequate resources directed at research and development, and poor management. They argue instead that research on the Sheffield metal trades shows that sustained economic success could be achieved on the basis of the network of small firms in the area. They continue: 'the firms formed a network of competing units, which exploited Sheffield's outwork system. The firms could retain a nucleus of skilled outworkers, knowing that costs could be cut during downswings by laying people off.'[20] According to this line of thought, local industries based on a network of small firms, 'little mesters' and outworkers are economically viable today as in the last century and are more resilient to downswings than large concerns because of their flexible employment structure.

Such an argument is obviously open to challenge by those who are concerned not only with economic survival rates but with other economic and social indicators in their reading of nineteenth-century history. Put simply, it highlights the advantages of outwork for the employer and completely ignores the realities for the worker. It is, however, useful in that it exposes the confusion that has arisen in the wake of the industrial districts debate, confusion inherent in Sheffield's industrial history and class structure. It is the purpose of the remainder of this essay to attempt to unravel such confusion and to put the debate into a different perspective.

## II

At first glance, it would appear that Sheffield's light industries indeed prospered during the nineteenth century. The various sources indicate a dramatic increase in the number of firms in the cutlery and edge-tool trades from the late 1790s to 1914. A closer examination reveals that some of the most marked increases in small firms were at times of economic recession. For instance, between 1837 and 1843 – a period of both local and national depression – there was an increase in the numbers listed under the heading 'Merchants and Manufacturers' in the Sheffield trade directories, with forty-three new ventures appearing in 1841, the worst year of the depression.[21] Such figures appear to vindicate those who point to the survival rates of small firms as indicators of their economic viability.[22]

But who were these merchants and manufacturers? And are these entries in fact synonymous with our concept of a firm? The 'firms' alluded to in the foregoing quotation may, in Sheffield terms, have been no more than one- or perhaps two-person concerns. While the annual report of the Chief Inspector of Factories and Workshops might note in 1887 that in Sheffield and Rotherham there existed 3,110 factories and 1,242 workshops, the historian G.I.H. Lloyd has pointed out that in the context of nineteenth-century Sheffield a 'factory' normally meant a small-scale concern comprising an average of four to six workers.[23] A workshop was by implication even smaller, consisting of perhaps a father and son. It should also be noted that any individual could have his or her own entry in the Sheffield trade directories under any heading he or she might choose. Indeed, it was by no means uncommon to appear under more than one heading: for instance, a 'manufacturer' might also be listed elsewhere as a 'pen-knife cutler'. The firm of George Wostenholm, a large and well-known Sheffield employer, is one example of this; but there are many others, far smaller and often virtually unknown.

Terminology, therefore, needs to be treated very carefully in the Sheffield context. This applies not only to 'firms', but to other words such as 'masters' and 'manufacturers', which occur frequently and often interchangeably in the literature, thereby causing a great deal of confusion as will be further demonstrated.

## III

Behagg begins his study of the social structure of nineteenth-century Birmingham by challenging the statement made by Timmins in 1866 that out of all industrial workers in the country, those in Sheffield and Birmingham enjoyed the greatest degree of social and personal freedom: 'The large number of small manufacturers are practically independent of the numerous factors and merchants they supply.'[24] Far from being independent of such people, as Timmins suggests here, the evidence of a wide variety of nineteenth-century sources indicates that the small manufacturers became ever more indebted to them. For instance, the *Sheffield Independent* in 1872 noted that 'in quiet times merchants are able to barter the "little mesters", as they are called, almost to starvation prices, and thus compete on most unfair terms with the larger manufacturers, who continue to pay ordinary prices'.[25] In a number of instances the evidence presented to the Select Committee on the Sweating System in 1889 described 'little mesters' either as outworkers or as dependent on merchants, factors or larger manufacturers. Similar examples may be found in the evidence compiled by the Royal Commission on Labour in 1894.[26] Timmins's comment refers to 1866, but the increasing dependence of Sheffield workers on those who controlled the industrial capital of the city, and which he failed to observe, was in fact established well before then. Lloyd notes with reference to the depression of 1820, that when as many as 1,600 spring-knife cutlers were unemployed, Sheffield was nevertheless 'thronging with little masters while the regular workshops were empty'; and that at the height of the recession from 1842 until 1844, when four out of five workers were unemployed, 'the trades were swarming with little masters, there being more than 500 in the spring knife trade alone'. During such times, while wages and prices both became depressed, output continued to increase.[27]

These little masters were not, in the vast majority of cases, themselves factors. Factors generally comprised a separate group, although the two are often confused. For instance, Taylor writes that the little masters might be small-scale producers, merchants, or both; and moreover that the 'working' little masters always outnumbered the 'factor' little masters. However, she acknowledges that 'one factory inspector characterized the little mester not as an "intermediary" but as a "workman", forced by circumstances to "sweat" those who worked for him'.[28] In 1936 Dyson defined a little master as 'a master cutler working on his own, but in a rented room in a factory, paying his own rent and dealing through a factor'.[29] This definition not only makes a distinction between the two groups but indicates that possibly the only genuine independence the little masters enjoyed was that afforded by physical privacy at work.

Who then were these factors and merchants in the Sheffield context? Unlike Leeds, to take one example, there was no traditional merchant class in Sheffield.[30] Factors are often alluded to in the nineteenth-century sources on Sheffield but rarely defined, which adds to the confusion surrounding them. In his evidence to the Select Committee on the Sweating System, Stuart Uttley describes them in the following terms:

> These factors or merchants in many instances do not employ workmen direct, but they obtain orders and give them out to the little master, who is himself a workman. . . . A factor or small merchant is a man who will either go direct into the market or will take orders from a larger merchant for certain classes of goods, and of course give them out to the small masters to execute for him. . . . Many of these persons who set up as factors are as a rule those that have had some experience in the larger warehouses, and under the system of apprenticeship or service that exists, they very often find themselves . . . compelled to get along as best they can, as the larger firms do not require their services after they get up to 21 or 22 years of age. . . . The small factor in the first instance is a man who possibly does not understand the work; he is not a workman, but understands something of it from the routine of his service in some factor's warehouse.[31]

So a factor, like the little master whom he exploited, was often forced into self-employment through his own economic hardship. Apart from this similarity, Uttley draws a clear distinction between the two groups in terms of their respective roles. Moreover if there was a difference between the functions of a little master and a factor, there was also a difference in their economic and social origins. In her study of the West Yorkshire woollen industry, Hudson notes that evidence suggests that the merchant-manufacturer, who personified the alliance of mercantile and industrial capital, was increasingly the product of industrial rather than mercantile circles.[32] If this was the case in the Leeds area, where even before large-scale industrialization a traditional merchant class had existed, it is still more likely to have been true of Sheffield, where such a group was virtually non-existent.[33] Small factors could have originated from among the numerous attorneys and retailers in the town. Behagg observes that it is essential to distinguish between 'the petit-bourgeois small manufacturer, who drew strength from the image of the entrepreneur as created and modelled by the highly individual values of political economy', and 'the small master, who related the economic structure to an artisan-oriented set of collective values'.[34]

By the end of the depression which had lasted from 1837 to 1843, there did indeed exist in Sheffield a distinct and growing *petite bourgeoisie* whose influence was increasingly felt not only in the town's economy but in local affairs generally.[35] Less than fifty years later Stuart Uttley, in his evidence to the Select Committee on the Sweating System, described the factors as Sheffield's middle classes: 'I believe that there are too many people today who are making a living out of it, what we may term middle-class men who themselves go in to obtain orders and get their living out of the workmen.'[36] Inherent in Sheffield's nineteenth-century class structure, therefore, was an exploitative class relationship that manifested itself not in the workplace but at the warehouse, at the point of commodity exchange.[37]

There is one additional complication in the Sheffield terminology. There has been a tendency for some writers to take the phrase 'proximity of men and masters', which occurs very frequently in a wide variety of nineteenth-century sources, out of context.[38] As already indicated, the word 'masters' in Sheffield does not normally mean large-scale employers, of whom there were very few in the light trades, George Wostenholm and Joseph Rodgers being among the largest. On the contrary, it generally means the 'little mesters' who normally worked alongside those whom they hired, whether as employees or outworkers. Masters and men alike worked in appalling conditions. In his *Report on the Trades of Sheffield*, Symons writes that:

> orders for inferior cutlery are given by a species of merchant termed 'factors', who . . . merely give orders (sometimes supplying steel) to very small cutlers, who . . . perform all the operations except grinding. . . . These men are in the position . . . of small manufacturers; and indeed it is not easy to draw the line in Sheffield between men and masters.[39]

This statement not only serves to underline the distinction between factors on the one hand and little masters on the other, but puts the phrase 'proximity of men and masters' in its proper context.

It is apparent that the 'little mesters' themselves were increasingly being reduced to the status of outworkers as the century progressed, indicating that downward social mobility, not upward, was the norm. Towards the end of the nineteenth century, the terms 'manufacturer', 'little mester' and 'outworker' were certainly being used ever more interchangeably. As Uttley commented in a masterpiece of understatement in his evidence to the Select Committee on the Sweating System, 'it is rather complicated I am aware for persons that are not accustomed to it'.[40] The fluidity of Sheffield's social structure is illustrated by the following exchange between Joe Gale, a scissor grinder, and George Chance, one of the commissioners appointed in 1867 to investigate the Sheffield Outrages:

> 2588 (Mr Chance). What are you? – A scissor grinder.
> 2589 How long have you been in the trade? – I was apprenticed in the year 1850.
> 2590 When did you become a journeyman? – In 1858, nine years ago.
> 2591 Are you a journeyman now? – No, a scissor grinder; as a rule we are master grinders, though you might term us journeymen. I am employed for a scissors manufacturer in the town.
> 2592 You employ journeymen? – Sometimes.
> 2593 And you also work yourself? – It is the rule in the town that scissors grinders are master grinders because they find their own tools and pay for power, and can leave at a moment's notice.
> 2594 You sometimes employ journeymen and sometimes not? – Yes.
> 2595 Then you work for yourself, and are at the same time an employer, and also a scissor grinder? – Yes, and also a journeyman.[41]

Moreover, both masters and outworkers were increasingly dependent on, rather than independent of, the factors, merchants or large manufacturers who ultimately paid them. The employer might be a manufacturer, but was more likely to be a factor or small merchant who had his own warehouse and sold, in his turn, either to a variety of manufacturers or directly to customers. There was constant competition for work, especially in times of recession, which only slackened during periods of economic growth.[42]

The problem originated with the ease – officially after the Cutlers' Act of 1814, unofficially before it – with which an unemployed worker, or indeed any worker, could set himself up as a master or small manufacturer in his own right. Little if any capital, and probably no new tools or equipment, were required.[43] It was precisely the large numbers of new entrants to the market, particularly at times of depression when workers were laid off in their thousands, that caused oversupply of goods and downward pressure on both prices and wages. Far from encouraging upward social mobility, the result was sweated labour on an unprecedented scale. Thus the increasing numbers of small firms in the Sheffield trade directories and the increasing poverty in the city were directly related to each other. Contrary to some interpretations, the first was not a panacea for the second but an immediate cause of it.[44] Behagg has summarized it thus:

> At the start of our period the economic and social nexus between the artisan and small master was strong: by the mid-nineteenth century that between capital and the producer was stronger . . . the small master . . . had been marginalized.[45]

'Proximity of men and masters' therefore has nothing to do with egalitarianism or upward mobility but in nineteenth-century Sheffield, as in Birmingham, was a result of the exploitation of small masters and artisans by the emergent and increasingly dominant factor class.

## IV

The lack of a clear distinction in nineteenth-century Sheffield between masters and men, or manufacturers and employees, did not mean that there was no cause for conflict among those engaged in the city's light trades. The mere fact of the Outrages, and the appointment of a Royal

Commission in 1867 to investigate what had become a regular feature of life there, attests to the contrary. Taylor's concluding statement to her recent study of the Sheffield cutlery industry from 1870 to 1914, that 'the small-scale [sic] of the industry, the intense competition and commensurate absence of large fortunes helped to ensure the proximity of most manufacturers to their men', is misleading in that it creates an impression of general economic and social harmony, echoing the work of Alfred Marshall previously cited.[46]

To those historians seeking by contrast to account for the high incidence of friction among Sheffield workers, as exemplified by the Outrages, the unions have provided a convenient explanation. In his comparative study of Birmingham and Sheffield, Smith writes that in Sheffield there was considerable overlap between the workplace and the household, allowing the local community an exceptional degree of control over its members.[47] He cites the example of an edge-tool maker who, having left Sheffield for Birmingham in 1838, observed that 'in Sheffield I have known the children hoot a workman who did not belong to the union of his trade'.[48] According to Smith, it was the unions that were responsible for impeding the moves to mechanization that were taking place in other industries. The same worker is quoted as remarking: 'the strikes among the workmen are very numerous at Sheffield. . . . Machinery is much more extensively employed at Birmingham than at Sheffield, and the prejudice against it is so strong at Sheffield that I have known an instance of a man being obliged to leave the town because he substituted a bellows for a blow-pipe.'[49]

Smith cites as evidence of their strength the greater number of trade unions in Sheffield than in Birmingham, despite the larger population of the latter city. The Trades Union Directory for 1861 listed sixty unions in Sheffield, as opposed to forty-two in Birmingham. Moreover, the meeting times were listed for all the Sheffield unions, suggesting 'a higher degree of activity and closer communication among union members in Sheffield than in Birmingham'.[50] In contrast, Lloyd uses similar numerical evidence to observe that 'the dispersal of the trades through a multitude of small workshops robbed the men of that stimulus to industrial solidarity which congregation in a few large establishments affords'.[51] Indeed, it had been the primary purpose of the 1814 Cutlers' Act to weaken the unions by allowing the workforce to increase in size.[52] So the number of unions in Sheffield, which Smith interprets as an indicator of their strength, may in fact have been quite the reverse.

In a detailed discussion of the unions or trades societies in Sheffield, Lloyd states that excepting short periods of comparative strength, usually at times of rapid economic growth, most of the Sheffield unions remained weak and disorganized throughout the nineteenth century.[53] Every branch of every trade had its own organization. Thus there was not a single grinders' union, but a saw grinders' union, an axe grinders' union, a pen- and pocket-knife grinders' union, and so on. The sheer number of unions in nineteenth-century Sheffield bore no more relationship to the strength of the union movement than the number of cutlery firms to the health of the local industry. On the contrary, the relationship in both cases may well have been an inverse one. The unions did not unite the workers in the cutlery trades, and did not act as a surrogate for class in disputes with employers.

The reason for this disunity lies, again, in Sheffield's social structure. If there were fewer socio-economic gulfs in Sheffield than in other industrial cities of nineteenth-century Britain, this is due neither to a total absence of wealthier classes,[54] nor to a greater degree of philanthropy on their part in Sheffield than elsewhere, but because the majority of workers in Sheffield's major industry until mid-century, that of cutlery and tool production, were either outworkers or very small manufacturers. It would follow that unions as such might have been inhibited from taking part in Sheffield trades disputes because in general they would have been opposing their fellow workers. Many employers were themselves union members and at least one union was actually also an employer.[55]

The Outrages were not in general a reaction by the unions to changes in production, pay or conditions introduced by employers, but a reaction by individuals, sometimes but by no means always acting with the union's knowledge, usually to the employment by 'little mesters' of non-union members. To talk about general obstructiveness by the unions to innovations in technology, as various writers including Smith, Sabel and Zeitlin do, is to miss the point made by Lloyd and earlier observers that the nineteenth-century cutlery unions in Sheffield were the successors of the guilds, whose primary concern was to maintain standards among their workers. 'The conduct of the unions . . . constituted in many respects an appeal to the old principle of regulated trade. . . . Even the practice of "rattening" was in its essence a relic of the ancient legal right of the guild to enforce the observance of trade rules by distraining upon the property of defaulting members. . . . Nowhere was the spirit of loyalty to industrial traditions stronger than in Sheffield.'[56] It also overlooks the possibility suggested by Tweedale in his study of the firm of George Wostenholm that some of the opposition to innovation that inevitably did occur may have originated not with the workers but with their employers.[57]

In contradiction of Smith and other writers cited earlier, it may be argued that together with the increase of factors it was the proliferation of the 'little mesters', not of the unions, that caused divisions and tensions in nineteenth-century Sheffield society. Lloyd observes that the little masters were not only a considerable disadvantage to the manufacturers, but were even more detrimental to the development of the union movement.[58] The increase in the numbers of little masters in the city, especially at times of recession such as that from 1837 to 1843, has already been observed along with the consequent erosion of standards and quality of workmanship due to overproduction and price undercutting.[59] The *Sheffield Iris* reported on 10 December 1842 that 'a great many of these outrages had been committed by individuals in no way connected with Trades Unions . . . [which] had been equally beneficial to masters and workmen'.[60] Taylor, writing of the number of small trade societies formed from 1814 onward within the framework of the old Cutlers' Company regulations, observes that there was a greater degree of similarity between the trade unionists and the main manufacturers in the town than there was between union members and the unskilled workers who were rapidly proliferating there, but who were nevertheless free to call themselves little masters too.[61]

Crossick has also noted increasing tensions among workers during this period. He questions the very existence of the 'supposedly close relationship between masters and men' in small workshops, an assumption which has extensively influenced the historical interpretation of society and politics in Birmingham, and which has then been extended to include other industrial towns. According to Crossick, little evidence has ever been advanced to illustrate such closeness. He continues: 'the economic difficulties of small masters, and the way that so many people responded by . . . behaving less and less according to the artisanal expectations of their trade, made increasing conflict between masters and journeymen unavoidable'.[62]

This is a different type of conflict from that hypothesized by Smith. Crossick is not discussing militancy on the part of the unions but increasing factionalism among the workers themselves. He notes, in common with Berg, Hudson and Deane, that the Industrial Revolution was characterized at least as much by commercial change as by the building of factories and mills. He observes that this change particularly affected small producers who became increasingly dependent on factors and on merchant operations, in turn effectively perpetuating the fragmentation of whole industries and furthering their own internal weaknesses.[63] Thus, while it may be true that in nineteenth-century Sheffield fewer individual fortunes were 'amassed' than in other industrial cities, it is hard to justify the statement that 'few major gulfs developed between masters and men'.[64] In socio-economic terms these gulfs may indeed have been negligible, but in terms of credit relationships they were both apparent and widening. The title of a chapter of Baxter's thesis, 'Freedom to Become Slaves', is an apt summation of the social and economic consequences for Sheffield cutlery workers of the removal by Parliament in 1814 of the restraints hitherto imposed on entry to the industry by the Cutlers' Company.[65]

<h2 style="text-align:center">V</h2>

Crossick has written that, in nineteenth-century Britain, upward social mobility was not necessarily the experience of all who made the transition from wage-earners to little masters.[66] In the context of nineteenth-century Sheffield, the almost universal experience of the small master appears, rather, to have been downward – his ranking on the social scale was gradually replaced by the growing if ill-defined group of factors, who were increasingly being perceived as Sheffield's middle class.[67]

Several conclusions may be drawn from the preceding discussion. Firstly, the subject is an important one for understanding the process of industrialization in nineteenth-century Britain, for the observations made here are not limited to Sheffield. They can be applied to any number of other industrial towns. For example, it has been written of Nottingham:

the supposed contrast between the delights experienced by the domestic worker and the grim conditions of the factory worker is no longer acceptable . . . it is clear that [the independent stocking-knitter] of the early nineteenth century was working harder than ever before for lower wages and that his children were working at an earlier age than ever before. The independence associated with working at home or in a neighbour's small workshop meant nothing if a fifteen-hour day had to be worked. . . . There is little reason to suppose that Henry Hollins of Mansfield was wrong in claiming in 1816 that the lot of a child in a well-run cotton-mill was better than that of a twelve-year-old operating a stocking-frame.[68]

A person engaged in industrial work at home or in a workshop in nineteenth-century Britain rarely remained, if indeed he had ever been, master of his own destiny. And if, as Deane has stated, it is indeed the case that workshops proliferated faster than factories until the late nineteenth century, then it must also be the case that the worsening conditions of much of the industrial population were due to their situation not as factory workers but as outworkers. Small wonder, then, that the majority of the early Factory Acts were so ineffectual in redressing the conditions of the majority of British industrial workers.

Secondly, it has been suggested elsewhere that 'the more important the identity of the independent small producer became in both working- and middle-class self-perceptions, the more of a myth it became in economic reality'.[69] Neither that essay nor this has addressed the validity of such self-perceptions. Even if it were only an illusion, did the feeling of independence offset the problems caused by chronic indebtedness, poor working conditions, long hours and ill health? As long as Sheffield workers adhered to 'Saint Monday', for instance, they were able to some extent to regulate their own working hours, even if by doing so they had to recoup any time lost during the remainder of the week.[70] To what extent moreover was there a sense of class interest and identity among the artisans?[71]

This essay has sought to clarify some of the divisions in Sheffield society and has indicated a large degree of fragmentation among its workforce, but none of this necessarily implies that there was more friction in Sheffield than in other industrial towns. The extent to which workers in the Sheffield light trades were content with their lot and laboured under at least an illusion of independence necessitates further investigation. In an earlier work on Kentish London, Crossick paved the way for such a study by writing of Victorian society there that while 'too firm a line must not be drawn between small masters and the élite of skilled workers from which they came . . . nevertheless the distinction is relevant, not for the reality it portrays – that reality offered little escape for most skilled workers – but because it allowed the view of economic opportunity to remain a partially opened one'.[72]

Finally, the debate on class relationships in nineteenth-century Sheffield may be of immediate relevance to our own era. John Major's 'classless society' was based on the ideal of upward social mobility for all individuals, among other means through the impetus given to small businesses by successive Conservative governments. His last government tended to equate the growth in the numbers of small businesses with economic recovery.[73] This increase is synonymous with the rise in self-employment throughout the country. Yet far from indicating an economic upturn, it may – as in nineteenth-century Sheffield – mean quite the reverse. Self-employment today often stems from unemployment, and from a last desperate attempt to avoid the poverty trap caused by the benefits squeeze or by the withdrawal after only six months of unemployment of the 'job-seeker's allowance'. Recent falls in unemployment and the survival in registers of small firms from one year to the next are on their own no indication, any more than they were in nineteenth-century Sheffield, of the condition of the workforce or the revival of the local or national economy. Dependence on an employer has been replaced by dependence on bank or government loans: the modern equivalent of factoring. Moreover, as more and more employers take advantage of part-time, freelance or self-employed workers in order to minimize their own overheads, and as more and more overseas firms move into Britain to take advantage of relatively low wage rates, it may be postulated that upward social mobility is again becoming increasingly elusive for much of the working population.

CHAPTER

4

# SECOND METROPOLIS:

## THE MIDDLE CLASS IN EARLY VICTORIAN LIVERPOOL

JOHN BELCHEM AND NICK HARDY

From its exponential growth to its current decline Liverpool has been notorious for its proverbial exceptionalism. Once the second city of the empire (now descended by seemingly irreversible economic and demographic decline into Objective One European Union status), Liverpool has defied historical categorization, standing outside the main narrative frameworks of modern British history. Revisionism promises rehabilitation. Labour history leads the way: scouse exceptionalism has been called into question as attention has shifted from the old paradigms and preoccupations based on the narrow confines of the 'traditional' working class in the industrial districts.[1] This essay carries such interrogation further by applying revisionist perspectives on economic history – and on the Irish in Britain – to the Liverpolitan (to use the genteel inflexion) middle class. Specifically, how useful are such revisionist motifs as 'gentlemanly capitalism' and 'ethnic fade'? As we shall show, nineteenth-century commercial Liverpool, the nation's 'second metropolis', remains difficult to locate even in the emerging orthodoxy which now recognizes Victorian England more as the clearing-house than the workshop of the world. There is no entry for Liverpool in the index for either volume of Cain and Hopkins's much-praised study of 'gentlemanly capitalism'.[2] Its large Irish population notwithstanding, Liverpool is similarly overlooked in studies which now insist on the socio-economic success and assimilation of the Irish in Britain.

From the construction of its innovatory wet-docks system in the early eighteenth century, Liverpool, the 'western emporium of

Albion', identified its prosperity with commerce, not with manufacture.[3] Incoming merchants, Scottish and otherwise, continued to avoid industrial investment even when 'surfeited with capital'. John Gladstone, father of the future prime minister, typified the attitude: a leading merchant in the West India interest (an efficient slaveowner though never a slavetrader), he possessed an outstanding business brain, but took no interest in the Industrial Revolution.[4] Guidebooks duly welcomed the absence of industry, noting with relief that the curse of the factory system stopped short of Liverpool and its independent workers.[5] Having overhauled Bristol, Liverpool was proud of its commercial image and provincial pre-eminence: it sought to rival London in its commercial infrastructure, to establish itself as a 'self-dependent financial centre'.[6] Vaunting its status as 'second metropolis',[7] nineteenth-century Liverpool, the 'modern Tyre', aspired to combine commerce, culture and civilization. A kind of city-state, it craved recognition as 'the Florence of the north', a fitting tribute to William Roscoe, self-made role model and icon for the mercantile élite.[8] Subscription societies attended to the promotion of literature and the arts, supplemented by a number of voluntary associations specifically geared to the education and recreation of young clerks, 'Liverpool gentlemen' – not 'Manchester men' – in the making.[9] Through the hasty invention of tradition, Liverpool acquired a number of 'old families' to attest to the nobility of commerce.[10] The ethos was to endure, preventing a wider (and much-needed) industrial diversification.

A northern outpost of gentlemanly capitalism with a flourishing extra-European trade, early Victorian Liverpool defined itself against industrial Manchester and in rivalry with commercial London. Thomas Baines's *History of the Commerce and Town of Liverpool* (1852) provided the requisite historical perspective to confirm the port's commercial pre-eminence:

> . . . the commerce of Liverpool extends to every port of any importance in every quarter of the globe. In this respect it far surpasses the commerce of any city of which we have a record from past times, as Tyre, Venice, Genoa, Amsterdam, or Antwerp, and fully equals, if it does not surpass, that of London and New York, the one the avowed capital of the first commercial state in the world, the other the real capital of the second.[11]

By the 1840s, as the push for the free-trade economy gathered strength, Liverpool's credentials as a major commercial centre were unquestionable.[12] By mid-decade customs revenue collected at the port amounted to £4.5 million per annum[13] while dock revenue was running at about £250,000.[14] By the end of the decade Liverpool was clearing more than twice the export business of London, shipping out nearly £35 million worth of goods a year, while imports were valued at £37.5 million (£5 million less than London).[15] Faith in the efficacy of *freer* trade as an economic stimulant was expressed in a dock committee recommendation (endorsed by the town council) in June 1847 that rates be reduced on cotton, iron, coal and shipping, in some cases by almost a half.[16]

By the mid-1840s there were about 8,000 businessmen engaged in activities of a commercial nature in Liverpool.[17] Revenue figures indicate the presence of substantial personal wealth among the most successful individuals while the aggressive pricing of facilities within the port economy indicates strong competition against the capital. Significant personal wealth elevated the individual into the local plutocracy while the general wealth of the town resourced its prestige on the national stage. Civic architecture, institutional endowment and domestic luxury, derived from a virile commercial economy, sustained the 'second metropolis' status. Here was a site where gentlemanly capitalism – that 'complex of economic, social and political influences even more powerful and dynamic than the forces released by the Industrial Revolution'[18] – appeared truly to flourish.

Forced by jealous commercial rivalry of London into conditional alignment with the 'industrial' north, Liverpool brought a special angle to the north–south divide. London was much resented for its monopolistic privileges and practices, anachronistic obstacles in the path of Liverpool's rise to commercial pre-eminence. When James Morris, a director of the Bank of England, came up from London as Ewart's running mate in the 1835 parliamentary election, he was immediately stigmatized (and offered for auction) as:

Lot 2: COCKNEY: a South Country Horse, 11½ hands high, sent here with a <u>false pedigree</u>; Sire stated to be <u>Free Trade</u>, but though <u>quite unknown</u> here, he is ascertained to have been got by <u>Monopoly</u>, trained in Threadneedle-street, where he has been used by an <u>Old Lady</u>, who has got a Patent, for making Rags into

Money, and who prosecutes with the utmost rigour anyone else that attempts to follow the same trade. Though not vicious in other respects, 'COCKNEY' like all <u>London</u>-bred Horses, is very <u>jealous</u> of those bred in the <u>North</u>, particularly <u>Liverpool</u>.[19]

Rivalry and jealousy were as significant as differences in political economy between the capital and the 'second metropolis'. As in London, where gentlemanly capitalists with shipping, timber, tea and sugar interests preferred to reap the benefits of monopoly rather than rush headlong into an open and risky market, some of Liverpool's merchant princes in the West India trade, the old Tory élite, were staunchly protectionist, committed to the retention of the Navigation Laws.[20] By the 1840s, however, the initiative had passed to the more progressive (often Unitarian) merchants in the American trade. Fed by the expansionist fervour of Bramley-Moore and Hartley, the grandiose plans for extensions to the docks (and hence displacement of the old Tory-protectionist riverside artisan trades) were premised on the anticipated freeing of trade.[21]

Within commercial Liverpool itself, divisions over political economy should not be overdrawn: there was no fundamental fracture in the mercantile élite. The 'community' of capitalist entrepreneurs which ran Liverpool did not endorse a 'free trade' in commercial practice. Soon after the Navigation Laws were repealed, merchant groups set former differences aside to cooperate in the newly established Liverpool Chamber of Commerce, in defiance of predictions that 'it was impossible for gentlemen of different political opinions, having different commercial interests, and different commercial views, to meet and act for a common object and a common good'.[22] Such collective self-regulation was designed to impose discipline and curb excesses. Stability of prices was highly prized. 'Alarm' in the markets created unease at the dining tables of the élite.[23] Admittedly, when the share and stock market was 'in great agitation' many people stood to gain (one 'gentleman', in one year, was said to have gained £100,000),[24] but speculation was not seen as a good thing for the business community as a whole. For the individual, 'share mania' (to use George Holt's phrase) carried with it the taint of moral degeneracy besides the risk of economic catastrophe, particularly when it caused merchants to neglect 'their ordinary occupations'.[25] Serious and substantial businessmen, especially those of Nonconformist beliefs, deplored such activity.[26] William Rathbone was uninterested in making a great deal of money in a short space of time; such wealth was insecure and the scramble to acquire it left nothing for the contemplation of the purpose behind having it.[27] Of Rathbone's rationalization of personal wealth it was said only that:

> in order to fulfil the possibilities which he saw for himself, it was necessary that he should command a fairly ample fortune. He had no taste for personal luxury, and a strong sense of the duty of frugality.[28]

Indicative of a sense of personal self-worth, and implying a sense of responsibility to something wider than himself and his own, this assessment of Rathbone also implies a perception on his part of a potential prejudice against which commercial entrepreneurs had to fight. He knew that:

> the weight which was given to a man's words or principles was greatly determined by the skill which he had shown in managing his own affairs, and . . . this skill, in the case at any rate of men of business, was inevitably roughly measured by the amount of his wealth.[29]

Thus, holding important formal positions in local government and in bodies to which 'gentlemanly' businessmen were inclined to direct their philanthropic contributions, was an indication, if not a certificate, of commercial success.

Philanthropy was an important credential for a member of the plutocracy, while indiscriminate charity, including cash handouts by individuals, on the street or at the house, was frowned upon. This latter – 'the national error of Englishmen' – was mischievous and ostentatious: 'the readiest, the easiest, and the coarsest medicament which naturally approved itself to a people at once rich, tender-hearted and lazy'. The 'frightful spectacle . . . of a number of people tumultuously rushing to do good' was counter-productive, for want was caused by high prices and high prices were a symptom of scarcity. Charity could not augment quantity, only adjust distribution. Voting money to the famine-stricken Irish, for example, amounted to no more than voting it into the pockets of corn growers.[30] Ahead of the London urban gentry, Liverpool's gentlemanly capitalists appreciated the need for 'scientific charity'.[31]

In the 'perfected state of society' which free trade would herald, public charities would become unnecessary, a point underlined at Renshaw Street (Unitarian) chapel by Revd John Hamilton Thom in a 'charity' sermon – on behalf of the Dispensaries – which addressed 'the bearing of free trade on the condition of society as well as government in general'.[32] In the meantime, however, constructive philanthropy was a necessary ingredient in the concept of a 'commercial aristocrat'. Thus, William Brown received the accolade of 'merchant prince' from the *Liverpool Mercury* in March 1849, for his contributions of £250 to the Mechanics' Institute and £1,000 to the Northern Hospital, plus 'many other munificent subscriptions to our local charities and institutions'.[33] Contributions in times of crisis could legitimately be sent to 'approved' institutions, like Mr Barclay's Refuge for the Destitute, in Mount Vernon, which also fostered a programme to look into and engage with the problem of juvenile delinquency,[34] to the Domestic Mission fostered by Unitarians like Richard Vaughan Yates,[35] or to the Night Asylum, of whose management committee George Holt was the chair and a report for which organization showed that, in 1844, it sheltered 14,700.[36]

The extent of general poverty prompted discussions in the local press, but the discourse served only to confirm free trade as a moral imperative.[37] 'The prosperity of the working classes is inseparably dependent on that of their employers', the editor of the *Liverpool Times* opined: 'the only way they can place it on a firm basis is by cooperating zealously with their employers in the war against monopolies of all kinds'.[38] While there was careful guard on charitable expenditure, economic depressions and social crises did not arrest the commercial class's drive for cultural adornments. The 1840s was a significant decade for advancements in the provision of music, for though in the past celebrities had occasionally visited, there was now an aspiration for Liverpool to become a regular station on the circuit of every internationally renowned musician. Momentum built throughout the decade for a project which resulted in the building of a concert hall. The opening festival in 1850 was graced by 'The Swedish Nightingale', Jenny Lind.[39] This new hall (costing £30,000 – a sum which was raised with ease from among the local élite) was said by the London *Times* to be 'one of the best in Europe' (this notwithstanding that another large space under construction in Liverpool – St George's Hall – promised to be a 'musical hall . . . the first, without comparison, in all Europe'). Each proprietor (there were 700) purchased a box or a stall *ad perpetuum* binding themselves to an annual subscription. At the opening all sixty-five boxes had been purchased as well as 600 stalls. *The Times* devoted a good deal of space to the occasion, noting especially that 'the object of the society is described as the culture of the highest order'.[40]

At the same time individuals were entering the art markets.[41] They also indulged their vanities, commissioning portraits of themselves and their families, in 'little girl with lap-dog' mode.[42] Shipping magnates committed the immortalization of their favourite vessels to local marine artists. But it is arguable that though the wealth produced at the quaysides may have been sufficient to support the pretensions of a supreme cultural centre, a 'Florence of the north' as Roscoe would have had it, the intrusiveness of social disorder and the disproportionate ratio of poor and starving[43] to the rest of the population did not produce an atmosphere conducive to the comfortable public display of art and cultural opulence. While there was an obvious necessity ultimately to embellish the lives of the business élite or soften the harsher realities of the entrepreneurial environment with delicate and diversionary artefacts, doing so only emphasized wealth differentials locally and possibly added to the 'guilt' of the well-off. To indulge their cultural fantasies more fully it might have been necessary for them to do so not as a local élite nursing a redoubt mentality but in a national society distanced from the upsetting rudeness of local contingencies, and oriented, inevitably, to the capital.[44]

How significant in percentage terms merchants and other occupational groups were in the hierarchy of the town may be shown from a closer look at the bodies responsible for local government. The three most important of these were the justices, the town council and the dock committee.[45] In 1845 there were thirty-five Justices of the Peace listed for Liverpool.[46] Nineteen of these were described by *Gore's* as 'merchants'. The remainder were two brewers, a timber merchant, an iron merchant, an insurance broker, two cotton brokers, a corn merchant, a commission merchant, and a coal proprietor, plus one 'gentleman' and four for whom no occupation was given (but who were probably also gentlemen-cum-retired businessmen). Justices were appointed for life, so although investiture was the product of governmental and political choices of the time they, of all the governors and executives of town life, were the least accountable. Twenty-three merchants, so-named, held places on the local bench, while of the five more senior members it may be guessed that some were of a mercantile background. It is likely therefore that as much as three-quarters of the summary justice in the borough was handed down by members of the mercantile fraternity. The remaining decisions were made by men so closely allied to the merchants as to be indistinguishable as far as practical interests were concerned.

Of the forty-four ordinary town councillors twelve were merchants, six were gentlemen, four were timber merchants, three were attorneys, two were surgeons and while four gave no occupations, the rest were a merchant and shipbroker, a cotton broker, a wine broker, a wine merchant, a wine and spirit merchant, a civil engineer, a warehouse keeper, a commission merchant, a printer and publisher, a brewer, a rectifier, a shipbuilder, a merchant and agent, an architect and surveyor and an attorney and insurance agent. At least twenty-nine of the forty-four were following commercial careers and again the merchants were by far the dominant group. The sixteen aldermanic councillors consisted of six merchants, two brokers, a banker, a broker and agent, a barrister, a shipsmith, a gentleman, a brewer, an attorney and one with no occupation given.

The twenty-seven members of the dock committee were almost all merchants. One broker, one shipbuilder, two gentlemen, and two members whose occupation was not given, were the only exceptions. Given that the election of committee members was by quota from the body of town councillors and the body of dock ratepayers, it is not surprising to find it packed with merchants (the former body was overwhelmingly dominated by merchants and it must be assumed that the latter was exclusively mercantile in nature).

In their residential preferences, the members of these important local bodies displayed aristocratic aspirations, although at this time the mercantile élite divided into two distinct categories: those who lived within the borough of Liverpool, and on the developing edges of it, at Everton and Toxteth Park in a distinctly urban environment; and those who had initiated the retreat from their place of work into villadom and rurality. The second group, exhibiting élitist and aristocratic pretensions most conspicuously, favoured residences in Wavertree, Aigburth, Woolton, Allerton, West Derby, Dingle, Linacre Marsh and Roby. The Cheshire migration was also noticeable at this time with residences appearing at Oxton, Seacombe, Tranmere, Birkenhead, Rock Ferry, New Brighton, Wallasey and Liscard.

The names which these migrants selected for their new idyllic homes had aristocratic or Arcadian overtones[47] and occasionally they reflected the personal vanity of their owners. Some of the residences in the leafy hinterland were in fact second homes. While the most popular place of residence out of town appears to have been Aigburth, with twenty-five members of the élite sample having homes there, for those who lived in the town the prestigious addresses were indicated as Abercromby Square, Rodney Street, Hope Street, Mount Pleasant, Oxford Street, Islington, Falkner Street, Upper Parliament Street, Shaw Street, Low Hill, Pembroke Place, Netherfield Road North, Great George Square and the beginning of Edge Lane.

Of the Liverpool JPs, sixteen lived within the borough while twenty-four had retreated. The residences of the Liverpool ordinary town councillors reveal that twenty-seven of the forty-nine addresses were outside the borough limits. Eight of those, however, were at Everton, within the fringe of the built-up area, while a few were on the Liverpool margin of Toxteth Park, which was now becoming built-up.[48] The aldermanic councillors appear to exhibit slightly more loyal tendencies towards the town, with 50 per cent residing in the town proper. Five of them lived in Rodney Street alone, the others in Hope Street, Abercromby Square and Upper Parliament Street. Apart from two who lived in Everton, the rest of the commuters lived at Aigburth, Childwall, Mossley Hill, Toxteth Park and Birkenhead. The twenty-seven addresses of the dock committee present similar evidence, with fifteen (including the Evertonians) beyond the boundary, three of which were in Cheshire. Such residential evidence raises questions about the commercial class's commitment to Liverpool *per se*. On the one hand it was a good place to work and make huge profits, and to raise an edifice to one's own memory, but on the other it was not a suitable place to live; the atmosphere was too stifling. The aristocrats of commerce evidently felt the same as Hawthorne when, on account of its air quality, he found Liverpool 'the most disagreeable city in England'.[49]

An important member of Liverpool's plutocracy in the 1840s was George Holt, cotton broker, banker, insurance broker and father of shipping magnates Alfred and George, of the Blue Funnel Line and Lamport & Holt respectively. The estate of the Holt family residence at Edge Hill was, in the 1840s, still undergoing development. It sustained some kind of farm, with cattle, horses, smaller animals and fowl, some arable areas, and a garden devoted to both horticulture and the kitchen. Holt's interest in land was conspicuous from his inheritance through marriage, his buying, selling, renting out, and supporting cottages and houses from which he derived a rent income.[50]

His own house was substantial, judging by the scale of entertainment it could handle – occasionally as many as 100 guests to a party with buffet supper, music and dancing. It had a 'front', with gravel drive, and a full complement of staff and personal servants to maintain it and its occupants. Holt spent a good deal of time developing his estate and making up public roads bordering it, but besides buying land for cultivation he also bought it to control developments within the vicinity of his house. Because he maintained and let much of the local property many of his neighbours were also his tenants.[51]

The preservation of an impressive and refined domestic environment was of key importance to the propagation of the identity of the class which in ruling Liverpool secured its 'second metropolis' status. More than the institutions of local government, more than the Exchange, the commercialist's home was where he networked most significantly with his peers. Through the medium of hospitality, in socially exclusive circumstances, it was here that he communicated the cultural values which underpinned the local plutocracy.

Over a forty-four month period George Holt and/or other members of his immediate family were involved, as hosts or guests, in at least 155 dining engagements which could be described as socially exclusive occasions.[52] This represented an average of 3.5 per month. Some months, however (June, July and September 1845, May and June 1846, June and July 1847 and May 1848), had none, while in others (December 1845, February 1846, December 1846 and January 1847) there were eight or nine. The social year, in respect of dining at least, fell into two distinct parts, the more important being the winter season. The months from October to March had thirty-eight such occasions in 1845/6, twenty-seven in 1846/7 and twenty-one in 1847/8, while April to September had seven in 1845, eighteen in 1846 and twelve in 1847. Dining would normally be for about ten males or for about five couples, though the sample includes extreme variations. Distortions in the general frequency pattern occurred as when, for example, Holt's son William, on returning from America, was dined in short succession by the Finch House Mathers, by Richard Rathbone, and by Lawrence Heyworth at Yew Tree, during the summer of 1846. These hosts were interested in any intelligence he had acquired that might be of use to their American business. Conversely, the general evenness of the figures was distorted by the Holts' absence from the country for the whole of June, July and most of August 1847, during their 'grand tour' through continental Europe.

This evidence shows roughly the incidence of contact, within these circumstances, between Holt and his family and other members of the élite, although it is impossible to arrive at a satisfactory estimate of how many Holt ultimately shared table with. He himself hosted sixty-two such events, so the ratio of hosting to guesting for him over this period was about 1:1.5. Other prominent hosts in Holt's record were Thomas Bolton (four events), William Brown (four), Lawrence Heyworth (five), Christopher Rawdon (six), and Thomas Thornely (three). While these figures represent an average of about one visit per year by Holt to the tables of these men, there is no suggestion from the evidence that there was an annual ritual in force – some visits came in clusters, suggesting temporary intensifications of friendships. At his own and other people's tables, of course, Holt met these men more often: Bolton (nine times), Brown (eleven), Heyworth (five), Rawdon (seven), and Thornely (seven).

Holt's record is only useful up to a point. What was discussed at table was not revealed in the diary, probably because it was not very interesting, being perhaps a mannered exchange of trivia and some business intelligence. But it is not what members of the 'class' talk about which helps to give them a coherence and an identity so much as the fact that they are talking, in formally convened, socially exclusive circumstances and in an environment which they have created to reflect their idea of their own image in the world.

While 'gentlemanly capitalism' was a powerful motif in Victorian Liverpool, it would be wrong to judge the city's bourgeoisie, or its economic history, solely through this inevitably London-oriented focus. As a great commercial entrepôt, the leading export port, Liverpool was in the industrial north, but not of it – a distinction reflected in patterns of culture, diet and speech.[53] While safeguarding their distinctiveness, Liverpudlians respected the inventiveness, enterprise and mechanical prowess of the adjacent manufacturing districts. The symbiosis between commercial Liverpool and the industrial hinterland – a genuine two-way relationship, not a fundamental clash of economic and/or cultural values as implied in the gentlemanly capitalism thesis – underpinned Victorian confidence and ascendancy.[54] As the face of the old world turned to the west, Liverpool's future seemed secure:

It has been shrewdly remarked that Tyre, for many ages the greatest commercial city of the world, perished entirely, because it had not a productive, but merely a transit trade. It was a port, and nothing else. With us it is not so. The power of creating materials for trade exists at your very door.[55]

Significantly, these words come from Cardinal Wiseman's lecture, 'The highways of peaceful commerce have been the highways of art', on the opening of the Catholic Institute in Liverpool in 1853. Among the audience were a number of Irish-born, Liverpool-based merchants, a neglected group in studies of the local Irish presence. This is surprising as general studies of the Irish in Britain now insist on the diversity and general success of the migrant inflow. Coming from a variety of social, economic and religious backgrounds, the Irish were to distribute (and integrate) themselves throughout mainland Britain, taking up a number of occupational and residential opportunities within the urban hierarchy. A case (or class?) apart, the Liverpool-Irish – the 'dregs' who remained in the port of entry, unable, unsuited or unwilling to take advantage of opportunities elsewhere in Britain or the new world – have no place in the new optimistic reassessment. As the exception which proved the rule, Liverpool is disparaged as a sectarian redoubt, 'marginal to the cultural and political life of the nation'.[56]

Whatever its relationship to national patterns, the Liverpool-Irish community had a complex cultural and political life of its own which needs to be rescued from historical caricature and stigma. This is a difficult task but there are already some glimpses and suggestions of a significant middle-class contribution to Irish Liverpool. As in other major immigrant 'enclaves' – and here the size of the migrant population should compel historians of the Irish in Britain not to dismiss Liverpool – merchants, professionals, publicans and tradesmen provided an influential and respected leadership cadre for ethnic action. In 1848, for example, shipping agents, doctors and tradesmen revivified the Ribbonite culture of secrecy to penetrate deep into the migrant community, establishing a network of clubs in sympathetic pubs, temperance hotels and private houses. In Irish-Liverpool, indeed, middle-class nationalist leaders (most of whom were Ulster-born Catholics) enjoyed greater success than their counterparts in Ireland itself in enlisting their less fortunate fellow-countrymen in the Confederate cause.[57] On the economic front, a recent study of

Liverpool's mid-nineteenth-century coasting trade has underlined the dominance of the Irish trade and the crucial importance of the Liverpool–Dublin axis.[58] Historical attention has focused on the more exotic (and financially less secure) overseas transoceanic trade, but Liverpool's continuing prosperity owed much to its near-hegemony in the movement of goods and people within and around the 'inland' Irish Sea, trade which attracted and required a significant Irish mercantile presence.[59] Other aspirants to middle-class status – 'Micks on the make' to use Roy Foster's terminology – were attracted across the water to the 'second metropolis', a convenient testing-ground for their journalistic, legal, medical, clerical or other talents. When Justin McCarthy came to Liverpool as a 'stepping-stone on my way to London', he found that most of the staff on the *Northern Daily Times* were also Irish.[60]

Liverpool was an important staging-post in career development for the Irish middle class. For some who started lower and stayed longer, it offered upward mobility *into* the middle class, a socio-economic advance often topped off by political leadership. Biographical details of the Irish National Party (INP) councillors show three major groups, of which the first two had previously been prominent in the Liberal-oriented Catholic Club.[61] Firstly, there were the lawyers, doctors and other professionals whose practices covered the Irish community (for instance, there were no less than four INP councillors in the office of Irish-born solicitor W. Madden). Secondly, there were the traders who prospered and/or diversified as they took responsibility for the Liverpool end of the business: these included O'Hara, 'king' of the lucrative Irish egg trade, and Lawrence Connolly who branched out from the family fruit trade into substantial property speculation in New Brighton. The final group, new to political leadership, included the shopkeepers and others who attended to the daily needs of the Liverpool-Irish. Here there were some genuine 'rags to riches' stories, entrepreneurs who made their fortune supplying basic pleasures within the ethnic 'enclave' – for example, J. Clancy who began as a 'hotel boots' and then developed a lucrative tobacconist business, worth over £25,000 on his death; and 'Dandy Pat' Byrne who started work as a dock labourer, before acquiring a string of public houses.

Liverpool, then, presents important challenges for historians of the British middle class. As a non-industrial city, it took its mores and values from a commercial and cultural complex dominated by the figure of the 'merchant prince', a formation which was eventually (and inexorably) drawn away from civic prominence towards the capital: geographically, socially and culturally, the heart of commercial and financial capitalism was increasingly confined to London. As a human entrepôt, it contained ethnic enclaves where the exercise of middle-class leadership and authority took a very different and less rarefied form. In reminding us of the variety and diversity of the middle class, however, Liverpool is perhaps better characterized as exemplary rather than exceptional.

# 'A REPUBLIC OF QUAKERS':

## THE RADICAL BOURGEOISIE, THE STATE AND STABILITY IN LANCASHIRE, 1789–1851

### BRIAN LEWIS

During the campaign for the repeal of the Corn Laws, John Talbot Clifton of Clifton Hall, Lytham, who became Conservative MP for North Lancashire in 1844, wrote, 'I think those who suppose, that on the settlement of this question [Repeal], agitation is to cease, are quite mistaken as Mr Bright told me the other night (<u>Bless</u> him!!!!) – "We <u>will</u> have this and then go on for the rest." What he means by the rest I don't know, except a republic of Quakers.'[1] 'The rest' for the *Preston Chronicle* in a New Year's editorial in 1850 signified a new party to institute a thorough revision of the whole system of national government; to uproot the remaining obnoxious feudal laws – primogeniture and entail, copyholds and absurd tenures, game laws, naval and military chieftainships, dishonest sinecures; to complete the reformation of the Church; to reduce the Army and Navy; and to promote science, trade, commerce, industry and education without waiting to be coerced by outside agitation.[2]

This was to be a wholesale onslaught on the aristocratic state and the apparatus of Old Corruption. Such an agenda can be sewn together very neatly with the Messianic vision of triumphant middle-class ideology in the statements of a number of local millowners in the late 1840s and '50s. For example, Alderman John Baynes, a Blackburn manufacturer, Liberal and Evangelical Churchman, believed that:

THE MISSION OF THE COTTON TRADE is, to develop the resources of this nation – to multiply the springs of industry – to stimulate inventive genius – to encourage art and science – to increase profitably the employment of labour – to improve agriculture – to create large towns – to promote education – to elevate the moral and social status of the working population – to secure civil liberty – to confer political privileges – to check immorality – to encourage religion – to destroy monopolies – to give freedom to all – to enkindle a spirit of loyalty – to foster probity and honour – to discountenance war – to extinguish slavery – to promote peace – and to raise Britain to be the protector of the weak, the friend of the strong, a bright example to all nations, and the grand instrument for promoting the evangelization of the world.

In the missionary vanguard of God's Own Nation were the middle classes. Their rapid advance in wealth, power and influence had brought about repeal of the Test and Corporation Acts, Catholic emancipation, parliamentary reform, abolition of the slave trade and municipal reform. During the rise of manufactures, when great immorality pervaded the upper strata and social and moral degradation the lower, the middle classes 'were the salt which preserved society from falling to decay'. They had created the large towns, necessary for the establishment of representative municipal government which kept centralizing national governments at bay, and allowed opportunities for the better municipal regulation and improved living conditions of concentrated populations. Towns and factories helped inculcate discipline, order and regularity, all essential attributes of progress, civilization and intellectual superiority: 'No one need be reminded, how much more amenable to public opinion men are in cities than in remote hamlets; how much more easily are they brought under civilizing influences; and what superior advantages they possess for the improvement of their minds, and the acquisition of useful knowledge.'[3]

Here was a classic statement of urban-industrial bourgeois self-confidence, assured and didactic rather than defensive. But in spite of his sense of the middle class as 'the salt which preserved society', Baynes did not advocate the full radical programme. His attachment to the Church was later to take him into Tory ranks in protest at Gladstone's disestablishment of the Church of Ireland.[4] Nor were many others persuaded: after repeal of the Corn Laws, the Manchester School radicals failed to mobilize the middle classes as an independent political force against the aristocratic-military complex. Support for free trade in land, disestablishment of the Church, national non-sectarian education, further parliamentary reform, the Peace Society and the abolition of the East India Company, was sporadic.[5] These items did not rank high on the local middle-class agenda.

Baynes trumpeted the familiar refrain that trade and peace marched together, but he had come to terms with the state and its military machine as the means to that end. In breaking up the feudal system in Russia, in bringing religious freedom to Turkey and in producing considerable commercial advantages for Britain, the Crimean War had been utterly righteous.[6] For other liberal-radicals[7] the moment of truth came with the bombing open of the port of Canton in 1857 by Sir John Bowring, formerly radical MP for Bolton. Alderman Henry Marriott Richardson, a Bolton attorney, argued in 1852 that he and his Liberal colleagues 'did not believe in the system which sent missionaries on deck and the implements of death in the hold; they believed that commerce, free and unrestricted trade, was the great harbinger of peace and civilization'; but, in supporting Bowring five years later, he was not for having England's flag insulted or disgraced.[8]

Back in 1849, Henry Ashworth, a Bolton millowner, Quaker and bourgeois crusader, wrote to Richard Cobden, 'I think we have good and practical grounds for believing, that enlightened self-interest, and the social reforms which proceed from the use of the steam Engine whether Stationary or Locomotive, will one day be found to overpower the vainglory of the red-coated freebooter.' Having said that, he recognized with disgust how even members of the liberal-radical bourgeoisie were discovering what their more conservative brethren had known all along: that the aristocratic-military state was perfectly compatible with the progress of capital; as soon as foreigners threatened trading interests:

the first thing that crosses men's minds here is to set our 'Bull dogs' upon them. This reliance upon the Military has associated the Army & Navy with our industry; – a sort of wedlock has been recognised, and the unhallowed alliance has received too manifest a recognition by Manufacturers toasting, as Jno Potter [Mayor of Manchester] did the other day The 'Army & Navy'!!

Again in 1852 he blushed for Manchester after a proposal for a commemorative horseback statue of the Duke of Wellington: 'It is a desecration of Mill-got-money to subscribe it for any such unhallowed purpose.'[9] So much for a republic of radical Quakers. An alternative, perhaps more typical, image of the bourgeoisie in this period might instead be taken from the ceiling of Trinity Church in Blackburn. In 1846 the Revd Dr John William Whittaker, vicar of Blackburn, invited the local Anglican nobility, gentry and gentlemen to pay for their shields to be painted on to ceiling panels down the nave, at the crossing and in the transepts. Mingled with Church leaders, local baronets, local MPs and the older families of gentry are the families of relatively new wealth from commerce, manufacturing and the professions, inserted seamlessly into a timeless hierarchy, just as surely as their houses and halls slotted smoothly into the countryside without causing a rupture.[10]

Now, this might lend itself easily to a co-option thesis: the bourgeoisie was bought out – 'feudalized' – and therefore failed to develop and to implement an independent bourgeois politics.[11] But this would be misleading. What is more interesting and important is not to suggest the victory of one image over the other, one depiction of the bourgeoisie over the next, but to stress the building of contrasting narratives: a narrative of accommodation under the broad mantle of Church, state and the prevailing power structure, and a narrative defining itself in opposition to and seeking to supersede that power structure. Drawing on the bourgeoisie (the merchants, manufacturers, professional men, substantial retailers and their families) of Blackburn, Bolton and Preston roughly between the outbreak of the French Revolution and the Great Exhibition, this essay will sketch out the second of these narratives, paying particular attention to the impact of the state, often underplayed by community studies of the middle classes, and suggest some implications for the role of the bourgeoisie in creating order and stability in a volatile society of brutal inequalities of wealth and power.[12]

# I

As each bourgeois individual strove to make sense of his or her world, he or she juggled with a complex series of identities fabricated from positive alignments, negative barricading, and a medley of snippets of received wisdom and disparate discourses. Members of the bourgeoisie had to forge their own identities while striving to mould society and create stability. Many of them had to wrestle with status anxieties and financial insecurities in their own lives, and often responded by throwing up fences and defining themselves against 'inferior' others: the Anglican clergyman against the Nonconformist minister and the Catholic priest, the doctor against the apothecary or the quack, the well-spoken against the dialect speaker, the polite against the plebeian, the rational recreationist against indulgers in 'traditional' popular culture, the Sabbatarian against the defilers of Sundays, the lady against the working wife, the Manchester Man against the idle aristocrat. These identities were both restrictive (in the sense of curtailing the potential for autonomous decision-making) and empowering (in that a shared sense of a common identity or form of oppression could give rise to a challenge to those conditions). Such identities could be mobilized behind active political agendas through the construction of narratives that advanced 'a set of discursive claims about the social world' – narratives that sought to allow individuals to make sense of themselves in time and space.[13] Class was one such narrative, though it has now been dethroned as the master narrative of the nineteenth century and as the ultimate referent of all other forms of identity.[14] In the Blackburn–Bolton–Preston area, a liberal-radical bourgeois minority largely drew its inspiration, its notion of collective identity, its zealous sense that there were wrongs in the structure of state and society that needed to be righted, from the fact that most of them shared a common identity as religious Dissenters.[15] As well as helping to define the extent of marriage, business, social and political ties, this form of identity coloured an individual's whole sense of history and experience of second-class citizenship.[16] However much the religious distinctions might be attenuated in normal times, or the fluctuating bonds of common connections or ambitions stretch across denominational barriers, the Dissenting and Catholic sense of grievance was ever-present, and every time one of the religious crises punctuating the period raised its head the reminders, assumptions and stereotyping of religious others resurfaced. This narcissism of minor difference[17] was to have a major impact in British history. It meant that a middle-class group that stretched over a broad status and economic range was constantly defining itself and being defined as 'different' on key issues. It provided the basis and an agenda for a class-conscious crusade defined against the aristocratic state.

This religious identity ensured that bourgeois radicalism and liberalism would largely have a religious caste and avoid the scepticism of continental radicalism. It also meant that when a new Tory party began to develop in the 1790s, on the back of the campaign against the repeal of the Test and Corporation Acts and in response to revolution in France, the most important part of its programme would be the defence of the Church.[18] Much recent scholarship has stressed the extent and depth of loyalism during the French Revolutionary and Napoleonic Wars, measured in terms of patriotic displays and writings, donations to the war effort, and commitment to the Volunteer Corps.[19] The milltowns were no different. The wars strengthened the bourgeois commitment to an evolving Tory ideology. The sacred rights of property and an ordered hierarchy in Church and state were rhetorically buttressed through the contrast with a republican or usurping barbarism, and by the appropriation of a language of national identity. At the centre was the Protestant constitution and a suitably domesticated and unobtrusive monarch, and propping up the edifice ever more securely were the songs, the roast beef, the strong ale, the loyalist readings of history, and whatever else could be called into the service of the patriotic cause, particularly the twisting of the memory of William Pitt into a useful shape that rendered him historically unrecognizable.[20] The crowding out of the dissenting middle-class voice after 1792 was remarkable, especially given the severe divisions in middle-class ranks during the American War and the battle for the repeal of the Test and Corporation Acts.[21] Nevertheless, it did not die completely, just as Charles James Fox and the Whig remnant kept open a dissenting space in and out of Westminster.

An example from each of the towns must suffice for the war years. Firstly, in Preston, the roughly equal forces of the Whig Earl of Derby and the Tory Corporation reached an unofficial agreement in 1802 to field one candidate each at elections – a 'Coalition' that lasted until 1826. This was challenged by a string of 'Independent' candidates, beginning in 1807 with Joseph Hanson of Strangeways Hall, Manchester, a Unitarian, the son of a Manchester merchant and manufacturer, and Lt Col Commandant of the Manchester and Salford Rifle Regiment of Volunteers, who stood on a platform of independence, peace and a minimum wage for handloom weavers. He and his brother, who stood on a similar radical, anti-Coalition platform in 1812, attracted a limited amount of bourgeois support.[22]

Secondly, in Bolton in 1812, a body of leading inhabitants presented the zealous magistrate Ralph Fletcher with a silver vase in recognition of his services during the recent Luddite crisis of law and order, which had culminated in the burning of a cotton mill at Westhoughton. This provoked another group into presenting a piece of plate to Dr Robert Taylor, a Unitarian physician, for his exposure of the so-called Blackfacing spy system. In an address 'To the Friends of Freedom in the Town and Neighbourhood of Bolton', Taylor accused Fletcher and the Party of Order of wholesale violations of the law, of the deployment of *agents provocateurs*, and of the deliberate playing up and incitement of the lower-class radical threat to justify increasingly repressive measures and to precipitate the flight of the middle classes into conservative ranks.[23] This Blackfacing scandal subsequently became part of the histories of conservatism and political dissent, a fixed point of reference.[24] Thirdly, as part of a campaign against the Orders in Council during the economic slump of 1811–12, petitioners from Blackburn deplored 'the moral effects of war', lamented 'the miseries of their fellow-creatures', and were convinced 'that war is inimical to their interests' and 'injurious to a commercial Country'. Although this was swiftly countered by petitions placing full confidence in the men in power, the government responded to the agitation in the country and pressure from the opposition in Parliament, and to the danger of war with the United States, by revoking the Orders in Council.[25] The state proved its responsiveness to influential interests.

Throughout the wars, the majority of the local bourgeoisie associated bourgeois progress with the progress of the aristocratic state. This was not co-option, an early 'selling out' by the bourgeoisie even in the early stages of industrialization, but the calculation of interest and the economic and social advancement of themselves *vis-à-vis* their superiors and inferiors, a step in the 'quiet revolution' of the bourgeoisie. The wars tended to bolster bourgeois self-identity: commercial expansion and periodic trade disruption, the revolutionary stirrings of the lower classes, the chance to dress up in Volunteer Regiment uniforms to express both loyalty and a measure of independence from patrician control, *could* foster a more cohesive and coherent class awareness among the loyalists, *or* this same sectional self-assertion could be used as a vehicle for those who wished to climb into the ranks of the broadening band of mixed-wealth notables, *or* it could bolster the small knot of radicals in their opinions. The price members of the bourgeoisie demanded for their donations, mobilization and vocal support was a responsive and responsible state, and it was principally in judging this that the bourgeoisie displayed its divergent voices during the wars, ensuring that just as it had been heavily divided before 1792 it would not emerge in the 1810s pounded into a homogeneous Tory mould. The bourgeois radicals were confident enough to challenge the wisdom of the state's actions at home and abroad; the loyalists were still convinced the executive and legislature knew best.

In the postwar years an insistent bourgeois oppositional voice continued to be heard. At a county meeting in Preston in February 1817 to express outrage at an assault on the Prince Regent, Dr Taylor of Bolton and Dr Peter Crompton, a Liverpool reformer, effectively hijacked proceedings by carrying an alternative address: 'the Administration of Affairs by your present Councellors [sic], has diffused through this Country a degree of Misery never before experienced'.[26] It is difficult to tell how radical this opposition was. Home Office records in these years point to a number of committed reformers from the wealthier strata, apparently prepared to go some distance in the risky business of supporting the radicals.[27] But a later newspaper editor and local historian in Blackburn was no doubt near the mark when he wrote that during the postwar agitation, 'The moderate reformers held rigidly aloof, foreseeing the evil and danger. The Pilkingtons, Eccles's [sic], Turners, Haughtons [all millowners], and a few other respectable families who were not reckoned as Pittites or Tories, were too cautious and cool to think of joining hands with the admirers of Harry Hunt.'[28] Preston poll books indicate considerable broadcloth support for the milder versions of reform. When the Coalition broke down in 1826, John Wood, a Liverpool barrister and scion of Cross Street Unitarian Chapel in Manchester, was elected for the 'independent and reforming' Whigs. He picked up more élite support than any previous independent candidate, but the Derby and Corporation nominees still captured the bulk of the bourgeois vote.[29]

Vestry battles against Church rates, the repeal of the Test and Corporation Acts and Catholic emancipation kept politics charged with sectarian rivalries during the 1820s, hammering a more coherent conservative identity into shape, sharpening the Tory narrative against which reformers and radicals defined themselves. For every bourgeois *expression* of reform in these three milltowns there were many more statements of loyalty and conservatism. The Reform Bill was by no means carried upon a wave of bourgeois demand, slowly swelling during the postwar period as the political concomitant of increasing numbers and confidence through industrialization. Only after political conjuncture and contingency – the split in Tory ranks over emancipation, and the aftershocks of the July Revolution and the Swing riots, generating a crisis of governability – had placed moderate Reform on the agenda did it garner widespread bourgeois support, especially in unenfranchised Bolton and Blackburn.[30] The emphasis was still on moderate: in the Preston by-election in 1830 on the appointment of Edward Stanley as Chief Secretary for Ireland, his only challenger, Henry Hunt, out-polled him in a shocking upset; but élite voters voted for Stanley over Hunt by more than twelve to one.[31] Middle-class divisions remained deep throughout the Reform crisis, yet for the first time since before 1789 even prominent Tory-Anglicans were willing to proclaim their interest in at least some measure of reform and to attend public reform meetings;[32] and a more radical bourgeois element was willing to go much further and actually threaten the government with the consequences if Reform were not granted. As one small indication of the extent to which the government was drawing back from a precipice during the Days of May, 1832, Robert Segar, a Preston barrister, Catholic and leading reformer, said at a meeting in the Orchard in Preston, with Henry Hetherington of the *Poor Man's Guardian* on the same platform, that 'if circumstances had not fortunately taken a turn, the country would have been thrown into such a state, that he himself, (as well as others,) would have in all probability by this time been with arms in their hands'.

At the same meeting Segar argued that: 'It is essentially necessary that men should know, see, and feel that their interests are bound together, the highest and the lowest, the rich and the poor, there ought to be no distinction of interest or of classes, but tax-eaters and tax-payers.' He, like other bourgeois radicals, was sensitive to the charge that once they had been enfranchised they would leave the lower classes behind, and rejected the insinuation that the middle classes were not sincere in their desire for substantial reform.[33] The 1832 election largely proved him wrong: although various shades of reformer were elected in the three towns, the radical reformers did not find a great deal of support above the lower middle classes. In Preston the electorate was polarized between the Whig–Tory bloc of Stanley and

Hesketh Fleetwood, landowner, on the one hand, who picked up the vast majority of leading-inhabitant support, and Henry Hunt and a second radical on the other. The 'bourgeois-radical' candidate, Dr Charles Crompton, was squeezed out in the middle. In the more fluid setting of Blackburn and Bolton – short parliaments, further franchise extension, free trade, the separation of Church and state, drew a substantial number of shopkeeper-radical and some Nonconformist bourgeois votes.[34]

Even so, elements of a popular alliance can be detected through the 1830s and '40s, across Chartism and into mid-Victorian Liberalism.[35] The most sustained attempt to maintain the popular front came in Bolton, largely through the agency of a small circle of committed Dissenting bourgeois radicals and the *Bolton Free Press*. When the newspaper was first issued at the end of 1835 it set out its stall in favour of further electoral reform, the ballot, triennial parliaments, repeal of the Corn Laws, the reduction of the standing army, reform of the Church and the Lords, and an all round reduction of aristocratic corruption and power: a full radical agenda. Aristocrats were 'men born to consume and not to produce', men 'who fatten in idleness on the hard earnings of industry'.[36] The Bolton Reform Association was established in 1837 to organize the reform interest in a campaign for household suffrage, triennial parliaments, the ballot, national education, Corn Law repeal and incorporation of the borough. Some of these prominent reformers – people like Thomas Thomasson, Quaker-turned-freethinker millowner, and Charles James Darbishire, Unitarian manufacturer and first mayor of the borough – came out in support of the Charter in the autumn of 1838. A broader band of liberal reformers formed a local branch of the Anti-Corn Law League in 1839.[37]

In spite of this, the popular front was always an arm's-length alliance, noticeable as much for its ruptures as its cohesion. The Chartist leaders tended to view Corn Law repeal as a distraction and a diversion; the bourgeois reformers (including John Bowring, the most radical MP elected in the three towns, who had been a close disciple of Jeremy Bentham) tended to back the New Poor Law and to be outspoken partisans of the tenets of political economy. The popular alliance also split over the question of tactics. In the first serious Chartist disturbance in Bolton in the summer of 1839 the members of the Liberal administration – in office partly by virtue of a Tory boycott of the new council while the borough charter's legal validity was being tested – found themselves having to reconcile their principles with the need for law and order. The mayor had backed the Charter only a few months previously, but now he and local reformers were given the space by a Whig administration less jittery about public order than Liverpool and Sidmouth had been, and anxious to avoid any counter-productive débâcle like Peterloo, to see Chartist agitation as more of a threat than state violence. After the rioting was put down, the *Bolton Free Press* wrote:

> We believe that the Mayor, in common with the great majority of sincere and earnest Reformers, is of opinion that the suffrage ought to be extended to the labouring classes; but does it therefore follow, that he would not be as active and vigilant in repressing outrage and disturbance, as the most rabid Conservative?[38]

Most shades of bourgeois opinion recognized clearly enough that while in the short term the physical force of the state could tide a government over a troubling period, this merely provided an opportunity to work out a new agenda, to renegotiate legitimacy. For the radicals this meant continued hammering away at the need for Corn Law repeal, and further attempts to refocus on 'the common enemy': 'There is only one interest opposed to that of the people – the interest of the aristocracy.'[39] Again the united front proved ephemeral and foundered on the question of means: during the Plug Plot crisis of 1842 the Party of Order once more appeared the safer alternative. The *Free Press* reminded its readers: 'The insurrection may be put down by the great physical force powers which the Government possesses', but this could only be a temporary solution. 'The condition of the people must be improved, and then all apprehension of further disturbances will naturally subside.'[40] The Bolton Complete Suffrage Association attempted to re-knit the popular front in 1844, but the popular-radical division from the repealers was now accentuated by many of the bourgeois radicals finding themselves on the opposite bench on the question of Ten Hours. For Thomas Thomasson, short time was only feasible if accompanied by Corn Law repeal, and yet the working classes were opposing repeal. 'Can there be anything equal to the folly of complaining of your long hours of labour', he asked, 'and yet heaping abuse continually upon those who are seeking to remove the causes of the necessity of working those long hours?' He too found the spectacle of children torn from their beds and driven to the factories to 'fatten the coach horses of the landowners' objectionable. Thomas Brindle, secretary of the Operative Cotton Spinners, found such arguments risible. Our children, he said, only fatten the coach horses of the 'Cotton Masters'.[41]

This, then, was a frequently interrupted dialogue. In Blackburn and Preston the bourgeois Nonconformist presence (particularly Unitarian and Quaker) was smaller, the Conservative predominance stronger, and the level of cooperation between popular radicals and bourgeois liberal-radicals rather less. Still, there were signs of popular fronts in the 1830s and '40s during the campaign for the Municipal Corporations Act; in the attempt to elect liberal-radical candidates; around the Complete Suffrage Union; and in the pages of the *Preston Guardian*, the vehicle of Joseph Livesey, radical cheesemonger, journalist, Scottish Baptist and teetotaller. But if the pulse of the popular alliance was often weak and erratic (and practically no bourgeois leader voiced any support for the Charter), there was a significant base for bourgeois-radical vanguardism: as in Bolton, the Blackburn, Preston and Darwen Dissenting millowners contributed handsomely towards the League. The majority of the bourgeois votes in parliamentary elections went to the more conservative candidates, but the Liberal Free Traders won the two Preston seats and one of the Blackburn seats in both 1841 and 1847.[42]

Although the bourgeois-radical narrative continued to be pushed by many single-issue campaigners and the more ambitious, becoming an important plank in the Liberal platform from Gladstone to Lloyd George,[43] the optimistic vision of a 'republic of Quakers' or its equivalent soon evaporated after Corn Law repeal in 1846. Various bourgeois radicals or liberals accepted more and more facets of the state, not because of acquiescence in aristocratic values, but on either solid grounds of self-interest or because of successive governments' undermining of anti-aristocratic-state rhetoric.[44] Even at its height, during the anti-Corn Law campaign, the radical vision in the three milltowns was a creed for the few, a militant bourgeois minority grouped around a whole class-conscious agenda confronting and sometimes making contact with a much larger bloc of intertwined commercial, landed and professional opinion. But if the bourgeois radicals, like the Chartists, did not manage to storm the Establishment ramparts and plant their flags firmly on the top turrets, this did not betoken defeat so much as that push and pull of arm-twisting and accommodation which characterized the response of the state and its propertied classes to the long-drawn-out process of British industrialization.[45] Even Henry Ashworth, the man disgusted by the thought of a statue in Manchester to the Duke of Wellington, signalled this. In 1850 he expressed a degree of ambivalence and maybe a certain softening of his uncompromising opposition to the ruling class and all its attributes. He saw the approaching Great Exhibition as a sign that Court favour was no longer going to be confined to acres, and noted that a cotton manufacturer had been given a peerage and that there were now some 'cotton knights'. On the one hand he felt that this might result in a lessening of individual, titled-entrepreneurial drive, and evidently remained wary of expressions of loyalty. On the other, when Lord Granville (accompanying Queen Victoria on a visit to Manchester and vicinity in 1851) asked him why extravagant manifestations of loyalty had replaced the discontent of earlier years:

My reply was, that Class interests had been at the bottom of it – Her Majesty had been identified with measures which were based upon justice and which were in harmony with the spirit of Com$^{ce}$ [.] Favouritism & Class interests were done with, the people of Manch$^r$ were now reaping the benefits, and they had shewn Her Majesty that she could rely as safely upon those who were identified with Shuttles and spindles, as upon those who had to do with Turnips and Tup Sheep.[46]

Put another way, if property rallied when the Chartists came over the bridge and marched up the hill it was because the state had previously shown itself responsive to bourgeois interests and to be an evolving form worth fighting for, better than anything likely by its replacement. Without parliamentary reform, municipal reform and Corn Law repeal, without the gradual dismantling of the apparatus of Old Corruption, without a liberalizing state, without concessions to the Nonconformist and Catholic conscience, without a restrained military after the warning given by the outcry over Peterloo, one can speculate that members of the radical bourgeois minority would have found themselves on the popular side of the barricade in the event of a serious challenge to authority.

The bourgeois majority seemed happy enough with the reformed, repealed, ordered, 'liberal' state, allowing spheres of influence in the localities while providing laws, trade routes and military power at the centre.[47] Two symbolic moments in 1850 and 1851 can be seen as an acknowledgement of widespread bourgeois accommodation with the state, at least in the short term: the Great Exhibition and the death of Sir Robert Peel. An exhibition of industry and commerce under the patronage of a prince to bring nations together in a spirit of good will brought forth almost universal expressions of bourgeois praise. In Blackburn, a requisition for a public meeting in early 1850 to promote the Exhibition was signed by practically everyone of note in the town. The *Blackburn Standard* commented:

> we believe we are secure in saying that there is scarcely a political party, religious body, profession, manufacture, or trade, that is not directly or indirectly represented. . . . Such a requisition we believe to be a perfect novelty to the town, and in its comprehensiveness, freedom from all signs of political, sectarian, or professional difference, and complete unanimity of sentiment, may be regarded as no less honourable to the inhabitants, than it is in strict accordance with the project and purpose of the Prince Consort.[48]

Peel's untimely death enabled the Liberal newspapers to appropriate him as a symbol of a benign and responsive state, the meeting of the Establishment and Lancashire cotton within one body. '[W]ith a patriotism rarely equalled,' said Alderman Baynes, 'he sacrificed his own comfort and peace, his friends and connections, and by his consummate tact and ability, succeeded in carrying the repeal of the corn laws, and so saving the nation.'[49]

Brief unity in mourning, however, could not disguise the fact that bourgeois radicals expected *continued* movement in the direction of reform and liberalization in return for their support. As the *Preston Chronicle* had put it in a classic concessionist reading of recent British history at the end of the Year of Revolutions: 'The history of the last twenty years is a record of the progress of legislative measures, extending civil rights and ameliorating social evils; and herein is the true cause of England's freedom from the tide of revolution.' For 'revolutionary frenzy' to be averted, the process of 'Timely concession, seasonable reforms, the adaptation of institutions to the spirit of the age, and the extension of constitutional privileges' must not be halted.[50]

## II

I have described the building of a bourgeois-radical narrative defined in opposition to an aristocratic state at the national level and to a developing Toryism at the local level – a loyalist Toryism that was itself not unconditional but dependent on an accommodating state – and how the flexibility of a reforming state steadily undermined the bourgeois-radical message. What are the implications of this for the study of the bourgeoisie and stability?

Many leading scholars of the bourgeoisie or the broader middle classes in this period have argued that at some level – cultural, if not economic or political – a fair measure of class consciousness was forged, *had* to be forged, for the creation both of effective collective leadership and of a set of shared values to carry the towns and the nation through the traumas of early industrialization.[51] This undoubtedly *was* an era of middle-class formation in the sense that more and more people came to occupy the middle ground of wealth and status, and largely accepted such values as the sanctity of property, the work ethic, the market economy, the divinely ordained economic and sexual inequalities of life, the virtues of domesticity and the importance of independence. But in no sense were these the exclusive property of the bourgeoisie or the middle classes. The teasing out of liberal-radical and Tory strands, largely derived from religious identities, indicates that sections of the middle classes could be mobilized collectively behind shared narratives, damaging the prospects for class consciousness in the process. While sectional consciousness divided the bourgeoisie, and 'shared values' extended much more broadly, other equally unstable forms of identity could and did create alternative alignments in the political, economic and cultural realms. Given this, in attempting to explain social stability, focusing on the significance of the divisions rather than on the binding ties might be expected to pay dividends.

Members of the bourgeoisie – radical, liberal and conservative – were the people who exercised the most power locally and whose voice was loudest in the public square. While weaving together a patchwork of ideologies and identities to create order in and make sense of their own lives, they were directly involved in finding solutions to the dysfunctional urban-industrial society they were creating and in which their power could operate. The voices, responses and actions of the bourgeoisie formed the most critical aspect of the formation of urban

Britain, and the nation in the long run emerged closer to its multifarious norms and values than to those of any alternative groups or discourses.[52] Its detailed study is therefore essential, in spite of – *because* of – the fact that it was not a unitary actor and did not have a coherent identity.[53] A major part of the explanation of social stability lies in the very diversity and cross-cutting agendas of the disunited bourgeoisie. In a paradoxical sense, a lack of solidarity or rigidity actually helped maintain bourgeois pre-eminence at the local level during the most unstable period of modern British history – an inversion of commonsensical logic. A powerful hegemony, relationships of authority within the broader framework of the dominance of capitalism, and a pulsating civic and market culture do not need united class action, and the hunt for the class-conscious middle class might best be dispensed with. The variety of semi-contradictory organizational endeavours and conflicting ideological measures was a sign of strength, not of weakness.

This, on the one hand, de-emphasizes middle-class solidarity, and stresses the vast and fluctuating range of measures of coercion, concession and incorporation as various members of the bourgeoisie and fractions of capital in conjunction with the state devised their own halting, conflicting, cross-cutting and incomplete solutions. On the other hand it sets a relatively high value on the role of the state, and not only in relation to evolving bourgeois narratives. A number of theorists of 'modernity' argue that Enlightenment rationality bequeathed a dual legacy: the rhetoric and something of the reality of liberty and juridical equality, and the creation of a potentially vastly more coercive state.[54] In its most blatant form, state power meant armed force, the maintenance of authority through violence. It is by no means inconceivable that rebellion in the ranks or a bloody mess of a military operation – a Peterloo magnified – could have ignited a conflagration across the north and Midlands, especially in 1837–42. But military discipline held, and the bulk of the propertied classes of all stripes rallied sufficiently behind the flag of order. No history of the bourgeoisie and of the maintenance of order can ignore the barracks, the cavalry, the infantry, the yeomanry, the spies, the special constables, the selective use of the law to make examples, the web of information feeding back to the Home Secretary, and the ease of troop movements enhanced by better roads and by railways which could have reinforcements from other parts of the country or shipped over from Ireland in place within hours. A poorly manufactured pike never could be a match for a musket or the edge of a sabre wielded from the back of a horse. But repression could only be a short-term expedient with three possible outcomes: a failure to stem the tide of revolutionary upheaval with in all probability a short phase of popular libertarianism followed by an authoritarian crackdown, but with the contested memory of revolution kept alive (the French model); success in preventing upheaval but only by producing an even more repressive and unsheathed new order; or a search for alternatives (concession, incorporation, indoctrination) in order to reduce reliance on armed force. This last path was the one that was taken in Britain.

It is true that the state was retreating in the economic sphere, aided by the long period of relative peace after 1815 in which the need for revenue (in particular through taxes on consumption) to fight a war or to pay off war debts was substantially reduced, undermining the contention that the state was an organized conspiracy to enrich the landed classes.[55] But the era of warfare, the population explosion and the increased ease of communication created both a greater need by the state to keep a check on its citizens and the greater ability to do so. As theorists from Weber to Foucault to Giddens have argued (in very different ways), the modern nation-state operates by rendering its citizenry more 'legible', by increasing the means of surveillance, and by heightening the distance between conformist and 'deviant' elements. The poor felt the weight of this disciplinary and surveillant state before the benefits of the benign state. Policing, reformed prisons and the New Poor Law were all attempts to modify behaviour and to swell the ranks of the conformist and the respectable by inculcating self-discipline, the 'internalized gaze', meeting the agendas of the forces of order and the Christian moralist. But implementing such measures in the cotton district was only possible in moderated form, with hard bargaining, across a babel of competing voices and conflicting ideas and interests. The darker side of the era of enhanced discipline – the Foucauldian or Nietzschean nightmare – was always streaked with shades of grey.[56]

These were the coercive aspects of the attempt to create an ordered society. Alone they were insufficient. From a sense of fear, or Christian duty, or Enlightened thinking, or the desire to recruit as many as possible to one's party or denomination to undercut the opposition, different individuals and bourgeois fractions helped construct a relative stability from a vast range of alternative and often mutually incoherent solutions. One of these was short time, a concept bundled up with notions of happy hearths and homes, but dependent more on outside intervention from crusaders and legislators than from homegrown initiatives. A second was paternalism, a localist solution, combining a normative ideology of domesticity with an extension of time- and workplace-discipline, and either sending a message that factory civilization had reconstituted society on a higher moral plane, or attempting to recreate a pseudo-squirearchical reciprocity. A third possibility was the incorporation of the lower orders into hierarchical parties, either popular fronts or Operative Conservative Associations. A fourth was maybe to engineer the environment through sanitary reforms: clean bodies, clean minds. A fifth was simply indoctrination, from the pulpit or in the schoolroom: meddle not with them that are given to change, saith God the Lord. A sixth was religious paternalism, the creation of a jigsaw of denominational hierarchies.[57]

The list of solutions could continue. All of them were responses: to the prompting of religious teaching and conscience; to the unfamiliar industrializing, urbanizing and well-peopled landscape that had been created; to the inseparable forces of fear (of popular unrest, disorder and disease) and of optimism (in the creation of wealth, in progress, in the providential choice of the British nation to show the world by example a new civilization); and to the erecting of boundaries and barriers against ill-defined 'others', the better to begin to make sense of one's own identity, importance and place in the world. The attempts were confused, partial, contradictory, often unsuccessful. The price of contradictions and argumentation was often stagnation or tardy reforms, a grumbling inefficiency. Most of the attempts at incorporation or indoctrination did not work, at least in the sense of enfolding large numbers of the lower orders in the bourgeois mantle or of 'bourgeoisifying' working-class culture. But the divisions, the cross-cuttings and the polarities, by dividing and ruling the local rulers as well as the divided and ruled, prevented the cracks of class from yawning into chasms.[58]

The divisions were enough to disarm but not to paralyse. Competing business, political, cultural and social interests in their fluctuating formations could come together with sufficient frequency to achieve results. However they might undermine each other, political or denominational participation and voluntary associationism constantly reaffirmed a market and a civic culture, and kept open that public space in which bourgeois freedoms operated. The thrust and parry of debate, the rivalries and animosities reworked and reordered the relationships of power and authority upon each different layer, perpetually constructing and reconstructing the hegemony – the 'common sense' – of the liberal-capitalist system. It should be stressed that even within the most powerful hegemony (always involving coercion, concession and negotiation at every level), there is the potential not only for considerable dissent which might fundamentally alter its nature, but also for its complete overthrow. This is not a model that favours the consensual over the conflictual or presupposes that stability and the status quo are necessarily desirable or the norm. Hegemonies are constructed on a daily basis by human agents and can be deconstructed or demolished by them too. Nor is it an argument for the development of a consensual lib-labism.[59] This is a notion of hegemony that does not depend on a 'dominant class' but on the dominance of the system of liberal capitalism, drawing its support from ideas and beliefs cutting across class. The reason why members of the lower orders 'consented' to this system could have been out of ideological conviction or a recognition of the strength of the existing order combined with the debilitating power of 'dull economic compulsion', or a combination of both. Equally, the hegemonic model does not depend on a trickle down or imposition of ideas from upon high: the lower orders might seek accommodation with liberal capitalism from independent, bottom-up, ideological conviction.[60]

What I am suggesting here is that stability in the early to mid-nineteenth-century milltowns was maintained and the system sustained because of the lack of unity of the bourgeoisie or of a middle-class class consciousness, and because in the competing and conflicting agendas of fractions of the bourgeoisie there was room for the workings of cross-class alliances and rhetoric. This is the real significance of the liberal-radical bourgeoisie, not its failure to achieve a class agenda: it was one of the ways in which an oppositional voice was kept alive, however at times wavering and faint. Just as the rump of the Whigs at the national level kept open the channels of political dissent from the 1790s, ultimately providing the necessary flexibility in the constitution in 1832,[61] so the liberal-radicals at the local level helped keep open a space for the commingling of middle- and working-class ideals. This was only one factor in the building of stability, but a significant and enduring one. Without this division within bourgeois ranks one of the major streams forming Gladstonian Liberalism would not have existed.

Any interpretation that stresses the ideological cohesion – political, organizational, cultural – of the bourgeoisie misses this point. And this brings us back to the importance of the state and the impossibility of studying milltown communities only within their own borders. It was in arguments about the powers and scope of the state, and the rights of citizenship, that one of the major divisions in bourgeois ranks occurred, feeding back into and enhancing identity-based divergent narratives.

# 6

# OWNERS AND OCCUPIERS:

PROPERTY, POLITICS AND MIDDLE-CLASS FORMATION
IN EARLY INDUSTRIAL LANCASHIRE

MICHAEL WINSTANLEY

The terms 'propertied class(es)' and 'middle class(es)' are often used interchangeably by urban historians of the nineteenth century. This is not surprising. As Bob Morris has observed, 'If the middle class means anything it has something to do with property.'[1] It is somewhat paradoxical, therefore, that the structure of property ownership in Victorian Britain, remains, in Geoffrey Crossick's words, 'one of the great lacunae in the study of the urban fabric'.[2] Indeed, apparently straightforward questions such as, 'Who owned the physical infrastructure of Manchester, Leeds, or Birmingham?' in the early to mid-nineteenth century have rarely been asked, let alone answered.[3] Judgements about the relationship between property and the development of middle-class social consciousness and political allegiance have consequently been based on surprisingly little empirical evidence.

The reasons for this lack of interest are not difficult to find. Apart from a few relatively straightforward instances where development was promoted by a single landowner or commercial organization, patterns of property ownership in most towns remain extraordinarily difficult to assess. Estate records, land tax returns and tithe maps provide detailed information on the nature of land ownership and tenancy agreements in rural society but are of less use for urban areas. Many of the early rate books, the only source capable of reconstructing the changing nature of property ownership and occupancy over time, have not survived. Even where they have, they are dauntingly voluminous and defy easy analysis since, as John Foster recognized, 'rates are listed by street and occupier, making the calculation of any one man's aggregate liability almost impossible'.[4] The recent fashion for the 'linguistic turn' has done nothing to persuade social and cultural historians to abandon their preference for rather less daunting qualitative sources.

This chapter, therefore, represents a first attempt to assert the importance of property relations for our understanding of middle-class social formation and political consciousness in the early to mid-nineteenth century. In particular it seeks to challenge the assumption that most of the expanding middle class of Lancashire were 'propertied' in the sense of owning real estate, suggesting instead that, until possibly the closing decades of the century, urban growth fuelled the creation of a class of substantial middle-class occupiers whose numerical preponderance was to have profound political consequences at both local and national levels.

I

Ownership, control of, and access to property in the form of land or buildings has always conditioned every aspect of life, whether in the town or the country. Until relatively recently property, not income, profits, wealth or capital, also provided the major rationale for direct taxation in Britain at both local and national levels. Ownership or occupation of property in the nineteenth century was also the criterion which determined the nature and extent of an individual's contribution to and participation in the government of the community and country. It was the yardstick by which democratic reforms were debated and judged, defining eligibility to vote and serve in select vestries, Poor Law unions, improvement and police commissions, reformed municipal corporations, local health, burial and education boards, and the return of Members of Parliament.

Property ownership, burdens and tenurial relations also increasingly dominated the political agenda in the nineteenth century.[5] Four Royal Commissions considered the costly complexities of land transfer between the late 1820s and 1870 (1828–32, 1846, 1857, 1870), pamphlet literature kept the issue in the public eye, and a number of abortive private bills were introduced. In the late 1840s and early 1850s the extension of property ownership underpinned the campaign for 'free trade' in land, the subsequent creation of freehold land societies which sought to mitigate some of the legal and financial obstacles to the purchase of real estate, and the proliferation of building societies.[6] The level and incidence of local property rates remained contentious issues throughout the century, dominating election campaigns, generating numerous ratepayer revolts which ultimately impinged on central government fiscal strategy and encouraged the policy of making 'grants in aid' to local authorities for certain services.[7] From the 1870s property was 'swept into the mainstream of politics' symbolized by the 'new domesday' return of 1873. By the 1880s the Conservatives were deliberately fanning urban small property-owners' fears of Liberal or socialist encroachments on their rights, and both parties were actively wooing agricultural tenants with promises of land reform. The relative merits of tenant rights and owner-occupancy dominated attempts to find political and economic solutions to the perceived problems of Ireland and the Scottish Highlands.[8] Significantly, throughout the period, it was the Conservatives who asserted the rights of property owners and advocated the extension of ownership, while Liberals sought to strengthen the protection afforded to tenants while increasing taxation on owners.

This distinction reminds us that 'propertied' was an ambiguous concept throughout the nineteenth century. Not everyone who held significant amounts of property necessarily benefited from increases in its value which occurred over the course of the century. Much clearly depended on the function and location of property, but even more significant were the conditions under which it was held. The classic distinctions between landlords and tenants, fixed and working capital, were equally, if not more significant in the town than they were in the country, and the interests of the two groups cannot be assumed to be mutually compatible. As Avner Offer has explained, 'The great prize which urbanization offered to the traditional owners of land' was the possibility of increasing 'conversion rent. . . . The landowner farmed out economic opportunities [and risks] to agricultural and urban entrepreneurs; they provided the skills, management and working capital and took their chances; the landowner took the residue. . . . Landowners secured an income and capital gains primarily from the fact of possession; entrepreneurs had to rely on judgement, effort, skill and luck.'[9] Furthermore, except in the cheapest properties, it was the tenant not the owner who was responsible for paying rates on property. The level of rates, and the differential rating of agricultural land, agricultural buildings, residential property, shops, licensed premises, warehouses, manufactories, mills and mines, created numerous local disputes about the moral and financial equity of such taxation, more noticeably and spectacularly during the Edwardian years at a national level. In short, those who owned urban land and buildings enjoyed the prospect of becoming rich on the back of rising values while occupiers took the risks and paid the tax bills. Whereas the potential conflict of interest between landlords and tenants is widely regarded as central to rural society and to the urban working-class housing market, however, its potential significance for relations within the commercial and industrial middle class has never been seriously explored.

The assumption that most of the Victorian urban middle class were property owners probably accounts for this neglect. Whereas agricultural land was held by a wealthy élite, in urban areas the majority of investment in housing stock was provided by the lower-status members of the middle classes, the '"trading classes": builders, publicans, shopkeepers, etc . . .' who were 'in the main men of slender resources'.[10] This preponderance of small property owners is generally assumed to have been long-standing and their economic vulnerability has been portrayed as the bedrock of the emergent petit bourgeois radicalism of the 1830s and the local 'economy' parties of the 1850s and '60s.[11] As wealthier members of the middle class increasingly preferred to invest surplus funds in more mobile profit-seeking assets, in Britain, as in the rest of Europe, urban property remained a 'classic outlet for petit bourgeois savings'.[12] By the end of the century, therefore, the urban housing market was characterized by very low concentration levels of ownership.[13] The economic and social reasons for this have been explored by Geoffrey Crossick and its political ramifications in the decades leading up to the First World War have been explained by David Englander and Avner Offer.[14]

As these historians admit, however, judgements about the diffuse nature of urban property ownership for the early to mid-nineteenth century are based on very little systematic evidence. Overseers' replies to the Town Queries in the appendices of the Poor Law Commission of 1834 about ownership of working-class housing suggest that it would be premature to generalize. Small landlords appear to have been more prevalent in longer-established settlements, where a substantial class of freeholders were able to develop infill housing in courts and yards on small plots off the main thoroughfares, than in the newer dynamic industrial towns. This distinction was clearly evident within Lancashire. 'Tradesmen', 'persons of small property' and 'the middle class' accounted for the majority of working-class housing in Ormskirk, Padiham, Prescot, and the corporate towns of Lancaster, Preston and Wigan. In Everton and Liverpool, however, 'speculative builders with little or no capital' and other tradesmen connected with construction were most closely associated with house ownership. In Warrington, manufacturers and a rentier class of 'persons whose income chiefly arises from them' owned most of the houses. In Manchester there was a spatial division with 'the more ancient parts of town', primarily the city's commercial core, in the hands of 'older landed proprietors', while in the suburbs 'the more recent erections belong to tradesmen, shopkeepers, publicans, mechanics, and building or subscription clubs'. In emerging manufacturing towns, the absence of a substantial established trading class meant that employers were much more involved in housing provision. Masters, bleachers, spinners and manufacturers were listed as major landlords in Bolton alongside mechanics, shopkeepers, widows and weavers, while in Oldham, although some cottages were in the hands of 'publicans, small tradesmen and persons having small capital', they were 'principally owned by the manufacturers being built for the people employed by them'.[15]

This picture is congruent with John Marshall's analysis of factory colonization in the north-west which suggests that, although 'mill-owners in an already developing urban area very rarely made themselves responsible for building activities and house provision' it would be wrong to dismiss such employer provision 'even in the immediate vicinity of large and growing towns, before the third or fourth decades of the nineteenth century'.[16] Caroline Bedale's case study of Oldham provides convincing empirical evidence of their importance, concluding that it was only after mid-century that 'The provision of working-class housing [thus] passed from large industrialists, who were interested not only in making a profit from renting houses but also in attracting labour to the town, to the petty bourgeoisie, who saw the ownership of a few houses purely as a means of making small, safe investments.'[17] Shopkeepers only significantly increased their share of the housing market in the town after the mid-1880s and their holdings were always exceeded by men more closely associated with the building trades. Despite Patrick Joyce's lack of emphasis on employer housing provision, his analyses of Blackburn and Bury portray a similar picture. Although the majority of owners in Blackburn and Bury in the 1870s held only a few houses, the majority were still held in large blocks of between ten and fifty, and it was only in the closing decades of the century that employers' holdings were broken up.[18]

## II

We need to consider, therefore, whether the extension of right to participate in national elections and local government in the early nineteenth century was premised on the concept of a 'propertied' middle class as small property owners or one which visualized them as occupiers of relatively highly rated premises such as shops and manufacturing workshops. It is significant in this context that extension of the parliamentary borough franchise in the Reform Act of 1832, widely regarded as a defining moment in the politicization of the middle class, encompassed not just owners of £10 properties, but their *occupiers*.

The transformation in the qualifications for membership of the 300 Improvement or Police Commissions which were created from the mid-eighteenth century provides further evidence of this recognition of the existence of substantial occupiers and their rights. These bodies, largely ignored by historians, were possibly the most tangible manifestation of an emerging middle-class civic consciousness during this period. They represented a significant increase in the power of local authorities to control the appearance, use and enjoyment of what could be considered as 'urban commons' – the public streets – and to levy compulsory rates on inhabitants to effect desired changes in the provision of public amenities.[19] By the second quarter of the nineteenth century they were grappling with issues which continued to dominate local government well into the following century: the relative merits of municipal and private ownership of utilities like water and gas; whether such enterprises should aim to make a profit and whether it should be utilized for 'public improvements' or to reduce taxation; the control, purpose and financing of police establishments; municipal provision of social and recreational amenities; building regulations and by-laws; traffic management.[20]

These bodies were established in virtually every town in the first half of the nineteenth century. In Lancashire, Manchester (1792), Salford (1792) and Great and Little Bolton (1792) had established improvement commissions before the end of the eighteenth century. Other long-standing centres such Blackburn (1803), Warrington (1813) and Preston (1815) had acquired them by 1820, as had Burnley (1819), but the majority of initiatives occurred in a burst of activity in the mid- to late 1820s when, as Edwin Butterworth put it, towns 'entered into competition in right good earnest . . . in the race of public improvements, which at that period prevailed so generally'.[21] In the space of just six years Chorlton (1822), Ardwick (1825), Hulme (1824), Lancaster (1824), Rochdale (1825), Oldham and Stockport (1826), Ashton (1827) and Stalybridge (1828) all obtained private Enabling Acts. During the 1840s and early 1850s another rash of legislation established commissions in later developing industrial towns and the seaside resorts further to the west: Fleetwood (1842); St Helens (1845); Bury (1846); Southport (1846); Blackpool (1851); Chorley (1853).

In the absence of national blueprints such as those drawn up for later reforms of the Poor Law, municipal corporations and local boards, the property qualifications for membership of these bodies were determined by private local Acts of Parliament. As the Webbs observed, the definition of the 'propertied' class in this legislation did not remain constant over time, but shifted from one based primarily on ownership to one based on occupation:

> Among the thousand Local Acts, by which, during the eighteenth century, the three hundred or so bodies of Commissioners were established or amended, there was introduced first the qualification of ownership of real estate; then the alternative possession of £1,000 or other specified amount of any form of wealth; and in the late constitutions, first as a new alternative and latterly, in a few cases, as the only permissible form of qualification, the occupation within the town of premises of what was at the time a high annual value. . . .[22]

This transition was clearly evident in Lancashire between the 1790s and 1820s (Table 6.1).

*Table 6.1: Membership Qualifications for selected Lancashire Improvement Commissions, 1765–1846*

*Manchester*
1765    (with Salford): self-appointed body with power to co-opt new members
1792    owners or occupiers of property with rental assessment of £30
1828    240 commissioners with £28 property qualification, to be elected by £16 electors (values double for victuallers)

*Bolton, Great*
1792    40 trustees holding property to value of £1,000, appointed for life; vacancies filled by co-option
1831    vacancies to be filled from lists of candidates nominated by Great Bolton vestry meetings, but trustees reverted to electing themselves in 1833 on the grounds that no rates had been laid for two years

*Bolton, Little*
1792    30 trustees holding property to the value of £500, appointed for life; vacancies filled by co-option
1830    10 trustees to be elected annually by public meeting of ratepayers of 7 months' standing

*Blackburn*
1803    12 trustees, including the vicar of Blackburn, 'seized or possessed' of property rated at £20; new members to be elected or appointed by existing trustees, excluding victuallers

*Preston*
1815    mayor and aldermen of borough; owners of property to value of £100; tenants of inns, alehouses, etc. to £100; tenants of other property to value of £50

*Burnley*
1819    owners of property to the yearly value of £50, occupiers of property of £100 within 1,320 yards of the Merestone 'opposite the great Front Door of the Black Bull Inn'

*Rochdale*
1825    owners, occupiers and tenants of building of yearly rent or value of £35, excluding victuallers

*Oldham*
1826    resident owners of property of clear yearly rental of value of £50 and occupiers of property valued at £30, excluding victuallers

*Ashton*
1827    owners and occupiers of buildings rated at £35, excluding victuallers

*Bury*
1846    27 commissioners elected by occupiers of property assessed to the poor rate; commissioners to be male, resident and rated at £20; one-third to retire each year

*Sources*: Improvement Acts for Ashton 14 June 1827 (7 & 8 Geo 4); Blackburn 13 July 1803 (43 Geo 3); Burnley 19 May 1819 (59 Geo 3); Bury 27 July 1846 (9 & 10 Vic); Oldham 26 May 1826 (7 Geo 4); Preston 20 May 1815 (55 Geo 3); Rochdale 10 June 1825 (6 Geo 4). Details for Manchester and Bolton drawn from P. Taylor, *Popular Politics in Early Industrial Britain: Bolton 1825–50* (Keele University Press, 1995); S. and B. Webb, *Statutory Authorities for Special Purposes* (London, Longman, 1922)

Thereafter, the feasibility of Athenian forms of direct representation declined, especially in the larger towns like Manchester and Bolton, and there was a gradual move towards indirect forms of representative democracy which were to characterize later Victorian local authorities. These modifications adopted a variety of strategies: a straightforward property franchise as in Manchester; nomination by vestry meeting in Bolton; and plural voting on the basis of the Select Vestry Act of 1819 in Bury.

Changes to qualifications were not unconnected with the increasing presence of the 'middling ranks' and 'the trading middle classes' who mounted challenges to the authority of the 'self-elected and self-governing clique of "principal inhabitants"' in Manchester and Bolton in the late 1820s.[23] Peter Taylor has described how in Bolton a radical petit bourgeois onslaught against the Tory–Anglican oligarchy in the early 1830s succeeded, temporarily at least, in curbing expenditure and precipitating limited democratic reforms.[24] Michael Turner, Vic Gatrell and Derek Fraser have all shown how in Manchester in the late 1820s, a 'small but determined band', led by Archibald Prentice, 'presented themselves as the advocates of economy and the guardians of the public purse, performing a valuable service for ratepayers by keeping a tight control on expenditure'.[25] John Foster identified a similar challenge to Oldham's established élite in the early 1830s, although he portrayed their actions as being determined by pressure from the organized working class exerted through a mixture of 'outright coercion or exclusive dealing'.[26] Recent historians have tended to accept these men's portrayal of themselves as champions of the 'politics of the people', challenging privilege, corruption and extravagance.[27] The Webbs, however, were less generous to them, describing those in Manchester as 'a noisy and persistent minority of Radicals and nonconformists', who prevented the implementation of a 'vigorous municipal policy'.[28] However, precisely who these smaller men were and, more pertinently, whether they were, as is usually assumed, small property owners, or part of a growing class of occupiers is less clear.


## III


The membership book for Oldham's Police Commission between 1827 and 1848, sheds light on this issue. The Enabling Act of 1826 empowered the commission to levy up to 2s 6d in the pound each year and borrow up to £20,000 for 'policing' the township of Oldham, the word being applied in its older broader sense as appertaining to all civic affairs including 'paving, watching, lighting, cleansing and improving the township of Oldham'. Throughout its existence, membership was restricted to males over twenty-one years of age of six months' residence either 'in possession or enjoyment or receipt of rents and profits of any house[s], warehouse[s] . . . of clear yearly rent or annual value of £50' or occupying property of a clear yearly value of £30.[29] The value of a property, however, was calculated on land and buildings alone, exclusive of any money paid or received for application of steam or power for turning machinery, a clause which undoubtedly had the effect of reducing the potential number of recruits from the ranks of small textile producers who rented accommodation in mills inclusive of room and power. All retailers of alcohol and anyone holding 'office or place or profit under the commissioners' were also excluded.[30] Each new commissioner was obliged to confirm his eligibility in writing by signing a membership book, providing details of his address, occupation and whether he qualified on the grounds of ownership or occupation of property of the requisite value.[31] Such a source is clearly inferior to rate books in that it does not provide precise details of each individual's property or of possible tenurial relationships between individuals. It also fails to reflect the fact that some men both owned and rented property and it only records circumstances on the specific occasion in an individual's life cycle when he took the oath as a commissioner.[32] Nevertheless, the significant transformation in the structure of the town's propertied class over the period implied by its patterns of enrolment cannot be lightly dismissed.

Oldham township's extensive boundaries also had an exceptional influence on the commission's membership and political complexion in its early years. In marked contrast to commissions established in other sprawling townships such as Burnley, Rochdale and Ashton where the areas of urban jurisdiction were specifically delineated, Oldham Police Commission's powers applied to the entire township, a sprawling area of 4,617 acres which was neither urban nor a town in the sense in which these terms are generally conceived. As the parliamentary boundary commissioners noted in 1831, the township contained 'a large space of rural district', and it is likely that in appearance it closely resembled Samuel Bamford's portrayal of the textile districts as 'a vast city scattered amongst meads and pastures and belts of woodland', rather than a recognizable urban landscape.[33] Many of the industrial population lived in settlements like Greenacres Moor and Waterhead Mill to the east, and Hollinwood to the south, and it was not until the end of the nineteenth century that these separate communities were physically absorbed into a recognizable urban environment; even then they retained a strong sense of their own identities.[34] Residents in the settlement around St Mary's parish church, however, accounted for an increasing proportion of the township's population, up from approximately 50 per cent in 1821 to 66 per cent in 1841.[35] More significantly, service and retail functions were increasingly concentrated along its central thoroughfares. So, although the majority of employment in the township was dependent on manufacturing, Oldham's 'propertied' class was both more diverse and complex, incorporating an important, if declining, agricultural element, and an expanding service sector, both of which helped to define the political trajectory of the town during the 1830s and 1840s.

Property owners were in a clear majority at the inaugural meeting of the Police Commission in January 1827, outnumbering occupiers by sixty-one to twenty-six. As founder members they were also able to dominate the first General Purposes committee. These men were predominantly drawn from what John Foster described as the 'big bourgeoisie'; a small group of long-established families who owned the town's major hatting, coalmining and integrated textile firms which employed the majority of the population.[36] Their names continued to feature prominently in the rate books of the 1840s as owners of substantial industrial and mining premises and proprietors of extensive blocks of residential properties.[37] Other founding members included building merchants, metal workers, farmers, 'gentlemen' (usually retired members of these same families), and town-centre shopkeepers, most of whom were also property owners.

During the rest of 1827, however, occupiers of property outnumbered owners among new members by thirty-one to twenty-two. Thereafter they accounted for the majority of new members in every year of the Police Commission's existence except for a few in the depressed years of the late 1830s. By the 1840s the ratio of occupiers to owners had widened perceptively to around three to one. Their numerical preponderance was also reflected in the composition of the General Purposes committee, on which they comprised 40 to 50 per cent

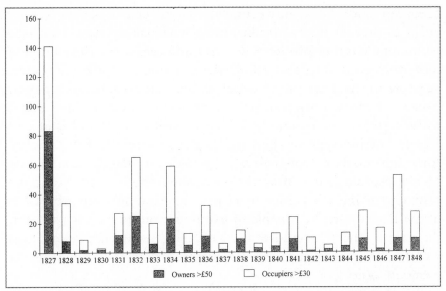

*Figure 6.1: Property Qualifications of New Oldham Commissioners, 1827–48*

of members between 1828 and the late 1830s, and 50 to 75 per cent in the 1840s.[38] Assuming that patterns of enrolment broadly reflected changes in the composition of Oldham's middle class, then it would appear the majority of the town's propertied class were primarily tenants not owners.

The commission's sprawling boundaries were the most significant determinant of its membership during the first six years of its existence in that tenant farmers constituted the largest single group of new enrolments. These men had sound reasons for taking an interest in urban affairs since they were liable to rates on the value of their land and agricultural buildings, unlike neighbouring Rochdale and Ashton where any 'yard, close, barn, stable or other building used for husbandry only, or arable, meadow or pasture land within the said town' were exempted. Not surprisingly they were opposed to contributing towards the cost of improvements from which they could envisage few, if any, direct benefits. In this they were initially relatively successful, forcing occupiers of properties which benefited from lighting and watching to pay an additional separate rate and, in alliance with retailers, removing the preferential treatment which manufacturing premises initially enjoyed in relation to agricultural and commercial property for other rating purposes.[39]

From the mid-1830s, however, their involvement declined. They failed to prevent the reintroduction of unequal assessment on land and manufacturing property in 1840 and, despite a final burst of recruitment in 1847 and 1848, were unable to muster sufficient numbers to challenge the proposal to hand the commission's powers over to the new corporation, a move which they rightly feared would erode their remaining influence still further and lead to a significant increase in the rate burden, especially for policing. Although the extent of their role in Oldham would seem to have been exceptional, it is nevertheless a reminder that we should not assume that the aristocracy or gentry were the only representatives of the landed interest capable of exerting influence in towns during the period, and that industrial Lancashire contained a numerically significant, tenant farming class which survived well into the twentieth century.[40]

The changing structures and mixed fortunes of local industries, however, were also evident on the commission over the period. The relatively small number of coal owners and coal merchants reflected the concentrated ownership of mineral rights in the area. Twenty-six hat manufacturers joined in the first eleven years but only six in the next eleven years, and half of the latter were small men who were also involved in retailing. The miscellaneous group of employers involved in the metal trades significantly increased their presence, ironfounders and machine makers supplanting representatives of small businesses such as blacksmiths, tinplate workers and ironmongers in the late 1840s.

There were also dramatic changes in the nature of the area's major industrial sector, textiles. By the mid-1830s the initial owners of integrated spinning and weaving concerns had been joined by representatives of smaller, single-process, coarse-spinning concerns who were generally described simply as spinners, or occasionally doublers or warpers, and who were increasingly occupiers, possibly renting room and power from more established textile manufacturers who were presumably also potential purchasers of their yarn. The majority of these spinners who joined in 1834 cannot be traced in the 1832 poll book and their surnames are also largely absent from the parliamentary voting lists of 1847 suggesting that their businesses were both of recent origin and relatively short-lived. Recruitment of small textile producers ceased entirely in the late 1830s as the industry moved into depression and only revived in the mid- to late 1840s. It was only in these final years that representatives of the town's waste dealers made an appearance on the commission and that these smaller, single-process producers came close to matching the number of property-owning textile manufacturers. More significantly, they never comprised more than a small minority of spinners listed in trade directories. As commissioners they had a poor attendance record and were almost totally absent from the numerous sub-committees established throughout the period. Their marginal interest in the management of the town and the improvement of its physical infrastructure possibly reflected the fact that many of Oldham's small producers had little in the way of property, and were closer to the workers in lifestyle and possessions.[41]

In relation to their contribution to employment in the town or the total rates bill, however, Oldham's industrial proprietors were significantly under-represented on the commission. But on these criteria shopkeepers were over-represented. They accounted for a significant proportion of early members, but their absolute and relative significance increased substantially during upswings in the trade cycle in the early 1830s and mid-1840s. Over sixty joined between 1832 and 1836, only twenty-eight in the eight years which followed, but another thirty-five between 1845 and early 1848.[42] Although most rarely attended except during times of social unrest, such as the riots in April 1834, or when major policy issues like the erection of a town hall or the purchase of the gas company were being discussed, they were nevertheless able to constitute the largest single occupational group on the General Purposes committee throughout the period. Shopkeepers had more reason than other sectors of the middle class to be concerned about the nature and cost of urban improvements. They were heavily taxed in comparison to both manufacturers, who were not rated on the value of machinery or power on their premises, and to farmers, both of whom enjoyed some relief from the separately levied watching and lighting rates because their premises were not situated on the main thoroughfares.[43] The business prospects and domestic lives of those who lived above their shops in the town centre, however, were directly influenced by activities which dominated the commission's regular business agenda: the provision of lighting; maintenance of public order; removal of pavement obstructions; traffic management, including parking; and the improvement and regulation of market facilities.

*Table 6.2: Oldham Police Commissioners, 1827–48: Property Qualifications of New Members by Occupational Category*

|  | 1827–31 | | 1832–6 | | 1837–42 | | 1843–8 | | 1827–48 | |
|---|---|---|---|---|---|---|---|---|---|---|
|  | Owners | Occupiers | Owners | Occupiers | Owners | Occupiers | Owners | Occupiers | Owners | Occupiers |
| Farming | 13 | 40 | 2 | 32 | 1 | 7 | 0 | 18 | 16 | 97 |
| Retailing | 20 | 25 | 19 | 41 | 5 | 18 | 6 | 36 | 50 | 120 |
| Textiles | 32 | 19 | 13 | 22 | 7 | 5 | 12 | 29 | 64 | 75 |
| Hatting | 7 | 7 | 2 | 7 | 1 | 5 | 1 | 2 | 11 | 21 |
| Metal trades | 5 | 1 | 5 | 2 | 2 | 4 | 5 | 10 | 17 | 17 |
| Building trades | 5 | 2 | 6 | 5 | 2 | 2 | 4 | 4 | 17 | 13 |
| Gentlemen | 20 | 3 | 13 | 4 | 3 | 1 | 5 | 3 | 41 | 11 |
| Professionals | 2 | 3 | 5 | 3 | 4 | 2 | 2 | 4 | 13 | 12 |
| Others | 3 | 7 | 5 | 3 | 3 | 2 | 0 | 0 | 11 | 12 |
| Total | 107 | 107 | 70 | 119 | 28 | 46 | 35 | 106 | 240 | 378 |

*Property Qualifications of Textile Trades, 1827–48*

|  | Owners | Occupiers | Total |
|---|---|---|---|
| Spinners and manufacturers | 27 | 38 | 65 |
| Spinners | 24 | 21 | 45 |
| Waste dealers | 6 | 10 | 16 |
| Others | 7 | 6 | 13 |

The overwhelming majority of these retailers qualified on the basis of their occupation of business premises, although a small majority of those who qualified in the first two years were property owners as were a significant minority of those in the surrounding industrial settlements who joined in the early 1830s, several of whom combined retailing with farming or small-scale textile production. Along the town's main thoroughfares, however, the shops were almost exclusively occupied by tenants. Of the twenty-three shopkeepers with outlets on Market Place who qualified for membership over the 22-year period, only four did so as owners, three of them at the inaugural meeting. Only six of the fifty commissioners with retail premises on High Street were owners. Five of the seven retailers from Yorkshire Street who qualified before 1842 were owners, but none of the nine who joined after that date was. Indeed, of the forty-three retailers who qualified in the last five years of the commission only six were owners. Not surprisingly, at the inaugural meeting of the Oldham Freehold Land Society in April 1850 the first committee was made up almost entirely from tenant shopkeepers in this central commercial district; land and residential property elsewhere in the township were still largely in the hands of a few established families.[44]

*Table 6.3: Oldham Town-centre Premises, 1827–48*

| | Qualifications of Retailers on Police Commission, 1827–48 | | Occupiers of Properties >£15 r.v. 1848 Poor Rate Book | |
| --- | --- | --- | --- | --- |
| | Owners | *Occupiers* | Owners | *Tenants* |
| High Street | 6 | *44* | 6 | *34* |
| Market Place | 4 | *19* | 2 | 27 |
| Yorkshire Street | 5 | *11* | 9 | *25* |

The expansion of this substantial group of middle-class occupiers had profound political implications for the town (Table 6.4).[45] In every parliamentary election between 1832 and 1852 tenants were more likely than owners to vote for Radical or Liberal candidates. This distinction cut across occupational categories and was evident even within sectors like retailing and farming which were consistently more radical during the period. William Cobbett's portrayal of a rural idyll inhabited by prosperous smallholders and his criticisms of urbanization clearly struck a chord with Oldham's tenant farmers who almost to a man voted for him in 1832.[46] Shopkeepers also voted overwhelmingly for Cobbett in 1832 but expressed a slight preference for his running partner, John Fielden. While farmers largely remained loyal to Fielden and William's son, John Morgan Cobbett, throughout the period, shopkeepers rapidly became disenchanted with Cobbett's brand of Anglican radicalism, as their less than wholehearted support of his son's cause in 1835 and 1847 bears out.[47] Only eleven of the sixty-five retail commissioners voted for the Fielden and Cobbett ticket in 1847, as opposed to seventeen for Fielden and the Liberal W.J. Fox, and twenty-one for Fox and the local, free trade Tory, John Duncuft. In the by-election of 1852 occasioned by Duncuft's death, shop-owning ex-commissioners voted two to one for the protectionist James Heald, but tenants voted four to one for Fox; several of the occupiers who voted for Heald were either butchers or had become involved in the licensed trades, both of which had strong agricultural connections. By this time out-of-town farmers had made common cause with a rump of Tories to oppose urban Liberal property holders who had voted for incorporation in 1848 after the Tory county JPs had imposed the rural constabulary on the town the previous year.[48]

*Table 6.4: Voting Behaviour of Oldham Police Commissioners, 1832–52*

Percentage Voting for each Candidate

**1832**

| | N= | Cobbett (R) | Fielden (R) | Bright (W) | Burge (C) |
|---|---|---|---|---|---|
| Owners | 111 | 35 | 43 | 51 | 29 |
| *Farmers* | 10 | 80 | 60 | 20 | 40 |
| *Shopkeepers* | 28 | 64 | 75 | 29 | 18 |
| *Others* | 73 | 18 | 29 | 64 | 32 |
| Occupiers | 126 | 72 | 74 | 21 | 12 |
| *Farmers* | 49 | 96 | 94 | 6 | 4 |
| *Shopkeepers* | 33 | 79 | 82 | 15 | 3 |
| *Others* | 44 | 41 | 48 | 43 | 30 |

**1835**

| | | Cobbett (R) | O'Connor (R) | Lees (C) |
|---|---|---|---|---|
| Owners | 132 | 28 | 4 | 68 |
| *Farmers* | 6 | 50 | | 50 |
| *Shopkeepers* | 33 | 27 | 9 | 64 |
| *Others* | 93 | 27 | 2 | 71 |
| Occupiers | 142 | 41 | 7 | 52 |
| *Farmers* | 33 | 61 | | 39 |
| *Shopkeepers* | 45 | 42 | 16 | 42 |
| *Others* | 64 | 30 | 5 | 65 |

**1847**

| | | Cobbett (R) | Fielden (R) | Fox (L) | Duncuft (C) |
|---|---|---|---|---|---|
| Owners | 107 | 31 | 22 | 61 | 69 |
| *Farmers* | 10 | 80 | 70 | 20 | 30 |
| *Shopkeepers* | 22 | 23 | 18 | 64 | 68 |
| *Others* | 75 | 27 | 17 | 65 | 75 |
| Occupiers | 196 | 40 | 41 | 60 | 48 |
| *Farmers* | 43 | 79 | 72 | 26 | 19 |
| *Shopkeepers* | 65 | 32 | 43 | 71 | 45 |
| *Others* | 88 | 26 | 24 | 68 | 66 |

**1852**

| | | Fox (L) | Heald (C) |
|---|---|---|---|
| Owners | 99 | 47 | 53 |
| *Farmers* | 6 | 17 | 83 |
| *Shopkeepers* | 19 | 32 | 68 |
| *Others* | 74 | 54 | 46 |
| Occupiers | 155 | 62 | 38 |
| *Farmers* | 28 | 21 | 79 |
| *Shopkeepers* | 59 | 80 | 20 |
| *Others* | 68 | 63 | 37 |

*Sources*: Police Commission Membership Book; Poll Books

## IV

The increasing emphasis throughout the period on the political rights of occupiers combined with this evidence from Oldham suggests that rapid urban growth in the early nineteenth century created not so much a class of small property owners, as a substantial middle-class urban tenantry. While property owners were predominantly Tory, this latter group was increasingly associated with the Liberal cause. We cannot as yet say whether Oldham's experience was typical of other developing towns during this period. The agricultural sector's prominence was probably exceptional, but there is circumstantial evidence to suppose that in other respects it was.

We know, for example, that retail businesses expanded more rapidly than those in any other sector of the urban economy and at a rate well in excess of population growth.[49] As in Oldham, in many towns the mobilization of this 'shopocracy' underpinned campaigns to reform local government in the second quarter of the nineteenth century.[50] In most parliamentary constituencies such men also comprised the largest single occupational group under the reformed electoral franchise and were loyal supporters of Liberal candidates from the 1830s to the 1860s.[51] Nossiter has also demonstrated that shopkeepers and small businessmen who qualified for the parliamentary franchise as £10 occupiers in corporate towns like Newcastle were also more likely to vote for Radical or Liberal candidates in 1832 than those who were freemen.[52]

If the expanding middle class of the early to mid-nineteenth century were occupiers rather than owners of property, then many of the features commonly associated with this group become more, not less, understandable: their sense of economic insecurity; heightened concern with the level of rent and rates; their militant individualistic Liberalism and faith in personal qualities; their antipathy towards rentiers. The Liberals' land societies in the late 1840s and 1850s, designed to expand the number of freeholders qualified to vote in county elections, were premised on the assumption that property ownership was not yet widespread among many sections of the urban *petite bourgeoisie*. More conservative supporters of the established order, however, also recognized the political advantages of creating a class of small proprietors such as existed in Western Europe, 'at least into the crowded manufacturing districts . . . in order thereby to create among the shopkeepers, and among those who would become owners of gardens and farms, a strong conservative class, capable of countering the immensely powerful democratic class, which is now nursing in those districts, and which is increasing there every day in strength and numbers'.[53] In view of small property owners' apparent attachment to Conservatism in the late nineteenth century this diagnosis would seem to have been broadly accurate.

We need, therefore, to revise our assumptions about the relationship between property ownership and the middle class for the early to mid-Victorian period. Perhaps, however, we also need to challenge our assumptions about the origins, nature and rationale of property ownership in the late Victorian period and the importance of the 'trading' classes as suppliers of working-class housing. Ownership of blocks of rented housing stock was much more evident among trades connected with the building industry than among retailers or white collar workers, and it was these groups that dominated many of the small property owners' associations which opposed the introduction of stricter building by-laws during the period and patronized early building clubs and societies.[54] As early as the 1840s savings banks were attracting significant savings from tradesmen and shopkeepers, and by the end of the century joint stock companies were becoming increasingly attractive investment options.[55] For many within the lower middle class, the desire to own property probably did not extend beyond owning their own residence. The combination of rising rents, low rates of interest, increased economic security and spectacular booms in speculative suburban building in the last quarter of the century provided both the incentive and means for them to achieve this.[56] A significant proportion of owner-occupiers by the late nineteenth century were small businessmen and the salaried lower middle class, and it is not surprising, therefore, that their family homes and business premises accounted for a relatively high proportion of their modest wealth at death.[57] Even without making allowance for the inclusion of owner-occupiers' properties in Daunton's tables of 'landlords' in the five late Victorian, northern industrial towns which he analysed, 1.8 per cent and 4 per cent of proprietors still accounted for between 19.3 per cent and 30.6 per cent of the housing market. Assuming that most of the cheapest properties were rented, this suggests that ownership of rented housing was rather more concentrated than current historiography suggests.[58]

Without further detailed research into the structure of property ownership and occupancy across a range of towns and periods, and the possible relationship between these and political allegiance, such observations must remain largely speculative. What is clear, however, is that we should not assume that the 'propertied' middle class in the industrial towns of the early nineteenth century were necessarily owners. Even if the majority of property owners and landlords of cheap rented accommodation were drawn from this class, it does not follow that the majority of property was held by them, or that the majority of them were property owners, let alone that they wished to be, or were able to become, landlords.

**APPENDIX**

Composition of Occupational Groups referred to in Table 6.2.

*Farming*: farmer, yeoman.

*Retailing*: shopkeeper, grocer, provision dealer, oil and colourman, butcher, greengrocer, flour dealer, corn factor, corn and tallow dealer, confectioner and seedsman, tea dealer, draper, lace dealer, haberdasher, tailor, clothes dealer, shoe dealer, shoemaker, boot and shoemaker, clogger, leather dealer, druggist and spirit dealer, chemist, watch and clock maker and jeweller, stationer, bookseller, pawnbroker, hairdresser and perfumier, tobacconist, china, glass and earthenware dealer, cabinet-maker, furnishing ironmonger, furniture broker.

*Textiles*: cotton manufacturer, cotton spinner, cotton spinner and manufacturer, cotton spinner and fustian manufacturer, cotton spinner and millwright, cotton spinner and doubler, warp manufacturer, cotton dealer, waste dealer, hosier, weaver, dyer.

*Hatting*: hat manufacturer, hatter, furrier.

*Metal Trades*: ironfounder, machine maker, roller and spindle maker, machine brush maker, brazier and gas fitter, tinplate worker, blacksmith, ironmonger, mechanic, engineer.

*Building Trades*: builder, timber merchant, iron dealer, plumber, glazier, painter, joiner, stonemason, mason, bricklayer, bricksetter, slater, flag merchant.

*Gentlemen*: gent, esquire.

*Professionals*: broker, surveyor, lawyer, attorney, solicitor, agent, manager, law clerk, clerk, accountant, schoolmaster, rate collector, commission agent, surgeon.

*Others*: constable, coal master, coal miner, coal merchant, labourer, unknown.

These occupations reflect the descriptions given at the time of joining the commission or in contemporary trade directories. In sixty-one cases entries in directories were either different from those given in the membership book or suggested individuals were, or had been, involved in more than one trade or profession. The occupation or status given at time of joining the commission has always been given preference for purposes of analysis.

CHAPTER

7

# READING THE WILL:

## CASH ECONOMY CAPITALISTS AND URBAN PEASANTS IN THE 1830S

R.J. MORRIS

The ability to make testamentary bequests, to transmit our property to those who occupy the chief place in our affections, or to whom we have been under obligations is indispensable to the advancement of society in wealth and civilization.

J.R. McCulloch

The reading and making of wills was a constantly recurring theme in that vast quantity of novels through which the nineteenth-century middle class of Britain explored their social being and social relationships. Wills provide a very particular access to the practices, strategies and structures of many societies. Death, especially the death of adults who have gathered some element of authority during their lives, always requires a society to remake itself. In the processes of that remaking and in the anticipation of that remaking societies, social groups and individuals affirm and develop a wide range of values, status positions and relationships. For the property-owning societies of the modern period, the will and its probate and execution are and were a major part of this remaking.

Historians have used a variety of ways of seeking to understand the nature and impact of the middle classes in Britain. Political progress and stability, economic structure, power and accumulation, the remaking of gender, the making and remaking of consumer society as well as the creation and development of languages and discourses have all received attention.[1] Judgements have been debated regarding their 'success' and their relationships with an aristocracy.[2] In any discussion of the middle classes property must play a central part. Property may be considered as an element in the structural relationships of capital or as a cultural construct essential to a power relationship, but few enquiries into the nature and importance of the middle classes proceed without attention to it.

This case study of the nature of property and property relationships is conducted through the wills and intestate property of 362 individuals from the parish of Leeds whose estates were brought to the ecclesiastical courts of York for probate in the early 1830s.[3] Each probate traced the transfer of property at death which was so crucial to the making and remaking of the middle classes. It involved the social relationships of property, family, friendship, gender and status – all central to accounts of the middle classes. This transfer involved law, morality, custom and emotion as well as the stark material factors of economic status and survival.

The sample in this study was brought for probate as British society was emerging from a long period of war and was coming to terms with a sense of rapid economic change and urbanization. It was a society seeking political and social balance. Deep individual insecurity, both demographic and economic, was coupled with a high sense of moral importance often linked to the remaking of gender relationships and sustained attempts to manage class relationships.[4] As yet property relationships were highly individualistic. Most were related to a legal personality, sometimes in partnership and on occasion mediated by a trust. Apart from the family there were few collective forms for spreading and evaluating risk. The modern collective forms of property such as life insurance, limited liability joint stock companies or corporate salaried employment were imperfect in both their nature and use. The harsh illuminating lens of the last will and testament revealed a variety of strategies and attitudes in the face of the opportunities and insecurities of this situation.

Until the reforms of 1856 probate, both testate and intestate, remained with the ecclesiastical courts. By the 1830s, no effective inventory was retained in the court records but two types of evidence do remain, the text of the wills and the sworn value of the probate. Sworn value was an estimate of the gross value of the personal property involved in the estate made towards the beginning of the executorship of an estate for tax purposes. For the historian it provides a useful but imperfect measure of economic status. This indicator and its aggregates have been much used in debates around the nature and importance of the middle classes.[5] It will be used in this study as an indicator of economic status, so it is important that the strengths and weaknesses of sworn value are recognized.

Among the most important obligations of executors and administrators was the payment of probate and legacy duties. These were required by legislation consolidated in the Stamp Act of 55 Geo. 3, c. 184 for the probate duty and c. 52 for the legacy duty. Executors and administrators were 'required by the Stamp Act to swear to the gross value of the personal estate without any deduction for debts'.[6] This had to be done within six months of death or a penalty of £100 was due. If the testator held property in both provinces then two sets of sworn values and probate duty had to be paid. Thus sworn values in the York records did not include property held in the province of Canterbury. The 'sworn value' included only personal property; all holdings of land and buildings were excluded. This again was important as many among the Leeds middle class had substantial holdings of freehold urban housing and cottage property. In his *Guide* of 1838, J.C. Hudson reminded executors that personal estate included all leasehold property and any freehold real estate that was contracted to be sold. The position with partnership capital was complex:

If the testator were a partner in any house of trade, his share in any real estate belonging to the firm, as having been purchased with partnership property is to be included. But in the case of partnership, the executor is not to include the whole gross amount of the testator's share of the partnership property, but must obtain from the surviving partners a balance sheet, exhibiting both the property and liabilities of the firm, and the sum to be included in the estimate of the testator's property will be his share of the net balance only.[7]

Once the sworn value had been notified, probate tax was charged under an irregular series of tax bands. The sum actually entered in the affidavit was thus not the estimated value but the upper bound of the tax band within which the executor believed the estate would fall. When the full estate had been gathered in and debts paid then the executors could claim a rebate from the tax office or pay extra together with a penalty if they had underestimated. Thus the sworn value was an indicator of economic status which must be used with great care. It was not a direct valuation of an individual's net assets, even at the time of death. The relationship might be expressed as follows:

Net Value of Assets at time of death = Sworn Value in province of York – liabilities + value of real estate + value of personal property held in province of Canterbury.

Nevertheless, this indicator is still a very usable one. When compared with other indicators of status, sworn value produced sensible results.

*Table 7.1. Sworn value and occupational status*

| Occupational status | Number of cases | mean | median | coefficient of variation* | participation in subscription 1829** |
|---|---|---|---|---|---|
| commerce | 34 | 4,842 | 1,500 | 1.30 | 5.08 |
| gentleman | 51 | 2,427 | 450 | 1.69 | – |
| professional | 13 | 2,077 | 800 | 1.25 | 4.83 |
| manufacturing | 46 | 1,443 | 100 | 3.29 | 0.78 |
| no title | 71 | 1,235 | 450 | 1.92 | – |
| distribution | 51 | 985 | 200 | 2.22 | 0.50 |
| miscellaneous | 8 | 740 | 325 | 1.80 | – |
| white collar | 12 | 720 | 200 | 1.53 | 0.81 |
| yeoman | 15 | 611 | 100 | 2.09 | – |
| craft | 56 | 460 | 100 | 2.12 | 0.18 |
| wage labour | 5 | 162 | 50 | 1.52 | – |
| total | 362 | 1,575 | 300 | 2.25 | 1.00 |

* standard deviation/mean
** This was a subscription for the relief of the poor in the economic depression of 1829. The indicator measured the percentage participation of the group in the subscribers' list (observed) divided by the percentage share of the group in the Trade Directory (expected).[8]

The ranking follows that of other status indicators with commerce leading followed by gentlemen and professionals. All groups follow the same pattern as the whole sample. They contained a large number of modest-sized estates with a few very small and a long tail of larger estates. The sample was characterized by this massively skewed inequality as was the distribution within groups. The variation was greatest among the manufacturers who had also shown greater range and variation according to other indicators.

Sworn value is likely to be a useful indicator of economic status for groups provided their circumstances and habits are understood. Two hypothetical examples will illustrate the difficulties. In the first a manufacturer dies in his thirties with an active business. He has substantial working capital and large liabilities to his suppliers, no partnership and has just begun to purchase real estate. His older brother dies aged sixty, a gentleman, retired from business with considerable household furniture, cash in the bank and extensive real property from which he draws his income. The merchant has a sworn value of £10,000, his gentleman brother £3,000, but once the merchant's executors have paid his trade debts (say £8,000), even with the addition of the net worth of his real estate (say £2,000), the net worth of the merchant would be only £4,000, while his retired older brother, sworn value £3,000 (he had no trading capital), had few debts (£1,000) and real estate with a net value of £10,000, net worth £12,000. Thus the relationship between sworn value and actual net worth must vary with life cycle stage. In the same way the relationship will vary with the propensity to invest in real rather than personal property. If this is a matter of personal preference then there would be little problem about estimating the relative economic status of groups but it seems likely that some groups, notably shopkeepers and craftsmen, did have a higher preference for real property, while in some areas of the country the prevalence of leaseholds might mean that a real property preference would be recorded in sworn value while in others it would not.

Of the 362 probates, 73 per cent were male. Those who made wills were 74 per cent of the total (77 per cent of the men and 66 per cent of the women). A large number of these wills were made close to death. Of the 252 wills for which both date of death and the date of the will were known, 36 were made within 10 days of death, 83 within 50 days while just over half were made within 6 months of death. The bulk of the men identified themselves by an occupational title or some other indicator of economic status such as gentleman or yeoman. Women rarely gave an occupation. When they did it was usually that of their husband. Women were identified by their civil status. The structure of the population whose estates were brought for probate showed important differences when compared with the structure of the Leeds population entered in the Trade Directory of 1834.

*Table 7.2: Occupational Status*

| status | male | wills female | total | % | total % | 1834 directory status group if different |
|---|---|---|---|---|---|---|
| yeoman | 14 | 1 | 15 | 4.14 | 2.1 | land |
| misc. | 8 | 0 | 8 | 2.21 | 1.6 | |
| distribution | 41 | 10 | 51 | 14.09 | 23.6 | |
| commerce | 30 | 4 | 34 | 9.39 | 7.7 | |
| white collar | 10 | 2 | 12 | 3.31 | 6.0 | |
| manufacturing | 43 | 3 | 46 | 12.71 | 17.0 | |
| craft | 51 | 5 | 56 | 15.47 | 28.2 | |
| professional | 13 | 0 | 13 | 3.59 | 2.3 | |
| wage labour | 5 | 0 | 5 | 1.38 | 0.7 | |
| | | | | | 4.3 | govt and service |
| gentleman | 48 | 3 | 51 | 14.09 | 8.3 | indep. income |
| no title | 3 | 68 | 71 | 19.61 | | |
| total | 266 | 96 | 362 | 100.00 | N=9101 | |

These two accounts of the middle-class population of Leeds in the early 1830s, one framed by the probates and the other by the Trade Directory, showed several differences. The most important was the number of 'gentlemen' among those whose estates came to probate. Despite some claims, this was not in itself an indicator of preference for land or deference to aristocratic social values but simply a product of the fact that those in the probate population by its very nature tended to be near the end of the life cycle and hence included many who had retired from business and described themselves as 'gentlemen'.

Among the 'gentlemen' were twenty-seven about whom further information could be gathered either from the trade directories of the 1820s or the internal evidence of the wills. Several different meanings of 'gentleman' emerged. Nine held some rural property, although many of these holdings were small. There were three professional individuals, including one who acknowledged that his father had transferred a small parcel of land to him, 'so as to qualify him to shoot game'.

The next group consisted of four who had been manufacturers in at least one of the 1820s trade directories and five who had craft or retail occupational titles or links. In addition, there was one clothier and a cloth dresser. In many cases, these individuals acknowledged their occupation in the 1822 Trade Directory but by 1825 called themselves gentlemen. In this group, the term gentleman is best understood to mean 'retired on rentier income'. Almost all of them listed the property, usually urban cottages, houses and warehouses from which they drew their retirement income. In these cases, 'gentleman' was a life cycle stage rather than an indicator of social status.

The last group consisted of four individuals linked to the building trades, including a joiner and a stonemason. One John Dufton was a major owner of working-class housing including the notorious Boot and Shoe Yard in central Leeds which was already being pointed to by public health reformers as a source of disease.[9] He had a large number of cottages in Richmond Hill, York Street and the Boot and Shoe Yard, as well as a tenement in Marsh Lane, 'where I now live'. In 1822, he was a furniture broker in Marsh Lane; in 1825, a general broker, at 9 Dufton's Court, Marsh Lane. His son, George Dufton was listed as a bricklayer living at 43 Bridge Street, Lady Lane. This group of gentlemen were property developers.

The term gentleman had begun its life in the sixteenth century with a fairly strict legal definition. By 1700, its meaning had already widened.[10] By the 1830s, it still implied someone who had an independent income or an income from property but this claim had lost all meaning in terms of links with traditional society. The gentlemen of Leeds ranged from a lawyer with a game licence, to retired merchants and a major slum landlord whose property entered Leeds history by way of every public health report produced between 1832 and 1850.

So far the discussion has concerned very specific items in the text of the will: name, an occupational title or civil status and the date on which the will was made. The bulk of the text was in essence a series of instructions regarding the disposal of property after death. The expressive religious declarations of earlier periods were gone. These were instructions about property and people. There were two groups of wills. Many, especially those which belonged to the commercial and professional families, were drafted in formulistic legal language and often included a lawyer's clerk among the witnesses and a lawyer as one of the executors. The others show through handwriting and phraseology that they were self-drafted or drafted by friends, but with a good knowledge of the legal context. For example, many would include the phrase 'of sound mind' showing that they understood that a will might be challenged on the grounds the testator was confused. The bleak and often utilitarian language of these wills does not provide a complete account of family and social relationships but it does catch the will makers participating in the anticipated process of remaking social relationships after death. They selected those aspects of property and the relationships of affection and obligation which were so important that they required the careful disposition of the will.

There were three types of influence upon this text, namely law, custom and practice. By the late eighteenth century, English law gave considerable freedom to the will maker. Direction was only given when an individual died intestate. In this case real property went to the eldest son and personal property was distributed according to the custom of the ecclesiastical court concerned, usually a third to the widow and the rest equally among children. Indeed, the purpose of making a will could be defined as stopping this form of distribution taking place. Custom was a powerful influence. Most courts assumed that a third was for the widow, a third for the children and a third was the 'dead's part', in other words the testator could dispose of this as they wanted. It is not clear what force this custom had in law but it was rare to find a will that deviated from it. It was practice which was crucial and here several behaviour patterns can be identified which can advance discussion and understanding of the middle classes.

The dominant form of the will was that of a married man making provision for a widow and children. Debates on inheritance, legal textbooks and advice manuals on making wills were all addressed to this group. Although they were the largest element among the will makers they were still a minority, albeit the minority around which ideology and law revolved.

*Table 7.3: The will makers*

|  | N | % |
| --- | --- | --- |
| men with widow and children | 100 | 37.6 |
| men with widow | 31 | 11.7 |
| men with children | 37 | 13.9 |
| other men | 34 | 12.8 |
| widow with children | 15 | 5.6 |
| widow | 17 | 6.4 |
| spinster | 18 | 6.8 |
| other women | 14 | 5.3 |

These men were guided by two principles: to make provision for their widow and to treat their children with strict equity. Phrases like 'equally amongst all my said children' and 'share and share alike' appear many times in these wills. The detailed operation of the principle of equity varied according to the resources which the will maker anticipated having at death, the age of the children and any preference which had been given to individual children while the testator was alive. The principle of equity was also heavily gendered. Sons would normally receive their fortune free of all restraint when and if they reached the age of twenty-one. Daughters normally received only the income flow from capital which had been invested in trust. Gendered equity thus produced two very distinctive forms of finance capital within the middle classes. The way in which this operated can be seen in the will of George Hepper, woolstapler who made his will on 13 May 1829 and died in December of that year.[11]

Hepper lived in Wortley, one of the weaving villages in the south of the parish of Leeds. He and men like him were central to the textile economy of Leeds. His eldest son, George, was a clothier. His three trustees were son George, the local schoolmaster and a fellow woolstapler. Residential community, occupational community and family were the social resources on which he drew. Death had caught the woolstapler before he had completed the child-raising middle part of the life cycle and he gave his instructions with care. Once his debts had been paid and his personal estate turned into cash, it was to be divided into four equal parts. One part was to go to George 'his executors, administrators and assignees . . . for his and their own absolute use and benefit'. The rest was to be invested 'in Parliamentary Stocks or Public Funds of Great Britain or at interest on Government or Real Securities'. The income from this relatively secure range of investments was to be divided into three parts. One part was for the support of Hannah his widow. The other two parts were for the 'respective maintenance and education' of two children, Hannah and William Edward. William Edward was to get his share of the capital when he reached twenty-one years of age, 'for his own absolute use and benefit', but Hannah when she reached twenty-one or married, whichever came first, was to get £100 and her share of capital was to be invested by the trustees. She was to get the income flow only and Hepper, with his eye firmly on the married women's property law of the period, instructed that the income 'shall not be subject to the debts, control or engagements of any husband with whom she may intermarry but shall be entirely at her own disposal'.[12] The will finished by covering a number of contingencies. When Hannah, his widow, died, her part of the trust was to be divided between all three. When daughter Hannah died, her share was to be divided equally between any children she might have or if she had no 'issue' then equally between George and William. The trustees were empowered to draw up to £100 from William's 'fortune . . . for binding my said son Apprentice or for his advancement in the World'. So in a very characteristic will, men got capital, women got an income flow and the legal personality of the will maker was to extend well beyond death. In all these matters equity dominated. In the process, age and gender created two very distinctive blocks of capital, one seeking a low-risk income stream, the other available for higher-risk investment in trade and manufacturing or in the human capital of education and training.

Although this practice of gendered equity towards children was nearly universal, there were many minor variants as will makers took account of circumstances, life cycle stage and previous family history. George Hepper had signed a codicil to his will three days before his death in which he cancelled a debt 'for wages for weaving on my account' of £240 which was owed by son George and added a further £260 to his eldest son's inheritance for 'he has not had such a liberal education as my younger children'. Another significant variant involved the will maker essentially bargaining from beyond the grave to ensure the continuity of a business which was to provide support for widow and younger children. Edmund Craister, boot and shoemaker,[13] devised his real estate in the Leylands to his eldest son, Edmund, and directed that his widow would either live with Edmund or she would have one of the ten cottages rent free plus £25 a year from the rents so long as she remained a widow. In return Edmund got the cottages, and the business assets plus 'my silver pint'. The other brothers and sisters got a legacy of £80 each plus a share of the silver spoons. William Harrison, spirit merchant,[14] sworn value under £7,000, assigned his business to his wife and son Thomas as trustees, with instructions 'to continue and carry on my said trade of a spirit merchant until the youngest of my children shall attain the age of twenty one years'. Thomas was to have a quarter of the profits for the first seven years and half thereafter. William's widow was to have an annuity of £200 a year reducing to £50 if she remarried. This annuity was a charge upon the 'rents and profits of the estate' to which the business, as well as the sale of real and personal estate, was to contribute. These arrangements did favour one son but always as part of an implicit bargain with the dead. This type of arrangement conformed with a model of inheritance as an economic bargain whereby one child gained an advantage in return for ensuring that the obligations of the dead towards widow and younger children were fulfilled.[15]

There was a clear preference among the middle classes for their own nuclear family. Almost no wills which mention sons and daughters make any provision for other family members. The extended family was important for those who had no living children. This group drew in a reserve army of nephews, nieces, brothers, sisters and cousins. Once the group had been identified, the same principles of gendered equity operated but with less rigidity. Charles Coupland, solicitor,[16] for example, left £200 to his grand nephew Richard Coupland, now a clerk in the office of Coupland and Shaw, to help with the stamp duty on his apprenticeship articles, but after that there was an equal division between a variety of nieces and nephews. James Noble, the surgeon, divided equally between four brothers and sisters but did not bother with a trust for the sisters.[17]

There were two important deviations from the practice of gendered equity. Of the twelve men who deviated from equity in the allocation of property to their children one group marked out a boundary of the urban middle class. Edward Brooke, merchant, was on the edge of the landed class.[18] Property relationships with his wife were governed by a marriage settlement and she was about to inherit land from a brother. His daughter had married John Gott, son of the wealthiest merchant-manufacturer in Leeds. Richard Kemplay, gentleman,[19] had in the early 1820s run an academy for young gentlemen in north Leeds but his sworn value of £16,000 suggested wealth which owed itself more to his links with land at Leavening in Yorkshire than to his schoolteaching. He clearly had a feeling for family continuity and identity through land and left his eldest sons £1,000 more than the other three children with the option of purchasing his 'estate' in North Street at valuation. Christopher may well have taken this up for he was established there as a member of a leading firm of Tory solicitors, Bolland and Kemplay, in 1834. Edward Armitage, gentleman,[20] lived at Farnley and under his father's will had the disposal of shares in the Aire and Calder Navigation. His eldest son got half of them while the other three got a sixth each.

The other important deviation from this practice was among the women who made wills. In general, widows who had property at their disposal tended to act like their husbands with equity towards children or towards selected groups of their extended family. At times they showed a preference towards daughters, especially when items and categories of property which they regarded as female were concerned. When Rachel Thackrey died the sworn value of her estate was £450.[21] For Rachael there were female things, and family things. The female things were 'my plate, linen, china, trinkets and wearing apparel' which were to be divided equally among her four daughters; the children of her dead daughter Rachael 'taking equally among them their mother's share'. Then there were family things; 'my household goods, furniture, wines, spirituous liquors, books, pictures, maps, prints, money securities for money debts. . . .' These were to be converted 'into money' and divided equally between her six living children and her son-in-law Richard Winter Hamilton.

There was a small group, mainly spinsters but including some widows with no children, who were able and prepared to move away from this practice of family-based equity. They patrolled the boundaries of friendship, family and cousinage making choices, expressing preferences and passing judgement. Mary Turner of Chapeltown had an estate with a sworn value of only £100 although she must have had some real estate.[22] She marked out a territory of friends, friends' children, godchildren and cousins with gifts of various small amounts before showing preference to two sons of cousins with £200 each. Hannah Bracewell was a widow with a sworn value of £20. Son James got the silver plate and daughter Lydia the feather bed but another daughter Ann, wife of Joseph Endcott, a weaver, got a life interest in four tenements, which were then to go to Ann's children. Here there is no indication why the preference; perhaps Ann had looked after her mother. In many cases it is clear that care or companionship was its basis. Priscilla Catlow[23] left a life interest to her 'dear friend Hannah Roberts' which included the co-partnership of a business in which they had shared. Lucinda Wilson[24] rewarded a number of family members but showed special preference to two nieces Mary Johnson and Dinah Lucinda Johnson 'who reside with me'. Sarah Arthington,[25] wife of a Quaker brewer, was one of the rare examples of a women who gained her independence from a marriage settlement. She left property and legacies to a wide range of relatives but one nephew John William

Elam was told he was to have £10 a year only, 'considering the loss I have sustained by part of my property being placed in his hands, with little chance of its being regained, and from which I acquit and release him'.

This world of gendered equity and the more discriminating and judgemental practices of women operated in a variety of ways. One reason for this was the existence of three distinct if overlapping ways of conceptualizing property. The text of the wills revealed three choices for the will makers. They could be *things* people; they could be *categories* people; or they could be *real property* people. Mary Moxon, spinster,[26] listed individual items with clear directions as to who should receive them: a chest of drawers to one nephew, 'my set of valuable books called *Devotional Comments*' to another, silver spoons to another, while a watch and half her clothes went to a niece and sugar tongs and more silver spoons to the wife of another nephew. Things people were very often women but James Noble, the surgeon, who died without children, gave his brother Thomas 'my watch and family bible' and listed his shares in some detail. These were people for whom individual items had a meaning which they wanted to link with specific people after their death. John French, merchant,[27] with one of the highest sworn values in the sample at £16,000, was very different. His executors were instructed to gather up his property by lawyer-made categories, 'all my freehold messuages, warehouses, closes, lands, tenements . . . , my stock in trade . . . real and personal estate. . .'. This was a utilitarian will which empowered executors and trustees. In some cases, a category usually listed as 'all my household goods, linen and furniture' was reserved for my 'dear wife' but that was all. Another group used categories for most types of property but carefully listed all their real property, often leaving specific instructions for that property. Joseph Rollinson, joiner and builder,[28] sworn value £100, listed his freehold dwelling houses and cottages in York Street and Marsh Lane. Charles Hopkins, a stuff piece maker,[29] was very careful about his real property rights:

> four several double houses cottages or tenements situate in or adjoining Edmund Street and Catherine St in Richmond Road in Leeds aforesaid being the most westerly of my cottages there situate three of which said double houses are occupied as six separate Dwellings and are now in the occupation of – Baxter, John Woodhall, Jane Holling, John Swalwell, John Pullan and

Richard Bates and the other now occupied by me as a single dwelling with the joint ownership use along with the other devisees of the three privies near thereto belonging to me and also the use of any well, or pump which I may put down. . . .

These different ways of conceptualizing property were related in turn to very different approaches to achieving equity and to the task of asserting the new relationships required by death. John French was a cash economy capitalist. After he had listed the categories of his property, he instructed his executors 'as soon as conveniently may be after my decease sell and dispose of all my said real estates and such part of my personal estates as shall not be in money . . .'. In this group there were many who clearly had deep feelings about the link between family and specific items of real property but in order to achieve equity these feelings were regulated through the market. The retired merchant Michael Thackrey[30] instructed his executors to take possession of his real estate 'upon trust when and as they shall think it most expedient to sell and absolutely dispose of all my said real estate hereinafter devised to them either by public sale or private contract, together or in parcels for the best price or prices that can be or may be reasonably had or gotten for the same'. The executors were to collect debts and rents due to him 'and convert all other personal estate and effects, and (at the death of my said wife) my said household goods and furniture, plate, linen and china into money and stand and be possessed of the money . . .'. That type of instruction was present in 50 per cent of the male wills and 25 per cent of the female ones. It was often linked to some contingency such as the widow's death. The equity which was sought was to be mediated by the cash values of the market economy. When Michael's widow, Rachel, died a few months later in February 1831 she had reserved female things for equal division among her daughters and the family things for equal division between her six surviving children and her son-in-law. Both categories of property were first to be converted 'into money'. In other words, money was the medium by which equity was to be ensured. But first an inventory and valuation were to be taken, and:

if any of the persons who under the trusts hereinafter declared shall become entitled to any part of share of the said trust money shall be desirous of purchasing any part of such articles comprised in such inventory and valuation he or she shall be at liberty to purchase and take the same at the price or respective prices at which the same shall have been so valued, the same to be taken in to such satisfaction and discharge of the share or respective shares of the trust money to which he she or they may become entitled by this my will.

The family had privileged access to their mother's possessions but this access was mediated by market values to preserve equity.

The 'urban peasant' took quite a different approach to achieving equity. John Topham, who died in February 1830,[31] had appeared in the trade directories of the 1820s as a currier, leather seller and hair dealer. The sworn value of £450 together with a substantial listing of real property suggests considerable success in lifetime accumulation. He had a son, a daughter and left a widow. He achieved equity not by the precise numerical division of a cash sum but by allocating categories and items of real property to specified functions within his strategy. His dwelling house at 45 Trafalgar Street together with 'household goods, plate, linen and other articles of furniture' went to his widow but only for her natural life or widowhood. His widow also inherited a life interest in a house, outbuildings and two closes of land in Ripon to the north of Leeds, thus assuring her of an income as well as a place to live. Son John got the 'stock in trade and all my utensils and implements used in and about my business' as well as the ready money and debts owing the business. He also received an interest in some land at Buslingthorpe. Thus John had a working business and a bit of real estate on which to raise credit if he wished. The daughter received ten cottages in Mabgate and ten shares in 'a building club or Society . . . known by the name of the Commercial Union Building Society'.[32] Thus, the son got the more active male capital with its potential for high risk and high profit while the daughter got the more passive property, although Topham, like many 'urban peasants' chose not to protect her with a trust arrangement. Finally, on his widow's death, son John got the Ripon and Trafalgar Street property on condition he paid outstanding amounts on the building club shares, thus rewarding John for managing this element of the estate and retaining some element of equity. There was no hint of using the market or the market-based valuation here. Equity was qualitative and functional.

Several features of middle-class property relationships were revealed by the sample of wills and the process of the transfer of property after death. The process concerned family, preferably nuclear family, although the extended family could be drawn upon for the 32 per cent of male and 75 per cent of female will makers with no children. Gendered equity was the dominant feature of the transfer. This was very different from patterns of primogeniture and entail observed among landed families and was one of the major differences between middle-class and landed aristocratic practices regarding property.[33] Within the middle classes there were two important divisions. The 32 per cent of the wills made by women show that where women had property rights they used them with much greater freedom. The male wills showed that many women gained property rights only in the attenuated form of an income stream derived from a trust fund.

The other major division which existed was between the cash economy capitalist and the 'urban peasant'. This was closely related to different ways of conceptualizing property, as things, as categories or as items of real estate. In general those who instructed their executors to turn their estate 'into cash' produced a form of capital which could be quantified and divided with precision through the market. It was a more flexible and mobile form of capital. The sworn value of those who gave the 'into cash' instruction was higher than that of those who did not. This imperfect measure was especially compromised here as the 'urban peasant' group almost certainly had a preference for real estate. Among the occupational status groups the 'into cash' instruction was used in about equal measure by shopkeepers (49 per cent of them used the instruction), commerce (52 per cent) and manufacturing (48 per cent). Use by the professions was high (80 per cent), evidence of their very distinctive use and attitudes to property. The craft groups (38 per cent) support the view that the practice of those with lower economic status was less likely to include 'into cash'. This reliance on cash evaluation had some link with the mode of conceptualizing property: 59 per cent of categories people used it but only 43 per cent of things people.[34] The use of the 'into cash' instruction was very closely related to the use of the trust fund to control women's property rights: 68 per cent of the 'into cash' people used the trust fund while only 16 per cent of others did so. The 'urban peasants' manipulated specific items of real property in order to achieve their aims. This title has been chosen because the group was dominated by men who gained an income by using their own capital and/or credit, their own labour and skill and their own real estate. Flexibility came from the changing balance of debt, labour and capital accumulation over the life cycle and from the manner in which specific items of real property could change their meaning as circumstances required. A house might be a dwelling place, a resource for raising credit, or a means of saving as mortgage or building club obligations were reduced. Other properties might be a workplace, a source of income for old age or a widow, or a source of liquid capital in a crisis.

The result of all this was not only the achievement of a variety of family aims of obligation and affection but also the creation of several different varieties of capital. This process provided capital for the creation of much urban real estate. Active male risk capital was created for trade, industry and the human capital of the professions. Accumulation for old age and the trusts which were designed to secure female income were both sources of passive capital for government stock, mortgages and the more secure forms of joint stock company capital, which was soon to be increased by railway building.

CHAPTER

8

# THE PLATFORM AND THE PULPIT:

CULTURAL NETWORKS AND CIVIC IDENTITIES IN
INDUSTRIAL TOWNS, *c.* 1850–70[1]

ROBERT GRAY

Studies of the Victorian middle class continue to replay metaphors of
space and place: north and south, metropolis and provinces, national
and regional and so on. Urban localities are seen as particularly
significant, both enabling and in some ways circumscribing middle-
class formation. A substantial body of work has focused on expanding
industrial towns as the sites of potential middle-class challenges to
longer-established élites.[2] More recently such accounts have been
qualified and revised by recognition of economic, social and cultural
continuities around empire, high finance and an associated complex of
what has been termed 'gentlemanly capitalism'. As land declined in
relative importance, the centre of gravity shifted to high finance and a
genteel service class of top professionals and officials, but not to the
new industrialism.[3]

Important as these revisions are, they may substitute one set of
stereotypes for another. For example a binary model of 'two middle
classes' condenses together a complex series of differences and
interconnections. I want to reconsider these interpretations, focusing
again on expanding urban industrial areas but treating the formation
of social identities, including the identities of place and of civic space
that were so important for the nineteenth-century middle class, as
implicated in wider networks and circuits. This more complex reading
has been suggested, with regard to economic relations, by Martin

Daunton. He argues that metropolitan 'gentlemanly capitalism', as much as provincial manufacturing, needs to be deconstructed; the broad sectors were *all* subdivided, with many cross-cutting interests and alignments and shifting balances of bargaining power.[4] Moreover, as recent case studies have indicated, middle-class 'family enterprises' operated across a range of sectors and activities, with local, regional and wider links.[5]

Debates about the middle class would also benefit from a more complex cultural analysis of identities and alignments. If industrial towns were important sites where 'social structure was remade and the power of the bourgeoisie displayed', this symbolization of power necessarily drew on wider cultural resources.[6] The local institutional framework sometimes required legislative empowerment and therefore access to the parliamentary process and to the official state, and it generally also drew on the cultural capital of rational knowledge (as well as contributing to the formation of that capital).

This chapter focuses particularly on the circulation of rational knowledge and its implications for middle-class identities. Here broader views of a shared middle-class culture, defined in terms of separations of private and public, gender and domesticity become relevant. This has of course to be understood not as rigidly fixed and set in place but as in process, a series of attempts to draw boundaries and enforce separations, which were necessarily contradictory in practice and sometimes contentious in principle.[7] The construction of public and private spheres and associated gendering processes can also be seen as part of a broader transition to modernity, not the property of any particular class. In so far as this was the case, the middle classes should perhaps be regarded as an expanding segment of society, strategically placed to position themselves on the moral high ground. It was the tensions of this process, rather than its accomplishment, that provided the dynamic of class formation.

Claims to authority based on rational knowledge were bound up with the role of professional men as potential 'modernizing' cultural brokers between localities and wider networks. The definition of professionalism was itself fluid and changing but it was probably acquiring clearer identity and clearer links to specific occupations during the period considered. The claim to rational authority emphasized here extended to a range of philanthropic 'moral entrepreneurs', as well as to key professional men in the occupational sense. In its appropriation by middle-class women, it became a contested boundary zone in the redrawing of gender.[8] Rational knowledge could also provide a legitimizing language for entrepreneurial activities and for the cultural and political aspirations of business leaders.

This chapter explores aspects of the culture of urban reform and the roles of professional and business groups. This suggests a focus on particular, broadly 'liberal', formations, and on those middle-class men who became publicly prominent within them. The Nonconformist pulpit, as well as various reform campaigns and associations, provide examples of this. This milieu is not implied to be synonymous with the middle class, or with some essential 'middle-class consciousness' within the communities considered, still less in Victorian Britain as a whole. But nor was it narrowly 'provincial', in the marginalizing sense of that term. It entered into the renegotiation of power and the reimagining of the nation that shaped mid-Victorian 'equipoise'.

## I

The mid-decades of the nineteenth century saw a proliferation of pressure groups and discussions concerned with urban reform. Local campaigns and civic identities were linked to national opinion networks and public platforms. Medical reform constituted one such area of debate.

On 25 February 1861 Florence Nightingale wrote to her uncle Samuel Smith: 'Adshead of Manchester is dead – my best pupil.' Joseph Adshead was a Manchester businessman and philanthropist, represented by Nightingale as 'Manchester man' *par excellence*:

Adshead was a man who could hardly write or speak the Queen's English (I believe he raised himself) & was now a kind of manufacturer's agent in Manchester. He was a man of very ordinary abilities; common-place appearance – vulgar but *never* unbusinesslike which is, I think, the worst kind of vulgarity.

But these deficiencies were compensated by moral rectitude, energy and determination, exemplary of 'the character which I believe is quite peculiar to our race'.[9] A Dissenter, Adshead was active in sanitary reform, ragged schools and various other endeavours (while the list of causes is predictable enough, his active involvement in all of them suggests a rather less common intensity of commitment). Variously listed in the Manchester directories as an estate, land and building agent with offices in George Street and a house in Withington, Adshead could turn his 'extensive information of a local character respecting this city and neighbourhood' to both business and philanthropic ends – indeed both urban development deals and philanthropic moral reform may have been regarded as aspects of a single process of improvement. His image was that of the benevolent local notable, 'as generally respected as known'.[10] He seems to have been in contact with Nightingale through a sponsored migration scheme for relocating distressed silk-weavers in the north (involving also her close friends the Bracebridges of Coventry) and, at the time of his death, an unsuccessful campaign to build a convalescent hospital on a greenfield site according to the 'pavilion' plan energetically promoted by Nightingale and by John Roberton, himself a Manchester medical man (and, like Adshead, a Dissenter).

As in other towns, the development of Manchester Infirmary was determined in a series of often fraught negotiations and alliances between professionals and lay patrons drawn from the business élite, marked also by divisions within both these groupings. The problems in Manchester were particularly acute in view of the cramped central site, the extreme pressure on vacant space in the city centre, the growth of the population served and high death rates attributed by reformers to the irredeemably insanitary nature of the existing building.[11] Nightingale's support for Roberton, a Manchester reformer nationally known as the leading medical advocate of the pavilion plan, suggests attempts to orchestrate a national expert opinion. Some of this is captured in the rather patronizing tone of her representation of Adshead ('dear old Addle-head') and what he was taken to stand for. Adshead's dogged pursuit of his causes, for instance the somewhat deferential covering letters that accompanied pamphlets he sent to Lord Brougham, does perhaps suggest some cultural insecurity (though scarcely inability to write the Queen's English).[12] Nightingale positions herself as the representative of a broader vision, a more self-assured philanthropy and expertise. At the same time, this claimed expertise was both enabled and limited by gender, by the strategies she adopted to circumvent the authority of male professional interests and by the controversial nature of her views on medical and administrative reform.[13] In that sense she needed allies like Adshead, as much as he may have needed her expert endorsement for his philanthropic projects. At the height of her Crimean fame Nightingale had some local impact, more particularly, according to Elizabeth Gaskell's account of a Manchester meeting, among the operatives, 'grimy hands . . . all ready to cheer and applaud *their* heroine – for they feel her as theirs, their brother's nurse, their dead friend's friend' while the ladies, 'stupid creatures', did not take up their allotted seats.[14] Nightingale's perceptions of Manchester may in turn have been influenced by Gaskell's writing; she expressed appreciation of *North and South* on its appearance (during the Crimean campaign itself), and wanted to reread it about the time she was in touch with Adshead.[15]

In the event the campaign for a relocated hospital was unsuccessful, and the Infirmary stayed in its Piccadilly location for the rest of the century. The reformers were more successful in Manchester with the Chorlton Union Poor Law Hospital at Withington and, further north, the new Blackburn Infirmary. The Blackburn Infirmary was the particular concern of the mayor, William Pilkington, a member of a major local Nonconformist cotton dynasty.[16] While the new Infirmary was a civic initiative attracting cross-party support, its most active protagonists seem to have been Liberal Dissenters. 'I will not here speak as your minister', the pastor of Pilkington's congregation declared at the stone-laying ceremony, but he none the less went on to claim that their denomination was 'everywhere acknowledged as the pioneer of progress and the bodyguard of freedom'. The hospital itself, located in a protected green space, 'whence healthful breezes would be wafted to the dormitories and convalescent wards', was to be a 'model Infirmary'.[17]

If campaigns for medical reform had limited and uneven outcomes, they were nevertheless important culturally, for the meanings they attached to urban and suburban space. Fresh air and regulated open space, as part of a rationalized therapeutic environment, had long been a preoccupation of Roberton's. In an early work on *The Mortality and Management of Children*, he noted the absence of green space as one of the evils of large towns like Manchester; and, like other liberal reformers, he used evidence to the 1833 Factory Commission to advocate urban improvement and especially the creation of public parks.[18] As Daniel Noble, another noted Manchester medical reformer, put it in a pamphlet some years later (1843), the poor health of operatives arose from 'the ill-conditioned localities in our large towns

. . . the evils will be considered to attain to their *domestic* rather than to their *industrial* relations'.[19]

Civic identities and the image of the town as the site of progress could be critically deployed in these debates. An article in the *Medical Times & Gazette* contrasted 'the application of high science in all matters of trade' with the 'medieval' condition of Manchester Infirmary; and Nightingale used similar language in a letter to Roberton, deploring the failure of Manchester 'with her high civilization . . . her advanced principles of progress' to adopt enlightened views on hospital reform.[20] Reference to the application of science to trade constructs the successful entrepreneur as agent of rationality and improvement, alongside the educated professional. In this language of rationality the town is defined as a site of dynamic progress but also of collateral risk and problems demanding surveillance and intervention.

Debates on medical reform provided one occasion for the elaboration of this perspective. The National Association for the Promotion of Social Science (NAPSS) and especially its annual congresses in provincial towns, provided another, more widely resonant forum for high-toned debates about appropriate forms of intervention and for the civic display of philanthropic concerns. As Lawrence Goldman has argued, the NAPSS represented a significant moment in the construction of the mid-Victorian political nation and the articulation of a national liberal culture.[21] The opinion of the 'great towns' was represented as a key element in national vitality, a symbol of British progress contrasted to the dominance of French affairs by Paris.[22] The association was in large part what would nowadays be called a 'think-tank', a gathering of the self-defined enlightened oriented to practical influence on policy-making. But it also, as Eileen Yeo has emphasized, involved a mutual discovery of new social subjects, a 'communion of labour' across functionally divided lines of class and gender, with consequent tensions over the precise lines of division.[23] Goldman argues that this helped prepare the ground for the hegemonic project of Gladstonian Liberalism; it may also, however, have provided some moral and intellectual underpinning for Palmerstonian 'equipoise' (as indeed did the development of Gladstonian finance).[24] Presided over by the charismatic figures of Brougham and Shaftesbury, representing continuities from different aspects of the cultures of reform in earlier, less settled decades, the association encompassed a range of figures from the Whig and Peelite centre ground to intellectual radicalism, trade unionism and feminism.

The practice of meeting in provincial centres linked in to wider constituencies; it 'brought "great men" to the provinces, and, in turn, it brought the provinces to the metropolis'. There is some overlap here, both in cultural form and in personnel, with for example the British Association or the local committees for the Great Exhibition and subsequent civic spectacles like the Manchester Art Treasures Exhibition.[25] As Yeo has shown, while the leadership of the NAPSS appears dominated by metropolitan professionals, intellectuals and rentier philanthropists, merchants and manufacturers from major industrial centres also formed a significant component.[26] The Association's council for 1866/7 included several textile industrialist MPs linked to this world (John Cheetham, Thomas Bazley, Edward Akroyd, Edmund Potter) and also William Fairbairn the engineer, Henry Ashworth (cotton manufacturer), H.W. Ripley (Bradford dyer) and Oliver Heywood (Manchester banker and civic luminary); professional men from the region included Daniel Noble (Manchester medic) and Samuel Steinthal (Unitarian minister). Among the metropolitan great and good, Edwin Chadwick and James Kay-Shuttleworth were of course associated with the culture of urban reform in industrial towns, and cited their past experience in some of the debates.[27] Local committees for the annual meetings helped underpin the links. For the 1866 Manchester meeting the committee included a range of businessmen, civic leaders, lawyers, medics and academics associated with Owens College, as well as some of the national council members already mentioned. At Bradford in 1859 there was a particularly strong overlap with the civic self-assertion of the town's ascendant Liberal grouping. The committee included six business leaders (a pioneer department store developer, in addition to worsted merchants and industrialists), four Dissenting ministers, one Anglican cleric, two journalist-publishers, two medics, three lawyers and an architect (whose work included the Wool Exchange and Saltaire).[28]

The meetings functioned as civic spectacle as well as think-tank. Welcoming the Bradford congress, the *Bradford Observer* particularly noted the provision of two working men's meetings (as compared to one at Liverpool the previous year): 'we shall be much mistaken if Yorkshire does not bear away the palm'. Brougham gave his address at the Mechanics' Institute and this venue, itself the product of a movement he had inaugurated forty years ago in the dark days before reform, symbolized the place of the event in a liberal narrative of national progress: 'Most earnestly we trust the richest fruits may, from this grand re-union, accrue to our English homes, and not least to the homes of the town which this year receives its visit.' This is represented, in almost millennial language, as a process of mutual recognition and social unity, 'our people's living contact and throbbing sympathies'. Summing up at the close of the proceedings, the *Bradford Observer* took particular exception to the suggestion ('all the way from London') that there was any element of condescension; the distinguished visitors were themselves workmen of a specific kind, 'who have gone from Bradford only to labour in other places'.[29]

The Revd J.R. Campbell, minister of the key Horton Lane congregation and a local committee member, marked the occasion by a sermon devoted to *Lessons in Social Science from the Life of Our Blessed Saviour*. As its title implies the sermon moves between the registers of evangelical religion and rational knowledge, sanctifying social enquiry and action with moral purpose. This is effected particularly through the powerful metaphor of the 'social body':

[Christianity taught the] fraternity of society – a fraternity which is not equality, and which is most beautiful in the absence of equality: when the 'body politic', from a figure, becomes a reality, and the diversity of function and harmony of working in the members reveals its general health and vigour.[30]

This fraternity is to be expressed in enlightened intervention to correct malfunctioning in the social body, directed particularly to the domestic; Christ, 'a wise master builder of the social structure' stipulated 'parental authority – the first form of government to which we all submit' as the 'foundation of all well-ordered society'. There is a characteristic move from this construction of domestic order to the town, the nation and indeed a world to be colonized by the civilizing mission. Campbell marks the difference between British Christian civilization and its others by reminding his hearers that Britain itself was once, before its early evangelization, among the 'nations sunk in pagan ignorance and debasement, of which this [a long quotation from Romans. i. 21–32 follows] is the fearful description'. National redemption is linked to a Christian message translated into some characteristically 'Victorian' values. As a model youth Jesus displayed 'filial piety' and 'an enquiring spirit' and in his ministry was to enjoin 'TEMPERANCE', 'FORTITUDE' and 'INDUSTRY'.[31]

The meetings of the Association therefore mobilized a range of local protagonists of moral and environmental reform around an emerging conception of the social and linked them to their counterparts elsewhere and to circles of national influence. As well as questions of more general concern (legal reforms, middle-class education, married women's property), the deliberations themselves aired a range of issues particularly associated with urban industrial areas: the health of towns, the education of the poor, Factory Act extension, trade unionism and industrial conciliation. Writing to Brougham about arrangements for the Bradford meeting, G.W. Hastings anticipated that the discussion on trades unions would prove 'the most important thing in all our subjects at the moment'.[32] This was a two-way flow of information and ideas, in which the industrial districts were by no means passive recipients; forums such as the NAPSS served rather to re-articulate the relations between urban localities and national publics. Its orchestration of informed opinion (which Goldman suggests did much to shape the legislative programmes of the 1860s and 1870s) was targeted on the legislature as much as on philistine local notables in the benighted provinces.[33]

The culture of urban reform therefore developed links between urban localities and wider networks, providing access to the cultural capital of rational knowledge. This defined a particular 'professional' voice in the making of the middle class, adopted by entrepreneurs and philanthropists (including some women) as well as by professional men in the narrower occupational sense. Discussions of trade unions or industrial legislation sought to mobilize the knowledge and experience of leading employers and to enlighten their colleagues.

While the policy solutions proposed might be contentious and unevenly implemented, the language used had wider cultural resonances. Particular civic identities and visions of urban space were linked – often through the metaphor of a 'social body' – to the imperial nation on the one hand and to domestic space on the other. The languages of the pulpit, the platform and the lecture hall echoed each other. Professional men, often themselves geographically mobile and connected to wider networks, were important agent⸱ in shaping these relations. The second part of the chapter considers their role, with particular reference to the Nonconformist ministry.

## II

The equation of Nonconformity, aggressive middle-class politics and the industrial north has rightly been subject to qualification and revision but it remains true that Dissenting congregations were important elements in the civic life of industrial towns.[34] For prosperous entrepreneurs and rising professional men, as well as for a wider social range of the 'respectable', they provided points of cultural identity. And for gifted preachers – themselves increasingly identifiable as part of a mobile and aspirant professional middle class – these large town congregations were important career moves.

The career of Joseph Parker may serve as an example. Born (1830) and brought up in Northumberland, Parker went (aged twenty-two) to fill in ('supply the pulpit') at the London Tabernacle, at the same time enrolling at University College. After a successful first pastorate in Banbury he attracted attention as a capable young preacher and was approached by Cavendish Street, Manchester, after supplying its pulpit on two successive Sundays. There followed some bargaining over terms in which Parker showed himself no less hard-headed than the Manchester men (no routine visitations, residence out of town for his wife's health, a clear month's annual vacation at his convenience, the pulpit to be supplied by his nominees at the congregation's expense, deacons to understand their offices as purely 'secular' and allow him to follow his reason and conscience in spiritual matters). Initial reluctance to abandon his present flock seems to have been part of the code in such negotiations. After ten successful years at Cavendish Street (1858–69), Parker made his last move to what became the City Temple in London, which he represents in his autobiography (published 1899) as the fulfilment of his calling. His account of Cavendish Street characterizes its leading members as rather dour but sterling characters – and as 'millionaires' (which most of them would certainly not have been; the word is anyhow perhaps more resonant of the time Parker was writing than of the mid-Victorian period itself). But, if there were few millionaires in the industrial districts, there was certainly new and unprecedented Nonconformist wealth. Parker's salary at Banbury was £130; Cavendish Street eventually paid him £425, plus bonus for increasing the seat lettings, and paid off the debt on the Banbury church building, thus honouring what Parker regarded as his obligations to the congregation there. He was later presented with a purse of 700 guineas to mark the completion of ten years at

Cavendish Street (by which time he was being head-hunted for the future City Temple).[35]

Other cases of the move from Lancashire to London include Robert Halley, Parker's predecessor at Cavendish Street (who went to be Principal of New College) and James Guinness Rogers (minister at Albion Chapel, Ashton, who moved in 1865 to a prosperous congregation in Clapham).[36] Guinness Rogers was born in 1822 in Ireland but brought up mainly in Liverpool and educated at a Dissenting school near Wakefield, then at Trinity College, Dublin before training for the ministry at Lancashire Independent College. More widespread than this kind of move to London were long associations with congregations in the textile towns, often by ministers who were themselves migrants. Analysis of ministers listed in the *Dictionary of Evangelical Biography* indicates the predominantly southern origin of those associated for ten or more years during the period *c.* 1830–60 with congregations (or in some cases posts at denominational colleges and the like) in the Lancashire and West Riding textile districts.[37]

These documented individuals were of course the most distinguished; less eminent ministers may in many cases have had more purely local formations. Professionalization did not go uncontested; both the concept of a specially trained ministry and particularly the exact nature of that training remained contentious. There might be tensions around the minister's understanding of his role and the demands of his deacons. The inspired preaching or liturgical innovation needed to fill the pews might not be to the taste of some long-standing adherents, while ministers often tried to keep the demands of pastoral visiting, tea meetings and the like at arm's length. However, as in other professions, there was a trend to greater formalization and a clearer identity from around the mid-decades of the century. There was a consolidation and rationalization of denominational colleges, with emphasis on an 'educated ministry' often justified in terms of keeping up with the times and the improved cultural level of the flock. Of the biographical cohort considered above, fourteen out of eighteen studied at various theological colleges, of whom one also attended University College London, while three others went to London or the Scottish universities (not all of these took degrees but this was probably not unusual).

The theological colleges were themselves important career openings. The Baptist Benjamin Godwin, born in 1785 in Bath of fairly poor parents, went to sea in his teens during the Napoleonic Wars.

Thereafter he worked as a shoemaker while furthering his education and starting as an itinerant preacher (not unusual at this period) under the patronage of ministers and denominational leaders. After studying under and assisting a minister in Cornwall and pastorates in Devon and Buckinghamshire, Godwin moved to a tutorial post at Horton College, Bradford and the pastorate of Sion Chapel. Eventually he returned to semi-retirement in Bradford, following an interlude (1838–45) with a congregation in Oxford, welcoming the personal space gained (among other things, to write his autobiography) by release from pastoral duties.[38] The governance of colleges drew together leading ministers and laymen on a regional basis. Guinness Rogers, himself trained at the Independent College in Manchester, subsequently served on its committee, together with 'a body of singularly able and intelligent men of business'.[39] This emphasis on the enlarged views of denominational leaders hints at a process of negotiating greater professional autonomy, also apparent in Parker's terms for going to Cavendish Street.

A more formal denominational structure went alongside the expansion and rationalization of training. Although congregational autonomy and the voluntary principle made this contentious and dictated a minimal superstructure, there was an emerging institutional framework providing occasion for formal and informal professional contacts. Guinness Rogers suggests that ministers, together with other elements of the middle class, identified with the region and with Manchester as its centre, while towns like his Ashton were 'a kind of manufacturing suburb'.[40] There was a regular circulation of preachers, especially on such occasions as anniversaries, missionary meetings, stone-layings and jubilees. Supplying the pulpit was, as we have seen, an important career stage. Such practices were reinforced by kinship or other connections. Daniel Fraser, who had a long and successful career at Airedale College, was first appointed there through his brother Alexander, a Blackburn minister with regular preaching contacts in Yorkshire.[41] Ministerial networks necessarily included denominational leaders. George Hadfield, the Manchester solicitor and politician, had numerous contacts with ministers; holidaying in Devon, he heard Jonathan Glyde preach at a village chapel and recommended Glyde for the vacant pastorate at Horton Lane, Bradford.[42] Hadfield himself owed his start in Manchester to the suggestion of a preacher visiting the Sheffield congregation to which his family belonged. Like several autobiographical writers, Hadfield sees his career moves as the work of a guiding providence, symbolized in his subsequent political success as MP for his native city.[43]

Such arrangements clearly depended upon and fostered intra-denominational sociability and friendships. Enoch Mellor, Guinness Rogers's close friend (from student days in Manchester), 'a sturdy Yorkshireman', was born and schooled in the West Riding then attended Edinburgh University and the Lancashire College before going to Square Chapel, Halifax, where he was to stay apart from a brief interlude in Liverpool. Guinness Rogers emphasized in his memorial sermon that Mellor's Liverpool ministry had not been a 'failure'; he had supposedly reversed the decline of a city-centre church emptied out by suburbanization, but was unsettled there because of his 'strong attachment to Halifax and his first church'. Mellor may in fact have felt displaced in a bigger city, after his acknowledged public role in Halifax and connections with the leading members of his congregation, 'that noble band of brothers . . . rejoicing in their increasing prosperity'.[44] This strong local identification was not incompatible with extra-regional links. Mellor's daughter Rosa became the friend and confidante of Robert Horton, the son of a Wolverhampton minister friend. Robert Horton in turn had a distinguished ministerial career with a new kind of professional trajectory; among the first Dissenters to take advantage of the opening of Oxford, he went to a long and successful metropolitan pastorate at Lyndhurst Road, Hampstead.[45]

The period therefore saw the development of formal and informal professional networks in which prominent ministers could retain national links as well as strong local and regional identifications. It remains to consider the significance of this for the cultures and identities of a broader middle class. The centrality of religious institutions and discourses for that class (and indeed for all levels of Victorian culture) has of course been widely noted. I want to explore particularly the ways in which biographical and autobiographical accounts of the professionalized ministry (on which much of the foregoing discussion has obviously been based) were linked to liberal narratives of self-making, material and moral progress and the growth of civilization. If the Victorian fascination with biographical writing was partly an interest in finding exemplary lives, then what life could be more exemplary than that of the learned and pious man of God, particularly when he also reveals himself as a modern man, reflecting on the changes he has witnessed in the society around him? And ministers (and their wives and daughters) were indeed prolific writers of biography and autobiography.

Parker represents his career as an odyssey, an exploration of the geographic space of modernizing England, beginning as a boy preacher 'from a sawpit on a village green . . . on and on to busy Banbury, to wealthy Manchester, to England's capital'.[46] Like several accounts, Parker's refers to the radical and Chartist ferment of the 1830s and 1840s, placing special emphasis on his own commitment to reasoned dialogue, including celebrated public debates in Banbury with Holyoake.[47] It was from this reasoned Christian response to popular discontent and the challenge of infidelity that 'social England' took shape. The language of the pulpit was, in Simon Gunn's phrase, 'an admixture of intellectual rationality and religious inspiration'. For example, sermons might enjoin due respect for other professionalized knowledges, such as the 'laws of health', both personal and environmental.[48] The foresight, prudence, technical and organizing skills of the successful man of business could also be celebrated in this register.

Such narratives were at the same time celebrations of the growth of the town, of the particular denomination and of British Christian civilization. Godwin describes his own role as public speaker, giving form to the inchoate civil society of the Bradford to which he came in the 1820s. The town's first venture into a public banquet in celebration of the Reform Bill, 'on the whole went off very decorously and agreeable [sic]', despite the expiry of certain local notables from imbibing wine in measures more suitable to their customary ale.[49] In the worsted boom of the early 1850s, the Revd Jonathan Glyde (minister at Horton Lane Congregational Chapel, and the migrant son of an Exeter merchant) preached a series of sermons addressing the moral duties of the newly prosperous and offered a prayer for the town of Bradford:

> O God, by whose providence towns and cities are multiplied and grow populous . . . let Thy blessing be on our mills and manufactories, on our homes, our schools, and our sanctuaries. Preserve us from fire and flood, from stagnation in trade and overmuch business; yet more earnestly do we beseech Thee to preserve and deliver us from irreligion and profanity.[50]

Place and civic identity could be defined by allusions to mobility and a sense of prophetic mission. The Revd Alexander Fraser, addressing his 'fellow-townsmen of Blackburn', referred to himself as 'a citizen of no mean city' (he was a Glasgow merchant's son and graduate of that university). Nevertheless:

> I have given the best part of my life to Blackburn. I have been set by Providence a watchman on the walls of Blackburn. Like Elijah from the heights of Carmel, I look down on the busy world. Day by day, I behold your tall chimneys with their cowling wreaths of smoke and I see a beauty in them, and I bless them.[51]

J.R. Campbell, another Glasgow graduate, spent twenty-eight years at Horton Lane; his funeral was a Bradford civic occasion, comparable to that of his much respected predecessor Jonathan Glyde some three decades earlier. Although Campbell's first pastorate was in Scotland 'overlooking the grey north sea', his life's work was in Bradford: 'Here was the church he loved. This place he built in joy, in faith . . . his best monument.'[52] As well as these ministers, several Nonconformist entrepreneurs and professional men had Scottish connections (including a number prominent in the Bradford business community and John Roberton, the Manchester medical reformer, who belonged to Parker's Cavendish Street flock).[53]

Certain tropes of 'Scottishness' – stalwart Protestantism, austerity and self-discipline – seem to have been particularly resonant in the industrial north of England. This may be linked to the recurring motif of 'north and south' in biographical narratives. Writing, after his return to Bradford, about his time in Oxford, Godwin represented the rudeness of the Bradford operatives as counterbalanced by a moral independence absent in the deferential university town. Earlier, commencing his autobiography in the epistolary form of letters to his son back in Bradford, he conveyed a strong sense of exclusion; the college gargoyles symbolized Gothic oppression, 'all manner of frightful, incongruous, fantastic, and odd shapes'.[54] Guinness Rogers expresses continuing identification with Lancashire, paying tribute to the 'strenuous and earnest men' he knew in Ashton and the moral equality that prevailed in the counsels of the church:

> Let me say here that while there were two or three magistrates of the highest standing amongst the deacons, no one secured more attention in our deliberations than those who were working men, and who were treated by their colleagues as Christian gentlemen.[55]

These narratives of place, identity and mobility defined a gendered male professionalism, established by occasional reference to femininity and the domestic. The domestic space of the minister's own home figured in professional self-representation. Both Parker and Guinness Rogers illustrated their autobiographies with photographs of domestic interiors in their current residences as well as of their wives. Parker, writing under the shadow of his second wife's death, devotes a rather formulaic chapter to her exemplary virtues (which were intellectual as well as domestic, for she was widely read and a language scholar). After Parker's own death a few years later his biographer hints at some of the tensions in this marital companionship; his wife had been apprehensive about leaving the house, lest he emerge from his study to find her gone.[56] The study was in fact a privileged site, a link between intellectual endeavour and public moral seriousness and the domestic sphere. Time spent in the study was often cited by ministers (as it is by modern academics) to demonstrate the hard work of their calling, as part of a rational and industrious middle class, who 'know full well what it is to "rise early and sit up late, and eat the bread of carefulness". . . . Ministers of religion are of necessity a laborious class'.[57] Godwin was able to devote more time to his autobiographical manuscript when he retired from pastoral duties and 'not having sermons to compose feeling that I must still be in my study about the usual time, I gradually . . . enlarged my plan'.[58]

Ministers' narratives of their self-making as successful professional men moved between domestic, urban and national space. Domestic values could, as Poovey has suggested, inspire aggressive colonizing projects, whether in Britain or in the empire.[59] These narratives were resonant for wider middle-class publics. Religion was significant for its claim to negotiate the boundaries of discursive domains, its shifting between rational and emotive registers, and this made an integral contribution to Victorian urban society.

## III

Industrial towns were significant venues for the making and enactment of a liberal middle-class culture. That culture was national in scope, defined by a series of intersecting formal and informal networks and institutions. Nation, locality and home were variable and interdependent spaces, defined in relation to each other. This essay has focused on particular professional and professionalizing groups, associated with liberal visions of urban space, as key links in these relations. That this is not synonymous with the middle class as a whole, nor with whatever might be thought of as its militant vanguard, should not in the light of an extensive recent body of work require further emphasis. But neither should it be assumed without inspection that metropolitan and provincial stood in some hierarchical relation of centre to periphery and that any linkages between them can be read as implying the capitulation of provincial middle-class liberalism to an aristocratic embrace.

If the mid-Victorian British (or indeed European) bourgeoisie may be seen as a class of local notables, this does not necessarily imply parochial isolation. While the span of contacts varied, and this may provide one measure of differentiation within the broadly regarded 'middle classes', some access to wider networks and to the circulation of cultural capital was itself an enabling condition of notability.[60] For example, businessmen's command of what John Morley called 'the information to be gathered in coaches and in the commercial rooms of provincial hotels' is too easily overlooked in this context.[61] George Hadfield made a point of attending the London courts at the beginning of his career, thus enhancing his qualifications and learning 'agency business' (he also met his wife there); he was to be influential in legal reform, in addition to his profile as a regional notable.[62]

The metropolitan end of the chain is also more complex than a simple centre/periphery model would lead us to suppose. The career of Guinness Rogers may again serve as a case study. He was a highly politicized minister and moved south at a time of growing Nonconformist self-assertion and opportunity. As the history of his Clapham church notes, the congregation 'recognised that he was marked out for a leader . . . and were prepared to give him some freedom to devote himself to the wider work of the church'.[63] Less delicately put, he was the Dissenting equivalent of an Erastian pluralist with political ambitions. But if Guinness Rogers needed a metropolitan location to orchestrate a political pressure group, the constituency he had to deliver was largely provincial. His autobiographical references to the moral qualities of Lancashire folk, to his own Puritan ancestry and to the political education he acquired through participation in Anti-Corn Law League meetings – part of the foundation myth of Victorian Liberalism – may have a strategic political function.

In his London years Guinness Rogers went regularly to the seaside retreat of the Norwich Colmans in East Anglia, where J.J. Colman liked to convene high-minded house parties of ministers, businessmen, politicians and others in the cultural orbit of Nonconformity and Liberalism, including several leading members of Guinness Rogers's own congregation at Clapham. Norwich at the turn of the century was an expanding industrial town, with a base of 'new industries' and a close-knit grouping of Nonconformist business and civic leaders not unlike those of some northern towns in earlier decades. Colman and his like were no less successful industrialists than the Ashton cotton masters, and 'everyone who knew anything of English commerce knew him as one of its distinguished representatives'.[64]

The differences between north and south were more complicated than simple binary oppositions will allow. The negotiation of power and influence was correspondingly complex, subtle and, perhaps, ultimately ambiguous in its processes and outcomes.

# CRAFT, PROFESSIONAL AND MIDDLE-CLASS IDENTITY:

SOLICITORS AND GAS ENGINEERS *c.* 1850–1914

JOHN GARRARD AND VIVIENNE PARROTT

In recent decades, several historians have asserted the existence, distinctiveness, even society-shaping importance, of a professional middle class.[1] In this essay, we will explore this claim by testing the strength of broad professional identity against the two most obvious economically based alternatives – those of occupation/craft and generalized middle class. We will examine two contrasting types of professional: solicitors, primarily fee-earning and essentially pre-industrial; and gas engineers, primarily salary-earning and, as off-shoots of civil engineering, by-products of technological and urban expansion. Their origins and mode of payment are different but they are similar because, like all professionals, they greatly benefit from accelerated social change – gas engineers from ever-increasing demands for lighting, heating and cooking facilities in industries and towns; solicitors from heightened rates and complexity of property transfer, and from greatly enhanced litigation levels released by urban complexity and conflict.

We will not wholly discount the nineteenth-century presence of a professional middle class. However, its existence is more narrowly perceptible than other middle-class groups – say, entrepreneurs or shopkeepers. Moreover, of the three identities available to solicitors and gas engineers, professional identity was markedly weaker than those of either craft or broad middle class. Furthermore, partly underlying their incoherence in professional terms and clearly tying them into middle-class identity, was the hazy borderline between each and entrepreneurial activity.

First, however, we need to define how we conceive each alternative (though not mutually exclusive) identity might exist. Occupation, professionalism and middle 'classness' may be severally distinguishable. One way is through the possession of common and distinctive life circumstances – relationship to capital, property, type of income, skills, etc. Another is by the possession of a common and distinctive culture – in terms of attitudes, values, ideas, lifestyles, activities, etc. Identity is also observable through self-identification and/or recognition of a group by others as distinctive and perhaps distinctively valuable. Finally, we can look for conscious articulation of common and distinctive interests via language, ideas, organization – or, for the unchallengeably powerful, mere unstated assumptions. Broadly speaking, a professional class could be said to exist in that many professional groups shared substantial (though not all-embracing) and distinctive objective circumstances and possessed strong, though not all-encompassing, elements of common culture. However, a professional class is much harder to locate in terms of self-identity, and virtually impossible in terms of collective mobilization. Broad middle-class identity works rather better in all respects; occupational or craft identity best of all.

It is also necessary to provide some sense of the size of the two professions. Precision is difficult since, as we shall see, both are decidedly hazy at the edges and both comprise a considerable range of status and well-being.[2] Of the two, solicitors are easier to estimate and far more numerous. In 1865, in England and Wales alone,[3] approximately 10,200 solicitors were practising with certificates issued by the courts. Of these, some 2,035 were members of the London Law Society, although many more belonged to local law societies. By 1911, these figures had risen to 16,739 and 9,039 respectively.[4] By comparison, in 1868, some four years after its foundation and with many still 'holding aloof', the British Association of Gas Managers had 208 members while its Scottish counterpart (the North British Association) had 70. By 1911, the Institution of Gas Engineers, as it now was, had some 843 members and the North British 260.[5] This contrast is somewhat skewed by the far greater tendency of engineers to divide into specialized sub-categories: the 1861 census for England

and Wales lists 4,400 civil and mining engineers (who would include gas engineers); that for 1911 lists 7,208 along with 1,034 'professional engineers and surveyors'.

## I

It seems logical to start the comparison where the two groups' identity seems weakest, or at least most narrowly based – professionality itself. We are not suggesting this was absent; indeed, it was quite important for both groups. Though different in origins and historical longevity, solicitors and gas engineers shared significant objective circumstances – and ones that were distinctively professional. Admittedly, their payment mode was different – one being primarily fee-earning, the other normally salaried. However, as already noted and with later qualification, this merely makes them representative of the two central objective trends among professionals, helping label them as 'old' and 'new'. To some extent, moreover, whatever we say later about the contrasts this helps produce between them, we can admit Perkin's argument[6] that both payment modes represented societal admissions that their services were sufficiently valuable to require significant market protection, with money being 'set aside' for them.

Underpinning this and their power over others was their expertise, their privileged access to extensive and, particularly for gas engineers, rapidly expanding, technical knowledge and, wherever possible, accompanying mystery. This was crucial to everything: their ability to make gas for consumers and manipulate the law for clients; their sense of worth; their status and power. Thus the gas manager's (and probably the solicitor's) expertise placed him 'above the common level of his fellow townsmen and [made] his power felt . . . [proving] the truth of Lord Bacon's aphorism that "knowledge is power"'.[7] Given such understanding, it was unsurprising that both professions showed increasing pride in what they believed themselves uniquely to possess. For solicitors, enlarged expertise separated them from laymen.[8] Gas managers constantly hailed the increasing scientific understanding and technological skill they needed as works became larger and gas-making more complex. At their most ecstatic, they could claim the need for expertise in almost every field of scientific and civil endeavour.[9]

Knowledge exchange was a primary function of the many journals produced by these and other professions.[10] Particularly for gas engineers, it underpinned professional organization at all levels and helps explain why professionals, far more than any other middle-class segment, were such talented creators of organization. At the various gatherings of their national[11] and local associations, members could meet, mostly beyond clients' and employers' hearing. They could commune with doyens of the profession, hear learned papers and generally act so that 'the experience of one became the property of all'.[12] Such meetings allowed them access to 'the revivifying company of . . . professional brethren.'[13] These expertise-enhancing possibilities solemnized such gatherings – occasionally even excluding frivolous pleasure; sometimes nearly overcoming decent national inhibition with 'a zeal which fell only just short of enthusiasm'.[14]

While mutually sharing knowledge, both groups were naturally careful to cultivate their professions. At greatly differing speeds, with solicitors far more eager than gas engineers, both sought professionalization – attempting to formalize training, systematize knowledge and control entry, and with varying success establish clear borderlines between themselves and various peripheral irregulars. By the 1729 Judicature Act, every aspirant solicitor was enrolled on appropriate court lists and was articled for five years to an attorney or solicitor. All articles were registered and an affidavit produced to a judge on completion. Gas engineers were far slower to attempt regularization and control. They were a newer profession, attached to ideals of practicality and mobility from artisan bottom to well-paid and knowledgeable top. Nevertheless, by around 1900 the Institution of Gas Engineers was helping examine specifically designed City and Guilds courses and trying to establish its membership hierarchy as the sole high road into the profession. As we shall see, it was also making vigorous, if faltering, efforts to delineate 'real' gas engineers from hosts of variably respectable others.

There were also other objective circumstances and consequent cultural traits which these two occupational groups held distinctively and in common. Like many other professions, and deriving from the essentially service-oriented character of this 'class', solicitors and gas managers were brought into contact with public needs and desires – solicitors directly with clients, and gas engineers indirectly (via boards of directors and municipal committees) with growing numbers of gas consumers. Indeed, their fortunes partly depended upon successful mediation of this relationship. Consequently, though to widely contrasting extents important later, each profession worried about its public reputation. Gas engineers were periodically exercised about their prestige, and the 'very general impression . . . that . . . gasmaking is . . . little more than throwing coal into an oven and allowing gas to flow away through a pipe'.[15] They even fractionally relinquished their control of knowledge by periodically mounting public lectures on 'the art of gas making'. Meanwhile scandals involving gas engineers produced concern about 'the great cloud cast upon the profession'.[16] Solicitors, particularly before 1850, were deeply preoccupied by reputation and especially respectability. They were perceived to have a shady and pettyfogging past which needed living down by constant elimination of malpractice and of unqualified practitioners. Indeed, this concern primarily encouraged professional organization. Thus the Law Society's promoters in 1825 saw their organization, and its resplendent headquarters, as impressing 'the Public with a higher opinion . . . of the . . . respectability of the profession'.[17] Overall, both professions were aware that expertise, unlike hierarchy, did not guarantee public deference, and might entail hostile scrutiny.[18]

Also shared with other professions, arising from reliance upon expertise, and sitting uneasily alongside desires to regulate entry, were attachments to social mobility and meritocracy.[19] If value rested upon knowledge, the job must be open to anyone capable of acquiring it, irrespective of birth and even competitiveness. These ideals were reinforced by both professions' character, particularly gas engineering, and indeed engineering as a whole. Gasworks varied greatly, ranging from tiny one-man works powering a village to those supplying whole cities. Managers also varied greatly from high status, high-salaried engineers at large urban works controlling many workers, down to individuals barely above skilled and knowledgeable artisans earning 'thirty shillings a week plus house and fuel' (and who in Western Scotland were regrettably called 'wee managers'). Particularly before specific training arrived in the late nineteenth century, one needed, if disasters were to be avoided, to be able to move from bottom to top of this profession by graduated steps, acquiring knowledge and experience as one went. Reinforced by Victorian ideology, this possibility became proudly traditional. Even when formal training courses emerged, the profession still complimented itself upon being 'peculiarly democratic' with 'many and varied steps' upwards.[20]

Finally, members of both groups periodically identified themselves as 'professional men' – without being exactly clear what this implied, nor that it always meant the same thing. Rather more often, individuals said they belonged to 'the Profession'.

## II

Yet here we reach the limits of commonality. Furthermore, in the self-categorization described above, what was being honoured was clearly the occupation itself. The same is evident from the earlier proclamations by solicitors and gas engineers about their central ideals, ones we have so far located in professional culture. Significantly, neither solicitors nor gas engineers, nor other professionals, ever apparently sought common cause with other groups of their kind. Nor was any overarching professional organization ever formed – before or after 1914. In this professionals were dissimilar to any other class. They were unlike the working class with the TUC and Labour Party; unlike entrepreneurs who, for all their individualistic competitiveness, regularly proclaimed commonality in regional and industrywide employers' organizations, and after 1918 in several nationwide 'peak organisations'.[21] Professionals were also unlike all sectors of the highly individualistic lower middle class: the shopocracy (local small-traders' associations, National Federation of Shopkeepers); house landlords, builders, etc. (myriad local property-owners' protection associations); and clerical workers (National Union of Clerks). Admittedly, the British lower middle class as a whole is harder to locate collectively – certainly far harder than its continental counterparts.[22] Nevertheless, it regularly proclaimed its aggrieved existence locally by identifying itself as 'the middle class' against 'the aristocracy' (normally entrepreneurs) and through countless ratepayers' associations. The middle class as a whole admittedly had no embracing organization, other than the vast network of nineteenth-century charity.[23] Nevertheless, political collectivity was certainly contemplated by aspirant leaders such as Cobden and by the 1930s middle-class men and women were regularly expressing commonality through solid Conservative voting. Finally, even landed proprietors, though long hostile to common organization, were nevertheless lured into vulgarity in 1909 via the Country Landowners Association.[24] Professionals did none of this, nor apparently contemplated it, even though they were far earlier and more talented organizers at occupational levels than any other group.

Such limited commonality is unsurprising, to judge by these two professions' very different occupational circumstances. Although we have so far treated their fee- and salary-earning status as justification for choosing them as representative examples of dominant professional trends, this actually produced crucial experiential differences. Most fundamentally, it meant that while solicitors were, or might hope to become, partners in firms, gas engineers were mostly employees. Even the exceptions to this contrast, to be reviewed later, emphatically do not enhance notions of common professional consciousness.

The nearest solicitors approached employee status was as articled clerks ('under' qualified practitioners) or somewhat later as junior solicitors. Thereafter, they either acquired their own practices or became partners in larger 'firms'. Autonomy was inbuilt; solicitors were subject only to the profession's own rules of conduct. They ceased practice only after misconduct or because practices failed or terminated. By contrast, gas managers, except sometimes late on when eminent enough to become consultants, were employees – applying for jobs, subject to terms of service, and liable to dismissal. They could also resign and move on to other 'positions'. Thus their autonomy was essentially limited, expandable only through expertise. Theoretically, they were subject to their employers' policies and, in their own often victimized eyes, to their 'whims', misunderstandings and under-valuations.

However, objective differences between these professionals went beyond fees and salaries. For one thing, their respective operational fields produced very different relationships with central government. Since solicitors' business was the law, Parliament and government naturally sought early and extensive regulation. The first legislation affecting them emerged in 1292 and thereafter they were more regulated than any other occupation.[25] Thus governmental relationships were always fundamental to their lives – a fact, as we shall see, with important consequences for the functions of their professional organization. For gas managers (and other engineers), apart from growing safety regulations, law and government barely impinged at all.

Meanwhile, although 'serving' it, the relationship of both professions with 'the public' was very different. For solicitors, it was intensely personal. They serviced individuals, families or companies, and their power was partly derived from personal knowledge. They dealt with 'clients', almost invariably person-to-person, and hopefully in a spirit of 'trust'. They barely possessed a conception of 'the public' beyond something that damned them if they failed the respectability test. Gas managers' relationships with those they served were fundamentally different. In introspective nineteenth-century towns, particularly with municipalized gas undertakings, they might be highly visible figures to many 'consumers', but managers knew them as individuals barely at all. Unlike solicitors, public opinions and suspicions of them were constant features of their lives and imaginations. Yet, their relationships with 'customers', 'consumers' or 'the public' were distant and negotiated indirectly by boards of directors or gas committees.

Finally, and influentially, objective circumstances differed in that these two professionals deployed very different sorts of knowledge. Whereas the parameters of legal knowledge, in detail and even fundamental principle, were largely national, those of gas-making, like all engineering, were international and universalistic. Law differed greatly from country to country. By contrast, gas was made by the same processes, using the same known laws of chemistry, the world over. Local circumstances varied even within Britain but only within limits understandable by competent gas engineers everywhere.

Broad circumstantial differences made for equally important articulatory and cultural contrasts, ensuring that identity and interest would always be expressed primarily at a craft, rather than pan-professional, level. Each craft was admittedly professional, and thus possessed an additional aura. However, professional identity was rarely more than implicit, and had few articulatory and no mobilizational consequences. What was explicit and with profound collective results was the sense of being a distinctive occupation with a special and, particularly for gas engineers, proud role.

However, it should first be noted that articulation, even at craft level, was never easy. Gas engineers commenced professional organization in the 1860s. Earlier, 'almost every manager seemed as though he possessed a secret . . . to his disadvantage to disclose'.[26] Even after their associations appeared, both professions were riven by regional jealousies. The troubled history of English gas engineering organization was heavily underpinned by rivalries and suspicions between northern and Midlands managers, with predominantly municipal employers, and those in metropolitan and southern England, primarily working for private companies. Meanwhile, amalgamation was never seriously possible between English and Scottish managers, nor until the 1890s between the 'North British' (embracing most of Scotland) and the particularly 'wee managers' in Western Scotland. Indeed, most managers' strongest loyalties lay with regional associations which were only distantly affiliated with national organizations before around 1900. As late as 1890 apparently, 'gas managers [with] anything . . . to communicate . . . choose the . . . friendliness, of a district association [where] . . . nobody seeks to make points at anybody else's expense'.[27]

This was a frequent refrain. At work were several factors: differing types of ownership; friendship networks; travel problems even given railways; seasonal rhythms at gasworks making them impossible to leave outside of summer; vibrant regional loyalties;[28] hazy borderlines between professional and entrepreneurial activity; and finally clear regional differences in available fuel, average gasworks size, and concomitant gas-making techniques.[29]

For similar reasons, solicitors also experienced severe cohesion problems. This is not surprising in a far older profession – the Law Society was formed (in 1825) well before the British Association of Gas Managers.[30] However, from the start, its London-dominated council was beset by provincial fears of 'centralization', which rapidly heightened and persisted as it emerged as the profession's mouthpiece and regulator.[31] Local societies remained vibrant and jealously autonomous, often tempted into forming rival alliances.[32] Indeed, not until around 1900 could the Society claim to represent most solicitors. Even then, the council was suspected of being 'a nice family party . . . of London solicitors'.[33]

Occupation was nevertheless the only level at which identity and interest were regularly enunciated. Moreover, in many respects, each profession's internal divisions reinforced rather than undermined solicitors' and gas engineers' taste for collectivity: after all, provincial or regional disgruntlement led not to organizational disbandment but proliferation.

In fact, both occupations expressed identity and interest in at least two ways. First, in the frequent production of several million printed words: the *Solicitors' Journal* started in the 1840s, and appeared regularly thereafter. It contained advertisements for positions, legal information and provided a forum for airing professional concerns. Meanwhile, by the 1890s, gas engineers' interests were being explored in no fewer than four journals.[34] The *Journal of Gas Lighting* was the senior publication. Founded in 1852, it was appearing weekly by the 1870s with thirty pages or more – of adverts for gas appliances and jobs across the world, learned articles on gas-making, reports of managers' association meetings and gas company proceedings, relevant legislation and long editorials about the problems of the industry and its practitioners.

Secondly, collectivity was expressed even more fervently in the increasing membership and meetings of the national and many regional associations of gas managers and solicitors. Again, we should emphasize that in congregating so frequently they primarily expressed commonality as members of two distinctive occupational groups, and only secondarily as particular examples of a professional class. This was partly because their respective organizations, while having professional things in common, had very different primary purposes, arising from each occupation's distinctive, objective circumstances. For gas engineers, the central purpose of organization was exchange of practical and scientific knowledge, not just because it yielded professional power, but also because gas production was complex and difficult, and pooled knowledge was important if efficiency, cheapness and safety were to be delivered to employers and consumers. This explains why both national and regional gatherings mostly occupied themselves with learned papers on the gas engineer's art. It also explains why these papers, the subsequent discussion, and the proceedings of meetings overseas, were reproduced verbatim in the journals.

This learned purpose was constantly emphasized as the primary function of association. It was all very serious, though rarely sufficiently intense to prevent that second purpose of associating with one's brethren – increasingly extravagant sociability. All meetings were accompanied at least by a dinner and generally some 'delightful excursion' – initially to earnestly 'inspect' the local gasworks (though equally to sumptuously dine there) but then increasingly to sample the pleasures of river, countryside or seaside. This at first occupied an afternoon, but later an entire abandoned day. In 1883, the Institute even discovered pleasure in Sheffield: so great were the Corporation's entertainments that the *Journal* forecast improbably that 'after this, Sheffield will be recognized as a pleasure resort'.[35]

The forces creating this secondary, but crucial, associational purpose were powerful, for they too arose from the circumstances of gas managers' lives. Essentially lonely creatures – there was rarely more than one in any town, gas being naturally monopolistic – they often believed themselves surrounded by people ignorant and uncaring about their heroic indispensability. Meetings were 'the happy occasions when they can . . . [meet] professional brethren from whom they are perforce separated during fifty one weeks of the year'.[36] Furthermore, 'the gas engineer is companionable . . . so are [his] . . . family'. Without sociability, 'the annual meeting would lose much of its charm'.[37]

The primary associational purposes for gas engineers were thus knowledge exchange and conviviality – both responses to the objective circumstances of managers' lives. The first purpose is of course classically professional and might seem to undermine the case for distinctive occupational consciousnesses. Yet equally significant is the fact that knowledge exchange was, at best, a secondary aim of solicitors' associational lives. Their spokesmen sometimes acknowledged it, for example when contemplating the Law Society's resplendent London headquarters where solicitors could meet, exchange information about legislation, legal cases and court business.[38] However, the organization's primary purpose was political. As Sugarman has pointed out, due to their concern with the law and the complex governmental regulation surrounding solicitors, the Law Society mainly sought to act as an occupational pressure group. This was evident from the start[39] and by 1893 was sufficiently important for 'the untiring zeal with which the Society watches over the fortunes of solicitors' to be extensively noticed by *The Times* which called it 'the best organised and intelligent trade union in the country'.[40] This ambivalent tribute was equally applicable to provincial societies. Manchester's had long ago declared as a primary object 'to . . . watch over . . . general measures affecting [the profession] or producing changes of law or practice'.[41] Indeed, national and provincial societies, however mutually suspicious, increased their political clout by cooperation and exchange of intelligence about current parliamentary Bills. Furthermore, so extensive was the society's legislative involvement that it rapidly became a trusted governmental adviser on planned legislation, particularly law reform. As Sugarman observes, it helped 'fill a void at the heart of the state, namely, the absence of an adequate system for the preparation and revision of legislation'.[42]

The Law Society and its provincial allies had another associated and complementary role – formalized by the 1844 Solicitors Act – namely, regulating the profession and more particularly safeguarding its membership. They quickly acquired crucial roles in expelling corrupt or sham practitioners. These powers increased over the decades, greatly expanding the Society's more general role in maintaining and enhancing respectability. Taken together, these various functions clearly produced a quasi-corporatist relationship with government, and solicitors could cloak their pursuit of self-interest in the mantle of protecting the public interest.

Such possibilities were barely contemplated by gas engineers. The profession prided itself upon members being able to rise from artisan bottom to prestigious top, and was long reluctant even to establish educational entry qualifications. Gas engineers were also less troubled by concerns about respectability than solicitors.[43] For these and other reasons, it is unsurprising that their associations showed little interest, until the end of the period, in policing the gates to the profession. Nor, until near the end, did they seek politically to defend its interests, doing so even then only with great heart-searching and to considerable opposition.[44]

Reinforcing these differences in organizational function were contrasts in culture, or more specifically self-image, values and orientation – all stemming partly from contrasting objective situations. Solicitors and gas engineers had very different images of themselves, resting upon different views of the qualities required for successful job performance. To heighten public estimations of their expertise, both certainly cultivated professional mystique but in different ways. For solicitors, the idealized image was changing and varied according to professional level, but by the 1870s for most middle-rankers it was of the discreet and trusted family counsellor and friend, or loyal company adviser. This picture arose naturally from the solicitor's professional functions and personal relationship with 'clients'. It implied attachments to values of discretion and trustworthiness. To these, of course, can be added the crucial quality of respectability, stemming from a desire to counter the public's hostile alternative image of solicitors as venial pettyfoggers – people who deliberately extended legal processes, and thus their fees, by raising esoteric and minor legal points.

Gas managers' self-images were different in content and complexity. At least partly, this resulted from having two masters rather than one, and because their relationship with each was different from that between solicitors and clients. Firstly, managers served 'consumers', or 'the public', with whom, in their own eyes anyway, relationships were intense, though essentially impersonal. To them, they brought an increasing range of necessary commodities: the means of cooking, heating and lighting. The last was much the most important, particularly in the dark and fearful nineteenth-century urban environment. The other master was the board of directors or municipal gas committee, who might admire and fête managers, but who, like the public, were always apt to misunderstand, criticize, and offer ignorant advice. Finally, relevant to self-perceptions was the fact that, due to the natural monopoly all utilities possessed, there was generally only one manager per urban location.

As a result of this complex relationship, managers' self-images gave little importance to respectability, trust or discretion, values arguably emerging from knowing and personal relationships. Instead they emphasized charisma and lone heroism against the odds, and perpetual martyrdom to unjust persecution, undervaluation and underpayment. The image flowed quite naturally from consciousness of serving a dependent but critical public and unpredictable boards of directors or gas committees.

The heroism and the way this focused upon gas engineers' multi-talented roles as bringers of light were evident during the bitter labour disputes in the London gas industry during 1872 and 1873. The achievements were celebrated at the Association of Gas Managers' subsequent AGM. After customary reference to managers' multiple talents and polymathic knowledge, particularly evident during the late crisis, the president suggested that, 'no word . . . can express . . . the consternation . . . [at] London being left in darkness'. Undeterred by verbal incapacity, he prognosticated that, had gas production ceased, 'many of our most important industries would have been crippled . . .; the police . . . paralysed; life and property [left] . . . at the mercy of the dangerous classes'.[45] Fourteen years later, heroism and mystique remained sufficient for 'a lady correspondent' – possibly some long-suffering wife – in the *Gas World* to liken gas engineers to high priests:

> The colleges and temples in which the neophytes study and worship before becoming ordained . . . are to the outside world known as 'the Gas Works'; the high priests as engineers and managers. Little knows the 'consumer' . . . of the severe training . . .

the gas manager is subjected to before he can be trusted with . . . keeping 'the Sacred Fire' alight in the streets, public buildings and homes of the community.[46]

Gas managers also felt persecuted, misjudged and undervalued. Although they might be revered, even allowed considerable influence over gas policy,[47] as heads of what were increasingly very large capital plants, managers were natural spendthrifts, impinging upon the public via rates and gas prices. Thus they were frequent objects of critical suspicion from directors and councillors on the political make. Such sniping elicited streams of aggrieved hauteur. Gas committees were particularly culpable. The *Journal of Gas Lighting* expressed steady contempt for 'the handful of pawnbrokers and publicans' whom it saw as the most common component of such bodies, and who 'think they know all about the business'.[48] It compared their 'dwarfed capacities' to those of 'tribes of savages . . . whose powers of numeration do not exceed four'.[49] The *Journal*'s correspondents bemoaned insults from ignorant and salary-pinching committees of 'retired old clothesmen, pawnbrokers, jerry builders, or what not', determined to prevent their manager from 'becoming a gentleman'.[50] These emotions could lead into strange places, for one manager to the moors above Stockport, there to duel (with fortunate inaccuracy) with a council critic.[51]

Such hauteur partly derived from the cosmopolitan orientation of gas engineers, and here we come across another major contrast in the 'culture' of the two professions.[52] Solicitors' horizons were local, or national at best, while gas managers justifiably prided themselves on being an international profession. Solicitors were strongly articulated at both local/regional and national levels. However, judging by the activities and rhetoric of their professional associations and journals, they had little interest in comparable occupations beyond British borders. Their work might sometimes produce interaction with lawyers abroad, but this led to no feeling of fraternity. Gas-making was different. Though local conditions varied, production everywhere rested upon the same scientific principles and gas engineering knowledge was universal. Managers were thus internationally oriented, strongly attached to their 'brothers' abroad – again not as fellow professionals but as fellow gas practitioners.

This orientation was apparent from at least the commencement of their journals in the late 1850s, emerging in several ways. It was evident among job advertisements. These related to positions all over Europe, the empire and beyond. Gas managers seeking new positions also advertised, portraying themselves with phrases like 'no objection to going abroad', or 'can speak Spanish fluently',[53] or 'can speak and write French . . . prefer situation in France'.[54] The trend warranted proud comment from the *Journal of Gas Lighting*, and was incorporated into a self-image as 'citizens of the world'.[55]

The tendency stemmed partly from Britain's pioneering role in gas-making, 'the boarding school of the entire profession'. Its practitioners were in widespread demand, and 'a few years abroad' were 'a fine discipline for a young man'.[56] Such international orientations extended far beyond the termination of Britain's gas hegemony. Indeed, they steadily strengthened. From at least the 1870s, gas journals increasingly provided extensive reportage of association meetings throughout Europe and North America. There was also much coverage of new foreign gas inventions – about which there seems to have been no attempt at national secrecy. The Institute, meanwhile, eagerly facilitated attendance at each other's meetings. Leading continental gas engineers were made honorary members and from the 1880s few annual meetings were complete without 'friends from the United States and Europe which we do not like to speak of as a foreign land'.[57] British managers were also regularly treated with 'extreme kindness' at European meetings.

There was indeed increasing brotherhood among gas managers everywhere. They frequently used fraternal terminology to describe each other, persisting even during periods of international tension. In 1900, the Institute's president urged his entirely sympathetic members not to turn against 'our French brethren' because of 'the vapourings of the lower sections of the French press over South Africa'.[58] Fraternity continued into the First World War. For some years, what was now the Institution had been increasingly friendly with 'our confrères' among the German Gas and Water Engineers, with much learned and sociable intervisiting. Now, in the early months of war, the *Journal* carried extensive, even affectionate, reports of the German association's annual meeting, and long articles praising the German gas industry. On 18 August, an anonymous engineer commenced sad 'Thoughts on the War':

The . . . friendship with German gas engineers [has] become much stronger of late. . . . Our sympathies go out to them, . . . the marvellous progress [German engineers have] made stands as a protest against the dominant philosophy in Prussia.[59]

This spirit significantly contrasted with solicitors' attitudes. These were indistinguishable from the rest of the population. They might regret the war but not on professional grounds.

## III

While sharing some objective characteristics and values, the two professions therefore showed little professional consciousness but were strongly articulated occupationally, this being also the location where distinctive commonality of situation, values and consciousness were most evident. Both groups' affinities to the broader middle class are fairly clear. This is evident particularly in two ways: the hazy borderlines with entrepreneurial activity and the networks into which each was connected.

One fact eroding clear conceptions of a distinctive professional class – and even occupational solidarity – is the way many in each profession were at least partly entrepreneurs. For solicitors, formal codes of conduct and legitimized training admittedly distinguished them, as legal practitioners, from all laymen – including entrepreneurs. However, for many solicitors the borderlines between professional and entrepreneurial activity were decidedly hazy. Many combined practices with business interests – for example, investing in factories and railways, or operating as insurance agents and, particularly early in the century, as bankers. Just how extensive solicitors' investments could be is shown by Fenton Robinson Atkinson, a radical lawyer whose Manchester practice began in 1811. By his death, Atkinson had £11,000 invested in the London and North Western Railway, £7,500 in the London and South Western, plus substantial holdings elsewhere.[60]

Such investment was often highly speculative not just passive. Many solicitors not merely invested extensively themselves, but dabbled with trust money. Until the end of the century this was not a criminal offence and many were irresistibly tempted. Such habits were worrying law societies, both local and national, by the 1850s. Yet their regular malpractice actions failed to curb the practice. Nowhere was this more evident than in the scandalous revelations accompanying Benjamin Lake's prosecution in 1900, by which time professional identity had been firmly established, and the entry points clearly secured by obligatory training. Lake was declared bankrupt after speculating enthusiastically for many years, both with his own money and his clients' – particularly in Kent Coal Company shares – to the tune of at least £200,000. He was also director of several companies. What made the subsequent trial and conviction particularly scandalous, embarrassing and significant from our present standpoint, were two things: firstly, Lake was a distinguished member of the profession and sometime president of the Law Society. Secondly, in subsequent professional breast-beating, it rapidly emerged that Lake's financial activities were very common. Indeed, his was only the most spectacular of many similar prosecutions. According to the *Solicitors' Journal*, the practice was widespread even among 'very respectable solicitors'.[61]

Underpinning much of this speculative activity were two things: firstly, the expectations and social aspirations set by the middle-class social milieu wherein solicitors, like other professionals, moved; secondly, the temptingly extensive knowledge of the property market derived from the nature of solicitors' professional activities, central to which was conveyancing. The result, as Offer has noted, was that, 'As entrepreneurs, mortgage brokers, trustees, executors and property managers, they operated in the market in their own account.'[62]

Given such opportunities, and propensities to exploit them, solicitors unsurprisingly often talked about their professional activities in decidedly entrepreneurial ways. This emerged clearly in Lake's case. Lake himself referred to his practice as 'the business'.[63] *Journal* correspondents noted it was 'an old-established business . . . upon which [his] predecessors . . . built up fortunes'. What seduced Lake, like 'hundreds of others', were 'the attractions of new and exciting business', producing laxness during which, 'the so-called "capital" . . . has been . . . depleted'.[64] Several letters offered advice about avoiding future disasters, suggesting means of distinguishing 'working capital and realised profits'; quite unselfconsciously assuming solicitors were, 'like other men of business'.[65]

Gas engineers too appeared unsatisfied with 'money set aside by society' to reward their professional services. This was evident in several interconnected ways – again making the line between professional and entrepreneurial activity decidedly hazy. There was the seedy fact that, like solicitors, many gas engineers saw their profession not merely as yielding salaries but also opportunities for dubious exploitation. It was widely agreed that when Samuel Hunter, Salford's gas manager, was imprisoned in 1887 for taking extensive bribes on municipal contracts, he was as much unlucky as corrupt. In the subsequent professional breast-beating, it rapidly became evident (as in the Lake scandal) that 'commissions' were both widespread, and not necessarily regarded as immoral. They were so extensively offered and accepted that some suggested it was hard otherwise to do business. Even Hunter's chief accuser emerged as his most energetic seducer.[66]

What fundamentally underpinned commission-taking was the intimate way trading intermeshed with managerial activity. Association and Institute meetings were invariably attended by many gas commodity traders 'pouncing upon every opportunity for waylaying unwary managers, and, in the usual fashion, . . . turning a penny'.[67] They commonly attended as 'associates' and occasioned endless agonized debate, becoming the immediate reason why the Institute split in 1888 and was so difficult to reunite. There were many attempts to exclude traders who appeared likely to swamp the organization. Unfortunately, the roots lay deeper than managers' 'inadequate salaries' and high social aspirations. Equally important was the fact that gas engineers, particularly the élite, regularly slithered into entrepreneurial activity. Like solicitors, they acquired shares and accumulated directorships, in the gas industry and outside. Their jobs necessitated making profits – for companies, or municipal ratepayers. Most important, however, was the fact that the better engineers tended to invent gas appliances or pioneer gas-making techniques. These they patented and either franchised to private companies or formed their own firms to exploit. Almost imperceptibly, they became businessmen. Here lay the problem: 'scientific traders' were no longer professional gas managers. They might be pecuniarily interested in Institute participation. Yet in the nature of their achievements they were likely to be distinguished members of their kind, with much to contribute to meetings. As was freely admitted, they were 'interested' in several senses.[68]

As noted, the issue eventually caused the 1888 split. But this simply highlighted the confusion. Those most hostile to traders formed the Institution of Gas Engineers. Yet their new executive contained those whose alleged actions (allegations never legally challenged) had actually initiated the split. In 1882, they had organized the Combined Gas and Electricity Exhibition at Crystal Palace, giving pride of place to the appliances of a distinguished entrepreneurial ex-member – William Sugg and Company.

Equally indicative debates accompanied this long and tortured story. Few denied many associates 'were about as eligible as the Mahdi'.[69] The problem was always 'where they would draw a . . . line . . . the President [of the Institute] was more or less a trader'.[70] Moreover, if the gasworks were swept 'of anyone . . . [with] shares in a trading company doing business with a gasworks . . . [or without] interest in a patent exploited by a company, the residue would not be sufficient . . . to effectively carry on'.[71] It was pointed out that some engineers 'invented things, made them and sold them . . . others invented things and got others to make and sell them . . . England was a trading country'.[72]

The uneasy borders with entrepreneurial activity meant that these professional groups interacted at many points with the business middle class and indeed shaded into it. Such haziness buttressed more formal links with the rest of middle-class society by virtue of professional services: solicitors with their primarily middle-class clients;[73] gas engineers with their manifestly middle-class boards of directors and their primarily, though decreasingly exclusively, middle-class consumers. These economic interactions were greatly supplemented by social ones: solicitors and gas managers were linked into the broader social networks of the middle class, both professionally and individually. They belonged to the same clubs – for Manchester solicitors[74] particularly Shaw's, the Manchester Union and the Brazenose. They joined the same rival political parties – in the case of solicitors, offering their legal and electoral expertise.[75] They worshipped at the same churches and chapels – and were thus linked into the accompanying political, social and cultural networks,[76] often using those networks for professional and social advancement. They patronized the same charities, thus gaining access to central channels for the potential diffusion of middle-class, or at least middle-class élite, influence over large sections of the population. Charitable activity also gave these professionals access to one of the most important ladders to social status available in Victorian towns and cities.[77]

One local example will clarify the position. Prior to the scandal, Samuel Hunter's influence as Salford's gas manager in the 1880s –

besides his formidable expertise and personality – was enhanced by his linkage into the networks of Salford's and Manchester's middle class. He belonged to the Salford Liberal Club and indeed had been approached by several local leaders to fund a new sympathetic newspaper, their hopes clearly raised by his involvement elsewhere in the regional press. However, Hunter was also an active Wesleyan lay-preacher, and had sufficiently funded a large local chapel to warrant recognition upon the foundation stone – later thoughtfully removed. This connected him not just with prominent Liberal councillors but also key members of the Tory majority. He was connected with local theatres, and an enthusiastic Cheshire huntsman. Hunter's success among these networks, and the resulting social solidarities, was probably what prompted many of Salford's élite to petition for his early release, on the grounds that, being a gentleman, he had suffered enough.[78] In fact, he was part of a more general trend, noted at the time, whereby 'the manager of the long-past yesterday, who entered upon his duties unknown, is now . . . a highly respected citizen of the town'.[79]

## IV

On our evidence it seems unsurprising that the professional middle class should be 'forgotten'.[80] Its existence was more ephemeral than any other group for which class identity has been claimed. For solicitors and gas engineers, pan-professionalism had far less reality than either of the alternative identity choices available to them. It meant something: there was some commonality of situation and culture. Yet, there is little evidence of common consciousness and none of mobilization. It is hard to think these professionals would have seen each other as anything other than potential clients or part of a rather fractious body of consumers. If they had contacts with other professionals, it was with those most occupationally adjacent – respectively barristers (ambivalently) and other engineers.

However, occupational identity had real meaning for both. Situational commonality was extensive and clear-cut, even if not unlimited. Here, were the greatest number of shared values. Here, they mobilized eagerly and often – for sociable, intellectual and (for solicitors) political purposes. Meanwhile, each group had clear links with the broader middle class: along the hazy borderlines with entrepreneurs; and across the economic, social and cultural networks of the middle class.

In fact, the only things commonly *and distinctively* embracing most professionals were cultural: firstly, attachments to expertise, and secondly, (and uniquely among the middle classes) talents and appetites for collective *occupational* organization. Even respectability seems to have been far more important to solicitors than gas engineers, probably because the former's relationship with their clients was essentially personal. Anyway, respectability was hardly distinctively professional, but arguably preoccupied most people below the landed class and above the 'residuum'. What may have distinguished professional groups were concerns about *collective* rather than just individual respectability, preoccupations deriving from collective dependency upon the opinions of those receiving their professional services. However, while this distinguished professionals from some middle-class segments, it did not distinguish them from all – not from shopkeepers' organizations, for example, which showed similar desires to eliminate malpractice and for similar reasons. Meanwhile, collective preoccupations with respectability were also urgent concerns of most working-class organizations – for example, the artisan end of Chartism; the Reform League in the 1860s; friendly societies, co-ops and skilled trade unions throughout the century.

Given the ephemeral character of the professional middle class we may reasonably ask whether 'it' could be said to possess power. We suspect not, at least in the sense of the production of collectively intended effects. We find it hard to see the Fabians or the Charity Organisation Society as collective outriders of professionalism.[81] Society has undoubtedly become increasingly attached to expertise but mainly because of needs produced by its own growing complexity and expectations. This produces a further question: why was there so little collective pan-professionalism, particularly given the propensity for occupational organization? There are two equally useful, if contradictory, answers: firstly because professionals did not require such organization – the needs of industrial and urban society ensured considerable political, social and economic agenda-control and for any other need craft organization was sufficient, particularly given such bodies' willingness to become incorporated into self-regulation; secondly, because, their particular expertise aside, the professions had little in common.

## CHAPTER 10

# FROM PERSONAL PATRONAGE TO PUBLIC SCHOOL PRIVILEGE:

SOCIAL CLOSURE IN THE RECRUITMENT OF MANAGERS
IN THE UNITED KINGDOM FROM THE LATE NINETEENTH
CENTURY TO 1930

JOHN M. QUAIL

The history of the firm in the twentieth century is dominated by the development of companies of ever-increasing size. Such companies have been crucial to the economic development of nations: it has been convincingly argued that the relative ease with which individual national economies have produced giant firms able to take their place in global oligopolies is the key endogenous condition for national economic success.[1] These huge firms have not only survived but prospered (in the face of the direst warning by neo-classical economists that this was logically impossible) by the development of managerial hierarchies and administrative techniques which have allowed them to fully mobilize their inherent economic power and achieve sufficient flexibility to readily respond to market conditions.[2] The pioneers of these innovations were the US corporations General Motors and DuPont in the first quarter of this century. Parallel developments took place in Germany a little later.[3]

The development of managerial hierarchies requires an entrepreneurial and administrative division of labour which disaggregates the functions of the individual proprietor into a set of separate occupational skills: marketing, accountancy, manufacturing and so on. In the process these skills become less the products of personal creativity and particular circumstances and turn into an impersonal body of professional knowledge. In turn the recruitment of new members of the management hierarchy becomes impersonally concerned with aptitudes and potential rather than family provenance. Recruitment itself becomes an impersonal professional skill. Put schematically, then, recruitment to the managerial hierarchy, like the processes within it, moves from the proprietorial to the professional, from the personal to the impersonal.

It is not possible, however, to separate such a schema from its local context. The development – the much delayed development – of managerial capitalism in the UK did not follow the same pattern as in Germany or the USA. These other economies have been demonstrably more successful than that of the UK. It is not surprising therefore that the late development of managerial capitalism has been identified as a crucial determinant of the UK's relative economic decline.[4] It is not the only cause that has been suggested, however. The 'decline of Britain' debate is long-standing and wide-ranging and its scope can only be sketched in here. Some have argued that there was little such decline,[5] others that it has been catastrophic.[6] The key watershed has been given as either the last quarter of the nineteenth century[7] or the thirty years after the Second World War.[8] At the level of the firm decline has been blamed on: a failure of entrepreneurship;[9] the persistence of 'Personal Capitalism';[10] the failure to replace the 'practical man' with the professional trained manager;[11] or on a dysfunctional form of joint stock director control.[12] At the level of society the blame has been placed on the institutional consequences of a successful market co-ordinated economy which made change to a corporate society difficult.[13] Alternatively, decline has been attributed to an anti-industrial ideology among the nation's élites who were deeply infiltrated by aristocratic mores,[14] or to those élites favouring commerce and finance at the expense of industry.[15] It has also been suggested that attention might be better directed at the debilitating effects of clinging to free trade in a world of tariff walls – and just possibly at the destruction caused by two world wars.[16]

It is difficult to attach a precise weight to each of these explanations. The wide scope of the debate and the range in scale of the factors involved mean that there are almost as many positions as there are scholars. Whatever the terms of the debate, however, every historical discussion of the performance of UK companies, of their management and their recruitment to management, can be ready grist to the mill of the decline debate and the decline debate sets an inevitable context to every such discussion. Recruitment, our main topic, is clearly an expression of the firm's image of itself as it is or as it wishes to be. Recruitment is a buyers' market. New recruits are assumed to have the qualities and the potential to replace or improve upon existing staff. In their recruitment policies, therefore, we may read something of a firm's aspirations or lack of them. The resonance with the decline debate is thus perhaps with those discussions of anti-industrial culture briefly referred to above. More strongly, however, the recruitment of certain sorts of people, particularly where they are destined for high position, indicates very clearly the nature and skills of the administrative structure they are joining. For example, why should a firm recruit public schoolboys with no work-related qualifications rather than, say, engineers or accountants?[17] What structure are they trying to sustain when they recruit one kind of person rather than another? We will return to these issues once we have looked more closely at the recruitment of managers in our period.

At the beginning of the twentieth century it was possible to imagine the new large UK companies as emerging impersonal professional managerial hierarchies. In 1901 the Fabian H.W. Macrosty wrote that:

> A company which works on a sufficiently large scale permits, or rather demands, a more effective division of control or management than a small firm, and can afford to pay for it. There is a vast commercial civil service . . . rising in grade above grade from the copying clerk to the general manager. . . . And although its members have lost the expectation of 'setting up in business for themselves' that Early Victorian incentive to industry, they yet feel themselves to be on the side of the capitalist; the industrious apprentice or aspiring office boy may not become a merchant himself, but he may reach the dignity of secretary or manager.[18]

On this model, the period before the First World War was one where middle-class proprietorial ambitions were beginning to be transmuted into the concept of a career with management as its goal: 'the direction of ambition might shift. . . . [A]n able man, instead of looking forward to being a small manufacturer or a commercial man, may aim at being a sub-captain of industry. . . .'[19] But in the conditions of Victorian and Edwardian England there were distinct social bars to careers of this type. The 'commercial civil service' that Macrosty refers to would prove to be as subject to social closure as the civil service itself.

Studies of early examples of managerial recruitment show that it was largely through personal, social and business connections in the form of patronage or nepotism.[20] This continued to be the case throughout our period. The later nineteenth century, however, saw a rise in the number of large firms through organic growth or amalgamation and administrative structures also began to grow, potentially to a size beyond the capacity of personal recommendation to provide new managerial recruits. Macrosty, a key chronicler of the growth of UK firms, was clearly of the opinion that the bureaucratic/rationalist approach to recruitment that large firms with large administrative structures might be expected to bring to élite recruitment would break with this earlier tradition. It will become apparent, however, that where recruitment of potential managers was deliberate and impersonal, it favoured the public schoolboy despite some puzzling counter-indications of his aptitude and commitment. There was still patronage, but it was an impersonal, class patronage. We will look more closely at impersonal recruitment after an examination of the more widespread personal recruitment of public schoolboys to industry and the nature of the managerial hierarchies they joined.

The Acton Society Trust, in their study *Management Succession* published in 1956, found that the percentage of managers who had been educated in public schools rose from less than 10 per cent of those born before 1895 to 30 per cent of those born between 1920 and 1924.[21] Given that for most of the period recruitment of graduates was low,[22] we can assume that most of these managers started work at the age of sixteen or so and the Acton Society Trust study therefore covers recruitment from about 1910 to about 1940. During this period the proportion of public schoolboys within their age groups remained the same,[23] so the increase of public schoolboy recruitment to management was not caused by a simple relative increase in their numbers. The Acton Society Trust study shows also that once recruited, public schoolboys were more likely to achieve promotion and rise to top management than entrants from other kinds of school.[24]

This growth in public school recruitment to business is also reflected, as we would expect, in the destinations recorded for boys leaving these schools.[25] Significantly, however, the available studies show that 'most public school educated sons entered, broadly speaking, the same types of occupational fields as their fathers – the sons of professionals generally became professionals, the sons of businessmen became businessmen'.[26] Thus the growth of public schoolboy recruitment to business may simply mean that more businessmen were sending their sons to public school. This does not automatically mean that these appointments were nepotistic but there is strong circumstantial evidence that this was indeed the case, not so much because public schoolboys' families were particularly prone to the practice but because it was endemic in United Kingdom employment practice generally.

In 1927 a well-informed observer of British business wrote:

Broadly speaking, in ninety-nine hundredths of British industry there is no system of promotion. Family connections, ownership of capital, toadyism, seniority, inertia or luck decide which men shall be selected to rule their fellows. . . . A speaker . . . a few years ago told an industrial conference that the only principle of organisation he had been able to discover in English industry was 'myself, my father, my son, and my wife's sister's nephew'.[27]

The use of influence and patronage was pervasive. In the 1920s it could be asserted roundly that 'the promotion of able administrators is hampered by the necessity of finding jobs for representatives of family or financial interests'.[28] Banking and insurance were generally businesses where 'preference would be given in recruitment to those who were respectably connected . . . by recruiting only men who were known personally or were nominated by persons known to the employer'.[29] As one 1914 career guide put it, 'to get an introduction into a good Insurance office usually requires some personal recommendation or influence'.[30] In banking, the guide said, the best pay was at the Bank of England but such posts were only available through recommendation by a director. The Midland Bank was still taking people introduced by customers or directors in 1931, though they were subject to examination.[31] Another career guide suggested municipal appointments for accountants 'for those who have influence in that direction'. This guide also warned prospective solicitors that their career prospects were limited 'without contacts or capital'.[32] Railways generally made appointments 'by nomination not competition'.[33] While the general manager of the London and North Western Railway (LNWR) played down the significance of directors' nominations in the company, he was happy to admit to the preference given to the children of employees.[34] This evidently applied as much if not more to managers as it did to less privileged employees: examination of rolls of principal officers reveals a striking repetition of surnames in senior and junior management posts.[35]

It was in fact openly recognized that there was nepotism on the LNWR[36] but it was not alone.[37] Other family managerial dynasties were not unknown. Three generations of Burbridges, for example, were to occupy the highest positions at Harrods from 1891 until 1959, when the store was taken over by House of Fraser.[38] It was also said in the 1920s that a director 'on resigning frequently expects to be succeeded by his son', the dispersal of shareholders in large public companies preventing any opposition developing to cosy co-options by existing directors.[39] In 1926 the magazine *System* gave the example of the head 'of a great concern' who swore by all his gods that he had done with the idea of the 'family' business for ever. No more sons and nephews would jump into big positions in his firm. This course was loyally followed by colleagues until the head of the firm himself claimed 'a certain position for a young relative. . . . It seems to be the fact that blood is thicker than business to some of the older school in British industry, even today.'[40] A scheme to bring in cadets (management trainees) on the London Underground failed in 1930 in part because of the 'insuperable tendency of directors to bring in youngsters recommended to their patronage'.[41] Until the 1980s, 'only those who had some personal associations with the City [of London] were likely to consider it as a life's career. Hence these sons of comfortable families typically found their way into the City after leaving their public schools through family connections direct or indirect.'[42]

Many more examples can be given of this kind of personal patronage. But examples can also be found of a more impersonal form which gave specific advantage to public schoolboys. Entry to the upper ranks of the civil service and to Oxbridge was barred by entrance exams geared to the syllabus of public schools, especially classics. The civil service in particular was alleged to have reduced the age limit at which the upper grade exams could be taken to make it almost impossible for lower grade clerks to compete through private study.[43] Where entry was not personal a public school education seems to have been a requirement in insurance and accountancy.[44] Patronage and nepotism were therefore ingrained into recruitment in our period. But was there anything new about the large enterprises of the late nineteenth/early twentieth centuries which might in time change this?

The size of firms undoubtedly grew towards the end of the nineteenth century. There had been considerable amalgamation activity in service sectors like railways, banking and insurance, combined with organic growth, and considerable administrative structures had been created. There had also been a wave of amalgamations in manufacturing industry, but compared to the more integrated structures in the service industries the structures here were relatively loose, largely as a result of the persistence of proprietorial influence from the amalgamating firms. These were primarily horizontal amalgamations, formed to reduce competition by market sharing and with some hopes of monopoly rather than to achieve efficiencies and competition by cost cutting. Nevertheless, the extent to which their structures remained loose has been exaggerated. In order to compete effectively they too had to establish central offices able to demand and compare management information from, and appoint managing directors able to issue instructions to, subsidiary manufacturing units.[45]

While there was considerable disparity between the size of the *administrative* structures in manufacturing and services, in both cases their *management* structures were sparse and fragmented compared to large companies in the US and Germany.[46] I have argued elsewhere that this was the consequence of a pervasive proprietorialism in UK joint stock companies.[47] Directors though largely part-time and often amateur (in the sense that they were not expert in the business of the firm on whose board they sat) felt impelled to retain the greatest possible amount of decision-making in their own hands. The consequence was that as organizations grew so too did operational departments but top management did not keep pace. Instead of delegating power to senior full-time professional managers, boards of directors expanded, forming committees of directors to manage the increasingly complex departmental business. Management integration across departments was weak: managing directors, where they existed, were often part-time, plural and hedged round with checks and balances. Some firms had no managers more senior than departmental heads. In other words, the board, whose ambition was modified only by the requirement to remain commercially competitive, was to be the firm's sole integrating body.

There was, in consequence, a discernible tendency towards a strategy of divide and rule between departments. Departments such as accounting and engineering were kept narrow in scope and their technical skills were not encouraged to grow into management ones.[48] The consequence was that promotion of technical experts usually went no further than the top of technical departments. Even when there was no professional technical element the boundaries between departments were difficult to cross. One railway chairman described the departments on railways as 'watertight' with no opportunity for promotion from one to another.[49] There is also some evidence of the cultivation of a deliberately adversarial culture between departments, probably designed to preserve directorial power.[50]

Generally, the opportunities to rise to managerial positions were restricted. There were not many managerial positions in UK firms compared to the number of administrative workers who might compete for them. Opportunities were, it seems, reduced rather than increased as the size of the firm grew. Evidence given to the Royal Commission on the Civil Service in 1913–14 allows a measure of quantification. At John Brown and Co. of Sheffield there were perhaps 20 management posts out of an administrative staff of 400; at Cadbury about 50 out of 527; and at Alliance Assurance about 30 out of 300 or so. For the London and North Western Railway the figures are less clear but we can estimate perhaps 200 or 300 managers out of an administrative staff of 12,000.[51] On this rather general evidence we can say that, at most, managerial posts represented 10 per cent of administrative staffs but could drop to 2 per cent or so in large firms. Thus it may have been optimistic for a writer in a business journal to say that in large firms employing between 300 and 800 clerks:

> prospects for the rank and file of these are no brighter than prospects for factory workers; 60 per cent will never rise beyond the work they are doing at present; 30 per cent will never rise much further than a position involving a moderate amount of responsibility; a meagre 10 per cent may rise to be departmental or sectional heads.[52]

The opportunities for any entrant into such administrative structures were clearly limited. Any system that gave special preference to particular entrants radically reduced the prospects of the rest. For some sections of opinion there was little doubt who deserved such privileged access as a matter of right.

Public school educated men were well ensconced in the professions. Indeed, it has been stressed by one scholar that public schools, even the most élite, were essentially for the sons of professional men who were destined themselves to be professional men.[53] There is strong evidence that the professions were becoming overcrowded and that this was limiting salary prospects.[54] Certainly some of the salaries of administrative jobs described in the career guides matched those that a qualified professional might expect.[55] Imaginations may also have been fired by public accounts of the tempting of already well-paid public servants into private firms and references in the press to the '£10,000 a year man' that private industry was looking for.[56] We can therefore understand the enthusiastic tone of the following:

> Not many years ago a thick line of demarcation was drawn between the professions and business. The line today is very thin and it will soon disappear. . . . We are led to understand that there is a distinct opening for Public School and University men in the big commercial firms at home and abroad. We were recently informed that it is men of this type that hold the executive posts as heads of department in one of the most successful establishments in London. . . . At Oxford a large number of men are turning their attention to business. Congenial openings are being found in increasing numbers in Publishing, Industrial and Engineering firms.[57]

But if there was a sense of possibility, there was also a sense of the right of the public school man to high business positions, well displayed by a letter to *The Times* in 1914 where the correspondent asserted that for a man to be a success in the business world:

> he should have been educated on the broad lines adopted in our public schools and universities. Hitherto there has been a prejudice against public school and university men in business circles and the Headmaster of one prominent school is, I understand, elaborating a special course for those of his pupils who are

destined to work in the City. In other words, the public school is to be modernised and the atmosphere of the grammar school and the technical institution is to be introduced into it. This, I submit, is the one thing that is not wanted. The City will always require thousands of clerks and the grammar school system is an excellent preparation for the clerk but it is every way unsuitable for the higher positions which our boards of directors find it so hard to fill. If only the directors of our railways and other large industries would understand that public school and varsity men are not necessarily unqualified fools in business matters and endeavour to attract them by offering a fair salary at the outset and train them for managerial positions instead of trying to turn them into clerks.[58]

A popular journal could assert in an article entitled 'The Public School Man in Business':

An unfortunately large number of our Public School and University men have heard that they are no better than anyone else. . . . We maintain that they are and are intended to be superior to others who have not had their advantages. . . . [L]eadership by force of example is an absolute obligation imposed upon them by the social system which has guaranteed them their worldly advantages.[59]

Another writer urged the appointment of public schoolboys to all leadership positions:

. . . that which is desirable above all else in those who wield authority is that they should be of the class, the breed which commands easily and is obeyed willingly. . . . Fill the Civil Service with those who do actually represent the spirit of the public schools, the unclever [sic] boys whom other boys respected and followed and liked, and fill with these also the posts in industry where the management of men is more important than technical proficiency with a balance sheet or a machine and we should then have a reform in the right direction. Throw emphasis on character and not on examination craft, and make appointments accordingly, and efficiency will look after itself.[60]

There appears to have been a consensus among supporters of public schools that 'character' was the most important thing they produced: 'that almost indefinable mixture of pluck, knowledge, good humour, self-reliance, self-restraint, loyalty to institutions and readiness to "play the game according to the rules"'.[61] There also seems to have been agreement among even the strongest advocates that the average public schoolboy emerged from his education with little more than character to show for it.[62] For some this was a perfectly satisfactory outcome:

> The unrefuted accusation still is that boys are sent out into the world knowing practically nothing useful, or knowing it in an academic and useless form. The answer is of course that the schools and universities have drifted into being schools of character, and not of learning. Let us be frank and confess that the stock of knowledge imparted though not exactly nothing at all, is little more than an excuse for decently clothing the other sort of education, which is so admirably given, and which the whole world has envied, in the sphere of the training of character.[63]

And that character was 'noble, beautiful and splendid taken as a whole'.[64] Other sources were somewhat less impressed. A careers guide says of the potential stockbroking recruit:

> He must be well educated in the public-school sense of the term; that is to say, he must speak well, dress well, play games and have a smattering of other subjects. To be perfectly frank, he need not know much about the deeper side of learning or the classics, but he must have sufficient general knowledge to carry him through a conversation without discredit.[65]

But whether the result of a public school education was a superficial social style or a strong moral character, the public schoolboy was clearly a desirable recruit for business despite an apparent consensus that he was less well educated than board school boys.[66] This was openly admitted by an employer which had been a pioneer of preferential recruitment of public schoolboys, the London and North Western Railway. The general manager told the Royal Commission on the Civil Service in 1913 that white-collar recruits:

... prior to their acceptance ... have to pass a very simple qualifying educational test, in addition, of course to passing the doctor. The educational examination is a test in arithmetic ... dictation and composition. ... We find that the board school boy passes our examination well and the young boy from Eton or Harrow generally gets ploughed. ... [W]e find the spelling is better from the board schools than from the big public schools and the writing also.[67]

There were also indications that outside the type of institutions that reproduced the kind of group conformity of the public schools, public schoolboys were at something of a loss. In the Church, the home or colonial civil service or the services the public schoolboy might do well. But reports from the colonies[68] or elsewhere abroad[69] tell of low commitment to business and a greater interest in amusements. In particular there was little interest among public school recruits in studying either business or the country they were in, especially after working hours. At home the general manager of Alliance Assurance regretted the lack of ambition of his largely public school clerks.[70] One writer went so far as to say that: 'Cut off from his traditions, cut off from his ideals ... the gentleman recruit in business withers for lack of nourishment.'[71] Nevertheless, despite these failings of attitude and aptitude among public school men a number of firms were clearly determined to recruit them.

From the mid-nineteenth century, high administrative office on the railways was held by a disproportionate number of ex-public schoolboys. Of thirty-one general managers recruited after 1870 of whom anything is known, a third were from public schools.[72] The extent to which this was the result either of personal or impersonal recruitment is not clear. It is worth noting, however, that a special apprenticeship scheme had been set up on at least one railway as early as 1855 which 'involved entrance by examination and was designed to train "a class of youths who are, or appear to be, superior by birth and education"'.[73] It is not known whether or not or for how long this scheme survived or if there were others like it in railway companies in the 1850s and 1860s. There is some evidence, however, that social bias in impersonal recruitment was developing systematically during the third quarter of the nineteenth century. An inquiry into the civil service in 1874/5 was told by the secretary of the London and Westminster Bank that they now only recruited the sons of 'clergymen, military and medical men' and the like. The sons of shopkeepers may have crept in in the past 'when we were not so rigid as we are now, but I would say that now, as a rule, we should not introduce the son of a shopkeeper'.[74]

By 1875 the London and North Western Railway (which had provided a witness at the civil service inquiry) had evolved a scheme which recruited impersonally and largely on the basis of social bias. Clerks were already recruited on the basis of examination. The new scheme was set up to 'secure the services of a limited number of young men of a superior class and higher education'[75] who would become assistants to third or fourth tier staff with hugely improved chances of promotion. Recruits were supposed to have gained some distinction at their schools 'by scholarships or in other ways'[76] but it was also made clear that that quality of 'manner and demeanour' which distinguished the public schoolboy was essential:

To start with they must have it. When we examine them before they go through the ordinary examinations, they must have all those qualities to start with . . . otherwise we should not take them; we should not give them a trial.[77]

Companies continued to look for this quality in the interwar years and beyond. The Cambridge University Appointments Board in the 1920s stated that firms wanted 'the public school type' for management posts but 'at any rate [the] man must be a natural leader to avoid discontent with . . . clerical staff who may see themselves superseded'.[78] An ICI internal memo in the late 1920s specified that the sort of man required was:

a man who takes First or Second Class Honours, who plays Rugby Football or Cricket . . . for his University, who is president of the JCR of his College . . . who is not afraid of 'losing his dignity' because he would bring his own dignity to whatever work he finds himself put to do, and is one whom men inquire when he first appears in any gathering 'who is that man?'[79]

The pattern which many of the recruitment schemes took was clearly set at an early date. The LNWR scheme attempted to give these privileged recruits an overview of the operations of the company by moving them from department to department:

They start generally at the bottom on the bank of a goods shed and see goods loaded, invoiced and everything else . . . then they go into accounts and into the various workings of goods traffic and then into passenger traffic.[80]

No further examples of such schemes appear to have emerged until after the First World War but the scheme on the Underground in the 1920s was very similar. Here, recruits were moved between works, sales, costing and financial departments and could gain experience of working in senior management's offices. Interestingly this appears to have originated as an in-house scheme for promising clerical staff which was later opened to graduates but undermined by directorial nepotism.[81] A variation on this theme was in place at GEC in the 1920s installed by Hugo Hirst who was a 'fervent admirer of British public schools and made speeches about them as the ideal breeding ground for industrial managers'.[82] The scheme was more static in that 'our young men [chosen] with great care from the secondary schools' were first given a training in the counting-house before being moved more purposefully around and up the organization.[83] Other schemes mentioned by Keeble of a type similar to the Underground scheme were put in place by the Gas Light and Coke Company, United Steel and Tootal Broadhurst Lee.[84]

Keeble describes these schemes as 'fairly limited':

. . . many involved not much more than a 'Cook's tour' of the various departments of the company, relying heavily on the interest and ability of the senior men to provide the training, with no extra support. The numbers receiving the training were very small. Few firms had taken up the idea in any systematic way before the Second World War. Less than twenty firms can be identified as having attempted a formal scheme with a regular intake.[85]

From this distance it is hard to disagree. On the other hand we should recognize that these 'less than twenty firms' were, in the UK context at least, pioneers. They had clearly understood that systematic means were needed to replenish top management. They clearly had a model of preferred leadership style and pursued the recruits that would meet it. Furthermore the 'Cook's tour' gave advantages to the participants which young men other than the heirs of family firms could not normally expect. In particular these recruits were allowed to move across the boundaries of departments normally shut off from one another as far as the 'ordinary' recruit was concerned. In terms of the generality of UK firms with their narrow hierarchies and nepotisms such schemes were bold and new, however timid they may appear by international comparison.

The UK, like other metropolitan societies, was and is élitist. What distinguished UK élitism in impersonal management recruitment from some others, however, was its ineffectual nature. Firstly, there appears to have been no noticeable difference in the quality of management produced by these schemes. Secondly, many of the schemes simply appear to have been fairly quickly abandoned.[86] Thirdly, some of them appear to have been regarded by the companies themselves as embarrassing failures.[87] The 'Cook's tour' system and recruitment to it thus did not discover or nurture talent, the training it provided was ineffective and it excluded those with ambition but without influence. It was simply a systematic form of uncompetitive privilege. A railway clerk wrote to a business journal in 1921:

> The more capable clerk wishes to make the utmost use of his abilities. But he is not allowed to do so. He sees the so-called gentleman, or at least those with money and influence, given special opportunities of learning the business, and of developing what powers of organisation and administration they may possess, with a view to taking on the more important and responsible posts in due time. He often longs to try his own powers; but no! He is permanently classified – a mere clerk. He will admit that the so-called gentleman has, or ought to have, a better education at the time of entering business life but cannot see that this is a reason for giving him every subsequent advantage; or understand why one so fortunate to have a good start should be carefully protected from competition.[88]

UK management recruitment in our period did indeed protect the fortunate from competition. There was no difference between impersonal and personal recruitment in this respect but while a 'disorderly' patronage or nepotism might leave some opportunity for the lucky or talented without influence, deliberate class patronage left none. Unequal opportunities were a fact of British life. The impersonal recruitment of public schoolboys made unequal opportunities systematic.

Jobs were treated as 'billets' and their acquisition as the rent of influence. There seems to have been little sense of them as skilled occupations for which an education, privileged or otherwise, could prepare the recruit.[89] Promotion seems largely to have been a question of being the right face, in the right place, at the right time. The essential trick was to gain access, by whatever means, to the positions where one was likely to be noticed. This indeed was the clear advice offered by the career guides.[90] This system was certainly not a 'credentialist' élitism like that in the USA or Germany, where entry was conditional on the completion of (expensive) degree courses in science, engineering or business and promotion was, at least formally, based on notions of competence.

The protection of the fortunate was a general rule in UK business which went far beyond the way recruitment to management was carried out. The instinctive response of UK business from at least the third quarter of the nineteenth century was by and large not to invest in technical innovation and marketing and cut costs by amalgamation and rationalization but to adopt the tactics of market sharing, collusion and exclusion. Where amalgamations did take place, integration of the enterprise generally proceeded no further than the minimum required for commercial survival. Anti-competitive activity went largely unopposed by government and was greatly encouraged by tariff walls in the interwar years and the organized sellers' market of the First and Second World Wars. By the 1950s the ability of the UK to compete internationally was choked by a thick cross-hatching of domestic trade associations, agreements and cartels.[91]

This systematic uncompetitiveness was not produced by the pre-industrial ideologies of the landed gentry – it was endemic in the practice of UK business large and small. Within the more protected enclaves of this uncompetitive system, however, the values of the gentry could flourish. It is not necessary to accept Wiener's argument that the explanations for economic decline are cultural but one cannot ignore the weight of evidence he produces of the unbusinesslike attitudes of senior businessmen. Industrialists before the Second World War could celebrate the gentlemen's club atmosphere of senior management[92] as could City grandees of a later period.[93] It could be said in 1956 that 'people in Anglo-Iranian, in Nuffields [are] just like higher civil servants. They belong to the same clubs in Pall Mall. They come from the same schools – or pretend that they do. (If you meet a representative of one of the "peasant industries" – say a lock-maker from Willenhall employing a hundred or so men – it is like another world.)'[94] It was thus possible, it would appear, for a man to be in management and not be 'in trade'.

The gentrification of British management was a form of institutionalization of pre-existing uncompetitive practices in business and recruitment to business. It was not the original cause of lack of competitiveness but its continuation. If we have a desire to blame we may perfectly reasonably hold top managers, who as a class were the beneficiaries of uncompetitive recruitment, responsible to a considerable extent for the failure of British industry and finance to withstand the onslaught of foreign competition from the 1960s to the 1980s. They were, however, the heirs and perpetuators of a system not of their making. The failings of the system lie in the structures and practices of UK business over a much longer period.

# BRITAIN'S ELITES IN THE INTERWAR PERIOD, 1918–39

W.D. RUBINSTEIN

The aim of this essay is to examine the overall position – what one might almost term the geo-politics or state of health – of Britain's élites and middle classes during the interwar years. To a surprising extent, there are few good studies of élite groups during this period; in contrast, virtually all of those which exist, whether of civic élites in large cities, landed families, business dynasties, or other groups, end abruptly in 1914 or encapsulate the subsequent thirty years as an afterthought – the 'succeeding generation' – marked by irreparable loss and insuperable challenge, and underscored by generational change of a fundamental nature, as in the latter half of Galsworthy's *Forsyte Saga*. Accurate general conclusions about the nature of Britain's élites as a whole during the interwar years are perhaps even rarer. In so far as any general conclusion has been reached, it is hallmarked by a conviction that they were necessarily much weaker in the interwar period than before, the war having fatally weakened the old élite structure of Britain (as it destroyed so much of that of continental Europe), leaving Britain's élites, much reduced in power and self-confidence, to fight a continuing and eventually losing battle with labour and socialism at home and with a disintegrating Empire, in the context of ever-greater unrest in Europe and economic depression throughout the world. The year 1914 is almost ubiquitously seen as marking a break of the most fundamental kind; indeed, it is difficult to imagine any history of Britain which does not treat the war as a fundamental break.

However, a very different interpretation of the situation of Britain's élites during the interwar period, in my opinion more accurate than the common view, may be offered. It is the aim of this paper briefly to put this view and outline the reasons why it is a viable, indeed a compelling way of interpreting this subject. The central argument is that Britain's mainstream élites were *not* weakened by the First World War or by any of its attendant changes. During the interwar years, and especially during the 1930s, they were in fact stronger than ever before. By this interpretation, if one had to give a precise date to the zenith of Britain's élites, one might suggest 12 May 1937, the date of the coronation of King George VI, rather than some earlier date such as Queen Victoria's 1887 or 1897 jubilees or the coronation of Edward VII in 1901.

One must, of course, define fairly precisely what is meant by Britain's mainstream élites and their evolution. My own view of this subject, which has been set out in several articles and books, has been to divide Britain's élites from the late eighteenth until the twentieth centuries into three groups: the London-based commercial and financial élite, the landed élite, and the north of England/Celtic industrial élite, which competed for wealth, status and power.[1] Self-evidently this oversimplifies an enormously complex situation but in my opinion a unified élite, uniting both land and the older forms of commercial wealth as well as many professions, and often bound together by 'Old Corruption', which reached its apogee in the era of Pitt and Liverpool, came apart around 1831 and remained apart until the 1880s, each of these groups going their separate ways during the mid-nineteenth century. The industrial élite was never able to 'break through' to supremacy, and the party political divisions of the 1830–86 period witnessed a significant peculiarity: that the élite institutions characteristic of pre-1832 Britain, the established Church, Oxbridge, perhaps the older mercantile bodies like the chartered companies, and, of course, most of the landed aristocracy and gentry, remained within the minority Conservative Party. As a result, the Whig/Liberal ascendancy could not truly claim to be the vehicle of much of Britain's 'Establishment', despite its normal electoral dominance. In my opinion, the Liberal Unionist split of 1886 was a major turning point in the process of élite reformulation, heralding the increasing unification of the financial/commercial and landed élites. The First World War saw the completion of this process, with a much weakened industrial élite now integrated into the national élite.

Thus, by about 1925 or 1930 for the first time since the Great Reform Bill, *all* of Britain's élites were politically unified within the Conservative Party. This fact in itself gave to the interwar Conservative Party an élite consensual presence which no political party had enjoyed since about 1830 (if indeed one can properly speak of political parties at that time). Nevertheless, the balance of power within the unified interwar élite had now obviously changed greatly: landowners plainly were much less influential and numerous at the highest levels of the Conservative Party or within the highest realms of governance than forty years before, while industrialists were both crucially weakened by the war and its consequential economic changes and subsumed within a unified élite. The centre of gravity of Britain's élite structure was now clearly represented by the south of England commercial élite along with the London-based higher professional classes. Much of the perceived weakness seen by both contemporary observers and historians of Britain's élites during the interwar years is probably based upon overemphasizing either the decline of the great landowners – for instance in David Cannadine's *Decline and Fall of the British Aristocracy* – or the old industrial dynasties of the north of England and the Celtic areas. The continuing strength of London and the south-east (apart from the well-known examples of new industry in automobiles and consumer goods) is either ignored or taken for granted.

The newly unified British élite had by the 1930s also overcome both of the primary challenges which had confronted Britain's traditional London-centred élite. The first of these challenges was that offered throughout the nineteenth century by manufacturing and industry based in the north, whose champions were disproportionately Nonconformist, Liberal, and centred in the northern cities, a challenge which probably reached its apogee under Joseph Chamberlain prior to his Liberal Unionist conversion. Much of nineteenth-century British politics revolved around the challenge, especially in the interests of further democratization, made by this group. The second of these was the trade union-based Labour challenge, which appeared acute, even critical, just after (and possibly before) the First World War, but which had probably been constitutionally contained by the time of the 1926

General Strike. Britain's mainstream élite had absorbed these challenges by dynastic and cultural co-option, as well as benefiting from the secular overriding trends in the British economy; it contained the second, obviously more equivocally, through the co-option of some of its key leaders, the legitimation of its institutions within the processes of governance and, most importantly, by striking electoral success from 1931 onwards. By the late 1930s Britain's mainstream élite had literally no effective challenges to its authority, arguably for the first time since 1832. It was at once both unified and triumphant over everybody and everything, in a way which had not been true for over a century.

Both the composition and authority of Britain's mainstream élite also benefited from the economic trends of the interwar period. It is a truism that the economic Depression of the interwar years affected the staple industries of the north to a far greater extent than it affected London and the south. The interwar Depression in itself accounted for an important measure of the decline of Britain's industrial élite, helping significantly to remove it as a viable threat to London and the south. Internationally, the net effects of the war were in some respects to strengthen rather than to weaken the City – the heart of the mainstream élite – as world entrepôt *in relative terms*. By the 1930s, Britain had 'clawed back' a good share of its markets in places like Latin America, the Far East, and of course in the sterling area, which it had lost to Germany and the United States prior to or just after the war. Cain and Hopkins have summarized the economic status of Britain at this time:

> [her] relative position with respect to her main rivals and satellites remained strong. Germany and France suffered severely as a result of World War I and the slump of the 1930s. The United States was only beginning to emerge as a world power before 1939, and some of the ground she had made up on Britain during the war and in the early 1920s was lost again during the depression. . . . For their part, Britain's satellites were constrained by a lack of alternatives: even in adversity, they remained tied to sterling and to the London money market. Viewed from this angle, Britain's decline as an imperial power became effective only when these relativities changed.[2]

Within the British élite itself, most of the quantitative evidence suggests that the size of the wealthiest minority of the population was actually increasing during the whole of the interwar period, the Depression having only a limited effect upon British high income and wealth (although direct taxation rose considerably). The number of persons with an annual income of £5,000 or more averaged 13,134 per annum during the five-year period 1911 to 1915. Their average annual number rose to 26,805 during the five years 1920 to 1925 in line with inflation, and to 28,359 in 1925 to 1930. During the years 1930 to 1935 the average annual number fell to 22,572, a decline of 20.4 per cent – not so significant as it seems if price deflation of over 10 per cent at this time is taken into account – and then rose again to 25,182 on average during the years 1935 to 1940.[3] It will be seen that neither the twenty-year period of post-1918 industrial decline, nor the Great Depression ushered in by the Wall Street Crash, had a catastrophic effect on Britain's top income earners, whatever the situation might well have been in America, Germany or elsewhere. Indeed, the economic vicissitudes of the British economy as a whole during the interwar years, even the critical period of the early 1930s, appear to have had virtually no effect whatever on Britain's rich, although the composition of the wealthy class, its individual members at any one time, may well have changed considerably, and although direct taxes were certainly higher during the interwar period than before.

The equivalent figures for top wealth-holders, for estates of £100,000 or more passing by probate, showed an even more striking trend. In the golden days of the Edwardian age, an average annual total of 300 estates worth £100,000 or more were left during the five years 1900 to 1914. Their total rose to 352 per annum during the wartime years 1915 to 1919, but then kept rising, to 372 in 1920 to 1924 and to 495 in 1925 to 1929. During the five years of the nadir of the Depression, 1930 to 1934, there was a decline in the number of estates at this level of only 6 per cent, to an annual average of 466 such estates (indicating an actual *rise* in their number when price movements are taken into account, extraordinary as this may seem). In the improved conditions of the latter half of the 1930s, an annual average of 540 estates of £100,000 or more were left in 1935 to 1939, 80 per cent more than during the alleged golden age of the super-rich before the war.[4] Clearly, all such figures must be treated with great caution, but it seems apparent that neither long-term nor short-term conditions in the British economy affected the total number of rich or very affluent persons, although the occupational and sectional composition of the class, and the social background of its members, may well have changed.

This particular point, that the rich and very affluent were probably more numerous during the interwar period than before the war (and arguably at their very peak in the late 1930s), is often missed by both economic and political historians, whose inferences are normally drawn from the state of the British economy as a whole rather than from one small class. But the satisfactory position of the rich also arguably had a considerable impact upon events. It was probably a factor in the popularity of appeasement: rocking the boat and preparing for war could only harm the well-off, and if another war could be averted by reasonable or even unreasonable concessions to Hitler to revise the Versailles Treaty, this was preferable to bringing the whole house crashing down.[5]

To be sure, there are obviously areas where this argument is either misleading or unproven. Landed wealth probably declined substantially just after the First World War, and landowners without substantial investments, urban rentals, or mineral deposits were often forced to sell off their land, although here one must be careful to note that only a minority of landowners were forced to sell.[6] We also know little or nothing about the geographical or occupational distribution of Britain's affluent; it is, however, reasonable to assume that during the interwar years there were far more top wealth-holders and high income earners in London and the south-east than in the north, just as there had always been. Almost certainly the growth of the white-collar category of middle-class employees in business, the public sector, and the professions also took place disproportionately in London and the south-east; it is hard to imagine anything else given the overall economic trends of the period.

While wealth apparently flourished as never before, the official and unofficial organs of élite recruitment, legitimacy, and recognition remained intact but were more genuinely inclusive of new men than ever before. At the apex, the British monarchy is often said to have successfully redefined itself, emerging under George V as genuinely popular, the symbol of national and imperial unity and the one fixed point in a world of change. The institutions of the 'Establishment', from the House of Lords and the Honours lists to debutantes' balls and public school sporting occasions, remained identical or virtually identical to what they had been before 1914, with the proviso that they were now largely more open to outsiders, to new money, to professionals, and even to the Labour élite (as the creation of a dozen or more Labour peers in 1924 and 1929–31 suggests). This broadening of the social bases of élite recruitment, indicative of the flexibility of the British system, should be contrasted with the more common view, presented, for example, in David Cannadine's *Decline and Fall of the British Aristocracy*, of the relentless downward spiral of the old landed aristocracy in this period.[7]

The old landed aristocracy comprised a considerably smaller percentage of the Tory cabinets of the interwar period than it did prior to 1906, although it was still very significant.[8] But if the notion of the decline of the aristocracy is meant to suggest a takeover of élite positions by the middle classes, this is rather misleading, since the basis of upper-class composition, founded until the late nineteenth century chiefly in the ownership of land, was merely transformed into a more broadly based élite. Far more than in the past, its determining characteristics revolved around public school and university education, as well as simply being rich. These were characteristics in which landowners and scions of the business and professional groups could now share, centred around a continuation of the formal titled aristocracy in which the great landowners, with their senior titles, actually still remained superior. This transition was surprisingly effortless, and there was less grumbling about the 'good old days' by the traditional landowners than one might have expected. The landed aristocracy seemed to be perfectly happy to be chiefly represented in the political thicket by an élite now centred in the upper middle classes.

It is also important to take into account the fact, so often overlooked and so often denigrated, that during the interwar period the British Empire was larger than ever before in its history. Despite the emergence of both legally self-governing Dominions and major nationalist movements in India, Egypt, Palestine and elsewhere, the Empire was in many respects more powerful and unified than it had ever been before and in some respects still constituted the most important political unit in the world.[9] Only in 1918, and not before, did the British Empire extend to Jerusalem, Baghdad, Dar-es-Salaam, Rabaul and other places absorbed by Britain and its Dominions as a result of its victory in the war. In an age which still regularly judged national political strength in terms of coloration of the world map rather than by macroeconomic statistics, this in itself remained impressive and reassuring, apart from the vast manpower and economic reserves of a world empire on this scale. It is also a fact that all of the Empire, including its self-governing component, declared war on Germany together with Britain in September 1939. Robert Menzies's celebrated declaration of war on behalf of his country in 1939 – 'today Britain is at war and as a result Australia is also at war' – spoke for a generation of Dominion citizens for whom Britain was indubitably the Mother Country. One recent work on Australian attitudes to the Empire at this time notes that:

When journeying to England, the Australian, whether artist or not, already had an image of 'Home', instilled by upbringing and education. Robert Menzies, visiting England for the first time in 1935 to attend the Imperial Conference, recorded his arrival: 'At last we are in England. Our journey to Mecca has ended, and our minds abandoned to those reflections which can so strangely (unless you remember our traditions and upbringing) move the soul of those who go "Home" to a land they have never seen. . . .' Mecca, indeed: and the first beholding of England could have almost a religious awe to it. The study of English history and literature prepared the visitor, but the experience of the countryside, particularly in spring, was still often a revelation. The educator Frank Tate, making his first visit to Britain at the age of 42, marvelled at bluebells and primroses, and observed of the countryside that 'there was nothing ragged and unfinished and new', the farms seeming to have been 'fertilised for centuries by human contact'. Yet he pointed out that Buttermere was not new to him; he 'had been there often enough through the magic of Wordsworth'. Menzies, still under the spell of it all, professed to understand England anew: 'The green and tranquil country sends forth from its very soil the love of peace and of good humour and contentment'. He was also enchanted to have tea with the Duke and Duchess of York, and to watch the Royal children having a dancing lesson: amazingly, this was 'a real family, with real and intelligent people in it'.[10]

While the opinions of Menzies and his colleagues were perhaps extreme, even by the standards of Australian anglophiles, it also remained the case that Britain still exercised both ceremonial and, in foreign policy, effective control over virtually the whole of the Empire during the interwar years. In 1932, for instance, the Governor-

General of Canada was the Earl of Bessborough, of New Zealand Lord Bledisloe, of South Africa the Earl of Clarendon, while the Earl of Willingdon was Viceroy of India – British aristocrats representing the Crown, socially almost indistinguishable from their grandfathers sixty years before. In the rare cases when a Dominion governor was native-born (as was Sir Isaac Isaacs in Australia) he had inevitably received a knighthood and appropriate orders of chivalry, the Irish Free State's James McNeill being a notable and disconcerting exception. And while there was obviously pervasive unrest in India, both the extent of Indian nationalism and its eventual aims, and the aims of the British, require closer scrutiny. If Baldwin and others in the mainstream of the Conservative Party now conceded that Indian self-government in some form was inevitable, it was a very different kind of self-government from that which actually occurred in 1947. In all likelihood it would have included a British viceroy or governor-general, British responsibility for Indian defence, British paramountcy in the princely states (which would have continued to exist), a pro-British Indian mercantile and professional class, and Britain continuing to provide an impartial and neutral force between Hindus and Muslims. Absolute British withdrawal, if it was ever foreseen at all, was something for future generations, while it goes without saying that in Africa, the Caribbean and the Far East, life was to continue as before. No one in Britain in 1937 would have believed that virtually every British colony in the Third World would be independent within thirty years.

During this period, the empire still also functioned as it had done since the eighteenth century, as a central venue for the employment of the offspring of the upper and upper middle classes. No change occurred in this: indeed, if anything there may well have been more employment opportunities within the colonial administration of the empire during the interwar years than before, given the considerable growth in the infrastructure of the colonies and the range of activities for which its governments were responsible.

A final central point may well be even more controversial than the previous ones – that the interwar period, rather than the years before, saw a relative cultural and educational unity within, broadly, the British middle classes if not the whole of society. In general, most writers and intellectuals emerged from the same stratum of society, the educated upper middle classes, chiefly if not overwhelmingly educated at a public school and Oxbridge among its male adherents. This actually represented a considerable change from the equivalent situation seventy-five or even fifty years before, when many notable writers and cultural figures, from Dickens to Gissing, were drawn from outside the educated upper middle classes. By the interwar years most shared the same cultural assumptions, the same language and subtexts.[11]

Because of this similarity in background (and for other reasons, such as victory in the war), Britain during the interwar years failed to produce an adversarial cultural Bohemia in the same way as most other Western countries; the chief representatives of such sharp cultural novelty as existed were often, like T.S. Eliot, Ezra Pound and Jacob Epstein, foreign-born. Much of British high and popular culture during the interwar years was, in fact, not radical in any sense but explicitly conservative. The great renaissance of English serious music at this time, led by Vaughan Williams, Elgar, Bax and others, was invariably nostalgic and celebratory, always eschewing atonality. The most popular form of middle-class reading, the classical detective story, invariably demonstrated the triumph, through superior cleverness, of the forces of law and order over criminality. The style of English writing, complex and convoluted even in the most highly regarded writers (like Dickens) in the mid-nineteenth century, acquired its remarkably crisp, clear, and lucid style at this time, based in the classical education now ubiquitously offered at the public schools and universities.

Even the famous socialist intellectuals of the 1930s, the Audens and Cornfords, emerged overwhelmingly from the same upper middle-class public school and university background; as a result, while many intellectuals were on the left, few had not been socialized into precisely the same educational and social universe of discourse as had their conservative contemporaries. There was, indeed, probably less cultural disunity or subversion during the interwar period than before or since, certainly than before about 1890 or after about 1960 – that is, than before and after the institutions and social forces which reached their zenith during the interwar period had done so. This relative cultural unity was also reinforced by Britain's new cultural institutions like the BBC, the national Fleet Street press, and the cinema. It might also be noted that London grew to its largest-ever population during the 1930s, containing about nine million people – more than one-sixth of the entire British population – by 1939. Perhaps even more than previously, London at this time was both the governmental and cultural capital of Britain in the true sense, with Whitehall, Fleet Street and the BBC stamping London upon everything. As well, during the interwar years, crime, violence, antisocial behaviour and, conceivably, visible anti-conformist display were then at their lowest levels in modern times, notwithstanding the unemployment, residual primary poverty and class-based social codes of the period.

It was also probably the case that, for both Britain's élites and middle classes, the interwar years saw a decline in both insecurity and the hazards of risk compared with the nineteenth century, especially with *laissez-faire* capitalism of the individual entrepreneur or small partnership. The growth of large corporations as the characteristic mode of business life meant the growth as well of a class of managers and white-collar workers vastly larger than before, who in the main were reasonably secure in their employment and career prospects. Many of Britain's key institutions emphasized and reflected security, for instance and most notably, the clearing bank system, by then reduced to the 'Big Five' which were universally regarded as being as safe as the Rock of Gibraltar. Risk and insecurity may well have been seen as diminishing for the whole population, but especially for the middle classes, in the continuing decline of mortality rates, especially infant and childhood mortality rates, leading to much smaller families, often consisting of only children, becoming far more common than before 1914.

Several points arising out of this interpretation of the interwar years require more detailed discussion. Clearly the First World War and its effects must be examined. It is certainly true that, in terms of the arguments made here, the war was profoundly important: in the elimination of the provincial élites and in the weakening of Nonconformity, for example. Yet while the war is normally seen as marking a break with pre-war British society, and however appalling the murderous demographic effects and personal tragedies brought about by it, the net effect of the First World War was, relatively and perhaps absolutely, to strengthen Britain's mainstream élite. Because Britain was victorious in the war, no fundamental discontinuities occurred in British society such as totally transformed eastern and central Europe, replacing the age-old élite structures there with regimes which were either unprecedentedly radical or widely regarded as illegitimate. Because there was no fundamental discontinuity, Britain had neither communism nor fascism of significance. On the contrary, the few direct consequences of the war for Britain's political constitution were chiefly very beneficial to the mainstream élite, especially in eliminating southern Ireland's Westminster contingent, enfranchising women and, in particular, in dividing the British left into two parties, both normally smaller than the Conservatives and thus disadvantaged under Britain's electoral system. Without the First World War, it is very arguable whether the Conservative hegemony which occurred after 1918 would have taken place, and one recent study of the Edwardian Conservative Party suggests that the party was on the point of disintegrating in 1914.[12] The war of course left a legacy of personal and familial grief beyond calculation and, however much the term may be a demographic exaggeration, a sense of a 'lost generation' which viewed the survivors as inadequate substitutes for those who perished.

Nevertheless, it is crucial to realize what the war failed to do in Britain. The war did not mark a total break with the *ancien régime* such as occurred throughout Europe, eliminating and liquidating age-old regimes, their symbols and their supporters. Someone falling asleep in Britain in 1912 and waking up in, say, 1925, would find that none of the symbols of pre-war British society and, indeed, surprisingly few of Britain's institutions, had changed markedly, let alone irrevocably and totally, as would immediately strike someone awakening in Moscow, Berlin or Vienna.[13] Nearly all of the institutions of the British 'Establishment' were completely intact and almost precisely just as they had been before the war, with a largely unchanged public school, university and clubland scene to place beside the monarchy, the titled aristocracy and the rest. The lack of radical discontinuities is widely and rightly credited with the abysmal performance of British fascism and communism during the interwar years. Uniquely among major European countries, both political extremes remained marginalized, allowing a revivified liberal neo-Orthodoxy assisted by newly enacted tariff barriers to deal with the Depression.[14] Britain had, moreover, won the war and, therefore and most crucially, its élites failed to experience that intense and permanent sense of 'relative deprivation' which, in particular, was a hallmark of Germany's élites even long before the war, let alone after Germany's defeat, and which was in itself a most important cause of Germany's lamentable record. Britain's élites (and British society) experienced absolutely nothing like this. While 750,000 British soldiers died for a cause which within a few years of the Armistice many found pointless, at least the survivors knew that they were on the winning side and did not add the burden of vengeance to the burden of grief. The war, in short, failed to destroy or even crucially alter, Britain's traditional 'Establishment' but on the contrary actually strengthened the political forces of Conservatism in many important ways.

A second important area which remains largely unexplored and a matter of guesswork is the collapse of the provincial élites, especially in the old industrial areas. With a handful of exceptions we lack searching local studies in what is surely a rich field with accessible sources, awaiting its historians. It seems likely that the collapse of the provincial élites (where they did collapse) had at least four components. Firstly, the leading nineteenth-century local business élites suffered sharp, often irreversible economic decline, normally being engaged in business activities which were disproportionately affected by the decline of Britain's old staple industries. Secondly, the scions of the great Victorian provincial entrepreneurs, educated (unlike their forebears) at élite public schools and universities, became part of the national economic élite, no longer looking primarily to their old local community as the matrix of their affairs, if they remained there at all. Thirdly, the interwar years saw the decline of many of the sustaining forces of the old provincial élites, especially of Nonconformity of an adversarial kind, the backbone of nineteenth-century radicalism. This decline was probably the result in large measure of the social forces unleashed by the war, but may well have been likely to occur in any case. The war is normally seen as marking a profound climacteric in the fortunes of Nonconformity. Recognized (for the first time) as thoroughly legitimate during the war itself, Dissent saw a disproportionate decline after 1918, while its sustaining forces like temperance and old-fashioned radicalism now seemed to suffer from the new circumstances of postwar life far more than Anglicanism, Catholicism or atheism.[15] Dissenters were often presented during the interwar period with the stark choice of joining the Tories, homeland of Anglicans, or Labour; disproportionately, middle-class Dissenters chose the former, especially after the mid-1920s. Fourthly, as British politics, at both the national and local levels, became transformed into a battle between Tory and Labour, with Labour paying lip-service on paper to a far-reaching socialism, the old amateur gentleman-politician was increasingly replaced, among Tories, by advocates for their cause with at least a modicum of articulateness, who might be drawn from any part of the upper middle classes. After 1918, only seldom were

Conservative MPs in the large towns themselves major entrepreneurs and industrialists (and employers of labour) in their constituency, as had regularly been the case in both the Conservative and Liberal Parties down to the First World War. One suspects – with all too little evidence – that this was the case as well with the civic élites of the major cities.

As noted, this trend has been relatively neglected by historians and only a few works explicitly examine it. Among the few notable discussions of this process are *The Making of a Ruling Class: Two Centuries of Capital Development on Tyneside*, an anonymous quasi-Marxist pamphlet published in 1978 by the Benwell Community Project in Newcastle, and Barry M. Doyle's 'Urban Liberalism and the "Lost Generation": Politics and Middle-Class Culture in Norwich, 1900–1935', in the *Historical Journal* (1996). The process has also been considered in a number of recent local histories, for instance in the work edited by David Nash and David Reeder, *Leicester in the Twentieth Century*. The Benwell study views Tyneside's élite (comprising families like the Peases, Strakers, Joiceys, Cooksons and Armstrongs, based on coal, engineering and local banking) as having evolved from 'an area-specific ruling class' prior to 1914 to 'an organised regional bourgeoisie that was acting to protect and pursue its own interests *vis-à-vis* a wider national bourgeoisie . . . [with] many family members having interests outside the region altogether'.[16] Doyle's study of Norwich depicts a local élite which had been largely Liberal and radical in the Victorian sense but whose younger members had evolved into Tories and viewed themselves as members of a national 'Establishment' by the 1930s. In Leicester, while about 60 per cent of the members of its town council had been businessmen in 1881, this figure declined to 50 per cent in 1901 and then to only 33 per cent in 1931. In that year, only about 5 per cent of the town's council were 'wealthy', although about one-third of Leicester's aldermen who served in the period 1871 to 1891 had left £50,000 or more.[17] Despite the fact that manufacturing industry in Leicester remained relatively strong, with a hosiery trade now being modernized, 'the middle-class allegiance to Liberalism that had been so strong . . . was now being dissolved. It was not immediate but was nevertheless quite rapid in the 1920s', consistent with trends in many other towns.[18] In interwar Leicester, the city's wealthy élite remained prominent in charitable affairs, but no longer in local politics; local Conservative politics now became reorganized in defence of ratepayers, private property owners and small businessmen.[19]

A third matter which requires some special mention is the status of the Labour Party during the 1930s. It must be said that the Labour Party probably stood little chance of defeating the National Government in the general election which must have been held in 1939 or 1940, had there been no war. In 1939, Labour was only slightly more popular than it had been during the previous eight years. In 1931, of course, the National Government won the greatest electoral victory in terms of parliamentary seats since 1832, and the greatest electoral victory in terms of percentage of the vote cast since the mid-nineteenth century, with the possible exception of 1918 if both the Couponed candidates and their un-Couponed allies are counted together. It is less well known that in 1935 the National Government also won the second largest victory on the basis of either seats or votes since the mid-nineteenth century. In 1935 the National Government elected 432 MPs – more than the victors in 1895, 1906 or 1945 – and received 53.7 per cent of all votes cast, the only time, apart from the 1900 and 1931 general elections, that one party received more than 50 per cent of the vote at any general election in the twentieth century.[20]

It is also important to realize that there was little or no real sign of any swing of the pendulum which would have brought Labour closer to victory at any putative 1939 or 1940 general election. The first three Gallup polls of voting intention in Britain, taken in February and December 1939 and February 1940 with methods fairly close to those now employed, revealed support for the 'Government' at, respectively, 50, 51 and 54 per cent, with support for the 'Opposition' at 44, 27 and 30 per cent.[21] The February 1939 survey taken once the euphoria of Munich had worn off (although a month before Nazi Germany took over the residuum of Czechoslovakia, normally taken as a key turning-point in Western perceptions of Hitler's intentions) showed that the National Government still enjoyed the support of an outright majority of voters.

One should indeed be careful not to infer too much from the sharply politicized move to the left among so many writers and intellectuals during the 'devil's decade', the time of 'taking sides' which has become so legendary. While many leading intellectuals did indeed swing to the left, it is very doubtful whether this affected more than a small minority of the middle classes as a whole. An undergraduate poll at

Cambridge University held concurrently with the 1935 general election showed that the National candidate received 650 votes, the Labour candidate 275 and the Liberal 171.[22] At Oxford, an 'informed estimate of 1935' claimed that there were about 2,000 Conservative undergraduates compared with 800 socialist undergraduates: the left-wing contingent seemed far larger than it was because around 600 socialist undergraduates were 'active' compared with only 200 Tory undergraduates.[23] This, the forgotten face of the well-educated middle classes in the 1930s, must be placed beside everything which might be said on the other side, for instance that the Cambridge University Socialist Club in 1938 claimed a membership of 1,000 out of fewer than 5,000 undergraduates.[24] Indeed, the consensual One Nation face of the National Government, and the fact that it had unified all of the nation's élites under one banner, must itself have gone some way towards satisfying those longings for collective action among some who would otherwise and in other places have looked more longingly to Moscow.

Neither Labour's leaders nor its policies in fact appeared likely then, or perhaps in that generation, to challenge the hegemony of the National Government, and the radicalization which led to 1945 must truly be attributed wholly to the 'people's war', with Britain, perhaps, presenting a close parallel to the sharp radicalization which occurred throughout occupied Europe, leading to the triumph of the left almost everywhere on the continent by 1944 to 1946. It requires an effort of will to understand that Labour's leader, Clement Attlee, was, even at the end of the decade, virtually unknown to the electorate, one of the few heads of a major political party who had never held cabinet rank before becoming leader. Attlee was a mediocre speaker and it is difficult indeed to imagine Labour winning a general election under his leadership without either the social change brought about by the war or the trust in Labour inspired by its partnership in the Churchill government.[25] Labour's sophisticated economic policy adopted in 1937, and virtually identical to that which it adopted after 1945, apparently failed to impress the electorate; there is simply no indication that this was changing significantly when war came.

Surveying the British scene in 1937, a south of England upper-middle-class supporter of the National Government was entitled to feel a glow of satisfaction at how – perhaps most unexpectedly – sanguine it all seemed. There was one exception, of course: the maniac in Berlin who, for no obvious reason whatever, threatened to bring the whole house crumbling down. Shortly he did, but history should not be read backwards, and what now appears to us to be a time of weakness and decline seems very different indeed if viewed with contemporary eyes.

# NEITHER METROPOLITAN NOR PROVINCIAL:

THE INTERWAR MIDDLE CLASS

RICHARD TRAINOR

Among the most important dichotomies in the writing of British history is that between 'Town' and 'Country' or – for the modern period – between 'the metropolis' and 'the provinces'. Surprisingly modern in origin,[1] the latter terms – with their hierarchical connotations – pervade much of the burgeoning historical literature on the middle class and the élites largely drawn from it. Many recent writers have followed the lead of W.D. Rubinstein in casting doubt on the resources, the coherence, and the local as well as the broader influence of élites based in the provinces, especially in industrial towns.[2] Even in their supposed heyday of the nineteenth century, it seems, industrial élites were overshadowed by, and divided from, landed, professional, financial and mercantile leaders for whom London was the natural hub.[3] From the late nineteenth century, as British industry began to falter while the City of London consolidated its international position, the aloof superiority of metropolitan élites evidently became even more marked, laying the basis for London's apparent late twentieth-century dominance in British (and especially English) economic, political, cultural and social life.[4] A major further deterioration of the position of provincial élites apparently occurred during the interwar period as the economy of the industrial north and Scotland failed to match the 'new industries' of London, the south-east and the Midlands.[5] From this perspective the upsurge of provincial resources and influence which took place during the eighteenth and nineteenth centuries appears to some observers as an 'interlude' in the longer-term dynamic strength of London and its region.[6] Thus the modern reinforcement of the age-old superiority of 'Town' to 'Country' has become a major prop to the scaffolding of the 'divided middle class' and the assumptions about nineteenth- and twentieth-century British social development that go with it.

It is impossible to deny the centrality of London: the especially populous, wealthy and powerful position of the capital is one of the distinguishing features of British history. It would be astonishing, then, if the importance of London had not had major consequences for the structure and impact of the country's middle class. Nevertheless, in writing the history of the modern British middle class it is vital to avoid projecting backward on to the period before 1939 the geographical hierarchies of the United Kingdom at the end of the twentieth century. To do so is to risk not only anachronism but also a misunderstanding of the processes by which the provincial assertiveness of the later nineteenth century gave way to the more London-centred patterns of the later twentieth. In order to understand these processes better, this essay – a speculative early instalment of a social history of the British middle class 1850–1950 – explores the apparently pivotal interwar years. During this period, it will be argued, the middle class was characterized less by division than by unity which was the result as much of provincial strength as of provincial weakness. Between 1918 and 1939, this essay will suggest, the age-old rivalry between metropolis and province increasingly gave way to a *national* middle-class culture, particularly strong in the upper middle class, which transcended the dichotomy between 'Town' and 'Country'.

Such a development depended upon a strong provincial role in the evolution of the middle class in the century before 1914, when the group expanded with unprecedented speed. Rapid urbanization assisted the integration of the Victorian middle class by providing advances in transport and communication which eased effective links among the propertied classes of industrial towns, provincial regional capitals and London. Admittedly, the development of the economy had complex effects on the distribution of resources between classes, regions and types of urban settlements. Yet even relatively humble industrial towns usually developed middle classes which combined, on the one hand, at least a few very wealthy individuals able to deal on terms of near equality with regional and national rivals, with, on the other, a critical mass of those with the comfortable incomes that effective local social leadership required.[7] To look at the same issue in occupational rather than social terms, the capitals of so-called industrial regions and even industrial towns themselves developed middle classes with significant professional as well as manufacturing and retail elements; these middle classes were characterized at least as much by a shared ethos of high-minded capitalism as by divisions centred around the presence or absence of formal qualifications.[8] The urban élites arising from these middle classes drew on a mixture of social levels, occupational groups and partisan and sectarian factions; the social interventions of these leaders were increasingly coherent, transcending differences of background and linking economic, voluntary and statutory institutions. These unambiguously public activities drew on an increasingly secure middle-class identity which had its roots in social activities pursued in homes and clubs as well as in town halls and the boardrooms of hospitals and firms.[9]

Naturally there were important hierarchies even within the urban provinces, and these were reflected in significant differences in middle-class size, occupational composition and sophistication. But increasingly there was intense communication by the middle class up as well as down this urban hierarchy, whether we look to the relations between industrial towns and regional capitals, or to the connections between regional capitals and London. Regionally based associations of mayors, chambers of commerce, professional and political associations and employers' organizations provided the glue within provincial districts; meanwhile MPs, national voluntary societies, national professional and trade organizations, cooperative aristocrats and the broadening of metropolitan high society linked provincial capitals to London.[10] From this perspective, the famous campaigns of the nineteenth century, in which the provinces played a major part – notably the drives for the Great Reform Act, the repeal of the Corn Laws and the establishment of state-supported primary education – were the tip of a large iceberg of increasingly complex and decreasingly unequal provincial–metropolitan relations.[11] Admittedly, by 1914 the south-eastern middle class still retained some of its long-standing aloofness and superiority, in lifestyle as in economic and political power.[12] But evidently it was a good deal less aloof and superior than it had been at the beginning of the nineteenth century.

The interaction between provincial towns and London became part of a much broader web of relations between 'core' and 'periphery' which were denser, more flexible and more subtle in the United Kingdom than in many other countries.[13] As a result, by the turn of the century the barriers between London and other parts of Britain were beginning to break down.[14]

Even if this interpretation of the years down to the early twentieth century is correct, these trends might have been reversed in the subsequent period by a large shift in middle-class resources, confidence and power in favour of London and the south-east more generally as the metropolis overwhelmed the 'provincial cultures' of the Victorian decades.[15] Yet, as far as the interwar period is concerned, economic, social and political changes may have done more to break down the remaining barriers between the provinces and London than to make the latter's middle class a detached super-élite. On this reading, London's middle class did not so much come to *dominate* its provincial counterpart by 1939; rather, the London middle class was the leading instrument of a process of broadly based economic, social and political change producing a much more geographically *united* British middle class in which the distinction between 'the provinces' and 'the metropolis' lost much of its sting.

This essay is an attempt to explore the possibility that the geographical divisions within the middle class, waning before 1914, came to matter even less in the interwar years. While handicapped by changes in the recording of income tax data which disregard regional differences, such arguments are compatible with analyses of the decennial census indicating the persisting similarity of provincial towns to London in the relative size and occupational composition of their middle-class populations.[16] But the focus here is on qualitative sources, especially on J.B. Priestley's 1934 classic *English Journey*, a survey of provincial cities and towns, and on the recently published memoir of London in the interwar years by the journalist and broadcaster Paul Vaughan, the mysteriously titled *Something in Linoleum* (a reference to his father's position as secretary of the Linoleum and Floorcloth Manufacturers' Association!).[17] This essay also draws on interwar autobiographies and on interviews with upper-middle-class people from various cities born in the late nineteenth century taken from the Essex Oral History Archive assembled by Paul Thompson.[18] While most of the individuals analysed – all of whom were conscious of the geographical as well as the social pattern of their routines – did not use the terms 'metropolitan' and 'provincial', this is not surprising in a period when the distinction arguably was of diminishing importance.

The mechanisms by which the economic, social and political trends of the interwar years challenged the pre-1914 assertiveness of the urban provincial middle class can be clearly glimpsed in these sources. Priestley lays great emphasis on provincial industry being undermined not just by short-term slump but also by long-term structural change; meanwhile, Vaughan's book conjures up a London whose prosperity fed not only on the famous 'new industries' but also on the enduring vitality of the commercial and financial interests focused in the south-east.[19] Vaughan's father serviced an industry which was largely based in the provinces, yet his substantial personal income was spent in the cinemas, restaurants and – above all – the pubs and clubs of London and its suburbs. Also, the extent to which the organizational life of upper-middle-class Britain was shifting to the south-east is evident from these sources. For example, by the early 1950s, when Vaughan was a public relations spokesman for the British Medical Association, leading provincial doctors had to make regular journeys to London in order to defend their profession against the perceived horrors of the new National Health Service.[20]

Politically, too, the centre of gravity seemed to be shifting away from provincial local government. Priestley reports an intensifying version of the familiar complaint that wealthy people were not standing for their local councils. In part this phenomenon was both cause and effect of another Priestley theme: that localities were losing their power to central government.[21] The Essex Oral History Archive also reveals a generational factor: a strong revulsion, by the young upper-middle-class people of the interwar period, for their parents' pre-1914 commitment to civic affairs. A manager from the Potteries lamented that his father was 'always . . . either at a church meeting or . . . a Council meeting'; a Bolton doctor reported that his father's absorption in the council 'sickened' him; and a Keighley woollen mill owner argued that his father, who regularly missed his meals because of council meetings, 'spent so much time on public work that he filled me with a horror of it'.[22] In addition, as chapel-centred loyalties declined, the growing strength in the provinces of the Conservative Party at the expense of the Liberals undermined one of the major sources of leverage previously enjoyed by much of the middle class outside London.[23]

Another source of provincial middle-class difficulty evident from Priestley and from the Essex Oral History Archive is the increasing *detachment* of the upper middle class from the towns where it made its money. Too often historians have pointed to so-called 'gentrification' as a feature of the Victorian and Edwardian periods: in fact it was the interwar era when the previous trickle of gentrification arguably became a flood.[24] Priestley echoes many other sources – notably the Bolton doctor in the oral history archive – in suggesting that 'the country gentleman tradition is livelier to-day than it was twenty-five years ago'.[25] In Bradford the 'richer merchants and manufacturers' use their newly acquired cars to live outside the city, leaving the latter to the 'professional, clerking and working classes' – in contrast to a pre-1914 pattern of a resident 'aristocracy' of merchants and manufacturers.[26] Similar patterns emerge in Hull, where old substantial residential districts are 'given up to dentistry, corsets, boarders, and estate agents'. The result is 'social disintegration . . . in so many provincial cities', with bridge and radio preferred to music and drama: 'the various social and artistic activities of these towns are now chiefly organised by people who belong to the employed and not the employing class'.[27]

The portrait of London which emerges in Priestley and in Vaughan is of economic prosperity, political assertiveness and social dynamism. In contrast to what Priestley calls 'that terrible dreariness which is probably the chief curse of our provincial towns' are the 'waves of fashion, rising in Berkeley Square and then slowly travelling out until at last they ebb and dwindle into semi-detached villas outside Newcastle and farmhouses in Devonshire'.[28] The BBC, the cinema and the increasingly dominant London press seemed ever more effective in conveying London's influence to the provinces. The provincial cities appeared passive: well-off people relentlessly drifted to London, Priestley reported, from those proud centres of Victorian initiative, Birmingham, Manchester and Leeds. Likewise, the First World War had diminished the cosmopolitanism as well as the prosperity of Bradford.[29] By contrast, Vaughan's suburban London was prosperous, rapidly expanding and confident. His book focuses on a state school with private school airs that ruthlessly and successfully trained bright boys to take their place, first at Oxbridge, and then among the London-centred literati.[30]

Thus the mechanisms – differential economic growth, organizational shift, changing political structures, the beginnings of the mass media and the mushroom growth of south-eastern suburbia – behind London's rise to greater middle-class prominence emerge clearly from these two accounts. Yet Vaughan's book, combined with undercurrents in Priestley's text and a range of evidence from other sources, complicates any simplistic interpretation of a *predominant* London middle class in the interwar period, and does so in a way which reinforces a perception of the persisting, if decreasingly independent, contribution of the provincial bourgeoisie to an increasingly unified British upper middle class. Thus, while the latter theme is shared with Professor Rubinstein's chapter in this volume, this chapter differs from his in that, on the interpretation offered here, provincial élites did not collapse (at least not until after 1945), and the emerging national élite did not belong to the south-east in any exclusive sense.

Vaughan's is the story of how an unfashionable – in effect a provincial[31] – part of suburban south-west London (Raynes Park) was integrated into an emerging national middle-class culture through the energies of a headmaster of a successful school. John Garrett, a hairdresser's son from Trowbridge, induces his pupils to modify their cockney accents and assimilate themselves to Received Standard English as propagated by the BBC.[32] The humdrum social pattern of the boys' parents – every bit as 'provincial' as the routines derided in the regions by Priestley – were enlivened by summonses to sherry with the elegantly attired Garrett. Only occasionally did these suburbanites venture into the West End, even less often than the inhabitants of the wealthier, more sophisticated but still introverted Tunbridge Wells of Richard Cobb's interwar childhood.[33] Likewise, the growing Tory sympathies of the provincial middle class found their echo in the automatic political Conservatism of Vaughan's father and his friends – an obstacle Garrett had to overcome in generating a cosmopolitan outlook in his school. According to Vaughan 'my father, having been an officer in the war and now with a house of his own, plus a responsible job and a family was drawn ineluctably to the party of possession, privilege, and rank'.[34] When the boys held a mock general election at the school, the National Government won easily. These London pupils required far more 'remedial' acculturation than did the Bolton doctor or the Keighley manufacturer mentioned earlier, or their fellow Essex oral history subject Michael Hope, who grew up in Birmingham as part of the Chamberlain/Kenrick clan and read *The Times* as well as the *Birmingham Post* in a businessman's home with very strong links to London.[35]

Thanks in part to Garrett-like headmasters all over Britain – such as the Oxford graduate who transformed the Leicester City Boys' School to the benefit of the future historian J.F.C. Harrison, like Vaughan a 'semi' dweller[36] – by the 1930s there was easy social interchange among prosperous middle-class people from different regions, including London. Priestley, a Bradford native who had turned himself into a Londoner by 1934, finds himself on the same conversational wavelength as middle-class people, especially *upper*-middle-class people, from a variety of regions and occupations. In the lounge of a hotel in Lincoln, for example, he 'struck up an acquaintance with an engineer', just as he mixes over lunch with leaders of the Black Country's metal trades.[37] There was no male monopoly, though there was male privilege, in such interactions. E.L. Delafield's 'provincial lady', a popular semi-autobiographical literary character of the 1930s, has no difficulty making repeated transitions from her Devon village and the upper middle-class society of the vicinities of Plymouth and Exeter to literary London.[38]

Such interchange was facilitated by the significant prosperity, sophistication and initiatives remaining in the provinces even in the depths of the 1930s' depression.[39] 'England, even now', Priestley notes, is 'the country of local government, local politics, strong local interests'.[40] This seemed especially true of those provincial cities, such as Bristol and Norwich, more tightly tied to southern gentility than to northern industry. Bristol's wealthy had not abandoned their town, Priestley reported, just as Norwich's professional men pursued elegant lifestyles combined with a persisting appetite for public affairs that made their city a plausible site for a regional parliament. Norwich worthies did not migrate to London in large numbers. In contrast to Bradford, Bristol was 'not a dirty nineteenth-century hotch-potch, not merely an extended factory and warehouse, but a real city with a charm and a dignity of its own'.[41] Yet Priestley's recognition of provincial resources and vitality went beyond the genteel south. He was struck, though not pleased, by the brash prosperity of Coventry and Birmingham – a part of 'provincial' Britain which profited from the economic resilience of the period and a region influential enough to contribute two Conservative prime ministers between the wars.[42] Even Bradford, Priestley argued, was not markedly inferior in size or wealth to Bristol. Moreover, *within* the north Priestley detected differences of function and vitality that pointed to the persisting particular impact of the major provincial cities and towns. Thus Leeds had 'much greater local importance' than Bradford, partly because it was a 'great marketing centre' with its own university and law courts.[43] In a similar way, in the north-east, although Gateshead had few public buildings and was 'nothing better than a huge dingy dormitory', and while Jarrow was 'entirely a working-class town', Newcastle enjoyed grandeur and some wealth and even South Shields had 'a far larger middle-class population than most of the other neighbouring towns'.[44] Manchester rejoiced in the amenities of the Midland Hotel, and Liverpool had its University Club with a lively mix of journalists, barristers, shipping men – and even some academics!

Nor were these provincial towns bereft of prosperous residents and leaders. It is evident – from Priestley as from many other sources, notably the Essex archive – that many provincial business and professional people continued to live in or at least near their towns and to play a significant though reduced role in their public affairs. Thus a Leicester company director whom Priestley visited resided in 'a very pleasant residential quarter of the town, with wide streets and detached villas'.[45] Also, scattered evidence suggests that substantial middle-class people, though less often top economic figures, still served in significant numbers on at least some councils. Furthermore, it seems likely that upper-middle-class leadership of provincial voluntary societies lasted through the interwar period.[46] Thus, the Keighley mill-owner cited earlier remained in close touch with his workforce and their industrial villages, pursuing a lifestyle which was in his words 'another language' compared to that of the truly aristocratic class of the surrounding countryside.[47]

For him, as for Michael Hope, and as for London-based comfortable middle-class individuals in the Essex archive, the basic sense of social identity was of belonging to the upper reaches of a broad social stratum without clear geographical limits, sandwiched between a genuine but tiny upper class and a variety of lesser, mainly working-class social groups below. This upper-middle-class stratum was linked together by schooling as well as by other aspects of lifestyle: even in Bolton the genteel education purveyed had an ethos and aim very similar to that dispensed in suburban London.[48] Also, when this emerging *national* upper middle class gathered together in new London-based institutions these were not markedly biased against the provincial representatives: Michael Hope used his impeccable BBC accent to do business in London as well as in Birmingham, and Paul

Vaughan's British Medical Association was a happy hunting ground for formidable provincial doctors.[49] For the upper middle class and in particular for its élites, then, divisions between the provinces and London came to count for less and less. Broadcasting, which affected the middle class earliest and most thoroughly, played an important role in this process: the fostering of a common culture compatible with persisting local customs had more impact than did the irritation caused by the resemblance of the announcers' accents to those of educated southerners.[50] Similarly, the interwar upper middle class proved more successful than its Victorian and Edwardian predecessors in avoiding partisan and sectarian tensions: 'Although it was generally assumed (not always correctly) that everyone was a Conservative, politics were usually avoided, as was religion.'[51] These self-denying ordinances diminished the disruptive potential of differences which, before the First World War, had often separated provincial middle-class individuals from their metropolitan equivalents. Thus the participation of key members of the upper middle class in the Second World War's fostering of national culture reinforced previous trends.[52]

What seems to have emerged by mid-century, then, was not so much a middle class in which London dominated the provinces but an increasingly geographically unified middle class in which London institutions and fashions set the pace but to which the provinces made a major contribution. Distinct provincial influence declined in the face of the provinces' interwar difficulties and the growing impact of national forces,[53] but the provincial upper middle class was better integrated into national élites than before – an integration which built upon the pre-1914 assertiveness of regional urban élites as well as their residual interwar strengths.

There remained, of course, enormous diversity and considerable inequality within the middle class and even within its élites: for example, occupational divisions such as those between professionals and managers may even have become more marked during the interwar years.[54] But these divisions – represented, admittedly, in different proportions, tilted in favour of London – were found throughout urban Britain. Moreover, the London and south-eastern middle class suffered from many of the problems affecting its provincial counterparts, including the declining willingness of wealthy people to stand for their local councils.[55] Also, while London had far more wealthy individuals than did provincial towns, the provinces continued to have enough to make reasonably equal interaction possible.

In the mid-twentieth century British middle class, as in its earlier counterparts, London played a special role. However, it seems that – due to factors such as rapidly accelerating improvements in communication and to growing homogeneity in speech, education and outlook – this special role was even less socially divisive than before. By the 1950s middle-class Britons of a certain level of resources – people such as Sir Raymond Streat, successively secretary of the Manchester Chamber of Commerce and chairman of the Cotton Board – moved almost effortlessly between London and provincial towns and back again.[56] The upper middle classes of Scotland and Northern Ireland – and, perhaps, Wales – combined this ability to move effectively in metropolitan circles with even greater cultural confidence than their colleagues from the English Midlands and north.[57] By the late 1940s, for many upper-middle-class men and women throughout the United Kingdom, residual regional tensions mattered far less than did the perceived threat from common enemies such as 'the growing power of the trade unions and general flattening-out of British society which denied them the respect (and the domestic servants) they'd been brought up to believe was their due'.[58]

How well this new British upper-middle-class equilibrium of mid-century survived the further social, economic and political changes of the next fifty years – especially the last twenty with their deindustrialization, ruthless centralization and southern-accented Thatcherism – would be a subject for another essay.[59] If such a study confirmed a recent acceleration of post-1945 centralizing trends there would be a nice irony – reflecting the many achievements of the Victorian and Edwardian provincial middle class, and the unifying interwar trends to which they contributed – in the fact that the process was presided over by the daughter of the mayor of an East Midlands market town.

## CHAPTER 13

# SERVICE, LOYALTY AND LEADERSHIP:

THE LIFE TALES OF BRITISH COAL MASTERS AND THE CULTURE OF THE MIDDLE CLASS, c. 1890–1950[1]

MICHAEL DINTENFASS

For many years two great questions have governed the history of the British middle class after 1832. Did those Britons who were merchants, manufacturers and professionals emulate the beliefs and behaviours of the landed aristocracy and gentry and subordinate themselves to the rural élite in politics and policy? Were those who lived neither from land nor manual labour divided from one another along occupational, regional and sectarian lines, with a predominantly financial and commercial, southern and Anglican middle class at odds with, and generally superior to, a largely industrial, northern and Nonconformist middle class? These two questions in turn have derived their power from the presumption that answers to them would solve the two most significant problems in modern British historiography: the sources of Britain's political stability during a century when revolution and upheaval were commonplace elsewhere and the causes of Britain's relatively slow economic growth after its precocious industrialization and mid-nineteenth-century dominance in inter-national markets.

Historical attempts to make sense of the experience of the British middle class have by and large proceeded along two lines. Firstly, a great deal of scholarly work has been done on what we might call the social history of the economic life of the middle class – research concerned, that is, with how those who received neither rents nor wages earned their livelihoods, with the sizes of those livelihoods, and with how they were spent. The second approach has concentrated on the social history of the cultural life of the middle class. Here attention has focused on the public, and especially the voluntary, initiatives of professionals, manufacturers and merchants in Britain's rapidly expanding cities and on the spaces and activities allocated to middle-class men and women respectively.[2]

Both genres have contributed mightily to the restoration of the middle class to a proper place in nineteenth- and twentieth-century British history. Neither singly nor together, however, have they resolved the questions that inspired them, and the nature of the middle class's relationship to the landed élite as well as the internal coherence of the middle class itself remain hotly contested matters. Perhaps it could not have been otherwise. The social history of the middle class's economic life and the social history of its cultural life have both endeavoured to recover the interior world of manufacturers, merchants and professionals – the beliefs, values and unspoken assumptions which they held dear – by drawing inferences from inherently ambiguous activities. The purchase of a stately home might well have signified a desire to assimilate to the aristocracy, but a house in the country could have served equally well for a decidedly bourgeois pattern of business and recreation. Participation in a society to promote a circulating library might have been part of a bid to contest the authority of the local landowners, but it could just as easily have betokened an earnest desire to spread the bounty of civilization more widely.

This essay takes a different approach to the history of the British middle class. Instead of charting the activities of those who lived neither from land nor labour, it asks how such people understood their activities. Instead of looking at the lives they led, I look at the stories they told about their lives. My concern, in other words, is with the meanings that members of the middle class themselves attached to what we have come to think of as middle-class occupations.

The men whose autobiographical and biographical writings form the subject of this essay all passed their working lives in the service of the British coal industry. They were, in fact, among the most prominent participants in the trade, the *Colliery Guardian*, the leading journalistic voice of the mining world, featuring them as 'Men of Note in the British Coal Industry'.[3] Born between 1865 and 1888, they entered coalmining in the two decades before the First World War. By the middle 1920s they had proven themselves persons of consequence in colliery management, coal-related government service and mining education.

The life stories analysed here were composed when their authors were in the fullness of their careers. The earliest was published in 1927/8 and the latest in 1955/6. With one exception, all of these texts appeared in the periodical press of the coal trade itself. None was conceived as an objective 'warts and all' portrayal of its subject. Each was a commemoration of a prominent mining man. Together they disclose what the best and brightest of British coal thought a career in the industry was all about.

Both the content and the form of these narratives of industrial distinction demonstrate that for members of the mining middle-class service, loyalty and leadership were the keynotes of occupational life. The prominence of these motifs in memorials published decades apart and primarily for the edification of those active in coal makes it impossible to dismiss them as mere public relations exercises. The reality they represent is the ethic of industrial patriotism and civic commitment by which an important component of Britain's industrial middle class imparted meaning to lives passed in trade, and not the expediency of a particular political or economic moment. The imperative to active citizenship inscribed in the mining life histories authored by the leading figures in the business promoted the integration of industrialists with financiers, merchants, professionals and the landed élite, at the same time as it ensured that the position of the industrial middle class in these engagements was neither a deferential nor a subordinate one.

I

Let us begin with Sir R.A.S. Redmayne, perhaps the premier British mining engineer of the first half of the twentieth century. The son of a Tyneside alkali manufacturer, he attended the Durham College of Physical Science before serving his articles under William Armstrong, one of the great north-eastern colliery engineers of the nineteenth century. In the course of a career that extended over seven decades from the 1890s, Redmayne managed coal mines in Durham, Natal and Northumberland, was the first professor of mining at the University of Birmingham, the first chief inspector of mines at the Home Office, assistant to the coal controller during the First World War, chairman of the Imperial Mineral Resources Board and a freelance engineer whose practice, it was said, included most of 'the important legal or general mining consulting cases' between the wars and whose reputation was 'second to none'.[4] Along the way, Redmayne was also the managing director of two North Staffordshire colliery concerns, sat on the board of a South Wales coal company, and served as the director of a large British rope manufacturer. Throughout these different postings, Redmayne proved himself a staunch advocate of greater efficiency in mining, and in the debates after 1914 about how to improve the performance of the British coal industry he was a forceful proponent of colliery amalgamations, fuel conservation and the mechanization of extraction and haulage.

In 1942, at age seventy-seven, Redmayne published *Men, Mines, and Memories*, 'not an autobiography,' he insisted, 'but merely some swept leaves of memory-recollections and reflections concerning some of the happenings in a long, varied and active career – a record of incidents, which, it seemed, might prove of general interest'.[5] Looking back with the benefit of more than forty years' hindsight on the management of coal mines, he found the occupation in which he had spent the first phase of his working life to be a rewarding one. 'The life of a colliery manager,' he wrote, 'is extremely varied and interesting.' What made it so were the 'wide opportunities' it afforded 'for service to one's fellows. . . . Apart from the purely technical work which colliery management involved, there were schools to look after . . . the miners' cottages to inspect and repair . . . the farms to supervise . . . and Parish Council meetings to attend [as chairman and vice chairman]. There was also co-operation in the social-cum-educational life' of the miners, workmen's institutes to direct, lectures to arrange, and university extension courses to organize.[6]

For all that Redmayne emphasized the colliery manager's obligations to his community, he was not himself indifferent to money. He turned down the chief inspectorship of mines when it was first offered 'for its acceptance would entail a much greater sacrifice of income than I considered warrantable in the circumstances', and he relented only when the Home Secretary improved 'somewhat the financial conditions attaching to the post'. Similarly, he left the Imperial Mineral Resources Board because it 'absorbed the whole of my time and the emolument was inadequate to meet my requirements'.[7] Redmayne was none the less outspoken in his condemnation of acquisitiveness as a motive for action. It was, he said, 'one of the least admirable of human qualities'. 'Acquisitiveness of riches, worldly distinction, or of power, the acquirement of all . . . is frequently at the expense of friendship, and certainly tends towards depreciation of character.'[8]

The priority that Redmayne accorded service to society over the satisfaction of self-interest found ample expression in the gallery of eminent contemporaries with which he closed his recollections. The composition of the group of the great and the good whose pen portraits he presented there alone speaks volumes about the primacy of citizenship over entrepreneurship in Redmayne's understanding of the world. Fifteen of the twenty prominent figures whose acquaintanceship he documented had made their mark outside the confines of industry and trade. Twelve were politicians, among them two prime ministers, A.J. Balfour and Neville Chamberlain, and the seven home secretaries under whom Redmayne had served as the head of the mines inspectorate. The economist and civil servant Robert Giffen, the physiologist J.S. Haldane and J.M. Barrie, the creator of Peter Pan, also figured among the most remarkable men whom Redmayne had been privileged to know personally.

The five men with ties to industry among the contemporaries Redmayne chose to celebrate in print were the chemist J.T. Merz, his son Charles Merz, the eminent electrical engineer, Charles Parsons, inventor of the steam turbine, Robert Smillie, the Scottish trade unionist, and Austin Hopkinson, a manufacturer of coal-cutting appliances. There was not a single coal owner nor a single mining engineer on the list. In more than half a century in the British coal industry, Redmayne had not met a solitary figure connected with the business of raising and selling coal whose virtues he felt worthy of public notice. The best he could do was to endorse the tribute that Smillie, a president of the Miners' Federation of Great Britain, had paid to the Durham coal master A.F. Pease: a man of 'wide and kindly outlook', of 'high ideals and integrity'.[9]

Certainly Redmayne did not scorn commercial competence. Indeed, he judged J.T. Merz, whose accomplishments included a four-volume study of *The History of European Thought in the Nineteenth Century*, to have been 'a good man of business'.[10] It is clear, though, that Redmayne's idea of the good industrial life had much more to do with civic virtue than with operational efficiency or profitable balance sheets. Parsons, whose 'attainments in the world of invention and industry' Redmayne left to 'others much better qualified to discourse on' than himself, was 'in business . . . "straight as a die." He had, for instance, a hatred of secret commissions.'[11] About the younger Merz, a pioneer of electrical supply and railway electrification in Britain, an energetic promoter of electrical power the world over, and one of the great engineers in the early days of the electricity industry, Redmayne was concerned to emphasize his services to the state and the still greater service he might have done it. Before parliamentary committees 'he was a superb witness, calm and collected, and in his replies lucid, accurate, and penetrating'. 'He would have been supreme', Redmayne wrote of a man of exceptional industrial talent and accomplishment, 'as a Civil Servant had he entered the Government service.'[12] Smillie, the one figure among Redmayne's heroes who had been directly involved in the coal industry, gained his place in Redmayne's pantheon by virtue of his self-abnegation: 'he seemed devoid of ambition in the matter of personal advancement and acquisition of money. His one aim was the promotion of the interests of labour.'[13]

If self-denial was the essence of trade union leadership as Redmayne understood it, it was also the attribute he found most admirable in a businessman, as his portrait of Austin Hopkinson revealed. Redmayne first met Hopkinson, who turned out to be a friend for life as well as the long-time MP for the Mossley division of Lancashire, at the end of the First World War:

> when a tall soldierly figure stalked into my room at the Coal Control, a man unknown to me, dressed in khaki with a corporal's stripes. He was a cavalry man and had been right through the War. He informed me that in civil life he was a manufacturer of mechanical coal-cutting machinery and that he felt bound to call upon me to let me know that, although such action was against his own financial interests, he considered the course we had recently adopted at the production department of the Coal Control in requiring the collieries to obtain their coal-cutters from America in order to concentrate at home on the production of armaments was, in his opinion, the correct one in the circumstances and he hoped that adverse criticism would not deter us from sticking to it.[14]

For Sir R.A.S. Redmayne, one of the most successful and celebrated figures in the British coal trade in its last half century as a private enterprise, distinction in industry, it seems, meant serving the country and the community before the company.

## II

The Sir R.A.S. Redmayne who articulated an ethic of business citizenship was exceptional in his attainments, his literary inclinations, and his readiness to reflect philosophically on the conduct of industrial life. Most of his fellow men of coal were made of more practical stuff. Indeed, practicality was a virtue to which they readily paid homage. Thus G.P. Hyslop, the North Staffordshire mining engineer who managed the Madeley Collieries and sat on the board of Robert Heath and Low Moor Ltd, wrote in praise of HM Chief Inspector of Mines F.H. Wynne that 'he was distinguished by his practical outlook and thoroughness. He was no mere theorist, but sought facts and reality.'[15] The biographical essays that Britain's leading mining men undertook to write about one another were practical exercises. Occasioned by the deaths of coalmining friends and colleagues, these memoirs and appreciations were read at the meetings of Britain's regional institutes of mining engineers and then printed in the *Transactions of the Institution of Mining Engineers*. How did the understandings of industrial life to which they gave expression compare with the ideal of community service that informed Redmayne's account of his career and contemporaries?

The biographical tales that these eminent mining men told in their obituaries of their peers were woven out of three strands. The first consisted of the deceased's roots in the world of coal. G.P. Hyslop's appreciation of F.H. Wynne, for example, began with the late chief inspector's industrial genealogy. He 'came of a Mining family. His father, Richard H. Wynne, practised as a Mining Engineer in Staffordshire, and his grandfather, Thomas Wynne, was elected as Hon Member of the North Stafford Institute in 1873 and was one of the first group of Mines Inspectors appointed by the State.' Next these posthumous tributes surveyed the occupational histories of their subjects. Narrating the career of Robert Clive, Douglas Hay, managing director of the Barrow Barnsley Main Collieries, moved from Clive's apprenticeship with A.H. Leech, mining engineer of Wigan, and then T.Y. Greener, general manager of Pease and Partners, County Durham, to his sixteen years as the manager of Barber, Walker and Company's

Bentley Colliery and lastly to his secretaryship of the South Yorkshire Coal Owners' Association, in which capacity Clive spent the remaining twenty-two years of his life. The final basic element of these biographical constructions was an account of the deceased colleague's services on behalf of mining's professional societies. The consulting engineer, mineral valuer and colliery-company director Alexander Smith, whom the Black Country mining engineer Laurence Holland remembered, had been secretary of the South Staffordshire and East Worcestershire Institute of Mining Engineers for thirty-two years, president of its successor body the South Staffordshire and Warwickshire Institute, an active participant in the federation of the various regional institutes into the Institution of Mining Engineers, a vice-president of that organization and a member of the Institution of Civil Engineers.[16]

These almost ritualistic invocations of industrial lineages, mining-trade histories and voluntary-society activism worked implicitly to inscribe the men they memorialized within a community of coal. The presidential address that Dr J.S. Haldane, the scientist whose researches into human activity underground greatly advanced the understanding of miners' diseases and the development of safe working practices down the pits, delivered to the Institution of Mining Engineers in 1924/5, explicitly recognized the existence of just such a community, and it made loyalty to its members the first principle by which coal owners, mining engineers and colliery managers ought to live. It was, as J. Ivon Graham, Haldane's assistant director of the Mining Research Laboratory at the University of Birmingham, recalled in his brief life of Haldane, 'a philosophical address [and as such] unique in the Institution's history'. In it, Haldane 'emphasized comradeship as being the value which in reality embraces all the other values'. By comradeship he meant '"just action based on the placing of value upon the interests of neighbours. It carries with it respect, and the very highest kind of respect, for those who show it, whether they be rich or poor, known or unknown."' Lest all this be too abstract for his coal-hardened audience, Haldane explained that comradeship was '"part of the atmosphere of a British pit, and real pitmen seem always to carry some of it round with them"'.[17]

The comradeship that J.S. Haldane preached was a virtue that Britain's leading mining men found practised in the lives of some of their most distinguished contemporaries. It was at the heart of the eulogy that Douglas Hay delivered on behalf of Robert Clive. Clive was, Hay wrote, 'at all times prepared to go out of his way to help his brother Mining Engineers in the various difficult problems which faced them'. Comradeliness was also the benchmark by which Professor J.A.S. Ritson of the Royal School of Mines took the measure of Sir Henry Walker, like Wynne and Redmayne at one time head of the mines inspectorate. 'No Chief Inspector of Mines', he wrote:

> had so many friends among all classes of the Mining Industry. To the mine owners he was a strong and just administrator of the Mining Laws and Regulations; to the management he was a sound judge of mining practice and a personal friend willing to help, especially when trouble was in the offing; and by the miners' leaders he was respected to the full.[18]

The most practical expression of such a sense of responsibility to one's fellows in mining was a dedication to health and safety underground, and tributes to initiatives in this domain figured prominently in the narratives that members of this coal-trade élite composed about each other's careers. Indeed, comradeship of this kind added lustre to lives spent at quite different points across the spectrum of mining occupations. Where Laurence Holland told of the consulting engineer Alexander Smith's 'very active part in the formation of ambulance brigades and rescue-work in mines generally', Granville Poole of Armstrong College was attentive to how his colleague Professor W.M. Thornton had been 'impelled still further in his research to improve the safety of mining operations' by his investigation of the West Stanley Colliery explosion. Robert Clive's biographer recalled how this coal association official had 'virtually controlled the [Doncaster and District Rescue] Station, which is regarded as one of the most efficient in the country', as well as the 'important part' his experimental work played 'in solving the problem of dealing with gob-fires', while G.P. Hyslop's F.H. Wynne had been 'so transparent' in his methods and 'so frank and simple' in his character that he 'in no small degree . . . aided in the pursuit of safety in coal-mining' during his time in the mines inspectorate.[19]

The privileged place that loyalty to the trade occupied in the life stories that men of Britain's mining middle class told about their peers emerged with poignant clarity in the memoir that the Chief

Inspector of Mines F.H. Wynne published about his recently deceased friend Lord Cadman, the late chairman of the Anglo-Iranian Oil Company, in the 1941/2 volume of the *Transactions of the Institution of Mining Engineers*. The author and his subject had grown up together in the 'comparatively small and out-of-the-way mining township' of Silverdale in North Staffordshire. They had followed identical paths from the mining classes of the Staffordshire County Council Education Authority to the Durham College of Physical Science, the Silverdale Collieries, and the mines inspectorate. Their working lives diverged only when they were in their early thirties. While Wynne continued his climb to the top of the government service, Cadman left for the chair of mining at the University of Birmingham, from where he launched a most successful career in the British oil business. Wynne's obituary paid proper tribute to Cadman's 'great work', 'his activities in the world of petroleum and . . . his services to the State' (he had served on the Admiralty commission to the British government that reported on the Iranian oilfields in 1913 and had headed the Inter-Allied Petroleum Council during the First World War). The main point of Wynne's heartfelt appreciation, however, was that this great oilman had 'up to the last . . . remained faithful to Coal-mining'.[20]

## III

Leadership was the third virtue around which members of Britain's coalmining élite spun their stories of their colleagues' lives in the industry. We have seen something of this already in Laurence Holland's detailed account of the offices the company director Alexander Smith occupied at the top of the professional mining societies of the West Midlands and Smith's initiative in the creation of mine safety facilities in the region. Holland also recalled that Smith had been 'instrumental in bringing' the mining department of the University of Birmingham 'into being'. F.H. Wynne likewise remembered Lord Cadman's achievements at the head of the mining engineering profession. Noting that Cadman had begun a three-year stint as the president of the Institution of Mining Engineers 'when no more than 44 years of age', Wynne took pride in the leading part his lifelong friend had played 'in the movement to raise the status of membership of the Institution and its general prestige and authority'.

During his term in office, Wynne wrote, Cadman was chiefly responsible for 'two mile-stones in the history of the Institution'. He had established a 'joint Headquarters with the Institution of Mining and Metallurgy, with a common Secretariat', and he had inspired 'the movement for strengthening the bonds between the two mother Institutions and kindred Institutions in the Dominions and Indian Empire'.[21]

The biographers of Robert Clive – Professor W.M. Thornton and Sir R.A.S. Redmayne – were no less concerned to place their subjects at the forefront of the institutional life of British industry. The Clive to whom Douglas Hay paid tribute had 'guided the [South Yorkshire Coal Owners'] Association through a number of difficult problems' and had been president, treasurer and a member of the council of the Midland Institute of Mining Engineers. Professor Granville Poole's Thornton was twice chairman of the North-East Centre of the Institution of Electrical Engineers as well as president of the Association of Mining Electrical Engineers and the Institution of Electrical Engineers. 'The mere recapitulation of . . . [Redmayne's] many activities', J.A.S. Ritson assured readers of his memoir, 'would be too lengthy', but he none the less found space for his presidency of the Institution of Mining and Metallurgy, the Institution of Civil Engineers and, for thirty-three years from its foundation, the Institution of Professional Civil Servants.[22]

## IV

Where amidst this homage to service, loyalty and leadership did technological and managerial accomplishments fit into the obituaries that Britain's leading mining men penned about their compatriots in the trade? What did the authors of these appreciations have to say about the development of collieries, the founding or reshaping of mining enterprises, the introduction of new techniques, the enhancement of productivity and the generation of profits? Where, in short, did prominent figures from the industrial middle class place activities connected with the efficient raising and selling of coal in their rendering of mining careers?

Few, in fact, of these brief lives found space for their subjects' efforts on behalf of the business of coalmining. J.A.S. Ritson, for example, moved directly from the successful completion of Sir Henry Walker's apprenticeship to his admission to the mines inspectorate, passing over in silence the five years Walker spent managing the Liverton and Stanghow collieries. Nor were such references to managerial matters as appeared in these essays necessarily very substantial. Laurence Holland wrote expansively of Alexander Smith's 'large practice as a consulting engineer and valuer', his retention 'by many of the largest firms in the Midlands', his expertise 'in rating matters', and his appearances 'as an expert witness in a large number of important cases', but at no point did he give the reader any concrete idea of the actual deeds that had laid the foundation of Smith's repute.[23]

Where the life tales that British men of coal constructed in memory of their contemporaries in the industry did make a point of their contributions to private enterprise, it was as often as not for the sake of emphasizing their collegial qualities. Douglas Hay acknowledged that Robert Clive had pioneered modern mining practices in the deep seams of South Yorkshire while in charge of the Bentley Colliery and that 'the technical developments [he had] carried out' there 'attracted considerable attention', but he found it just as 'interesting to note that no less than twelve of these students [apprenticed under Clive at Bentley] attained important positions in the Mining Industry'. For J.A.S. Ritson, the importance of the nine years that Sir R.A.S. Redmayne dedicated to the management of the Seaton Delaval mines in Northumberland was that 'it was during this period that he mastered the Tyneside dialect and collected the repertoire of stories that afterwards delighted his friends'.[24]

## V

The narratives that members of Britain's coalmining élite fashioned about industrial life made responsibilities to private enterprise more a matter of good citizenship and good fellowship than good balance sheets. Indeed, the importance these tales attributed to the leadership of the trade's voluntary associations shows clearly that the men who composed them understood the assumption of public commitments to be an integral part of the discharge of workplace assignments. For these prominent members of Britain's industrial middle class, a career in coal was in the nature of a calling undertaken on behalf of mining's participants rather than a business whose fortunes depended on the efficiency with which the demands of employers, customers and clients were met.

The language of loyalty, service and leadership that these middle-class men of coal spoke was not simply the idiom of eulogy or the fraternal address of the brotherhood of mining engineers. It was also the discourse that the *Colliery Guardian*, the contemporary equivalent of mining's *Financial Times*, employed to present its 'Men of Note in the British Coal Industry' to their associates, competitors and subordinates in the business world of coal.[25] The language of citizenship to which the biographical appreciations that appeared in the *Transactions of the Institution of Mining Engineers* and Sir R.A.S. Redmayne's memoirs gave voice was the language of the British coal trade itself.

To be sure, a discourse of civic virtue was not unique to mining. In the languages of Millian liberalism, Nonconformity, a classically inspired idealism, liberal Anglicanism and Smilesian self-help, ethical action and citizenship were synonymous too, and those whose spoke in these accents included the owners and managers of other industries and the bankers, doctors, merchants, attorneys and clergymen whom we customarily designate the non-industrial middle class.[26] Thanks to the reformed public schools and ancient universities and to sermons, the monthlies and the quarterlies, the idioms in which 'the participatory values [of] the middle classes' found expression also entered into the vocabularies of the aristocracy and the gentry. The dialogue about distinction in coal, then, was just one of the many tributaries that fed the conversation about community betterment in which both the industrial and non-industrial middle class and the landed élite took part.[27]

The terms on which an R.A.S. Redmayne or a Laurence Holland, a G.P. Hyslop or a J.S. Haldane, or an F.H. Wynne or a Douglas Hay entered into such a pan-occupational, cross-class civic discourse would not have been those of deference or subordination. Such supine postures would hardly have been available to men who spoke as they did. The imperative they inscribed at the heart of industrial employment was the obligation to serve the community. The code of conduct their ethic of civic responsibility enunciated was an inherently activist, self-assertive one. The industrialist for whom eminence inhered in the stewardship of his trade and those dependent on it, rather than in the productivity-conscious administration of mining or manufacturing assets, would not have surrendered the *civitas* to those who merely owned land, worked bankers' hours or hung out their own shingles. Therefore, any explanation of the stability of British politics or the slow growth of its economy that puts the industrial middle class at the centre of these narratives will have to proceed on the basis of the ideals of service, loyalty and leadership that made lives devoted to industry meaningful.

# SNATCHING DEFEAT FROM THE JAWS OF VICTORY:

THE LAST POST OF THE OLD CITY FINANCIAL ELITE, 1945–95

PAUL THOMPSON

For much of the postwar era, and perhaps most of all in the 1980s, the financial success of the City of London was acclaimed by politicians and economists as a model of what Britain could achieve in the international market and had signally failed to achieve in industry. The City's success was portrayed as dynamic and modern, the fruit of a bold policy of financial liberalization which put London ahead of even its toughest rival, New York.

Such a self-congratulatory view is no longer possible in the late 1990s, following the near-mortal crisis of Lloyd's and the humiliating collapse of its two vanguard merchant banks, Barings and Warburgs. Nor was it ever more than partially true. The City did certainly make a very striking comeback after 1950, reclaiming its lost place in the international currency markets and leading some crucial innovations, above all, the eurodollar in the late 1950s and currency swaps in the 1980s. And Lloyd's was an important pioneer of reinsurance. But against that, one must set important failures to develop crucial new markets, most notably in allowing Chicago to take the lead in futures. The gains need also to be set in the balance with some unnecessary losses of once-strong commodity markets – in coal, fish, cotton, corn, wool and tea – and in the collapse of the unique Baltic Exchange international market in shipping space. Even Lloyd's failed to maintain its share of the world insurance market during these decades. We also have to ask why the City's innovation remained so narrowly based, centred on the merchant banks and Lloyd's. How was it that the London Stock Exchange failed, even into the 1980s, to compete internationally, its members preferring to remain a shrinking exclusive British club? Why did none of the great British clearing banks take the lead in becoming a multi-purpose global finance house on the German and American model?

Part of the answer must of course lie in the changing international economic context of London. Positively, the City's innovators were able to make the most of London's double relationship with America and Europe, creating a new informal dealing space as if they were operating from an island which was Europe's prime offshore finance haven. But negatively, the inexorable decline of the British manufacturing economy was all the time undercutting the City's home base. By the 1980s the local capital resources of London were dwarfed by those of Japan, and volume of business on the London stock market had shrunk to a mere tenth of daily activity in New York and Tokyo. Increasingly, therefore, the City was having to win business from outside its home context if it was even to stand still.

On the other hand, the historic economic success of Britain has lain precisely in a repeated ability to seize new outside markets in this way. Indeed, the City's postwar successes showed that this was still possible. But why were those successes ultimately insufficient? The answer, I believe, is to be found not only in changing economic structures but also in continuing influences from the historical cultural structure of the City.

Given its indisputable historical importance, there has been remarkably little historical study of the City of London's financial élite in the twentieth century. David Kynaston's admirable social historical volumes provide an overview which currently does not reach beyond 1914, and Youssef Cassis's meticulous statistical study of the City élite stops in the same year. For the period beyond that there is little research to draw on beyond a two-part article on merchant banking dynasties by Michael Lisle-Williams, which covers the whole period from 1850 until 1960; and the admirably shrewd contemporary pages published by Anthony Sampson in successive editions of *The Anatomy of Britain*.[1] There are also useful detailed histories of two merchant banks, one leading stockbroker, and of the Bank of England.[2]

The City does feature in a number of grand historical debates about the role of culture in British economic decline, most notably articulated by Martin Wiener, and recently further popularized by Will Hutton. Although these works, and others which explore notions of the impact of 'gentlemanly capitalism' on an imperial scale, single out the City as a bastion of such 'gentlemanly' economic culture – a position with which basically I certainly agree – they provide remarkably little research-based information on the City to back their interpretations.[3] The only major dissenting voice in this historical discussion is that of Bill Rubinstein, and his unsubstantiated depiction of the post-1945 City as internationally 'universally respected' for its 'total probity' seems even more dangerously speculative.[4]

One reason why experienced researchers are able to sketch the economic culture of the City in such a cavalier fashion is that there are strangely few published voices from within the City against which to test their interpretations. It is very striking how few leaders of the City have left written autobiographies. For the postwar period the three most noteworthy autobiographical works are by Russell Taylor, a modest figure who worked for two City merchant banks in the 1960s; Michael Lewis, American author of the exposé *Liar's Poker*, who only worked in London for two years and not for a British firm; and the clearly atypical Nick Leeson, whose rogue dealing in futures proved the downfall of Barings, almost the last-remaining family-controlled great merchant bank in the City.[5] Thus not a single one of the major City figures of the post-1945 years has left his own story. It was awareness of the lack of significant autobiographical documentation by this key British élite which inspired the National Life Story Collection in 1987 to launch the project on which this essay and my book with Cathy Courtney, *City Lives*, are both based.[6]

The project's methods were based on the oral history approach described in my book *The Voice of the Past*: that is to say, in-depth semi-structured life story interviewing. The core people we interviewed were men – all men – who had come into the City in the 1940s and 1950s, and were now at the top and close to retirement – indeed many of them have since been succeeded in their posts. At their recommendation we also recorded a few men of the older generation, already retired, who had been important models for them. As a contrast, and to get a sense of recent change from the inside too, we also recorded some younger City people, including women, who are now on their way up.

In many ways, interviewing top City financiers is just like life story interviewing anyone else: at the beginning they are usually not confident that their memories can be of any real value, but once started they become highly involved and set aside far more time than they had imagined possible: typically at least three or four hours and sometimes more than twenty. They vary from the laconic to the garrulous, and from those at one extreme who never forget the need to protect confidential information to a few at the other end of the spectrum who tell confidential stories before even being prompted. One sensed that it helped many of them that the sponsorship for their interviews came from within the City: it was almost as if they were making a record for the club. A few were reflective intellectuals and nearly all were quick-thinking with relatively full and clear memories. As always with this type of retrospective information, what they told us was a mixture of myth and direct eye-witness information, and both were of significant historical interest.

The 'myths' were stories, not necessarily factually untrue, but important not because of the facts they conveyed but as symbols and interpretations of the profound changes which have taken place in the City during their working lives. The City in the late 1940s was a wholly white British male workplace, governed by unwritten rules of trust and good conduct, in which knowing people and exchanging inside information was one of the keys to success. This was why even dealers spent a lot of their time and energy not strictly working but joking, drinking and socializing. The City in those days is nostalgically remembered as 'fun'. Caryl Churchill caught the tone of the typical City memories perfectly in *Serious Money*: 'The stock exchange was a village street./ You strolled about and met your friends./ Now we never seem to meet. . . .'[7]

The first clear signs of postwar fundamental changes in the City did not come until the late 1950s when Warburgs and Hambros led the creation of the eurodollar market outside the well-regulated established banking system. Siegmund Warburg himself is especially remembered as a harbinger of change and he was always seen as a newcomer – although he had trained in London at Rothschilds and had brought his bank to the City in 1933 – principally because he was both Jewish and German. Warburg nevertheless successfully pushed his merchant bank to the very top: for which he was viewed as 'an upsetter of the establishment', and was long ridiculed as 'a squirt, an upstart', for his foreign accent and the 'Prussian' style in which he ran his office. 'Jokes were not cracked at Warburgs – not more than once, anyhow.'[8]

The epic British Aluminium battle of 1958, in which Warburg trounced the whole British City establishment with a successful hostile takeover, is thus seen as a turning-point, a key victory for the new seriousness. His principal younger British rivals saw that they too had to become more serious. This is why they distance themselves in their memories not only from Warburg but also from earlier ancestral figures who had set the tone in the 1930s and 1940s: men who did little work and made little effort, read cattle herd books rather than account books, refused to converse with other senior partners, and left for home in the early afternoon. They uttered proverbial advice like, 'Buy something and sit on it'; or, 'Never read a balance sheet. . . . Look at the Board.'[9] Most of the generation of men at the top in the 1980s, by contrast, felt that they had earned their positions through serious work. They were nevertheless overwhelmingly an élite by inheritance. Although at the extremes, as we shall see, their paths were diverse, they were as a body solidly upper middle class or above. Only six had not been brought up in a very comfortable home with servants and some with substantial staffs: Sir John Baring recalls a cook, kitchen maid, scullery maid, butler, footman, housemaids, lady's maid and governess. A mere three had no more than the bare elementary school education which was typical of the national population as a whole: three-quarters had been to public school and over a quarter to Eton. The proportion going to Eton is probably more than double that for the British business élite as a whole in this period.[10] A little over half of them had gone on to university, a proportion probably typical of the national business élite, although well below the typical European level which is more than three-quarters.[11] At university, moreover, only a few performed well, and more importantly, they studied subjects with no direct relevance to business, such as classics or history. Indeed, only three entered the City with qualifications directly relevant to work in a finance capital, either in law or insurance.

It is clear too that at that time studying finance or even accounting would not have proved much help in opening City doors. In many City quarters there was a deep suspicion of professional trained men. For example, at the London Metal Exchange, when Francis Holford joined Rudolf Wolff in 1967 he found that his colleagues regarded accountants as 'parasites' and some of the partners were so 'anti-accountant' that at first he could not function at all. 'For the first six months I wasn't allowed to see the books or the accounts. . . . It was all considered so private and intimate to the partners that – I mean even the bank manager didn't see the firm's accounts.' And even twenty years later, when David King, an accountant, was appointed as its executive chairman, he was the first of its senior staff to hold a professional qualification.[12]

The service professionals in law, accountancy and insurance at the fringe of the City always had to become qualified but our main generation usually did this while on the job. Only some of the lawyers took university law degrees first and then completed their training in an office. These professionals stand out as trained experts from the true financiers we interviewed, none of whom had any formal qualifications. None had gone to business school or understood accounting. And, in contrast to the younger generation, only one boasted a mathematics degree. The most important exception is a group of seven leading bankers who had taken degrees in economics – but significantly, rather than full economics degrees, these were mixed degrees, typically combined with politics or history, at Oxbridge, with tutors who were often themselves rising stars, such as Harold Wilson. It would seem that here the content of the degree was less important than its context. Such attitudes proved extraordinarily resilient in the postwar City, despite the growing evidence of economic success by the much better-trained west European business élite. Even when Ross Jones came as a banker in the late 1970s, 'three A levels was considered overqualified'.[13]

This point of view was not simply naive. It reflected widely held views of the skills needed in financial business. Thus the distinguished Winchester and Oxford classicist Sir Jeremy Morse, as chairman of Lloyds Bank in the 1980s, maintained that his education had given him the:

> skills of logical thinking. . . . Banking is mainly to do with customers and people, and such figuring as there is in it is fairly elementary, and my School Certificate maths . . . it's perfectly adequate for straight banking with the customer.[14]

City men saw the two key skills needed as, on the one hand, finding and retaining clients and, on the other, dealing.

Some tried to explain the techniques required for effectively handling clients. Thus Warburg emphasized the interpersonal skills of listening to them and feeding back their own ideas; Lord Benson the centrality of good communication in clear written English. Most picked up the techniques on the job. Gareth Lewis recounts his discovery that Americans would talk insurance business any time, unlike the British: 'playing golf, anywhere. Quite an important spot is the locker room, where you change your shoes and one thing or another. . . . That's where you might make a friend.' Conversely Americans who came to work in London banking, like Charles McVeigh in the 1970s, would gradually realize that over the double-length English lunch, even when business was not being mentioned, opportunities were likely to be sized up: 'They were assessing whether they could rely on them, whether they were men of integrity, and whether the chemistry between the guest and yourself was right and would lead to a worthwhile business relationship.' Eating well could be good for the firm as well as for the digestion.[15]

If professional qualifications were thought unnecessary for bankers, it is hardly surprising that for dealers they were not even discussed. Direct dealing demanded a combination of genuine physical stamina, a thrusting personality, and an ability to calculate very fast. Especially before the spread of pocket calculators in the 1960s, a quick mind for calculations was a tremendous advantage. Thus one senior banker first made his mark in the family bank through dealing in international currency over the telephone, with one phone in each hand: the distance and the time taken to communicate with the operator gave the space for someone 'quick enough' to buy or sell at good prices. Precisely the same mental quickness was thought the key skill for starting as an underwriter. Peter Miller recalled how:

> You had to learn to translate an underwriter's quotation at 18/3*d* which is 0.9125% into that percentage, and multiply it out in your mind, to get the answer of how much money he was wanting, without any use of calculators. . . . Because otherwise, if you went to an underwriter and got a quotation, you couldn't, in discussion with him, assess at once, if you had to, whether it was good, bad, or indifferent.

Older City men feel wistful that such mental agility no longer counts for much: as one leading merchant banker put it, 'the back of an envelope is not popular now'.[16] Thus once again, skill was earlier seen as much more a question of personality than of paper training.

In tune with this spirit, until the 1980s none of our élite entered the City through formally applying for an advertised post and being interviewed to establish their job qualifications. They were taken on for unadvertised posts with at best informal interviews at which the topics ranged from cricket to T.S. Eliot, but avoided direct discussion of finance. Most of them were in fact following a family path. Half were introduced to the City by their fathers, and indeed many of them had been taken to see the office or even the bank's gold bars as children. Derek Walker, who followed his father as secretary of the Baltic Exchange, said: 'I was born into the Business as it were.' Altogether two-thirds had kin in the City, and some indeed had a great many of them: Gareth Lewis had at one time thirteen uncles and cousins all working at Lloyd's.[17]

There were, however, three other routes into the postwar City which brought in different types of recruit. The first, which required no specific financial experience of any kind, was to be appointed straight to the top in later middle age after a career in national or local politics: for example Lord Boardman, who became Chairman of the National Westminster giant clearing bank at the age of sixty-five – although he was subsequently forced to resign in the face of the bank's difficulties – and Robin Leigh-Pemberton, Governor of the Bank of England, had been leading Conservative figures nationally and on the Kent County Council respectively. In a rather similar way, at a lower level there were City niches for retired army officers: thus Peter Wildblood found his way into the Sugar Association through a former commanding officer of his regiment. He describes his first job there as 'a sort of grade three staff officer type of appointment in terms of application skills'.[18] It is symptomatic of the whole character of the postwar City that the first Governor of the Bank with financial qualifications, Sir Gordon Richardson, was not appointed until 1973, and right through to the end of the period it was not regarded as essential that this principal of all City posts should be held by a professional.

The second path was meritocratic. This was typically followed by boys from the less comfortable middle-class backgrounds, who had been educated at provincial grammar schools and went on to university and also, more often than entrants by the other routes, to professional training. They could join branch offices of the great clearing banks or the national insurance institutions like the Prudential, sometimes using local family influence to get an initial foothold, and then work their way up through these immense pyramidal administrative hierarchies to enter the City in much later years, already near the top. Examples include Sir Brian Corby, chief executive of the Prudential before he became head of the CBI, or Sir John Quinton, who first worked in a Norfolk branch of Barclays where his father was manager, and eventually became chairman of the entire bank. A rather similar opportunity was provided by the Bank of England itself, which below its highest levels was organized on the competitive civil service model with entrance examinations. In practice the examinations were little more than literacy tests, and what mattered more was getting a personal nomination from a member of the Bank's Court. However, this did not always require an intimate connection. The future Governor O'Brien, for example, was nominated because his father, a local government administrator, had regularly played cricket with one of the Baring family.[19]

Undoubtedly the rarest path to the top started at the bottom, from one of the poor working-class homes in inner London which not only provided most of the City's messenger boys but also, much more rarely, some of its successful dealers. Yet it was difficult even for a successful dealer to win through to the topmost level. 'It's all right having barrow boys doing the dealing – they're good at it, it's what they understand', one senior banker explained recently, 'but higher up, you've got to have people who are at ease in industrialists' drawing-rooms.'[20] Nevertheless, some did succeed. Among them was Jack Spall, an Edmonton bus conductor's son, who came in as an East India merchant's 'gofer', seized a lucky chance to start coffee dealing, and later switched to silver, rising to the top as a bullion dealer. Another was Leonard Toomey, a leading underwriter at Lloyd's, whose only family connection with the City was that his father, an Irish stonemason, helped to reconstruct the Bank – 'there's a lot of stone in that'.[21]

Along with different paths into the City came different underlying attitudes to the purpose of work there. They also helped to shape whether these entrants to the City workforce were likely to prove innovative or not. In upper-class households it was not the custom for fathers to discuss money matters with their wives or children, and they were in any case more often than not away. For a boy, going shooting might provide one of the few chances of being close to his father; and later too, if he followed him into the City, it was often in a spirit of 'fun' and adventure. Such men were likely to believe that a sporting chance was worth risking. A very different atmosphere was imbibed by Sir Brian Corby in his lower middle-class Methodist family which, by contrast, imbued him with a 'respect for other people and prudence' and which he carried appropriately into the Prudential.[22]

A man from a background of real poverty like Leonard Toomey, on the other hand, found his first job at Lloyd's through a tip-off when he was a West End club page-boy, and he worked his way up there, fired by his fear of slipping back into the destitution of his childhood: 'the terror of ever reverting back to it, nothing else'. He remembers those times when as a child he was refused food on tick at the corner shop: 'sometimes he'd say, "no", because you'd run up too many debts on the slate. And you'd have to slink out of the shop. It marked me. It's marked me for the rest of my life.'[23]

Broadly speaking, except in one respect the paths into the City had changed little for the younger generation born in the 1950s and 1960s, even though the balance of social origin may have been shifting a little. The big change was in the entry of women into genuine financial work from the early 1970s onwards. But recruits continued to come from a very diverse social range. Thus among the women, Valerie Thompson was the daughter of an East End market greengrocer and pub singer, who learnt her basic skills on the market stalls: 'trading apples and oranges is not too dissimilar from trading securities: the principles are the same as in the City. They're perishable goods, and if you don't sell them today you've lost everything – that's how I learnt to assess risk.' She started into City business as a telex operator. Philippa Rose by contrast first fell in love with the City through visiting her father's office and gazing at all the important-looking marriageable men in suits. And just as in the 1940s Sir Kenneth Kleinwort was taken to see the family bank vaults and was 'fascinated to try to lift a gold bar', so a quarter of a century later Ann Smith was 'taken to see the gold' as a child visiting her father's office at the Bank of England: 'it was a fantastic spectacle, thousands of gold bars gleaming yellow'.[24]

Once started in the City, the new recruit was expected to pick up techniques on the job. Firms did not run training schemes. At most they expected new staff to circulate from department to department, staying just long enough to grasp the workings of each. Sir John Baring remembered being 'put through the mill, put round all the various departments. Excruciatingly dull some of them were. . . . You learnt by sitting next to whoever it was.'[25] There clearly is a parallel in being 'put through the mill' in the similar insistence during this period that recruits for industrial management, and especially 'crown princes' in family firms, should work for a period on the shop floor. Or indeed, with serving one's time as a fag at Eton. When Lord Cromer, heir to Barings and future Governor of the Bank of England, started his City career, it was as a messenger boy.[26] If these customs offered little training, they did at least ensure that those who reached the top had some notion of what it was like to work below. They also provided ritual passages in the gaining of masculine power: rituals, interestingly, which were extended to the first high-flying women who penetrated this male redoubt.

In many other City firms the learning process was even more abrupt. Typically, new staff were simply left to pick up their new trades as best they could. When Murray Lawrence started as an underwriter at Lloyd's, the head of his syndicate made sure he had a desk to sit at and that he had met the others in the room, and then simply told him, 'Good luck, well good luck my boy, get on with it, and do what you can.' At Lloyd's, as Murray found for himself, 'you learnt how to negotiate by listening to people'. More recently, in just the same spirit, when Ann Smith was set to sell securities for a Japanese house in 1985, 'I'd never been taught how to read a balance sheet. . . . There isn't any training. I was just given a telephone.'[27]

Even so, once started our main generation, with very few exceptions, remained for long years loyal to the same firms. Seven got to the top as chairmen of the firms which they had originally entered at the start of their working lives in the City, and scarcely any moved more than twice over forty years. They are quite different from the competitively footloose young of the 1980s, like Smith, who worked for four different firms in five years. Up to the 1970s, partly because trading was so personal, it was regarded as unacceptable to take one's clients to a new employer. But in return for long loyalty, firms then offered secure and lasting jobs. Today they can no longer do this even if they wish to. Peter Spira, Deputy Chairman of NatWest, doubted the chances of long-term loyalty when 'you don't know whether the firm you are joining will be there in x years time'.[28]

When the older generation in the City evaluate the principal changes since 1945 they stress two above all: the decline of trust, and the opening of the City to outsiders. The two are organically connected. Immediately after 1945 the City finance workforce was not only white and male, but in the wake of victory more proudly 'English' than it had been earlier. George Nissen, Chairman of IMRO, describes how Smith Brothers were frozen out of the gilt market because 'they were strongly Jewish and regarded as rather spivvy. . . . They were regarded as outsiders.'[29] The Stock Exchange in particular was in its most insular phase, with an ageing and declining membership. The London Stock Exchange had originally been proudly open to all comers. But from the 1890s onwards, foreigners could only become members after seven years of residence; from 1918 Germans, Austrians and other former enemies were ruled out altogether; and so from 1936 were women. In the 1960s – by when half the members were aged over fifty, membership was little more than half of what it had been fifty years earlier, and the banning of foreign members meant that its international role had slipped away – proposals to admit both women and foreigners were roundly defeated. The members only gave way and lifted both bans under heavy government pressure between 1971 and 1973. Why were they so resistant to change?

The Stock Exchange, and also Lloyd's, had essentially become clubs where old public schoolboys could remain boys. The Stock Exchange had long called itself 'the House', as if the members were still part of a public school.[30] Sir Peter Averill Daniell describes the typical larking:

> There was a jobber who used to sit underneath a pillar, he sat there, and nearly every day he was reading a paper. And somebody would light it and the whole thing would go up in smoke, and he would be furious, and everybody danced round him and got frightfully amused. And then if a stranger came in, everybody shouted '1400', and he had his trousers removed and was bundled out of the house.[31]

At Lloyd's also Terence Higgins recalls much:

> larking around . . . like rolling blotting paper and lobbing to your neighbour's box, or – it was not unknown at the time for either a broker or an underwriter in the box to drop a stinkbomb somewhere and cause a disturbance. And if anybody made a noise – a loud guffaw or dropped a pile of books – everyone in the underwriting boxes would pick up their pen and hammer away rat-tat-tat-rat on their metal lampshades. You can imagine,

hundreds of lampshades being banged by pens. I mean it's so childish, so schoolboyish; but everybody did it.[32]

Given this atmosphere, not surprisingly, many Stock Exchange members felt 'passionately . . . that it was quite inappropriate for women to subject themselves to the rough and tumble of life on the floor', the 'scramble' in the 'hurly-burly' crowd. Some of the brokers did indeed make life very nasty for the pioneers, sticking things on their clothes, assaulting them with sexual innuendo and cruel nicknaming.[33]

Despite such attitudes, these young women fought through, and their presence has irrevocably changed the texture of the City's working culture. Even though they may come from similar homes to their masculine peers, the City can no longer sustain itself as the same type of club. More than at any time in the past, for both men and women the City has opened itself to careers based primarily on talent rather than on connection.

There is, however, one crucial problem arising from the waning of the power of connection. For work in finance, the club's greatest strength is that it allows easy trust. Fraud and crime were not big issues in the City of the 1950s. Key information was taken on trust. Thus before 1979 all Stock Exchange contracts were made orally, and only confirmed on paper the following day: 'The next morning, at a place called Blossom's Inn, all the clerks used to assemble and they used to check up and say, "Now I did 500 shares of ICI with you, didn't I?"' In the same spirit, although ultimately very large sums were at stake, the Bank of England simply relied on the word of the merchant bankers. Kleinworts, for example, as Lord Limerick recalls, never published profit information beyond the bare bones required of an Exempt Private Company:

As a young accountant I used to go with the General Manager along to the Bank of England, to see the Head of the Discount Office, and he'd say, 'How's business?' And we'd say, 'Well, quite good. We've added a few new good accounts, and the size of the balance sheet has expanded. . . .'

He'd say, 'How about trading? What sort of year?' . . . And we'd say, 'Well, perhaps it was a little better than last year.' And that was really the sum total of the information that he got. Underlying this informal relationship was the unwritten but vital expectation that we would tell the Bank immediately of the first sign of trouble. And in a simpler world this worked very well.[34]

It was not that there were no irregularities then: there certainly were. But they would be dealt with privately. The key point was that there was order. This was possible because the City was made up of enclosed circles where most people knew each other well. One of the most powerful of these circles was that of old Etonians. It was not just a matter of connections. Within each club the old City motto, 'My word is my bond' – which goes back to controversy over dealings in stock futures in the eighteenth century[35] – was enforced through blackballing those who failed to conform. 'Good Etonian standards means a total trust', as Michael Verey put it. 'During my time in the City, those who hadn't been to Eton were striving for Eton standards and the Eton ethos dominated from Kim Cobbold, Governor of the Bank of England, downwards.' So at the heart of the City was the 'inner circle' who 'saw that everything was properly run and orderly and if anyone misbehaved, they got rapped'. If there was a crisis, they simply 'rang each other up and fixed everything'.[36]

It was also, it must be added, a way of protecting financiers from each other: of limiting competition. Anthony Sampson noted in the early 1960s that there was:

a thick web of 'gentlemen's agreements' arranging for banks, insurance companies or lawyers not to steal each other's business, and the phrase 'it's not done' is always lurking to frighten the newcomer and console the mediocre.[37]

Antony Hornby, senior partner from 1954 until 1970 of Cazenove, the most distinguished of all stockbroking firms, issued several memoranda to his colleagues insisting how they should not be 'unduly mercenary. Obviously one wants to make money, but we are not greedy. . . . One must be generous as well as competitive.'[38] Even in the 1970s Peter Wildblood found his new job as secretary of the Sugar Association was like becoming:

the secretary of a golf club. It was very pleasant. . . . There were a very small number of companies, perhaps dominated by four or five companies, who had all been around a long time, and they all knew each other. It was I suppose quite a gentlemanly commercial business in those days. And people resolved things very much in a friendly way.[39]

In the end, however, this self-protecting world was to disintegrate spectacularly. Such clubbish City organizations – from the Sugar Association to the Stock Exchange – sooner or later had to choose between opening up to international competition or shrinking into commercial insignificance. Some, like the Baltic, preferred just to die comfortably. Most did try, although often too late, to change. Very soon they found that the new values of uncontrolled open competition were incompatible with their traditional system based on trust. Faith in oral bonds disintegrated spectacularly in the 1980s, with the highly publicized trials for Barlow Clowes' bondwashing, Guinness insider dealing, and Maxwell's pension thefts. Perhaps most wounding of all, because it had been the ultimate symbol of London's trustworthiness, was the internal dispute between 'names' and underwriters at Lloyd's.

Lloyd's draws its risk capital from the commitment of individual 'names' to unlimited personal liability for claims: there were six thousand of them in the 1960s but over 30,000 by the late 1980s. While originally chiefly the City's rich, by then they included many people of quite moderate wealth from the provinces, including farmers, who each pledged their life's capital or land in the expectation of regular good returns. In fact in the early 1990s the returns became very bad and substantial numbers of 'names' were threatened with bankruptcy. They reacted with anger and dismay; indeed, very large numbers of them have initiated cases against Lloyd's, alleging that the underwriters were careless and misled them. Many members' agents, who should have been able to warn the 'names', were easily misled because they were untrained: 'often they were retired service people, with no experience in insurance. The old boy network. . . . I don't think they ever read an insurance journal', as one disgruntled 'name' put it. He describes how many of the other 'names' have felt 'a terrible shock . . . not just losing money, but that these people that they trusted, and who often were friends over the years, were either incompetent: or worse'.[40]

There is certainly a danger in overstressing the weaknesses of the old gentlemanly capitalism of the City. It certainly had very real strengths too. Unlike British industry, the postwar City has gone on fighting for its place in the international market. It is also especially important to note that its key innovators and reformers have always been either insiders, or outsider-insiders, rather than pure outsiders. Thus, of the pre-1945 generation, Warburg had trained in London; while Benson, the most innovative of financial accountants, although South African was able to enter the City through English family connections. The young Hambro brothers, who pioneered the euromarket with Warburgs, were Etonians from one of the most blue-blooded of merchant banking families. And Goodison, architect of the Stock Exchange reform, was an established member's son, but exceptional in his intellectuality. Thus not only was the City's reform led from within, but it was led from the family-formed core of its élite. There were no crucial contributions from those who entered the City by other paths.

This is partly because there were fewer of them. But the latecomers were also too old to be innovators, while the grammar school boys who rose through the administrative hierarchies had got to the top partly precisely because they knew how to perform well in established ways. The working-class dealers rarely got high enough in the system to even contemplate changing it. This meant that the City relied on its family-recruited public school core to generate change and adaptation; and it did not entirely fail to do so. It needs also to be said, however, that while some public schools – pre-eminently Eton – certainly set out to encourage creativity in their pupils, many were set on turning out conformists as systematically as run-of-the-mill grammar schools. The City, moreover, at least until the 1980s, was not regarded as an attractive destination for their brighter pupils, who were pushed much more towards the professions and the civil service. As the educationist and grammar school head Harry Ree was told when a public schoolboy at Shrewsbury, 'Only shits go into the City.'[41]

In educational terms then, we can see clearly that the City was relying too narrowly on one stream of not very distinguished recruits. Paradoxically, in this situation the continuing family system of recruitment was probably a strength rather than a weakness. Families throw up a broad range of talents; so that where elder sons were expected to look towards the City for a living, they inevitably pushed forward bright as well as mediocre recruits.

There were, however, other equally serious drawbacks from the City's narrow traditional social recruitment base. One was a complete failure to imagine the kind of popular capitalism on the American model which was eventually imposed on it by the Thatcher government in the 1980s through the mass sales of privatization. Because City business was conducted on a social network basis, it was over-focused on a narrow group of socially similar clients or business partners. This was one important reason why the City moved too slowly towards a wider market for financial services in the postwar years. John Fairbairn, for example, recalled how when unit trusts were first set up they were regarded as 'for the mass market, what, in those days, was called the "cloth cap investor"'. Many stockbrokers thus looked down on them as socially 'not really for the likes of you and me, old boy. . . . A bit beyond the pale.'[42]

A closely related weakness sprang from the extraordinarily hierarchical social snobbery even within the City itself, which served to keep its various sections insulated from each other. As Peter Spira put it, 'Bankers used to despise stockbrokers. . . . Calling on a stockbroker was absolute anathema. . . . Jobbers – you didn't even know jobbers.'[43] The division on the Stock Exchange between stockbrokers and jobbers was founded on differences of social origin more than on function, for the jobbers, as dealers, included a minority of working-class origin, while successful brokers had to be socially confident enough to relate well to rich clients. The structural division was a peculiarity of the London exchange and the membership's entrenched attachment to it was one of the principal obstructions to reform. It was overcome too late and then only through the imposition – in response to overwhelming government threats, and through the skilful mediation of Sir Nicholas Goodison as Chairman – of Big Bang at the end of the 1980s.

Very probably similar social divisions underlie the still more crucial failure of the City to create even one multi-functional world-class bank while the chance remained, until the mid-1980s. In industry the firms which survive are giants capable and willing to invest through research and development in their own long-term future. In finance, scale is now also essential. Barings could not survive its crisis independently because its capital base was too small. Modern finance houses need to be able to operate in all aspects of financial business, on an international basis. This demands not only a great range of expertise, but vast resources. No British house today operates in the big league.

Lord Rothschild, who at the beginning of the eighties 'would have liked to have a go at keeping N.M. Rothschild in the global first eleven', asks why:

> I'm afraid it's not so very different to the story of other industries. There was a failure to compete internationally, a failure of management to come to terms quickly enough with all the changes that have taken place. . . . Partly to do with skills, partly to do with will. They did care, but I just don't think that they had the management talent, or steeliness of will to compete with people who care more, and had greater skills, a harder work ethic.
>
> There's been a failure of nerve and resolve. You would have thought that one of the British clearing banks would have decided that it wanted to be a force that would compete with the great banks of the world – Morgan Guarantee, Deutsche Bank, and the big Japanese banks – but none of them succeeded.[44]

This need not have been so. They were no doubt inhibited by the short-termism which characterizes City calculations. There were also regulations to overcome or circumvent – but that had been done before. The underlying problem was cultural. It was not so much the persistence of gentlemanly capitalism in itself, but rather the deep divides which split the British finance world socially. In the case of the banks, on the one hand there was the family world of gentlemanly capitalism of the City merchant banks, relatively small but innovative, and operating internationally. On the other hand were the meritocratic bureaucracies of the potentially much more powerful high street clearing banks and insurance societies. They remained much more cautious, routinized, domestic: slumbering giants. The merchant banks were dominated by Etonians, the clearing banks by men from lesser public schools and grammar schools. The Governor of the Bank had at crucial moments indicated to the Etonians his willingness to turn a blind eye to the development of new unregulated business, classically with the innovative creation of the euromarket.[45] The clearing banks were given no such encouragements. When they tried to make their share in the 1980s boom, their inexperience told against them; some suffered badly, even though their resources meant that they were never seriously threatened.

For an élite merchant bank, by contrast, as Barings found, one serious blow could be fatal. By the 1990s the world finance markets were not a safe place for an aristocratic Don Quixote to be tilting at windmills. Even thirty years ago, the City's gentlemanly capitalism still seemed very much alive. But in fact, the vigorous response which the old élite made to the challenge of the new global markets, which has kept London's lead as the financial capital of Europe, has also meant that it lost its ancestral control of the City. The secret of success has proved the road to self-annihilation. This time the bell has tolled finally for family capitalism in the international City.

# NOTES

## INTRODUCTION

1. For examples of local studies, see S. Nenadic, 'Record Linkage and the Exploration of Nineteenth-century Social Groups: a Methodological Perspective on the Glasgow Middle Class in 1861' and P. Jones, 'Perspectives, Sources and Methodology in a Comparative Study of the Middle Class in Nineteenth-century Leicester and Peterborough' in P. Jones, S. Nenadic, and P. Hills, 'Studying the Middle Class in Nineteenth-century Britain', *Urban History Yearbook*, 14 (1987), 22–50; R.H. Trainor, *Black Country Elites: the Experience of Authority in an Industrial Area 1830–1900* (Oxford, Clarendon Press, 1993); T. Koditschek, *Class Formation and Urban Industrial Society: Bradford, 1750–1850* (Cambridge, Cambridge University Press, 1990); R.J. Morris, *Class, Sect and Party. The Making of the British Middle Class: Leeds, 1820–50* (Manchester, Manchester University Press, 1990); J. Foster, *Class Struggle and the Industrial Revolution* (London, Weidenfeld and Nicolson, 1974) on Oldham; J. Field, 'Wealth, styles of life and social tone amongst Portsmouth's middle class, 1800–75' in R.J. Morris (ed.), *Class, Power and Social Structure in British Nineteenth-century Towns* (Leicester, Leicester University Press, 1986).
2. See P.J. Corfield, 'Class by name and number in eighteenth-century Britain' in *idem* (ed.), *Language, History and Class* (Oxford, Oxford University Press, 1991), p. 113.
3. P. Joyce (ed.), *Class* (Oxford, Oxford University Press, 1995) provides a useful starting point.
4. E.H. Carr, *What is History?* (London, Macmillan, 1961).
5. Postmodernists reject 'structures' altogether as categories created by discourse not objective realities. Contrariwise, a Marxist 'structural' explanation for their intellectual position might explain it by reference to, *inter alia*, the triumph of the capitalist West, the ascendancy of the New Right, and the crisis for Marxism and for class politics generally.
6. This is somewhat ironical given the radical promise of postmodernism to liberate those whose voices have been largely silenced by the dominant discourse. For the contradiction between theoretical promise and conservative practice, see R. Price, 'Postmodernism as theory and history' in J. Belchem and N. Kirk (eds), *Languages of Labour* (Aldershot, Scolar Press, 1997), ch. 1.

7. The use of the term 'identity' by social historians has increased quite considerably in recent times, but is overdue for interrogation and for subjection to the same sort of scrutiny hitherto afforded class consciousness.

8. The huge literature of mid-Victorian stability post-Chartism provides excellent examples of this. Foster's rare attempt to locate stabilization in the context of capital export may have been flawed but not misconceived. Foster, *Class Struggle*.

9. Whereas in the 1750s living standards in the global North were not significantly higher than in the South, over the next 230 years the average citizen of the developing North (the expanding capitalist countries) grew to be eight times richer than a citizen in the South (the under-developed non-capitalist world). By 1980 the richest 20 per cent of the world's people received 82.7 per cent of its total income while the poorest 20 per cent received only 1.4 per cent. The North, with one-quarter of the world's population, consumes 70 per cent of the world's energy, 75 per cent of its metals, 85 per cent of its wood and 60 per cent of its food. On average, around 40,000 people worldwide, mostly children, die each day from hunger and poverty. (See Tom Athanasiou, 'Wising Up to the New World Order' in *Guardian*, 19 Feb. 1997.) Nor should it be assumed that the progress of the former was bought without any cost to the latter. Quite the opposite.

10. A recent report has revealed that Britain today is a far more unequal society than it was twenty years ago with the gap between rich and poor widening in every region of the country. The bottom 10 per cent of the population receives less than 3 per cent of Britain's total earnings whereas the top 10 per cent receives over 25 per cent. See Alissa Goodman, Paul Johnson and Steven Webb, *Inequality in the United Kingdom* (Oxford, Oxford University Press, 1997). The introduction and afterwards consolidation of capitalist relations of production was a protracted process which produced wide disparities in regional economic development, overlapping systems of production, the survival of small capital alongside burgeoning big capital enterprises, and corresponding complex local class structures. The persistence of small-scale production was the norm not the exception, even if these small units did increasingly come under the sway of large capital.

11. No doubt his conclusion that a coherent 'middle class' was not visible as a distinctive cultural and political agent until the nineteenth century, and especially not before 1832, will be disputed. D. Wahrman, *Imagining the Middle Class. The Political Representation of Class in Britain, c. 1780–1840* (Cambridge, Cambridge University Press, 1995), esp. pp. 6, 9, 17–18, 408. Cf. G. Stedman Jones's emphasis on the centrality of the political language of Chartism in *Languages of Class* (Cambridge, Cambridge University Press, 1983), ch. 3.

12. See Corfield (ed.), *Language, History and Class*, p. 113.

13. J. Seed, 'From "middling sort" to middle class in late eighteenth- and early nineteenth-century England' in M.L. Bush (ed.), *Social Orders and Social Classes in Europe since 1500* (Harlow, Longman, 1992), p. 115.

14. See R. Williams, *Keywords* (rev. edn, London, Fontana, 1976), pp. 45–8 for a definitional history. As R.J. Morris has written: 'The British towns of the Industrial Revolution period were substantially the creation of their middle class, and in turn provided the theatre within which that middle class sought, extended, expressed and defended its power.' R.J. Morris, 'The Middle Class and British Towns and Cities of the Industrial Revolution 1780–1870' in D. Fraser

and A. Sutcliffe (eds), *The Pursuit of Urban History* (London, Edward Arnold, 1983), p. 286.

15.  For a full account of this process, see Peter Earle, *The Making of the English Middle Class. Business, Society and Family Life in London, 1660–1730* (London, Methuen, 1989).

16   S. Nenadic, 'Businessmen, the Urban Middle Class and the "Dominance" of Manufacturers in Nineteenth-century Britain', *Economic History Review*, second series, 44 (1991), 67. She uses the term 'middle class' to refer to those adult males who were neither manual workers, except where these were also employers, nor aristocrats, landed gentry or farmers: 'Middle class is a convenient shorthand and not intended to convey any notion of class identity.' (Ibid.)

17.  M. Savage, J. Barlow, P. Dickens and T. Fielding, *Property, Bureaucracy and Culture. Middle-class Formation in Contemporary Britain* (London, Routledge, 1992), p. 2.

18.  See, for example, P. Corfield, *Power and the Professions in Britain 1700–1850* (London, Routledge, 1995). Corfield calculates that, in the census of 1851, 2.6 per cent of males in England and Wales were located in the professional sector of the economy, having risen from about 2.1 per cent in 1688, and that the eighteenth-century professions were proportionately as significant in the workforce as were their Victorian successors (p. 33). For the increasing importance of the professional middle class in the twentieth century, see H. Perkin, *The Rise of Professional Society. England since 1880* (London, Routledge, 1989).

19.  For a succinct summary, see Savage et al., *Property, Bureaucracy and Culture*, pp. 49–55. They maintain that managers remained very dependent upon single organizations and separate from the professional middle class until the 1970s when employers increasingly looked to professionally educated workers to carry out specialist tasks.

20.  G. Crossick and H.-G. Haupt, *The Petite Bourgeoisie in Europe 1780–1914* (London, Routledge, 1995), p. 9.

21.  See, for example, Leonore O'Boyle, 'The Classless Society: Comment on Stearns', *Comparative Studies in Society and History*, 21 (1979), esp. p. 412.

22.  See, for example, Earle, *Making*, p. 5.

23.  For Bourdieu, see *Distinction* (London, Routledge, 1984) and *In Other Words* (Cambridge, Polity Press, 1990) and the exposition of his work in Savage et al., *Property, Bureaucracy and Culture*, pp. 16, 42–4. The result was that 'the professional middle class were more closed to outsiders than any other social class in Victorian Britain, excepting only the dominant capitalist class'. Ibid., p. 44.

24.  Morris, *Class, Sect and Party*; *idem*, 'The Middle Class and British Towns', esp. pp. 303–4. Habermas's work on the public sphere was slow to be taken up by historians – *The Structural Transformation of the Public Sphere* was originally published in 1962 – but work on local institutions, charitable bodies, improvement organizations and the importance of the separation of spheres for gender relations has now begun to proliferate. See A. Kidd and D. Nicholls (eds), *Gender, Civic Culture and Consumerism: Middle-class Identity in Britain, 1800–1940* (Manchester, Manchester University Press, forthcoming 1999) for examples of, and further comment on, the new directions in social history.

25.  L. Davidoff and C. Hall, *Family Fortunes: Men and Women of the English*

*Middle Class, 1780–1850* (London, Hutchinson, 1987). Their account has been questioned for the period before 1832 by D. Wahrman, '"Middle-class" Domesticity Goes Public: Gender, Class, and Politics from Queen Caroline to Queen Victoria', *Journal of British Studies*, 32 (1993), 396–432.

26. M.C. Finn, *After Chartism* (Cambridge, Cambridge University Press, 1993), esp. p. 260; L. Colley, *Britons. Forging the Nation 1707–1837* (New Haven and London, Yale University Press, 1992). Cf. those cultural explanations of economic decline which have sought to locate it in the construction by the dominant classes of a rural nostalgic 'Englishness' (in the late nineteenth century) and which have been subjected to a recent critique by Peter Mandler, 'Against "Englishness": English Culture and the Limits to Rural Nostalgia, 1850–1940' in *Transactions of the Royal Historical Society*, sixth series, VII (1997), 155–95.

27. Cf. J. Barry, 'The Making of the Middle Class?', *Past and Present*, 145 (1994), 208.

28. See especially, Corfield (ed.), *Language, History and Class*; Earle, *Making*; J. Barry, 'Bourgeois Collectivism? Urban Association and the Middling Sort' in J. Barry and C. Brooks (eds), *The Middling Sort of People. Culture, Society and Politics in England, 1550–1800* (Basingstoke, Macmillan, 1994). The special edition of the *Journal of British Studies*, 32 (1993) provides a good summary of the revisionist view on the eighteenth-century middle class.

29. Seed, 'From "Middling Sort"', p. 126.

30. These arguments are elaborated in Colin Barker and David Nicholls (eds), *The Development of British Capitalist Society: a Marxist Debate* (Manchester, Northern Marxist Historians Group, 1988). For classic statements and discussion of what has come to be called the 'gentlemanly capitalism' thesis, see P. Anderson, 'The Figures of Descent', *New Left Review*, 171 (1987), 20–77; W.D. Rubinstein, *Elites and the Wealthy in Modern British History* (Brighton, Harvester Press, 1987); Will Hutton, *The State We're In* (London, Cape, 1995); P.J. Cain and A.G. Hopkins, *British Imperialism* (2 vols, London, Longman, 1993); S. Gunn, 'The Failure of the Victorian Middle Class: a Critique' in J. Woolf and J. Seed (eds), *The Culture of Capital: Art, Power and the Nineteenth-century Middle Class* (Manchester, Manchester University Press, 1988).

31. Jones, 'Perspectives', p. 25. Likewise Morris, 'The Middle Class and British Towns' in Fraser and Sutcliffe (eds), *Pursuit of Urban History*, considers the varieties of social structure and middle-class composition across a range of towns.

## CHAPTER 1

1. John Brewer, *Party Ideology and Popular Politics at the Accession of George III* (Cambridge, Cambridge University Press, 1976), esp. ch. 8; John Money, *Experience and Identity: Birmingham and the West Midlands, 1760–1800* (Manchester, Manchester University Press, 1977); Kathleen Wilson, *The Sense of the People: People, Culture and Imperialism in England, 1715–1785* (Cambridge, Cambridge University Press, 1995); Karl Schweizer and Rebecca Klein, 'The French Revolution and Developments in the London Daily Press to 1793' in Karl Schweizer and Jeremy Black (eds), *Politics and the Press in*

*Hanoverian Britain* (Lewiston, NY, Edward Mellon Press, 1989), pp. 171–86.

2. Jürgen Habermas, *The Structural Transformation of the Public Sphere: An Inquiry into a Category of Bourgeois Society*, trans. by Thomas Burger with the assistance of Frederick Lawrence (Cambridge, Mass., MIT Press, 1989, originally published in German in 1962). Habermas argues that, as the principal vehicle of 'public opinion' through its battles with successive ministries over press freedom, the press played a vital role in the creation of the public sphere in eighteenth-century Britain. He also suggests that it was through the press, that a new bourgeois public came to define itself. The press served to establish the choreography of the public sphere, embodying and reflecting the conventions, practices, relationships and, not least, exclusions, that gave substance and shape to the public. In a recent essay, Roy Porter describes Habermas as the 'new cult figure' presiding over eighteenth-century British social history. R. Porter, 'The New Eighteenth-Century Social History' in Jeremy Black (ed.), *Culture and Society in Britain, 1660–1800* (Manchester, Manchester University Press, 1997), p. 32.

3. The debate is conveniently reviewed in Jonathan Barry, 'Introduction' in Barry and Brooks (eds), *Middling Sort*, pp. 1–27.

4. See esp. Kathryn Shevelow, *Women and Print Culture: The Construction of Femininity in the Early Periodical* (London, Routledge, 1989).

5. See, for example, Michael Harris, *London Newspapers in the Age of Walpole: A Study in the Origins of the Modern English Press* (London and Toronto, Associated University Presses, 1987); M.E. Craig, *The Scottish Periodical Press 1750–89* (Edinburgh, Oliver and Boyd, 1931).

6. P.M. Handover, *A History of the London Gazette, 1665–1695* (London, HMSO, 1965); R.L. Haig, *The Gazetteer, 1735–1797: A Study in the Eighteenth-Century Newspaper* (Carbondale, Southern Illinois University Press, 1968).

7. See e.g. L.W. Hanson, *Government and the Press, 1695–1763* (Oxford, Clarendon Press, 1936); F.J. Siebert, *The Freedom of the Press in England, 1476–1776* (Urbana, University of Illinois Press, 1952).

8. See e.g. Brewer, *Party Ideology and Popular Politics*; Robert R. Rea, *The English Press in Politics 1769–1774* (Lincoln, University of Nebraska Press, 1963); Marie Peters, *Pitt and Popularity: the Patriot Minister and London Opinion during the Seven Years War* (Oxford, Clarendon Press, 1980); Robert (Bob) Harris, *A Patriot Press; National Politics and the London Press in the 1740s* (Oxford, Oxford University Press, 1993).

9. For a good summary, see Michael Harris, 'The Structure, Ownership and Control of the Press, 1620–1780' in J. Curran, G. Boyce and P. Wingate (eds), *Newspaper History from the Seventeenth Century to the Present Day* (London, Constable, 1978), pp. 82–97.

10. *London Daily Advertiser*, 4 Mar. 1751.

11. For a discussion of these changes which tends to downplay their scale and impact, see Jeremy Black, *The English Press in the Eighteenth Century* (London and Sydney, Croom Helm, 1987) *passim*. For a different view, see Bob Harris, *Politics and the Rise of the Press, Britain and France, 1620–1800* (London, Routledge, 1996).

12. For the shifting languages of social description in eighteenth-century Britain, see Corfield, 'Class by Name and Number' in *idem* (ed.), *Language, History and Class*, pp. 101–30.

13. John Brown, *Thoughts on Civil Liberty, on Licentiousness and Faction* (1765), esp. pp. 112–13.

14.  Ibid., p. 87.
15.  Peter Earle, 'The Middling Sort in London' in Barry and Brooks (eds), *Middling Sort*, p. 155.
16.  See esp. the comments in my *Politics and the Rise of the Press*, ch. 1.
17.  For advertising in the press, see e.g. Cranfield, *Development of the Provincial Newspaper*, pp. 207–23; Christine Ferdinand, 'Selling it to the Provinces: News and Commerce round Eighteenth-Century Salisbury' in John Brewer and Roy Porter (eds), *Consumption and the World of Goods* (London and New York, Routledge, 1993), pp. 393–411.
18.  See n. 8 above.
19.  Solomon Lutnick, *The American Revolution and the British Press, 1775–1783* (Columbia, Mo., University of Missouri Press, 1967); I. Asquith, 'The Structure, Ownership and Control of the Press, 1780–1855' in Boyce et al. (eds), *Newspaper History*, p. 111; Schweizer and Klein, 'The French Revolution and Developments in the London Daily Press' in Schweizer and Black (eds), *Politics and the Press*.
20.  See esp. Michael Harris, *London Newspapers*, ch. 4.
21.  M.J. Smith, 'English Radical Newspapers in the French Revolutionary Era, 1790–1803' (unpublished PhD thesis, University of London, 1979).
22.  Stephen Botein, Jack R. Censer and Harriet Ritvo, 'The Periodical Press in Eighteenth-century English and French Society: A Cross-Cultural Approach', *Comparative Studies in Society and History*, 23 (1981), 464–90. A different view of at least one section of the eighteenth-century French press, the provincial *Affiches*, which implies similarities with the contemporary British press, is expressed in Colin Jones, 'The Great Chain of Buying: Medical Advertisement, the Bourgeois Public Sphere and the French Revolution', *American Historical Review*, 101 (1996), 13–40.
23.  Botein, Censer and Ritvo, 'The Periodical Press', p. 489.
24.  Black, *The English Press*; Cranfield, *Development of the Provincial Newspaper*.
25.  Wilson, *Sense of the People*, esp. pp. 38–40. See also the comments by Philip Lawson in '"The Irishman's Prize": Views of Canada from the British Press, 1760–1774' in *idem, A Taste for Empire and Glory: Studies in British Overseas Expansion, 1660–1800* (Aldershot and Brookfield, Vermont, Variorum, 1997), pp. 575–96; *idem*, '"Arts and Empire Equally Extend": Tradition, Prejudice and Assumption in the Eighteenth-century Press Coverage of Empire' in ibid., pp. 119–46.
26.  *Edinburgh Weekly Journal*, 28 Mar. 1798.
27.  See *Edinburgh Evening Courant*, 20 Mar. 1782.
28.  See e.g. the extent of the coverage given in March 1782 to discussions about changes in Scots bankruptcy law in *Edinburgh Evening Courant* (4, 6, 11, 18, 20, 25 Mar. 1782) or the amount of coverage devoted during periods of war in all papers to enemy privateering activity.
29.  Quoted in Black, *The English Press*, p. 71.
30.  See ibid., esp. pp. 66–79; see also Money, *Experience and Identity*, esp. chs 2 and 3.
31.  See e.g., *Leicester and Nottingham Journal*, 22 Apr. 1791; *Glasgow Advertiser*, 13–16 Apr. 1792; *Glasgow Courier*, 17 Jan. 1793.
32.  Nicholas Rogers, 'Confronting the Crime Wave: The Debate over Social Reform and Regulation, 1749–1753' in Lee Davison, Tim Hitchcock, Tim Kiern and Robert B. Shoemaker (eds), *Stilling the Grumbling Hive: The Response to Social and Economic Problems in England, 1689–1750* (Stroud, Alan Sutton Publishing, 1992), pp. 79–80.

33. Steve Poole, 'Scarcity and the Civic Tradition: Market Management in Bristol, 1709–1815' in Adrian Randall and Andrew Charlesworth (eds), *Markets, Market Culture and Popular Protest in Eighteenth-century Britain and Ireland* (Liverpool, Liverpool University Press, 1996), p. 109.

34. Porter, 'The New Eighteenth-Century Social History', p. 35.

35. See Peter Borsay, 'Image and Counter Image in Georgian Bath', *British Journal for Eighteenth-century Studies*, 17 (1994), 165–79, and Philip Lawson and Jim Phillips, '"Our Execrable Banditti": Perceptions of Nabobs in Mid-Eighteenth-Century Britain', *Albion*, 16 (1984), 225–41.

36. See John Sekora, *Luxury: The Concept in Western Thought, Eden to Smollett* (Baltimore and London, Johns Hopkins University Press, 1978); Wilson, *Sense of the People*, esp. chs 3–5.

37. The claim is made in Lawrence and Jeanne Fawtier Stone, *An Open Elite? England 1540–1880* (Oxford, Oxford University Press, 1984), p. 418.

38. The estimate of Denison's estate was too low; he actually left over £700,000. R.G. Wilson, 'The Denisons and Milnses: Eighteenth-Century Merchant Landowners' in J.T. Ward and R.G. Wilson (eds), *Land and Industry: The Landed Estate and the Industrial Revolution* (Newton Abbot, David & Charles, 1971), pp. 145–72.

39. *Bath Chronicle*, 11 Apr. 1782.

40. John Shebbeare, *Matrimony: A Novel* (1755), p. 39. Someone else who mocked such items was Henry Fielding in the 'Modern History' section of the *Covent Garden Journal*.

41. Charles Clark, *The Public Prints: The Newspaper in Anglo-American Culture, 1665–1740* (New York and Oxford, Oxford University Press, 1994), p. 257.

42. For the shrinking of the Atlantic in this context, see I.K. Steele, *The English Atlantic Community 1675–1740: an exploration of communication and community* (New York and Oxford, Oxford University Press, 1986).

43. See e.g. Arthur Aspinall, *Politics and the Press, 1780–1850* (London, Home and Van Thal, 1949), p. 379. See also the view expressed in D. Fraser, 'The Life of Edward Baines: A Filial Biography of the "The Great Man of the North"', *Northern History*, 31 (1995), 208.

44. J.E. Cookson, *The Friends of Peace: Anti-War Liberalism in England 1793–1815* (Cambridge, Cambridge University Press, 1982), p. 109.

45. Money, *Experience and Identity*, p. 56.

46. Hannah Barker, 'Catering for Provincial Tastes: Newspapers, Readership and Profit in Late Eighteenth-century England', *Historical Research*, 19 (1996), 42–61.

47. E.g., the *Glasgow Courier* argued in its first issue of 1 Sept. 1791 that by appearing three times a week, it would be able to provide the most complete account of international and domestic news of any Glasgow paper. It also pointed out that the timing of the arrival of mail in Glasgow would allow the *Courier* earlier access than any of the Edinburgh papers to intelligence arriving from England. In 1798, the *Edinburgh Weekly Journal* boasted at various times about its ability to furnish its readers with early news from London, Ireland and from continental papers, in some cases in advance of the London press (17 Jan., 14 Mar., 4 Apr., 13 June, 1 Aug., 8 Aug. 1798).

48. For several leading London papers of the later eighteenth century, see I.R. Christie, 'British Newspapers in the Later Georgian Age' in *idem, Myth and Reality in Later Eighteenth-century British Politics and Other Papers* (London, Macmillan, 1970), pp. 311–33. For developments in the provincial press, see

D. Clare, 'The Growth and Importance of the Newspaper Press in Manchester, Liverpool and Leeds between 1780 and 1800' (unpublished MA thesis, University of Manchester, 1949), pp. 39–46.

49. We currently lack a modern systematic survey of the impact of the French Revolution on the British press, but much can be gleaned from I.R. Christie, 'British Newspapers in the Later Georgian Age'; Schweizer and Klein, 'The French Revolution and Developments in the London Daily Press'; L. Werkmeister, *A Newspaper History of England, 1792–1793* (Lincoln, University of Nebraska Press, 1962); Smith, 'English Radical Newspapers'.

50. Harris, *Politics and the Rise of the Press*, p. 19.

51. *Edinburgh Evening Courant*, 20 Feb. 1782. See also Money, *Experience and Identity*, p. 56, where he describes the efforts of the printers of the *Birmingham Gazette* to 'remain all things to all men'.

52. *Observer*, 4 Dec. 1791.

53. Jeremy Black, 'Politicization and the Press in Hanoverian England' in Robin Myers and Michael Harris (eds), *Serials and their Readers 1620–1914* (Winchester, St Paul's Bibliographies, 1993), pp. 75–6.

54. E.g. *Edinburgh Advertiser* declared on 8 Oct. 1782, 'The Essay entitled "Abolition of Property", would involve us in both a religious and political controversy, which we have not room for.'

55. Quoted in Haig, *The Gazetteer*, p. 199.

56. John Dwyer, 'The Caledonian Mercury and Scottish National Culture, 1763–1801' in Schweizer and Black (eds), *Politics and the Press in Hanoverian Britain*, p. 159.

57. See e.g. *General Evening Post*, 3–5 Oct. 1750; *Whitehall Evening Post*, 12–14 July, 26–8 July, 9–11 Aug. 1751.

58. Reprinted in the *Ipswich Journal*, 18 May 1754.

59. For attitudes towards aristocratic manners and behaviour, see Paul Langford, *Public Life and the Propertied Englishman, 1689–1798* (Oxford, Clarendon Press, 1991), ch. 8. See also Donna T. Andrew, '"Adultery à la Mode": Privilege, the Law and Attitudes to Adultery 1770–1809', *History*, 82 (1997), 5–23; Phyllis Deutsch, 'Moral Trespass in Georgian London: Gaming, Gender and Electoral Politics in the Age of George III', *Historical Journal*, 39 (1996), 637–56.

60. Wilson, *Sense of the People*, p. 40.

61. Quoted in Black, *The English Press*, p. 40.

62. See e.g., David Vaisey (ed.), *The Diary of Thomas Turner 1754–1765* (Oxford, Oxford University Press, 1985).

63. Roger Chartier, *The Cultural Uses of Print in Early Modern France*, trans. by Lydia G. Cochrane (Princeton, Princeton University Press, 1987).

64. *Ipswich Journal*, 16 Mar. 1754.

65. Jonas Hanway, *The Defects of Police: the Cayse of Immorality and Continual Robberies Committed Particularly in and about the Metropolis* (1775), p. 18.

66. David Eastwood, *Government and Community in the English Provinces, 1700–1870* (London, Macmillan, 1997), pp. 76–7.

67. See esp. Cookson, *Friends of Peace*, ch. 4.

## CHAPTER 2

1. Although anachronistic, the name of the short-lived modern county of West Yorkshire is the most appropriate designation for this portion of the historic

West Riding of Yorkshire. It was always quite separate from the other main West Riding industrial zone around Sheffield.

2.  The best complete account remains H. Heaton, *The Yorkshire Woollen and Worsted Industries*, (2nd edn, Oxford, Oxford University Press, 1965).

3.  E.P. Thompson, *The Making of the English Working Class*, rev. edn (Harmondsworth, Pelican, 1980), explicitly acknowledged Yorkshire influences, p. 13; R.J. Morris, *Class, Sect and Party: The Making of the British Middle Class, Leeds 1820–1850* (Manchester, Manchester University Press, 1990); T. Koditschek, *Class Formation and Urban-Industrial Society: Bradford 1750–1850* (Cambridge, Cambridge University Press, 1990).

4.  J. Smail, *The Origins of Middle-Class Culture: Halifax, Yorkshire, 1660–1780* (Ithaca, Cornell University Press, 1985), see esp. ch. 8.

5   P. Earle, *The Making of the English Middle Class: Business, Society and Family Life in London, 1660–1730* (London, Methuen, 1989), p. 12.

6.  L. Davidoff and C. Hall, *Family Fortunes: Men and Women of the English Middle Class, 1780–1850* (London, Routledge, 1987).

7.  M.J. Dickenson, 'The West Riding Worsted and Woollen Industries, 1679–1770: An Analysis of Probate Inventories and Insurance Policies', (unpublished PhD thesis, University of Nottingham, 1974); D. Gregory, *Regional Transformation and Industrial Revolution: A Geography of the Yorkshire Woollen Industry* (London, Macmillan, 1982); P. Hudson, *Genesis of Industrial Capital: A Study of the West Riding Wool Textile Industry, c. 1725–1850* (Cambridge, Cambridge University Press, 1986).

8.  It was posthumously published by his grandson as *The Autobiography of Thomas Wright of Birkenshaw, in the County of York, 1736–1797*, ed. T. Wright (London, John Russell Smith, 1864). This is the text used here.

9.  Wright, *Autobiography*, p. 83.

10. See Earle, *Making*, p. 238 and Davidoff and Hall, *Family*, pp. 20, 114, 229, 334 on the strength of the sense of responsibility to the next generation as a motivating force.

11. Wright, *Autobiography*, pp. 117, 266.

12. Ibid., pp. xxiv–xxv and see n. 63 below.

13. Thompson, *Making*, p. 13. Davidoff and Hall, *Family*, pp. 34 and 51, acknowledge their bias towards success. Manufacturers formed only 12 per cent of their middle class, see p. 233 and table 4.

14. Davidoff and Hall, *Family*, constantly refer to the importance of networks, e.g. pp. 13, 23, 100–2, 200, 207–8, 215–18. They also acknowledge the importance of this type of kinship web, e.g. pp. 32–3, 196, 355–6.

15. D. Fraser, *A History of Modern Leeds* (Manchester, Manchester University Press, 1980), pp. 35–41; Heaton, *Yorkshire Woollen*, pp. 238–47.

16. R.G. Wilson, *Gentlemen Merchants: The Merchant Community in Leeds* (Manchester, Manchester University Press, 1971) is an excellent study of the most substantial merchants, but as wealthy and powerful men they tended to prefer the status quo to radical change.

17. See J. Garrard, *Leadership and Power in Victorian Industrial Towns 1830–80* (Manchester, Manchester University Press, 1983), p. 10 on the survival of a significant nineteenth-century woollen sector in Rochdale.

18. S. Caunce, 'Complexity, Community Structure, and Competitive Advantage Within the Yorkshire Woollen Industry, *c.* 1700–1850', *Business History*, 39 (1997), 27–43. See also Koditschek, *Class*, pp. 53, 62–3.

19. See Caunce, 'Community Structure', pp. 29–32 on Birstall parish. See also

Heaton, *Yorkshire Woollen*, pp. 363–4, Dickenson, 'West Riding', pp. 140, 155, 186; Gregory, *Regional Transformation*, ch. 3. On Rawfolds, see Thompson, *Making*, pp. 611–15, and Wright, *Autobiography*, pp. 74, 184.

20. Ibid., pp. xxviii, 141–2; Davidoff and Hall, *Family*, pp. 15, 19, 442; Dickenson, 'West Riding', pp. 128–30.

21. See M. Chaytor, 'Household and Kinship: Ryton in the Late 16th and Early 17th Centuries', *Past and Present*, 10 (1980), 25–60 for a discussion of the merits of kinship webs as against static analysis.

22. Wright, *Autobiography*, pp. 7–8, 20.

23. Ibid., pp. 13, 24.

24. Ibid., pp. 9–14, 37–9. See Earle, *Making*, pp. 161 and Davidoff and Hall, *Family*, pp. 282–8 on the vulnerability of widows.

25. Ibid., pp. 28–34, 37, 40–1. See Heaton, *Yorkshire Woollen*, pp. 301–8 on Yorkshire apprenticeships; also A. Randall, *Before the Luddites: Custom, Community and Machinery in the Woollen Industry, 1776–1809* (Cambridge, Cambridge University Press, 1991), pp. 33, 205. J. Lane, *Apprenticeship in England, 1600–1914* (London, University College London Press, 1996) is the best account of the national apprenticeship system.

26. Wright, *Autobiography*, p. 47–8; Earle, *Making*, pp. 8–9, 15.

27. Ibid., pp. 77, 89, 97. D. Defoe, *A Tour Through the Whole Island of Great Britain* (1738; Harmondsworth, Penguin edn, 1971), pp. 500–4 is a graphic description of Leeds cloth market, and the use of public houses by the clothiers.

28. See Earle, *Making*, pp. 68–9, 73, 143, 328. In contrast Davidoff and Hall, *Family*, pp. 266–7, comment on the scarcity and inadequacy of salaried positions, especially before 1780.

29. Wright, *Autobiography*, pp. 71–89.

30. Ibid., p. 98.

31. Ibid., pp. 99, 116, 246.

32. Ibid., p. 246.

33. Ibid., pp. 117, 151.

34. Ibid., pp. 148–9.

35. A local official appointed by the justices to measure and assess the quality of cloth, see Heaton, *Yorkshire Woollen*, pp. 405–16.

36. Wright, *Autobiography*, p. 160.

37. Ibid., pp. 49, 66–7, 72–83, 108–16, 184–90.

38. Ibid., pp. 160–1. See Davidoff and Hall, *Family*, pp. 234–5.

39. Koditschek, *Class*, pp. 69–70.

40. Wright, *Autobiography*, pp. 242, 247, 249–50.

41. Ibid., pp. 32–3.

42. Ibid., pp. 32–3, 50–2, 254.

43. F. Peel, *Nonconformity in the Spen Valley* (Heckmondwike, Senior, 1891).

44. Davidoff and Hall, *Family*, p. 99, believe that Anglicanism could only be seen as a sect in Birmingham after 1860, and they describe the parish as the basis for a successful Anglican revival in the nineteenth century, pp. 42–3, 83.

45. See Koditschek, *Class*, pp. 50–1 on the intertwining of Anglicanism and Old Dissent in West Yorkshire; Davidoff and Hall, *Family*, pp. 120–2 on the monetary ties between ministers and congregations.

46. Wright, *Autobiography*, pp. x–xi, xiv–xvi, 258.

47. Ibid., pp. 260–4.

48. All totals exclude Wright.

49. Wright, *Autobiography*, pp. 244, 249.

50. Ibid., p. 10.
51. Ibid., pp. 243–4.
52. Ibid., pp. 22–3, 35–6, 77, 122, 142, 166, 192. See Davidoff and Hall, *Family*, p. 390 on the odd situation of single men and widowers with regard to servants.
53. Wright, *Autobiography*, pp. 5–6; see also Earle, *Making*, ch. 6 on the position of women and their high profile in running inns, an activity also discussed by Davidoff and Hall, *Family*, p. 241.
54. Wright, *Autobiography*, p. 211.
55. Ibid., p. 41.
56. Ibid., pp. 253–4.
57. Ibid., pp. 6, 56–7.
58. Ibid., pp. 243–4. See Earle, *Making*, p. 192; and Davidoff and Hall, *Family*, pp. 218–19 on the tendency of their sample to marry along occupational lines.
59. Wright, *Autobiography*, p. 249.
60. See Chaytor, 'Household', pp. 25–60 on the weakness of the strict nuclear family model in reality despite its strength as an ideal. K. Wrightson, 'Household and Kinship in Sixteenth-century England', *Past and Present*, 12 (1981), 151–8; and O. Harris, 'Households and their Boundaries', *Past and Present*, 13 (1982), 143–52 explore this further. See also Davidoff and Hall, *Family*, p. 31.
61. Wright, *Autobiography*, pp. 247–8. See H. Medick, 'The Proto-industrial Family Economy: the Structural Function of Household and Family During the Transition from Peasant Society to Industrial Capitalism', *Social History*, 3 (1976), 292–315, esp. pp. 304–5. Davidoff and Hall, *Family*, p. 224 argue that large families reinforced networks, but this is not true here.
62. Wright, *Autobiography*, pp. 121–2.
63. Ibid., pp. 214 and 221 onwards. The records of the lunacy investigation fully support Wright's account, Borthwick Institute of Historical Research, York, Cause and Testamentary Papers, CP1797/1.
64. Wright, *Autobiography*, p. 240.
65. Ibid., p. 247.
66. Ibid., pp. 244–5. See Earle, *Making*, pp. 235, 314 as a contrast.
67. Ibid., pp. 257–8. Earle, *Making*, p. 315. Davidoff and Hall, *Family*, pp. 19–20, 198, 213.
68. For instance, Wright, *Autobiography*, pp. 210–14.
69. See Harris, 'Households', pp. 145–6; and contrast Davidoff and Hall, *Family*, pp. 13, 218.
70. G. Redmonds, *Yorkshire, West Riding*, ed. R.A. McKinley, English Surnames Series, vol. I (London, Phillimore, 1973), esp. pp. 59–64, 206–8, 216–19, 224–9.
71. See Caunce, 'Community', pp. 30–2.
72. Wright, *Autobiography*, p. 68.
73. Contrast Earle, *Making*, p. 7. Would-be Northampton entrepreneurs left for London because of the lack of opportunity locally.
74. Medick, 'Proto-industrial Family', pp. 292–315 has a brief but thorough description of the proto-industrial model which does not fit West Yorkshire at all, especially the assumption of rural land shortages. There was plenty of land in the West Riding: the problem was quality, but W.B. Crump, 'Ancient Highways of the Parish of Halifax, VIII – Sowerby Highways', *Transactions of the Halifax Antiquarian Society* (1928), 2–6 shows how textiles removed this barrier to settlement. P. Hudson, 'Proto-industrialisation: the Case of the West Riding',

*Past and Present*, 12 (1981), 34–61 draws out the incompatibilities. Caunce, 'Community Structure', pp. 26–43 and J. Garrard, *Leadership*, pp. 6–7, both stress the diversity of these types of textile-led economy.

75. Davidoff and Hall, *Family*, pp. 21–2, 100–2, 200, 215–17, on general hostility to pure profit seeking.

76. Wright, *Autobiography*, p. 1. See also F. Peel, *Risings*, p. x; J. Lawson, *Letters to the Young on Progress in Pudsey During the Last Sixty Years* (Stanningley, J.W. Birdsall, 1887). Contrast Davidoff and Hall, *Family*, p. 190.

77. Wright, *Autobiography*, frontispiece is a drawing of Lower Blacup Farm. See also Royal Commission on Historical Monuments of England, *Rural Houses of West Yorkshire* (London, HMSO, 1986), pp. 127–31, 247–51. Davidoff and Hall, *Family*, p. 359 discuss the use of polite architecture to define new social divisions.

78. See Davidoff and Hall, *Family*, pp. 205–7, 335.

79. Heaton, *Yorkshire Woollen*, ch. 11. He records that while merchants built the third White Cloth Hall in Leeds, they handed it over to the clothiers to run, pp. 368–70. Koditschek, *Class*, p. 92 shows that between 1830 and 1850 there was almost a complete turnover of firms even in capitalist Bradford. Contrast Earle, *Making*, pp. 40–1 on the small number, dominance, and stability of Blackwell Hall factors.

80. The decentralized production system adapted remarkably well into the twentieth century in the heavy woollen district, including most of Birstall. It continued to innovate in technology, processes and products, D.T. Jenkins and J.C. Malin, 'European Competition in Woollen Cloth, 1870–1914: The Role of Shoddy', *Business History*, 32 (1990), 66–86. On industrial districts, see F. Pyke, G. Becattini, and W. Sengenburger (eds), *Industrial Districts and Inter-Firm Co-operation in Italy* (Geneva, International Institute for Labour Studies, 1990), esp. G. Becattini, 'The Marshallian Industrial District as a Socio-economic Notion'.

81. Davidoff and Hall, *Family*, pp. 162–4, 188–90, 361.

82. Contrast Earle, *Making*, p. 9; Davidoff and Hall, *Family*, pp. 35, 74, 110, 182, 198.

83. See Davidoff and Hall, *Family*, pp. 121–2 on the role of Anglican clergy as cultural missionaries in the regions; pp. 19–20, 73, 85 on the continuing sense of exclusion among Dissenters and the middle class in general.

84. Wilson, *Gentlemen Merchants*, ch. 10.

85. Smail, *Origins*, pp. 31–4; Morris, *Class Sect and Party*, pp. 165–7, 329–30; Earle, *Making*, pp. 3, 329.

86. Morris, *Class, Sect and Party*, pp. 167–8, 250–3.

87. R. Brook, *The Story of Huddersfield* (London, Macgibbon and Kee, 1986), chs 3–11. See Koditschek, Class, pp. 42–53.

88. Contrast J. Foster, *Class Struggle and the Industrial Revolution: Early Industrial Capitalism in Three English Towns* (London, Weidenfeld and Nicolson, 1974), p. 12, but this different conclusion is probably the result of his looking backward from the factory era.

89. Timothy Crowther's business career is detailed in H. Heaton, 'Yorkshire Cloth Traders in the United States 1770–1840', *Thoresby Society Miscellany*, XXXVII (1944), 225–87. It is hard to imagine a greater contrast with Wright.

90. Contrast Earle, *Making*, pp. 327, 331–2.

91. Thompson, *Making*, pp. 604–59 puts Luddism firmly at the heart of his analysis.

92. Earle, *Making*, pp. xi and 10. Defoe, *Tour*, pp. 484–94 is the classic description

of this densely populated countryside in the eighteenth century. Fraser, *Modern Leeds*, p. 46, records that private censuses put the Leeds population at *c.* 17,000 in the early 1770s. The 1801 census put its urban core at 27,000, with a similar number in nearby out-townships. Halifax town then had a population of *c.* 9,000. Koditschek, *Class*, p. 21, states that urbanization made the proletarians, yet comments pp. 38 and 57 on the very slow initial rate of urbanization in Bradford, which had a population in the central core of only *c.* 3,000 in 1801, and *c.* 7,000 in Bradford township, though it reached 100,000 by mid-century. Birmingham already had 75,000 people in 1801, and even Colchester had 10,000.

93. See Davidoff and Hall, *Family*, pp. 416–20 on the urban nature of the voluntary associations which they see as essential for escaping from aristocratic patronage.

## CHAPTER 3

1. This essay is based on a study during 1993–4 of the industrial structure of nineteenth-century Sheffield directed by Dr Alan White at the University of East London.
2. P. Deane, *The First Industrial Revolution* (Cambridge, Cambridge University Press, 1969, repr. 1981), p. 162.
3. Ibid., pp. 292–3.
4. R. Samuel, 'Workshop of the World: Steam Power and Hand Technology in Mid-Victorian Britain', *History Workshop*, 3 (Spring 1977), esp. pp. 20, 51–2, 57–8.
5. R. Grayson and A. White, '"More Myth than Reality": the Independent Artisan in Nineteenth-century Sheffield', *Journal of Historical Sociology*, 9, 3 (1996), 337.
6. See R.M. Ledbetter, 'Sheffield's Industrial History from about 1700 with Special Reference to the Abbeydale Works' (MA thesis, Sheffield University, 1971), p. 2.
7. P. Hudson, *The Genesis of Industrial Capital* (Cambridge, Cambridge University Press, 1986); R. Lloyd-Jones and M.J. Lewis, *Manchester and the Age of the Factory* (London, Croom Helm, 1988); C. Behagg, *Politics and Production in the Early Nineteenth Century* (London, Routledge, 1990).
8. M. Berg, P. Hudson and M. Sonenscher, *Manufacture in Town and Country Before the Factory* (Cambridge, Cambridge University Press, 1983), p. 4.
9. M. Berg, *The Machinery Question and the Making of Political Economy 1815–1848* (Cambridge, Cambridge University Press, 1980), pp. 1–2.
10. Pollard's study of Sheffield predates the revisionist historiography under discussion here. See S. Pollard, *A History of Labour in Sheffield* (Liverpool, Liverpool University Press, 1959).
11. Grayson and White, '"More Myth than Reality"', pp. 337–40.
12. Samuel, 'Workshop', pp. 57–8: 'Steam power and hand technology may represent different principles of industrial organization. . . . But from the point of view of nineteenth-century capitalist development they were two sides of the same coin. . . . Few objects [at the Great Exhibition of 1851] excited more attention among foreigners than the displays of Sheffield cutlery and edge tools.'
13. A. Marshall, *Industry and Trade* (London, Macmillan, 1919), p. 282–8.
14. See E.H. Carr, *What is History?* (Harmondsworth, Penguin, 1961), p. 36: 'The

historian is part of history. The point in the procession at which he finds himself determines his angle of vision over the past.'

15. A. White, '"We Never Knew What Price We Were Going to Have Till We Got to the Warehouse": Nineteenth-century Sheffield and the Industrial District Debate', *Social History*, 22, 3 (1997), 307–17.

16. C. Sabel and J. Zeitlin, 'Historical Alternatives to Mass Production: Politics, Markets, and Technology in Nineteenth-Century Industrialization', *Past and Present*, 108 (1985), 133–76.

17. White, '"We Never Knew"', pp. 307–8.

18. F.H. Hill, 'An Account of Trade Combinations in Sheffield', in *Trade Societies and Strikes* (London, National Association for the Promotion of Social Science, 1860), pp. 530–1. See G.C. Holland, *The Vital Statistics of Sheffield* (London and Sheffield, Tyas and Greaves, 1843), pp. 46 ff.; and E.R. Wickham, *Church and People in an Industrial City* (London, Lutterworth Press, 1957), p. 59.

19. J.C. Symons, *Report on the Trades of Sheffield and on the Moral and Physical Condition of the Young Persons Employed in Them* (Sheffield, 1843), pp. 3–4.

20. R. Lloyd-Jones, M. Lewis and V. Gore, 'Sheffield History Proves Small is Beautiful', *Guardian*, 7 February 1994. Contrast this with A.D. Chandler, *Scale and Scope: Dynamics of Industrial Capitalism*, (Cambridge, Cambridge University Press, 1990).

21. Grayson and White, '"More Myth than Reality"', p. 343.

22. See n. 20; also M.J. Lewis, 'The Growth and Development of Sheffield's Industrial Structure 1880–1930' (PhD thesis, Sheffield City Polytechnic, 1989).

23. *Annual Report of HM Inspector of Factories and Workshops*, 31 October, 1887; G.I.H. Lloyd, *The Cutlery Trades* (London, Cass, 1913, repr. 1968), pp. 181–2.

24. Behagg, *Politics and Production*, p. 27.

25. *Sheffield Independent*, 17 February 1872.

26. *Select Committee on the Sweating System*, Parliamentary Papers (1889), XIII; *Royal Commission on Labour*, Parliamentary Papers (1894), XXXV. See D. Bythell, *The Sweated Trades: Outwork in Nineteenth-century Britain* (Newton Abbot, Batsford, 1978).

27. Grayson and White, '"More Myth than Reality"', p. 341. See also G.C. Holland, *A Treatise on the Progressive Improvement and Present State of the Manufactures in Metal*, vol. II (London, Longman, 1833), pp. 12–13; Lloyd, *Cutlery Trades*, pp. 194, 342.

28. S.A. Taylor, 'The Industrial Structure of the Sheffield Cutlery Trades 1870–1914', in C. Binfield et al. (eds), *The History of the City of Sheffield*, vol. II (Sheffield, Sheffield Academic Press, 1993), p. 198.

29. B.R. Dyson, *A Glossary of Sheffield Trade Terms and Dialect* (Sheffield, Society for the Preservation of Old Sheffield Tools, 1936, repr. 1977), p. 29. For a more detailed definition of a little master, see M.J. Unwin, *The Sheffield Pen and Pocket Knife Industry* (MA thesis, Sheffield University, 1989).

30. See R.G. Wilson, *Gentlemen Merchants: The Merchant Community in Leeds, 1780–1830* (Manchester, Manchester University Press, 1971); and P. Hudson, *Genesis*.

31. Select Committee on the Sweating System, Qs. 24710–29.

32. Hudson, *Genesis*, pp. 36, 261.

33. Grayson and White, '"More Myth than Reality"', p. 345. See also, B.A. Holderness, 'A Sheffield Commercial House in the Mid-Eighteenth Century: Messrs Oborne and Gunning around 1760', *Business History*, 15 (1973), 32–44; and D. Hey, 'Sheffield on the Eve of the Industrial Revolution', *Transactions of the Hunter Archaeological Society*, 14 (1987), 1–10.

34. Behagg, *Politics and Production*, pp. 59, 103.

35. A. White, 'Class, Culture and Control: the Sheffield Athenaeum Movement and the Middle Class 1847–64' in J. Wolff and J. Seed (eds), *The Culture of Capital: Art, Power and the Nineteenth-century Middle Class* (Manchester, Manchester University Press, 1988), pp. 83–115.

36. Select Committee on the Sweating System, Q. 24852.

37. White, '"We Never Knew"', p. 313. See also E.O. Wright, 'What is Middle About the Middle Class?' in J. Roemer (ed.), *Analytical Marxism* (Cambridge, Cambridge University Press, 1986, repr. 1988), pp. 114–40.

38. Grayson and White, '"More Myth than Reality"', pp. 344–6.

39. Symons, *Trades of Sheffield*, p. 3.

40. Ibid. See evidence by S. Uttley to the Select Committee on the Sweating System (n. 36).

41. S. Pollard (intro.), *The Sheffield Outrages* (Bath, Trades Unions Commission, 1971), p. 52. The Sheffield Outrages were a series of violent incidents by trade unionists against 'blacklegs'.

42. R. Grayson, *Knifemaking in Sheffield and the Hawley Collection* (Sheffield, Sheffield Hallam University, 1995), p. 8.

43. Grayson and White, '"More Myth than Reality"', p. 342. See also Lloyd, *Cutlery Trades*, pp. 193–4; Hudson, *Genesis*, p. 190; J. Benson, *The Penny Capitalists: A Study of Nineteenth-century Working-Class Entrepreneurs* (London, Gill and MacMillan, 1983), p. 51.

44. Select Committee on the Sweating System, Qs. 25250–3; 25326–25417.

45. Behagg, *Politics and Production*, p. 103.

46. S.A. Taylor, 'Tradition and Change: The Sheffield Cutlery Trades 1870–1914' (PhD thesis, Sheffield University, 1988), p. 319. See n. 13.

47. D. Smith, *Conflict and Compromise: Class Formation in English Society 1830–1914. A Comparative Study of Birmingham and Sheffield* (London, Routledge & Kegan Paul, 1982), p. 42.

48. Quoted from *Morning Chronicle* in ibid., p. 43.

49. Ibid.

50. Ibid., p. 39.

51. Lloyd, *Cutlery Trades*, p. 212.

52. White, '"We Never Knew"', p. 312.

53. Lloyd, *Cutlery Trades*, ch. XII.

54. See n. 33.

55. Pollard, *Sheffield Outrages*, p. xi.

56. Lloyd, *Cutlery Trades*, p. 248.

57. G. Tweedale, 'Strategies for Decline: George Wostenholm and Son and the Sheffield Cutlery Industry', *Transactions of the Hunter Archaeological Society*, 17 (1993), 43–59.

58. Lloyd, *Cutlery Trades*, p. 196.

59. See n. 25.

60. Lloyd, *Cutlery Trades*, pp. 193–4.

61. Taylor, *Tradition and Change*, p. 16.

62. G. Crossick, 'The Petite Bourgeoisie in Nineteenth-century Britain: The Urban

and Liberal Case' in G. Crossick and H.-G. Haupt (eds), *Shopkeepers and Master Artisans in Nineteenth-century Europe* (London, Methuen, 1984), pp. 84–5. See also Behagg, *Politics and Production*.

63. Crossick, 'Petite Bourgeoisie', p. 69.

64. Taylor, *Tradition and Change*, abstract.

65. J.L. Baxter, 'The Origins of the Social War in South Yorkshire: a Study of Capitalist Evolution and Labour Class Realization in One Industrial Region *c.* 1750–1855' (PhD thesis, Sheffield University, 1976), ch. 4.

66. Crossick, 'Petite Bourgeoisie', p. 86.

67. See n. 36.

68. M.I. Thomis, *Politics and Society in Nottingham 1785–1835* (Oxford, Blackwell, 1969), pp. 21–2.

69. Grayson and White, '"More Myth than Reality"', p. 336.

70. See Symons, *Trades of Sheffield*, for a discussion of 'Saint Monday', the term used to describe the difficulty employers had in getting workers to turn in at the beginning of the week.

71. Crossick and Haupt, *The Petite Bourgeoisie in Europe*, pp. 216–17.

72. G. Crossick, *An Artisan Elite in Victorian Society: Kentish London 1840–1880* (London, Croom Helm, 1978), p. 59.

73. E.g. Michael Heseltine on the BBC Radio 4 Programme *Today*, 21 November 1995.

## CHAPTER 4

1. See, for example, John Belchem (ed.), *Popular Politics, Riot and Labour: Essays in Liverpool History 1790–1940* (Liverpool, Liverpool University Press, 1992), and Belchem's essay, '"An accent exceedingly rare": scouse and the inflexion of class' in John Belchem and Neville Kirk (eds), *Languages of Labour* (Aldershot, Ashgate, 1997), pp. 99–130; and Sam Davies, *Liverpool Labour* (Keele, Keele University Press, 1996).

2. P.J. Cain and A.G. Hopkins, *British Imperialism: Innovation and Expansion 1688–1914*, and *Crisis and Deconstruction 1914–1990* (London, Longman, 1993).

3. *Liverpool Repository of Literature, Philosophy and Commerce*, Jan. 1826. See also M.J. Power, 'The Growth of Liverpool' in Belchem (ed.), *Popular Politics, Riot and Labour*, pp. 21–37.

4. See John Vincent's review of a number of books on the Gladstone family in *Victorian Studies*, 16 (1972), 101.

5. See, for example, *The Stranger in Liverpool: or, An historical and descriptive view of the town of Liverpool and its environs* (Liverpool, 1846), pp. 108–9.

6. *Chamber of Commerce. Report of the Select Committee appointed to consider what steps can be taken for the purpose of constituting Liverpool a self-dependent financial centre* (Liverpool, 1863). As early as 1698, Liverpool had appeared to Celia Fiennes as 'London in miniature'; see Power 'Growth of Liverpool' in Belchem (ed.), *Popular Politics*, p. 21.

7. Liverpool's pretensions were acknowledged by outsiders: see, for example, the entry on Liverpool in *Mitchell's Newspaper Press Directory* (1847), p. 161: 'Situated near the mouth of the Mersey, this *second metropolis*, has rapidly advanced in opulence and importance. . . . The public buildings are in a style of liberal expense and tasteful decoration, superior to those of almost any

provincial town in England; and several of its institutions are honourable testimonials of the enlightened spirit by which commercial prosperity has been accompanied.' For the extension of the 'second metropolis' motif into popular fiction, see Anon., *The Life, Adventures and Opinions of a Liverpool Policeman, and his Contemporaries* (Liverpool, 1841).

8. See Arline Wilson, 'William Roscoe and the Cultural Identity of Liverpool' in A. Kidd and D. Nicholls (eds), *Gender, Civic Culture and Consumerism: Middle-class Identity in Britain, 1800–1940.* (Manchester, Manchester University Press, forthcoming 1999).

9. For a useful survey of societies and institutes, see *Roscoe Magazine*, March 1849.

10. Tony Lane, *Liverpool: Gateway of Empire* (London, Lawrence and Wishart, 1987), ch. 2.

11. Thomas Baines, *History of the Commerce and Town of Liverpool, and of the rise of manufacturing industry in the adjoining counties* (London, 1852), p. 840.

12. Sir Robert Peel, in an address to merchants of Liverpool at a town hall dinner in his honour, was reported to have referred to Liverpool as 'this great commercial community – the greatest, probably, that the world knew', *The Economist*, 23 Oct. 1847, p. 1224.

13. Ibid., 11 Jan. 1845, p. 26.

14. Ibid., 23 Oct. 1847, p. 1224.

15. Baines, *History of the Commerce and Town of Liverpool*, pp. 743–5.

16. *The Economist*, 26 June 1847, p. 735.

17. *Gore's Directory*, 1845.

18. From the blurb on the back covers of Cain and Hopkins, *British Imperialism*.

19. Posting-bill in British Library, call-mark 10349f8.

20. A.C. Howe, 'Free trade and the City of London, *c.* 1820–1870', *History*, 77 (1992), 391–410.

21. *Report of the speech of J. Bramley-Moore . . . on the subject of dock extension addressed to the Liverpool Town Council* (Liverpool, 1846).

22. Liverpool Chamber of Commerce, *First Annual Report of the Council, presented to the Chamber at the General Meeting, held February 3, 1851* (Liverpool, 1851), p. 6.

23. Liverpool Record Office (LRO), 920–DUR /1/2, Holt Diaries, 25 Oct. 1844.

24. Ibid., 26 Jan. 1845.

25. Ibid., 29 Aug., 1844.

26. 'The cold-blooded pursuit of profit was deeply suspect on moral grounds', Leonore Davidoff and Catherine Hall, *Family Fortunes. Men and Women of the English Middle Class, 1780–1850* (London, Hutchinson 1987), pp. 21–2.

27. Eleanor F. Rathbone *William Rathbone: a Memoir* (London, Macmillan, 1905), p. 114.

28. Ibid., p. 113.

29. Ibid.

30. *The Economist*, 29 Nov. 1845, pp. 1192–3.

31. Margaret Simey, *Charity Rediscovered: a study of philanthropic effort in nineteenth-century Liverpool* (Liverpool, Liverpool University Press, 1992), chs 4 and 6.

32. LRO, Holt Diaries, 30 Nov. 1844.

33. *The Economist*, 24 Mar. 1849, p. 340.

34. LRO, Holt Diaries, 29 Nov. 1844.

35. Ibid., 24 Mar. 1844.

36. Ibid., 14 Jan. 1845.
37. *The Economist*, 18 Jan. 1845, pp. 48–9.
38. Ibid., 1 Feb. 1845, p. 96.
39. Ibid., 24 Aug. 1850, p. 937.
40. *The Times*, 28 Aug. 1849.
41. *The Economist*, 15 Nov. 1845, p. 1131. Art purchases of 'considerable price' by private individuals in Manchester and Liverpool of work by the English landscapist Mr J.W. Allen.
42. LRO, Holt Diaries, 2 Apr. 1845.
43. 'I have long been of the opinion that hundreds die in this town from *gradual* starvation.' Owen Williams, house agent, 5 March 1842, quoted in *Statistics of Vauxhall Ward, Liverpool, shewing the Actual Condition of more than Five Thousand Families, being the result of an inquiry recently instituted at the request of the Liverpool Anti-Monopoly Association, with observations and explanatory letters. Compiled and edited by John Finch Junr., merchant.* (Liverpool, 1842).
44. The development of a 'national society' incorporating for the first time merchants and commercialists, who had traditionally been confined to a provincial identity is discussed by Dror Wahrman in 'National Society, communal culture: an argument about the recent historiography of eighteenth century Britain', *Social History*, 17 (1992), 43–72.
45. M.J. Daunton shows these institutions to have been the principal pillars of urban society; see *Progress and Poverty. An Economic and Social History of Britain 1700–1850* (Oxford, Oxford University Press, 1995), p. 481.
46. *Gore's Directory*, 1845.
47. E.g., Eton Lodge, High Pastures, Park Hill, Woodlands, Etruria Villa, Beaconsfield House, Rose Mount, Elm House, Lavrock Bank, Springwood, Poplar Grove, Fair Lawn, Grove House, Rock Villa, Summer Garden, Green Bank, Richmond Hill.
48. Paul Booth, 'The background: people and the place' in Sefton Park Civic Society, *Sefton Park* (n.d.), p. 41.
49. Hawthorne to Henry A. Bright, 10 March 1860 in Thomas Woodson et al. (eds), *Nathaniel Hawthorne. The Letters, 1857–1864* (Athens, OH, Ohio University Press, 1987), p. 248.
50. LRO, Holt Diaries, 11 Jan. 1846; 21 June 1846; 24 June 1846.
51. Ibid., 7 Feb. 1845–1 May 1847.
52. The time-span of the sample was from 11 November 1844 to 18 June 1848.
53. Belchem, '"An accent exceedingly rare"' in Belchem and Kirk (eds), *Languages of Labour*, pp. 99–130.
54. For the importance of such symbiosis to national economic well-being, see Geoffrey Ingham, 'British capitalism: empire, merchants and decline', *Social History*, 20 (1995), 339–54.
55. *The highways of peaceful commerce have been the highways of art, an address delivered at Liverpool . . . August 30, 1853, on occasion of the opening of the Catholic Institute, by His Eminence Cardinal Wiseman* (Liverpool, 1853).
56. Steven Fielding, *Class and Ethnicity: Irish Catholics in England, 1880–1939* (Buckingham, Open University Press, 1993), p. 5.
57. John Belchem, '"Freedom and Friendship to Ireland": Ribbonism in early nineteenth-century Liverpool', *International Review of Social History*, 39 (1994), 33–56; and 'Liverpool in the year of revolution: the political and

associational culture of the Irish immigrant community in 1848' in Belchem (ed.), *Popular Politics, Riot and Labour*, pp. 68–97.

58. Valerie Burton, 'Liverpool's mid-nineteenth century coasting trade' in Burton (ed.), *Liverpool Shipping, Trade and Industry* (Liverpool, National Museums and Galleries on Merseyside, 1989), pp. 26–66.

59. See the interesting portrayal of 'Liverpool and the Celtic Sea' in Robert Scally, *The End of Hidden Ireland* (New York, Oxford University Press, 1995), ch. 9.

60. L.W. Brady, *T.P. O'Connor and the Liverpool Irish* (London, Royal Historical Society, 1983), p. 37.

61. Biographical details can be obtained from the appendices of C.D. Watkinson, 'The Liberal Party on Merseyside in the Nineteenth Century' (unpublished PhD thesis, University of Liverpool, 1967); and B. O'Connell, 'The Irish Nationalist Party in Liverpool, 1873–1922' (unpublished MA thesis, University of Liverpool, 1971).

## CHAPTER 5

1. Clifton to James Fair, n.d. Quoted by John Kennedy, *The Clifton Chronicle* (Preston, Carnegie Press, 1990), p. 75.

2. *Preston Chronicle*, 5 Jan. 1850, p. 4.

3. Mr Alderman Baynes, *The Cotton Trade. Two Lectures . . . delivered before the members of the Blackburn Literary, Scientific and Mechanics' Institution* (on 2 April and 11 June 1857; Blackburn, 1857), II, 'Its Mission: Politically, Socially, Morally, and Religiously', pp. 56–7, 60, 66–8, 74–7.

4. Obituary, *Blackburn Times*, 11 Oct. 1873, p. 6.

5. As noted by, for example, D.A. Farnie, *The English Cotton Industry and the World Market 1815–1896* (Oxford, Clarendon Press, 1979), p. 40; Wendy Hinde, *Richard Cobden. A Victorian Outsider* (New Haven and London, Yale University Press, 1987), pp. 70–1, 282; Norman McCord, *The Anti-Corn Law League 1838–1846* (London, George Allen & Unwin, 1958), pp. 208–12; W.H. Greenleaf, *The British Political Tradition* (London and New York, Methuen, 1983), vol. 2, *The Ideological Heritage*, pp. 38–42; Geoffrey Best, *Mid-Victorian Britain 1851–1875* (London, Weidenfeld and Nicolson, 1971), p. 239; Gary S. Messinger, *Manchester in the Victorian Age. The Half-Known City* (Manchester, Manchester University Press, 1985), pp. 73–8.

6. Baynes, *The Cotton Trade*, pp. 88–9. For similar reactions, see Paul Adelman, *Victorian Radicalism: The Middle-Class Experience, 1830–1914* (London and New York, Longman, 1984), ch. 2.

7. The distinction between milltown radicals and liberals along a spectrum of reforming opinion is not clear-cut, though the more radical tended to be especially exercised by aristocratic privileges and values. For a useful attempt at clarification, see T.A. Jenkins, *The Liberal Ascendancy, 1830–1886* (New York, St Martin's Press, 1994), pp. 10–14.

8. Bolton Archives and Local Studies, Bolton Biographical Notes B1, pp. 147–9.

9. British Library, Cobden Papers, vol. VII, Add. MS 43653, Ashworth to Cobden, 22 Sept., 3 Oct. 1849, 12 Oct. 1852.

10. BL, Peel Papers, Add. MS 40589, Whittaker to Peel, 15 Apr. 1846; Lancashire Record Office, Coucher Book of Trinity, PR 1549/14.

11. For a good summary of the 'feudalization'/'bourgeoisification' debate, see Simon Gunn, 'The "Failure" of the Victorian Middle Class: A Critique' in Janet

Wolff and John Seed (eds), *The Culture of Capital: Art, Power and the Nineteenth-century Middle Class* (Manchester, Manchester University Press, 1988).

12. This is what is attempted in Brian Lewis, 'Bourgeois Ideology and Order: Middle-Class Culture and Politics in Lancashire, 1789–1851' (unpublished PhD thesis, Harvard University, 1994). For a critique of the exclusion of the state and politics from a number of notable studies, see Adrian Wilson, 'A Critical Portrait of Social History' in Wilson (ed.), *Rethinking Social History: English Society 1570–1920 and its Interpretation* (Manchester and New York, Manchester University Press, 1993), pp. 19, 26–7; and John Seed, 'Capital and Class Formation in Early Industrial England', *Social History*, 18, 1 (Jan. 1993), 17–30.

13. Nicholas B. Dirks, Geoff Eley and Sherry B. Ortner (eds), *Culture/Power/History: A Reader in Contemporary Social Theory* (Princeton, Princeton University Press, 1994), intro., pp. 13–32.

14. Patrick Joyce (ed.), *Oxford Readers: Class* (Oxford and New York, Oxford University Press, 1995), intro., pp. 3–16.

15. This applied to most, but by no means all, and was truer among local than national leaders. For one indication of the denominational split reflected in voting patterns, see *Bolton Free Press*, 14 Aug. 1847, p. 3. This begs the important question of the direction of causality: did people become radical because they were Dissenters, or vice versa? During the eighteenth century this is difficult to determine (see John Rule, *Albion's People. English Society, 1714–1815* (London and New York, Longman, 1992), pp. 94–6); but in the period under discussion, so far as I can tell, conversion to Dissent was rare.

16. See Jan Albers, '"Papist traitors" and "Presbyterian rogues": religious identities in eighteenth-century Lancashire' in John Walsh, Colin Haydon and Stephen Taylor (eds), *The Church of England c. 1689–c. 1833. From Toleration to Tractarianism* (Cambridge, Cambridge University Press, 1993), pp. 319–20.

17. A phrase brought to mind for another context by Michael Ignatieff, *Blood and Belonging. Journeys into the New Nationalism* (Harmondsworth, Penguin, 1993), p. 14: 'Freud once argued that the smaller the real difference between two peoples the larger it was bound to loom in their imagination. He called this effect the narcissism of minor difference. Its corollary must be that enemies need each other to remind themselves of who they really are.'

18. Frank O'Gorman, 'Pitt and the "Tory" Reaction to the French Revolution 1789–1815' in H.T. Dickinson (ed.), *Britain and the French Revolution, 1789–1815* (Basingstoke and London, Macmillan, 1989); James J. Sack, *From Jacobite to Conservative. Reaction and Orthodoxy in Britain, c. 1760–1832* (Cambridge, Cambridge University Press, 1993); Geoffrey Holmes and Daniel Szechi, *The Age of Oligarchy. Pre-industrial Britain 1722–1783* (London and New York, Longman, 1993), p. 332.

19. Notably Linda Colley, *Britons. Forging the Nation 1707–1837* (New Haven and London, Yale University Press, 1992); H.T. Dickinson, *Liberty and Property: Political Ideology in Eighteenth-century Britain*, (2nd edn, London, Methuen, 1979); Dickinson (ed.), *Britain and the French Revolution*; Gerald Newman, *The Rise of English Nationalism: A Cultural History 1740–1830* (New York, St Martin's Press, 1987); Robert R. Dozier, *For King, Constitution, and Country. The English Loyalists and the French Revolution* (Lexington, KY, University Press of Kentucky, 1983); David Eastwood, 'Patriotism and the English State in

the 1790s' in Mark Philp (ed.), *The French Revolution and British Popular Politics* (Cambridge, Cambridge University Press, 1991).

20. See Lewis, 'Bourgeois Ideology', ch. 1. On the appropriation of Pitt see Sack, *From Jacobite to Conservative*, pp. 85, 88–90. He was relatively liberal regarding reform, religion and Catholic emancipation, and held a Whiggish outlook on history, philosophy and theology, but his press turned him into something quite different.

21. Colley, *Britons*, p. 138; O'Gorman, 'Pitt and the "Tory" Reaction', pp. 114–15; Albert Goodwin, *The Friends of Liberty: The English Democratic Movement in the Age of the French Revolution* (London, Hutchinson, 1979), chs 3, 5, 7; Dumas Malone, *The Public Life of Thomas Cooper 1783–1839* (New Haven, Yale University Press, 1926), ch. 1.

22. William Dobson, *History of the Parliamentary Representation of Preston*, (2nd edn, Preston, 1868), pp. 54, 64–5; Stephen W. Urbanski, 'Parliamentary Politics, 1796–1832, in an Industrializing Borough: Preston, Lancashire' (unpublished PhD thesis, Emory University, 1976), pp. 58–60; H.W. Clemesha, '"The Weaver's Friend." A Short Account of a Former Parliamentary Candidate for Preston (MS in LRO, [1927?]); *Parliamentary Papers*, 1811, II, 'Report on Petition of Several Weavers: Evidence of Joseph Hanson, Esq.', pp. 2–3, 13; *Preston Election Squibs*, 1807, pp. 4, 9, 23–4, 50; *An Alphabetical List of the Electors Polled* (Preston, 1807); *Preston Chronicle*, 10 Oct. 1812.

23. 'The Blackfaces of 1812 . . .' (Bolton, 1839), pp. 8–18, repr. in Kenneth E. Carpenter (ed.), *British Labour Struggles: Contemporary Pamphlets 1727–1850. The Luddites* (New York, Arno Press, 1972).

24. See, for example, Bolton Archives and Local Studies, Heywood Papers, ZHE/18–27, 15 Mar. 1828; Thomas Grimshaw, *The Cogitations of Thomas Grimshaw Esq.* (Bolton, 1839), p. 7; *Bolton Free Press*, 28 Nov. 1835, p. 7, 18 Aug. 1838, p. 2.

25. *Blackburn Mail*, 4 Mar. 1812, p. 1, 18 Mar., p. 3, 25 Mar., p. 3, 1 Apr., p. 2; François Crouzet, *L'Économie Britannique et le Blocus Continental (1806–1813)* (Paris, Presses Universitaire de France, 1958), vol. II, pp. 793 ff, 809–29.

26. Lancashire Record Office, Hulton of Hulton Papers, DDHu 53/55. The addresses and loyalist rejoinders were published together by William Addison, Preston, 1 May 1817, to demonstrate that Lancashire still retained a high character of loyalty.

27. For example, Public Record Office, HO 40/17, Major Eckersley to Lt Gen Byng, 19 Feb. 1822.

28. William Alexander Abram, *Blackburn Characters of a Past Generation* (Blackburn, 1894), p. 17.

29. Dobson, *Parliamentary Representation*, pp. 72–4; LRO, QDE/3, '1826—List of Voters'; *Manchester Guardian*, 22 Oct. 1856, obituary of Wood; Lewis, 'Bourgeois Ideology', pp. 328 ff.

30. Roland Quinault, 'The Industrial Revolution and Parliamentary Reform' in Patrick O'Brien and Quinault (eds), *The Industrial Revolution and British Society* (Cambridge, Cambridge University Press, 1993), pp. 196–201.

31. Dobson, *Parliamentary Representation*, pp. 75–6; Winifred Proctor, 'Orator Hunt, MP for Preston, 1830–32', *Transactions of the Historic Society of Lancashire and Cheshire*, 114 (1962), 131–44; *An Alphabetical List of the Electors Polled* (Preston, 1831).

32. For example, *Bolton Chronicle*, 12 Feb. 1831, p. 4, 26 Feb, pp. 1, 3.

33. *Preston Chronicle*, 26 May, p. 3.

34. Dobson, *Parliamentary Representation*, pp. 78–80; *A List of Persons Entitled to Vote* (Preston, 1833); *Autobiographical Recollections of Sir John Bowring* (London, 1877), *passim*; W. Brimelow, *Political and Parliamentary History of Bolton* (Bolton, 1882), pp. 125–46, 150–92; Lewis, 'Bourgeois Ideology', pp. 348 ff.

35. See P.J. Cain and A.G. Hopkins, *British Imperialism: Innovation and Expansion 1688–1914* (London and New York, Longman, 1993), pp. 141–2. For Bolton, this is dealt with in depth in Peter Taylor, *Popular Politics in Early Industrial Britain: Bolton 1825–1850* (Keele, Keele University Press, 1995).

36. *Bolton Free Press*, 21 Nov. 1835, p. 2. This manifesto was signed 'A. W. P.' – presumably A.W. Paulton, soon to be a prominent anti-Corn Law speaker.

37. *Bolton Free Press*, 18 Aug. 1837, p. 3, 22 Sept. 1838, p. 3, 2 Feb. 1839, p. 3.

38. *Bolton Free Press*, 16 Feb. 1839, pp. 2–3, 24 Aug., p. 2, 31 Aug., p. 2; *Bolton Chronicle*, 10 Aug., p. 2, 17 Aug., p. 2, 24 Aug., p. 2; Robert Sykes, 'Physical-Force Chartism: The Cotton District and the Chartist Crisis of 1839', *International Review of Social History*, xxx, 2 (1985), 220, 235.

39. *Bolton Free Press*, 14 Sept. 1839, p. 2.

40. *Bolton Free Press*, 13 Aug. 1842, p. 2, 20 Aug., p. 2, 27 Aug., p. 2.

41. *Manchester Guardian*, 20 Jan. 1844, p. 7; *Bolton Free Press*, 16 Mar., p. 3, 23 Mar., p. 3.

42. Lewis, 'Bourgeois Ideology', pp. 382 ff. In Preston, apparently the only leading inhabitant to address a Chartist demonstration was Alderman John Noble, a prosperous Catholic maltster. According to the *Preston Pilot*, 10 Nov. 1838, pp. 2–3, this was why he was not re-elected as an alderman; he had forfeited 'every claim to become a member of any body that is composed of gentlemen'.

43. This especially needs stressing in the light of recent studies of radicalism that emphasize continuities over the mid-century period. See Eugenio F. Biagini and Alastair J. Reid (eds), *Currents of Radicalism: Popular Radicalism, Organized Labour and Party Politics in Britain, 1850–1914* (Cambridge, Cambridge University Press, 1991); Margot Finn, *After Chartism: Class and Nation in English Radical Politics, 1848–1874* (Cambridge, Cambridge University Press, 1993); David Nicholls, 'The English Middle Class and the Ideological Significance of Radicalism, 1760–1886', *Journal of British Studies*, 24 (Oct. 1985), 415–33; Miles Taylor, *The Decline of British Radicalism, 1847–1860* (Oxford, Oxford University Press, 1995).

44. See John Breuilly, *Labour and Liberalism in Nineteenth-century Europe. Essays in Comparative History*, (2nd edn, Manchester, Manchester University Press, 1994), p. 208 and *passim*.

45. Martin J. Daunton, *Progress and Poverty: An Economic and Social History of Britain 1700–1850* (Oxford, Oxford University Press, 1995), chs 18–20; J.R. Dinwiddy, 'Chartism', *Radicalism and Reform in Britain, 1780–1850* (London and Rio Grande, Hambledon Press, 1992), pp. 416–20.

46. BL, Cobden Papers, vol. VII, Add. MS 43653, Ashworth to Cobden, 25 May 1850, 22 Oct. 1851.

47. See Patrick O'Brien, 'Political Preconditions for the Industrial Revolution' in O'Brien and Quinault, *Industrial Revolution*, pp. 125–51; John Brewer, *The Sinews of Power. War, Money and the English State, 1688–1783* (London, Unwin Hyman, 1989); Lawrence Stone (ed.), *An Imperial State at War* (London and New York, Routledge, 1994), intro.; John Prest, *Liberty and Locality.*

*Parliament, Permissive Legislation, and Ratepayers' Democracies in the Nineteenth Century* (Oxford, Clarendon Press, 1990).

48. *Blackburn Standard*, 27 Feb. 1850, pp. 1–2.

49. Baynes, *The Cotton Trade*, I, 'The Origin, Rise, Progress and Present Extent of the Cotton Trade', pp. 30–1.

50. *Preston Chronicle*, 15 Apr. 1848, p. 4, 22 Apr., p. 4, 18 Nov., p. 4; *Preston Guardian*, 15 Apr., p. 4. This should be borne in mind alongside the contention of John Saville, *1848. The British State and the Chartist Movement* (Cambridge, Cambridge University Press, 1987), that the events of 1848 demonstrated for the first time beyond question that the propertied ranks stood behind constitution and state. See also his *The Consolidation of the Capitalist State, 1800–1850* (London and Boulder, Colo., Pluto Press, 1994), ch. 6.

51. Notably Leonore Davidoff and Catherine Hall, *Family Fortunes. Men and Women of the English Middle Class, 1780–1850* (London, Hutchinson, 1987); Theodore Koditschek, *Class Formation and Urban-Industrial Society. Bradford, 1750–1850* (Cambridge, Cambridge University Press, 1990); R.J. Morris, *Class, Sect and Party. The Making of the British Middle Class, Leeds 1820–1850* (Manchester, Manchester University Press, 1990).

52. Jürgen Kocka, 'The Middle Classes in Europe', *Journal of Modern History*, 67, 4 (Dec. 1995), 804.

53. This interpretation differs quite markedly from, for example, that of Michael Mann, *The Sources of Social Power*, vol. II, *The Rise of Classes and Nation-States, 1760–1914* (Cambridge, Cambridge University Press, 1993), pp. 529–31, 541, 724. In his bold attempt to understand the sources of social power he argues, rightly, that Chartism did not fail because of its own weaknesses, since in scope, intensity and organization it more than matched anything comparable before the revolutions in France. It failed, he claims, because there was no weakness or division on the other side: the working class encountered an equally resolute, class-conscious and self-righteous ruling regime and capitalist class. They clashed head on, and there was no dialectical resolution. The working class lost, as it has lost all such head on clashes.

54. See, for example, Anthony Giddens, *A Contemporary Critique of Historical Materialism*, vol. I, *Power, Property and the State* (Berkeley and Los Angeles, University of California Press, 1981), vol. II, *The Nation State and Violence* (Cambridge, Polity Press, 1987); Charles Tilly, *Coercion, Capital, and European States, AD 990–1990* (Oxford, Basil Blackwell, 1990); Ernest Gellner, *Nations and Nationalism* (Oxford, Basil Blackwell, 1983), pp. 55–7.

55. Michael Winstanley, 'Oldham Radicalism and the Origins of Popular Liberalism, 1830–52', *Historical Journal*, 36, 3 (1993), 642–3; Gareth Stedman Jones, 'Rethinking Chartism' in *Languages of Class. Studies in English Working Class History 1832–1982* (Cambridge, Cambridge University Press, 1983), pp. 174–7; Miles Taylor, 'Rethinking the Chartists: Searching for Synthesis in the Historiography of Chartism', *Historical Journal*, 39, 2 (1996), 488–92.

56. See, for example, Michel Foucault, *Discipline and Punish. The Birth of the Prison* (New York, Pantheon Books, 1977); Foucault, *The History of Sexuality, vol. I, An Introduction* (New York, Vintage Books, 1990); Giddens, *Nation-State and Violence*; Michael Ignatieff, 'Total Institutions and Working Classes: A Review Essay', *History Workshop*, 15 (Spring, 1983); and for a discussion of the literature, Lewis, 'Bourgeois Ideology', chs 3–4.

57. Fleshed out in Lewis, 'Bourgeois Ideology', chs 5–9, 11–13.

58. Brian Harrison, *Peaceable Kingdom. Stability and Change in Modern Britain* (Oxford, Clarendon Press, 1982), pp. 3–4, reaches a somewhat similar conclusion, though couching the debate in different terms.

59. See Richard Price, 'Historiography, Narrative, and the Nineteenth Century', *Journal of British Studies*, 35 (Apr. 1996), 231–2.

60. See Patrick Curry, 'Towards a post-Marxist social history: Thompson, Clark and beyond' in Wilson (ed.), *Rethinking Social History*, pp. 165–87; and contrast Stephen Hill, 'Britain: The Dominant Ideology Thesis after a decade', and Bryan S. Turner, 'Conclusion: peroration on ideology' in Nicholas Abercrombie, Hill and Turner (eds), *Dominant Ideologies* (London, Unwin Hyman, 1990).

61. A point argued by, for example, L.G. Mitchell, *Charles James Fox* (Oxford, Oxford University Press, 1992); Peter Mandler, *Aristocratic Government in the Age of Reform. Whigs and Liberals, 1830–1852* (Oxford, Clarendon Press, 1990); Jenkins, *Liberal Ascendancy*, p. 7.

## CHAPTER 6

1. R.J. Morris, Paper at conference on Middle Class, Manchester Metropolitan University, September 1996, which appears as chapter 8: 'Reading the Will' in this volume.

2. G. Crossick, 'Urban Society and the Petty Bourgeoisie in Nineteenth-century Britain' in D. Fraser and A. Sutcliffe (eds), *The Pursuit of Urban History* (London, Edward Arnold, 1983), p. 319. He repeats the same point about the 'anecdotal' nature of the evidence twelve years later in Crossick and Haupt, *The Petite Bourgeoisie in Europe*, p. 203.

3. C.W. Chalklin, *The Provincial Towns of Georgian England: a Study of the Building Process, 1740–1820* (London, Edward Arnold, 1974) provides material for the eighteenth century. R. Lloyd-Jones and M.J. Lewis, *Manchester and the Age of the Factory: the Business Structure of Cottonopolis in the Industrial Revolution* (London, Croom Helm, 1988) provides details on property assets but not who owned them.

4. J. Foster, *Class Struggle in the Industrial Revolution* (London, Methuen, 1974), p. 271.

5. A. Offer, *Property and Politics, 1870–1914: Landownership, Law, Ideology and Urban Development in England* (Cambridge, Cambridge University Press, 1981), pp. 23–35.

6. M. Chase, 'Out of Radicalism: the Mid-Victorian Freehold Land Movement', *English Historical Review*, 106 (1991), 319–45.

7. E.P. Hennock, 'Finance and Politics in Urban Local Government in England, 1835–1900', *Historical Journal*, 6 (1963), 212–25.

8. E.A Cameron, *Land for the People? The British Government and the Scottish Highlands, c. 1880–1925* (Scottish Historical Review/Tuckwell Press, 1996).

9. Offer, *Property and Politics*, pp. 113–14, 120.

10. R.J. Morris, 'The Middle Class and British Towns and Cities of the Industrial Revolution 1780–1870' in Fraser and Sutcliffe, *Pursuit of Urban History*, p. 295.

11. D. Englander, *Landlord and Tenant in Urban Britain 1838–1918* (Oxford, Clarendon Press, 1983), pp. 51–2.

12. Crossick and Haupt, *Petite Bourgeoisie*, p. 203.

13. M.J. Daunton, *House and Home in the Victorian City: Working-Class Housing 1850–1914* (London, Edward Arnold, 1983), pp. 108 ff.

14. G. Crossick, 'The Petite Bourgeoisie in Nineteenth-century Britain' in G. Crossick and H.-G. Haupt (eds), *Shopkeepers and Master Artisans in Nineteenth-Century Europe* (London, Methuen, 1984), pp. 62–94; Offer, *Property and Politics*; Englander, *Landlord and Tenant*.

15. *Poor Law Commission*, Appendix B2, Answers to Town Queries, QQ50–52, *PP*, 1834, XXXVI, pp. 75 ff.

16. J.D. Marshall, 'Colonisation as a Factor in the Planting of Towns in North-West England' in H.J. Dyos (ed.), *The Study of Urban History* (London, Edward Arnold, 1968), p. 221.

17. C. Bedale, 'Property Relations and Housing Policy: Oldham in the Late Nineteenth and Early Twentieth Centuries' in J. Melling (ed.), *Housing, Social Policy and the State* (London, Croom Helm, 1980), pp. 50–1.

18. P. Joyce, *Work, Society and Politics: The Culture of the Factory in Later Victorian England* (Brighton, Harvester, 1980), p. 122.

19. S. and B. Webb, *Statutory Authorities for Special Purposes* (London, Longman, Green and Co., 1922), pp. 235–349; B. Keith-Lucas, *The Unreformed Local Government System* (London, Croom Helm, 1980), pp. 108–21.

20. Webbs, *Statutory Authorities*, p. 246.

21. E. Butterworth, *Historical Sketches of Oldham* (Oldham, 1856), p. 190.

22. Webbs, *Statutory Authorities*, p. 473.

23. Webbs, *Statutory Authorities*, p. 245; J. Garrard, *Leadership and Power in Victorian Industrial Towns 1830–80* (Manchester, Manchester University Press, 1983), pp. 14–19.

24. P. Taylor, *Popular Politics in Early Industrial Britain. Bolton, 1825–1850* (Keele, Keele University Press, 1995), p. 40.

25. M.J. Turner, *Reform and Respectability: the Making of a Middle-class Liberalism in Early Nineteenth-century Manchester* (vol. 40, Chetham Society, 1995), pp. 119–46; D. Fraser, *Urban Politics in Victorian England: the Structure of Politics in Victorian Cities* (Leicester, Leicester University Press, 1976), pp. 95–100; V.A.C. Gatrell, 'Incorporation and the Pursuit of Liberal Hegemony in Manchester, 1790–1839' in D. Fraser (ed.), *Municipal Reform and the Industrial City* (Leicester, Leicester University Press, 1982).

26. Foster, *Class Struggle*, pp. 56–61.

27. Crossick, 'Petite Bourgeoisie', pp. 72–4.

28. Webbs, *Statutory Authorities*, pp. 251–2, 264, 271.

29. For the difference between rental and rateable value see Fraser, *Urban Politics*, p. 97.

30. Oldham Police Act, 7 Geo IV 1826.

31. Oldham Local Studies Library, Oldham Police Commission Membership Book, (OLSL), PCO. Details on individual members have been supplemented by reference to trade directories of the period.

32. R.J. Morris, 'The Middle Class and the Property Cycle during the Industrial Revolution' in T.C. Smout (ed.), *The Search for Wealth and Stability* (London, Macmillan, 1979).

33. Report of Parliamentary Boundary Commissioners, vol. 3, 1832, p. 67; S. Bamford, *Walks in South Lancashire and on its Borders* [1844] (Brighton, Harvester Press, 1972), p. 10; Lancashire Record Office (LRO), Oldham Tithe Award 1845, DRM/1/74.

34.  M. Smith, *Religion and Industrial Society: Oldham and Saddleworth, 1740–1865* (Oxford, Clarendon Press, 1994), pp. 9–12.

35.  Estimates from Butterworth, *Oldham*, pp. 193–4, 213.

36.  Foster, *Class Struggle*, pp. 177–86. See also K. Honeyman, *Origins of Enterprise: Business Leadership in the Industrial Revolution* (Manchester, Manchester University Press, 1982), pp. 87–97. All bar two of the twenty textile producers among the founding members were listed as 'manufacturers' indicative of their ownership of large integrated firms. For an estimate of employment patterns, see R. Sykes, 'Some Aspects of Working-Class Consciousness in Oldham, 1830–1842', *Historical Journal*, 23 (1980), 168–9.

37.  LRO, Oldham Poor Rate Book, 1848.

38.  OLSL, Police Commission Minute Books, PCO1/1 & 1/2.

39.  Commission Minutes, June 1829, Mar. 1830, June 1830, Oct. 1831.

40.  T.W. Fletcher, 'The Economic Development of Agriculture in East Lancashire' (MSc thesis, Leeds University, 1954).

41.  This aspect was widely commented on at the time, see e.g. A.B. Reach, *Manchester and the Textile Districts in 1849*, ed. C. Aspin (Helmshore Local History Society, 1972), p. 80. One-third of textile concerns in Oldham parish employed less than 20 workers; Reports of the Inspectors of Factories, PP 1842, vol. xxii.

42.  Several, including the radical leader William Knott, would appear to have lost qualifications during the depression of 1838–42.

43.  OLSL, Commission Minutes Aug. 1830. Subsequent meetings saw large numbers of manufacturers appealing against payment of these rates. The fact that all watching costs were consequently borne entirely by town-centre residents led to the decision to disband the night watch on 2 February 1831, not working-class pressure as Foster suggests: Foster, *Class Struggle*, p. 59.

44.  *The Freeholder*, 1 May 1850.

45.  The following paragraphs are based on an analysis of Oldham Poll Books in OLSL: 1832, 1835, 1847 and 1852 (by-election).

46.  Sykes, 'Working-Class Consciousness', pp. 174–5.

47.  For analysis of this split, see M. Winstanley, 'Oldham Radicalism and the Origins of Popular Liberalism, 1830–52', *Historical Journal*, 36 (1993), 619–44.

48.  The motion was carried 100–53; farmers voted 5–20 against it. OLSL, Commission Minutes, December 1848.

49.  D. Alexander, *Retailing in England During the Industrial Revolution* (London, Athlone Press, 1967); R. Scola, *Feeding the Victorian City: the Food Supply of Manchester, 1770–1870* (Manchester, Manchester University Press, 1992), pp. 180, 190, 197, 206; M. Hewitt, *The Emergence of Stability in the Industrial City: Manchester, 1832–67* (Aldershot, Scolar Press, 1996), p. 33.

50.  Taylor, *Popular Politics*, p. 27; Fraser, *Urban Politics*, p. 121; Turner, *Reform and Respectability*, pp. 106–11.

51.  T.J. Nossiter, *Influence, Opinion and Political Idioms in Reformed England: Case Studies from the North East, 1832–74* (Brighton, Harvester, 1975), pp. 166, 169; J. Vincent, *Pollbooks: How Victorians Voted* (Cambridge, Cambridge University Press, 1967).

52.  Nossiter, *Influence*, p. 151.

53.  J. Kay, *The Social Condition and Education of the People in England and Europe* (1850), quoted in Offer, *Property and Politics*, p. 149.

54.  Garrard, *Leadership and Power*, p. 131.

55.  V.A.C. Gatrell, 'The Commercial Middle Class in Manchester, 1820–1857'

(DPhil thesis, Cambridge University, 1972), pp. 85–9; Bedale, *Property Relations*, p. 59 drawing on D. Farnie, 'The English Cotton Industry, 1850–1896' (MA thesis, Manchester University, 1953).

56. B. Weber, 'A New Index of House Rents for Great Britain 1874–1913', *Scottish Journal of Political Economy*, 7 (1960), 232–7.

57. Daunton, *House and Home*, p. 103.

58. Owner-occupiers appear to have accounted for between 11 and 27 per cent of property values in Daunton's tables; *House and Home*, pp. 106–17. Offer, *Property and Politics*, p. 122 estimates that 6.11 million dwellings accounted for 85 per cent of the housing stock in 1904 but only 45 per cent of its value.

## CHAPTER 7

1. John Smail, *The Origins of Middle-Class Culture, Halifax, Yorkshire, 1660–1780* (Ithaca, Cornell University Press, 1995); Theodore Koditschek, *Class Formation and Urban Industrial Society. Bradford 1750–1850* (Cambridge, Cambridge University Press, 1990); Janet Wolff and John Seed (eds), *The Culture of Capital: Art, Power and the Nineteenth-century Middle Class* (Manchester, Manchester University Press, 1988).

2. Richard H. Trainor, *Black Country Elites. The Exercise of Authority in an Industrial Area, 1830–1900* (Oxford, Clarendon Press, 1993).

3. The sample of wills was drawn from the archives of the Borthwick Institute of Historical Research in York. I thank the staff for their help. I have received support in this work from Edinburgh University and the Nuffield Trust and thank them both.

4. Leonore Davidoff and Catherine Hall, *Family Fortunes. Men and Women of the English Middle Class, 1780–1850* (London, Hutchinson, 1987); R.J. Morris, *Class, Sect and Party. The Making of the British Middle Class, Leeds 1820–1850* (Manchester, Manchester University Press, 1990).

5. W.D. Rubinstein, 'The Victorian Middle Classes: Wealth, Occupation and Geography', *Economic History Review*, 30 (1970); W.D. Rubinstein, 'Wealth, Elites and the Class Structure of Modern Britain', *Past and Present*, 76 (1977).

6. J.C. Hudson, *The Executors Guide* (London, 1838), p. 21.

7. Ibid.

8. R.J. Morris, *Class, Sect and Party*, p. 221.

9. M.W. Beresford, 'East End, West End: The Face of Leeds during Urbanization, 1684–1842', *Publications of the Thoresby Society*, vols LX and LXI, nos 131 and 132 (Leeds, 1985–6), p. 393.

10. Peter Earle, *The Making of the English Middle Class. Business, Society and Family Life in London, 1660–1730* (London, Methuen, 1989).

11. Will of George Hepper, woolstapler of Wortley in the parish of Leeds, court of Ainstey, 24 Apr. 1830. All the wills are in the Borthwick Institute of Historical Research, York. They will be referred to by the date of probate and the court to which they were presented. The court of Ainstey dealt with estates that contained property limited to the Leeds area, while the Prerogative Court dealt with estates which had property in several areas of the Ecclesiastical Province of York.

12. R.J. Morris, 'Men, women and property: The reform of the Married Women's Property Act 1870' in F.M.L. Thompson (ed.), *Landowners*,

*Capitalists and Entrepreneurs* (Oxford, Oxford University Press, 1994); Lee Holcombe, *Wives and Property. Reform of the Married Women's Property Law in Nineteenth-century England* (Toronto, University of Toronto Press, 1983); Mary Lyndon Shanley, *Feminism, Marriage and the Law in Victorian England, 1850–1895* (Princeton, Princeton University Press, 1989).

13. Edmund Craister, boot and shoemaker, Ainstey, 5 Dec. 1831.

14. William Harrison, spirit merchant, Ainstey, 7 Oct. 1831.

15. Liam Kennedy, 'Farm Succession in modern Ireland: elements of a theory of inheritance', *Economic History Review*, XLIV (Aug. 1991), 477–99.

16. Charles Coupland, solicitor, Ainstey, 13 June 1831.

17. James Noble, surgeon, Ainstey, 1 Mar. 1830.

18. Edward Broke, merchant, Prerogative, 1 July 1831.

19. Richard Kemplay, gentleman, Prerogative, 16 May 1831.

20. Edward Armitage, gentleman, Prerogative, 15 Feb. 1830.

21. Rachel Thackrey, widow, Ainstey, 6 May 1831.

22. Mary Turner, spinster, Ainstey, 21 Nov. 1831.

23. Priscilla Catlow, spinster, Ainstey, 17 Feb. 1831.

24. Lucinda Wilson, spinster, Ainstey, 31 Oct. 1832.

25. Sarah Arthington, wife of James Arthington, Ainstey, 25 Aug. 1830.

26. Mary Moxon, spinster, Ainstey, 23 Apr. 1830.

27. John French, merchant, Prerogative, 3 Apr. 1830.

28. Joseph Rollinson, joiner and builder, Ainstey, 8 June 1830.

29. Charles Hopkins, stuff piece maker, Ainstey, 10 Nov. 1832.

30. Michael Thackrey, Esq., Ainstey, 16 Feb. 1830.

31. John Topham, currier, Ainstey, 8 June 1830.

32. Beresford, 'East End, West End', p. 186.

33. Barbara English and John Saville, *Strict Settlement. A Guide for Historians* (University of Hull, Occasional papers in Economic and Social History, no. 10, Hull 1983); Sir John Habakkuk, *Marriage, Debt and the Estates System: English Landownership, 1650–1950* (Oxford, Oxford University Press, 1994).

34. In allocating individuals to these categories, those who used 'things' in only part of their instructions were allocated to this category even if they used categories and cash in the rest of their will.

## CHAPTER 8

1. This chapter uses material drawn from research in progress on 'autobiographical writing and the Victorian middle class' and I wish to acknowledge the support of the Humanities Research Board, British Academy, as well as the University of Portsmouth. I am also indebted once again to Bradford and Manchester central libraries, to Dr Williams Library and to the Angus Library, Regents Park College, Oxford. I benefited greatly from discussion of this, and other, papers at the Manchester conference and from discussion with Eileen Yeo about her own work on the social science movement.

2. This tradition can be traced from the pioneering work of Asa Briggs, reprinted in *The Collected Essays of Asa Briggs, vol. 1: Words, Numbers, Places, People* (Brighton, Harvester Press, 1985). More recent studies include R.J. Morris (ed.), *Class, Power and Social Structure in Nineteenth-century Towns* (Leicester,

Leicester University Press, 1986); R.J. Morris, *Class, Sect and Party: the Making of the British Middle Class, Leeds, 1820–50* (Manchester, Manchester University Press, 1990); R.H. Trainor, *Black Country Elites: the Exercise of Authority in Industrial Areas, 1830–1900* (Oxford, Oxford University Press, 1993); T. Koditschek, *Class Formation and Urban Industrial Society: Bradford, 1750–1850* (Cambridge, Cambridge University Press, 1990); S. Gunn, 'The Manchester Middle Class, 1850–80' (PhD thesis, University of Manchester, 1992); and cf. M. Savage, 'Urban History and Social Class: Two paradigms', *Urban History*, 20 (1993), 61–77.

3.  See the extensive work of W.D. Rubinstein, esp. *Men of Property: the Very Wealthy in Britain since the Industrial Revolution* (London, Croom Helm, 1981), *Elites and the Wealthy in Modern British History* (Brighton, Harvester, 1987) and his recent *Capitalism, Culture and Decline in Britain* (London, 1993); also P. Cain and A.G. Hopkins, *British Imperialism: Innovation and Expansion, 1688–1914* (Harlow, Longman, 1993).

4.  M.J. Daunton, '"Gentlemanly Capitalism" and British Industry, 1820–1914', *Past and Present*, 122 (1989), 119–58.

5.  L. Davidoff and C. Hall, *Family Fortunes: Men and Women of the English Middle Class, 1780–1850* (London, Hutchinson, 1987), pt II; Morris, *Class, Sect and Party*; Koditschek, *Class Formation*.

6.  Daunton, 'Gentlemanly Capitalism', p. 152; cf. M. Ogburn, 'Local Power and State Regulation in Nineteenth-century Britain', *Transactions of the Institute of British Geographers*, new series, 17 (1992), 215–26.

7.  See esp. L. Davidoff, *Worlds Between* (Cambridge, Polity Press, 1995); M. Poovey, *Uneven Developments: the Ideological Work of Gender in Mid-Victorian England* (London, Virago edn, 1989); M. Poovey, *Making a Social Body: British Cultural Formation, 1830–1864* (Chicago, Chicago University Press, 1995).

8.  Poovey, *Uneven Developments*.

9.  M. Vicinus and B. Negaard (eds), *Ever Yours, Florence Nightingale: Selected Letters* (London, Virago, 1989), pp. 218–19.

10. Obituary, *Manchester Examiner and Times*, 19 Feb. 1861.

11. J.V. Pickstone, *Medicine and Industrial Society: a History of Hospital Development in Manchester and Its Region, 1752–1946* (Manchester, Manchester University Press, 1985), ch. 6, to which I am much indebted.

12. J. Adshead to Brougham, 11 March 1847, 8 Feb. 1859, Brougham Papers, UCL.

13. Poovey, *Uneven Developments*, ch. 6.

14. J.A.V. Chapple and A. Pollard (eds), *The Letters of Mrs Gaskell* (Manchester, Manchester University Press, 1966), no. 446a, p. 588.

15. E. Cook, *The Life of Florence Nightingale*, (2 vols, London, 1913), vol. I, pp. 140, 500.

16. Pickstone, *Medicine and Industrial Society*, pp. 125–6, 142–3.

17. *Blackburn Standard*, 26 May 1858.

18. J. Roberton, *Observations on the Mortality and Physical Management of Children* (1827); Factory Commission, Supplementary Report, *PP*, 1834 XX, D.3, p. 247.

19. D. Noble, *Facts and Observations Relative to the Influence of Manufactures upon Health and Life* (1843), p. 79.

20. Pickstone, *Medicine and Industrial Society*, p. 127; F. Nightingale to J. Roberton, 7 Oct. 1861, Wellcome Institute, MS 8999/37.

21. L. Goldman, 'The Social Science Association, 1857–86: a context for mid-

Victorian Liberalism', *English Historical Review*, 101 (1986), 95–134; E. Janes Yeo, *The Contest for Social Science: Relations and Representations of Gender and Class* (London, Rivers Oram, 1996), pt II.

22. Goldman, 'Social Science Association', p. 112, quoting *Birmingham Daily Press* on the first congress.

23. Yeo, *Contest for Social Science*.

24. Goldman, 'Social Science Association'.

25. Ibid.; and cf. I. Inkster and J. Morrell (eds), *Metropolis and Province: Science in British Culture 1780–1850* (London, Hutchinson, 1983); J. Wolff and J. Seed (eds), *The Culture of Capital: Art. Power and the Nineteenth-century Middle Class* (Manchester, Manchester University Press, 1988).

26. Yeo, *Contest for Social Science*, pp. 152–5.

27. *Transactions of the National Association for the Promotion of Social Science*, 1866; and for Chadwick's interventions, see ibid., e.g., 1865, p. 362, 1871, pp. 443–4.

28. Ibid., 1866, 1859. Committee members were identified from directories and secondary sources including Pickstone, *Medicine and Industrial Society*, Koditschek, *Class Formation*; also A. Howe, *The Cotton Masters, 1830–1880* (Oxford, Oxford University Press, 1984); J. Reynolds, *The Great Paternalist: Titus Salt and the Growth of Nineteenth-century Bradford* (London, Temple Smith, 1983).

29. *Bradford Observer*, 6, 27 Oct. 1859.

30. J.R. Campbell, MA, *Lessons in Social Science from the Life of Our Blessed Saviour* (1859), pp. 8–9; cf. Poovey, *Making a Social Body* and Yeo, *Contest for Social Science*.

31. Campbell, *Lessons*, pp. 4, 6, 7, 11; and see S. Gunn, 'The Ministry, the Middle Class and the "Civilizing Mission" in Manchester, 1850–80', *Social History*, 21 (1996), 22–36.

32. G.W. Hastings to Brougham, 20 Sept. 1859, Brougham Papers, UCL; I have benefited from discussion with Donna Loftus about her research in progress on these debates.

33. Goldman, 'Social Science Association, 1857–86'.

34. Gunn, 'The Ministry, the Middle Class'; R. Gray, *The Factory Question and Industrial England, 1830–60* (Cambridge, Cambridge University Press, 1996), pp. 112–21; J. Seed, 'Theologies of Power: Unitarianism and the Social Relations of Religious Discourse, 1800–1850' in Morris (ed.), *Class, Power and Social Structure*, pp. 108–56.

35. J. Parker, DD, *A Preacher's Life* (1899), chs 1–7; W. Adamson, DD, *The Life of the Reverend Joseph Parker, DD* (1902), pp. 53–5.

36. D.M. Lewis (ed.), *The Dictionary of Evangelical Biography* (2 vols, Oxford, Blackwell, 1995) for Halley; J. Guinness Rogers, *An Autobiography* (1903).

37. *Dictionary of Evangelical Biography*; the cohort comprised Baptists and Congregationalists (the former being more numerous; several prominent Congregationalists not included, e.g. Parker, also fit the pattern); fourteen of a total of eighteen were born outside the region and mostly south of the Severn–Wash line. See also K.D. Brown, *A Social History of the Nonconformist Ministry of England and Wales, 1800–1930* (Oxford, Oxford University Press, 1988).

38. B. Godwin, 'Reminiscences of Three Score Years and Ten', typewritten transcript in Bradford Central Library.

39. Guinness Rogers, *Autobiography*, pp. 85–6.
40. Guinness Rogers, *Autobiography*, pp. 107–8.
41. Lucy A. Fraser, *Memoirs of Daniel Fraser, MA, LLD (Glas): Half-a-century of Educational Work* (1905), pp. 16–18.
42. G.W. Conder, *Memoirs and Reminiscences of the Late Rev. Jonathan Glyde* (1858).
43. 'The Personal Narrative of George Hadfield, MP', MS in Manchester Central Library, pp. 43–4; and see the list of acquaintances, pp. 214–15 for a sense of such networks.
44. J. Guinness Rogers, *The Christian Standard-bearer: in Memoriam, Rev. Enoch Mellor, DD* (1881?).
45. R.F. Horton, *An Autobiography* (London, George Allen & Unwin, 1917), pp. 15–19; E. Neale, 'A Type of Congregational Ministry: R.F. Horton and Lyndhurst Road', *Journal of the United Reform Church Historical Society*, 5 (1994), 215–31.
46. J. Parker, *Tyne Chylde: My Life and Teaching* (1886), p. 6.
47. Parker, *Preacher's Life*, pp. 5–6, 136, 248–9. Other examples of such dialogues include: A. Gilbert, *Autobiography and Other Memorials of Mrs Gilbert*, ed. Josiah Gilbert, (2 vols, 1874), vol. II, pp. 70–6, 78; S. McAll, *Lectures Delivered at the Monthly United Service of the Nonconformist Churches in Nottingham* (1850), sermon IV on 'the anti-Christian character of the measures commonly suggested . . . to secure religious uniformity'.
48. Gunn, 'The Ministry, the Middle Class', p. 30; Glyde, sermon on 'the worth of life' in Conder, *Memoirs*, pp. 270 ff.
49. Godwin, 'Reminiscences', pp. 554–5; and see Gray, *Factory Question*, pp. 40–1.
50. Conder, *Memoirs*, p. 238; Gray, *Factory Question*, pp. 116–17.
51. *Blackburn Standard*, 26 May 1858.
52. *Bradford Observer*, 6 Dec. 1884, report on funeral.
53. Koditschek, *Class Formation*, p. 172; *John Roberton, Surgeon, 1797–1876* (1969; pamphlet in Manchester Central Library).
54. Godwin, 'Reminiscences', p. 8; the original MS (in Angus Library, Regents Park College, Oxford) has traces of several emendations and excisions (some possibly by Godwin's son, who edited the papers) in the prefatory letter of 1839, perhaps indicating that the Oxford experience was a sensitive one.
55. Guinness Rogers, *Autobiography*, pp. 107, 112.
56. Parker, *Preacher's Life*, ch. 10; Adamson, *Life of the Rev. Joseph Parker*.
57. McAll, *Lectures*, p. 126.
58. Godwin, 'Reminiscences', p. 3.
59. Poovey, *Uneven Developments*, ch. 6.
60. Cf. E.J. Hobsbawm, *The Age of Capital, 1848–1875* (Harmondsworth, Cardinal edn, 1988), p. 287.
61. J. Morley, *The Life of Richard Cobden* (London, T. Fisher Unwin, 10th edn, 1903), p. 8.
62. 'Personal Narrative', p. 46; and see the entry on Hadfield in *DNB*.
63. F. Reynolds Lovett, MA, *A History of the Clapham Congregational Church* (1912), p. 104; and see D.W. Bebbington, *The Nonconformist Conscience: Chapel and Politics, 1870–1914* (London, George Allen & Unwin, 1982).
64. Guinness Rogers, *Autobiography*, ch. 14; and see B. Doyle, 'Business Liberalism and Dissent in Norwich, 1900–1930', *Baptist Quarterly*, 35, no. 5 (1994), 243–50.

## CHAPTER 9

1. See, for example, H. Perkin, *The Origins of Modern British Society 1780–1880* (London, Routledge, 1969); and *The Rise of Professional Society: England Since 1880* (London, Routledge, 1989).
2. Moreover, only solicitors are separately listed in the census.
3. The office of solicitor does not exist in Scotland.
4. Figures taken from Richard L. Abel, *The Legal Profession in England and Wales* (Oxford, Blackwell, 1988), pp. 444–7.
5. The Institution's 843 comprised 706 ordinary members (the working professionals). The rest were honorary or associate members – often gas engineers who had converted into businessmen. Of the North British Association's membership of 260, 166 were ordinary members.
6. Perkin, *Origins*, p. 253.
7. Presidential address to British Association of Gas Managers AGM, *Journal of Gas Lighting*, 17 June 1877, p. 1004.
8. For full argument, see Vivienne Parrott, 'Pettyfogging to Respectability: a history of the profession of solicitor in the Manchester area 1800–1914' (unpublished PhD thesis, University of Salford, 1992).
9. See Neil Meikljohn, Letter, *Journal of Gas Lighting*, 22 May 1883, p. 765.
10. For solicitors, these included the *Solicitors' Journal*, the *Law Times*, and the *Legal Times*; for gas engineers, the *Journal of Gas Lighting*, *Gas Affairs*, the *Gas Engineer*, and the *Gas and Water Engineer*.
11. The Law Society, the British Association of Gas Managers and its successors – respectively, the Institute and Institution of Gas Engineers.
12. *Journal of Gas Lighting*, 22 Sept. 1863, p. 613.
13. Ibid., 14 Dec. 1887, p. 655.
14. Ibid., 17 May 1892, p. 324.
15. W.J. Warner, President, North of England Gas Managers Association, to AGM, ibid., 14 May 1878, p. 764.
16. President of Midland Association of Gas Managers, *Gas World*, 12 February 1887, p. 198. See John Garrard, *The Great Salford Gas Scandal of 1887* (Altrincham, British Gas Northwestern, 1988).
17. Quoted by David Sugarman, 'Bourgeois Collectivism, Professional Power and the Boundaries of the State – The Public and Private Life of the Law Society 1825–1914', *International Journal of the Legal Profession*, 3, no. 1/2 (1996). See also inaugural AGM of Metropolitan and Provincial Law Societies Association, *Law Society Journal*, 13 Apr. 1847.
18. Penelope J. Corfield, *Power and the Professions in Britain 1780–1850* (London, Routledge, 1995). For worries about respectability among engineers in general, see R.A. Buchanan, 'Gentlemen Engineers: the Making of a Profession', *Victorian Studies*, XXVI (1983), 407–29. It is our contention that gas engineers, at least by the 1860s when their journals start appearing, were less troubled by this problem than solicitors.
19. See Perkin, *Origins*, and Corfield, *Power and the Professions*.
20. M. Hunt, President of Institute of Gas Engineers, *Journal of Gas Lighting*, 17 May 1892, p. 375. In fact, he was arguing for more attention being paid to the provision of technical training. For more effusive and later praise of mobility, see 'The Future of the Gas Profession', *Journal of Gas Lighting*, 18 February 1900, p. 1508.
21. The National Union of Manufacturers, the Federation of British Industry, and

most vociferously of all, the National Confederation of Employers Organizations.

22. Crossick and Haupt, *Shopkeepers and Master Artisans in Nineteenth-Century Europe*.
23. See the persuasive argument of R.J. Morris in 'Voluntary Societies and British Urban Elites: an analysis', *Historical Journal*, 26 (1983).
24. Prompted by their sense of declining power.
25. Sugarman, 'Bourgeois Collectivism', p. 85.
26. Thomas Harwicke to South West England District Association of Gas Managers, *Journal of Gas Lighting*, 25 Mar. 1873, p. 455.
27. *Journal of Gas Lighting*, 4 Nov. 1890, p. 935.
28. See D. Read, *The English Provinces* c. *1760–1960* (London, Edward Arnold, 1964).
29. See, for example, paper on 'The Management of Small Gasworks' to AGM of British Association of Gas Managers, 1866, *Journal of Gas Lighting*, 12 June 1866, p. 490; see also comments at AGM of North British Association of Gas Managers, ibid., 1 August 1893, p. 215.
30. Its existence, moreover, was anticipated by several other organizations beginning as early as 1739.
31. See Sugarman, 'Bourgeois Collectivism', p. 89. The position was given legal recognition in the 1844 Solicitors Act.
32. For example, the Provincial Law Societies Association, 1844 and the Metropolitan and Provincial Law Associatio,n 1847.
33. 'Correspondence', *Law Times*, 11 November 1899.
34. See n. 6.
35. *Journal of Gas Lighting*, 19 June 1883, p. 1099.
36. Ibid., 12 April 1887, p. 665.
37. Ibid., 6 June 1905, p. 674.
38. Sugarman, 'Bourgeois Collectivism', p. 90; for another example, see Minutes, Manchester Law Association, 12 Dec. 1838.
39. Sugarman, 'Bourgeois Collectivism', p. 94.
40. *The Times*, 5 Apr. 1893.
41. Manchester Law Association Minutes, 12 Dec. 1838.
42. Sugarman, 'Bourgeois Collectivism', p. 100.
43. For a rather different view of engineers in general, see R.A. Buchanan, 'Gentleman Engineers'.
44. See the *Journal*'s contemptuous reaction to the Institute's decision to establish a political fund in 1894 – 'essentially the industry's job'. *Journal of Gas Lighting*, 9 June 1894, p. 1083.
45. Presidential address, ibid., 17 June 1873, p. 539.
46. *Gas World*, 26 Mar. 1887, p. 354.
47. See Garrard, *The Great Salford Gas Scandal*, ch. 2.
48. *Journal of Gas Lighting*, 17 June 1888, p. 540.
49. Ibid., 15 Nov. 1887, p. 869.
50. 'CE' in ibid., 8 May 1888, p. 823.
51. *Salford Reporter*, 26 Feb. 1887, p. 4.
52. For a possible counter-argument – that the culture of all professions was ultimately international – see Corfield, *Power and the Professions*.
53. *Journal of Gas Lighting*, 17 June 1862, p. 407.
54. Ibid., 26 July 1862, p. 501.
55. Ibid., 25 Sept. 1888, p. 540.

56. Presidential address to the AGM of the Institute of Gas Engineers, ibid., 9 June 1885, p. 1113.
57. Ibid., 26 June 1881, p. 1089.
58. Ibid., 1 May 1900, p. 1109.
59. Ibid., 18 Aug. 1914, p. 536.
60. Parrott, 'Pettyfogging to Respectability', p. 24 f.
61. *Solicitor's Journal*, 2 Feb. 1901, pp. 231, 233.
62. Avner Offer, *Property and Politics 1870–1914* (Cambridge, Cambridge University Press, 1981), p. 17.
63. *Solicitor's Journal*, 3 Nov. 1900, p. 15.
64. Ibid., 2 Feb. 1901, p. 237.
65. Ibid., 9 Feb. 1901, p. 255.
66. See Garrard, *The Great Salford Gas Scandal*, p. 4 f.
67. *Journal of Gas Lighting*, 25 June 1889, p. 1168.
68. Ibid., 26 June 1870, p. 481.
69. Ibid., 19 June 1883, p. 1099.
70. W. Carr, ibid., 19 June 1900, p. 620.
71. 'The Future of the Gas Profession', ibid., 25 Dec. 1900, p. 1558.
72. William Stelfox to the AGM of the Institute of Gas Engineers, ibid., 7 May 1901, p. 1181.
73. Some solicitors served working-class clients.
74. For further development of these points, see Parrott, 'Pettyfogging to Respectability', p. 166 ff.
75. See ibid., p. 114 ff.
76. See John Seed, 'Theologies of Power: Unitarianism and Social Relations in Religious Discourse' in R.J. Morris (ed.), *Class, Power and Social Structure in British Nineteenth-century Towns* (Leicester, Leicester University Press, 1986).
77. Ibid.; also John Garrard, *Leadership in Nineteenth-century Towns*, p. 31 f.
78. See Garrard, *The Great Salford Gas Scandal*, p. 33.
79. *Journal of Gas Lighting*, 15 Feb. 1887, p. 302.
80. Perkin's phrase, *Origins of Modern British Society*, p. 252.
81. See ibid., p. 262.

## CHAPTER 10

1. A.D. Chandler, *Scale and Scope* (Cambridge, Mass., Belknap Harvard, 1990); Bernard Elbaum and William Lazonick, *The Decline of the British Economy* (Oxford, Clarendon Press, 1986), particularly the editors' introduction.
2. Edith T. Penrose, *The Theory of the Growth of the Firm* (Oxford, Basil Blackwell, 1968); A.D. Chandler, *The Visible Hand* (Cambridge, Mass., Belknap Harvard, 1977); Chandler, *Scale and Scope*.
3. Chandler, ibid., pt IV.
4. See n. 1.
5. Leslie Hannah, *Rise of the Corporate Economy* (2nd rev. edn, London, Methuen, 1983).
6. Correlli Barnett, *The Collapse of British Power* (London, Macmillan, 1972); *idem*, *The Audit of War* (London, Macmillan, 1986); *idem*, *The Lost Victory* (London, Macmillan, 1995).

7.  P.L. Payne, 'The Emergence of the Large Scale Company in Great Britain, 1870–1914', *Economic History Review*, second series, XX, 3 (1967), 519–42.

8.  W.D. Rubinstein, 'Cultural Explanations for Britain's Decline: How True?' in B. Collins and K. Robbins (eds), *British Culture and Economic Decline* (London, Weidenfeld and Nicholson, 1990), pp. 59–90.

9.  D.S. Landes, 'Technological Change and Development in Western Europe, 1750–1914', *Cambridge Economic History of Europe*, vol. 4 (Cambridge, Cambridge University Press, 1965).

10. Chandler, *Scale and Scope*.

11. R.R. Locke, *The End of Practical Man* (Greenwich, Conn. and London, JAI Press, 1984).

12. J.M. Quail, 'Proprietors and Managers: Structure and Technique in Large British Enterprise, 1890–1939' (unpublished PhD thesis, University of Leeds, 1996).

13. Elbaum and Lazonick, *Decline of the British Economy*.

14. M.J. Wiener, *English Culture and the Decline of the Industrial Spirit* (Cambridge, Cambridge University Press, 1981).

15. Will Hutton, *The State We're In* (London, Cape, 1995); G. Ingham, *Capitalism Divided* (London, Macmillan, 1984).

16. Rubinstein in Collins and Robbins (eds), *British Culture*; L. Hannah, 'The American Miracle, 1875–1950, and After: A View in the European Mirror', *Business and Economic History*, 24, 2 (1995).

17. See, for example, the key role of engineers in the construction of new managerial techniques and new managerial structures in the USA: David F. Noble, *America by Design* (New York, Knopf, 1979); Chandler, *Visible Hand*.

18. H.W. Macrosty, *Trusts and the State* (London, Richards, 1901), p. 130.

19. Ibid.

20. Sidney Pollard, *The Genesis of Modern Management* (London, Edward Arnold, 1965).

21. Acton Society Trust (AST), *Management Succession* (London, 1956), p. 14.

22. See the evidence of Mr H.A. Roberts, secretary to Cambridge University Appointments Board, to the *Royal Commission on the Civil Service (RCCS)*, 12 December 1912; S.P. Keeble, *The Ability to Manage* (Manchester, Manchester University Press, 1992), *passim*.

23. AST, *Management Succession*, table p. 90.

24. Ibid., table p. 28.

25. T.J.H. Bishop and R. Wilkinson, *Winchester and the Public School Elite* (London, Faber & Faber, 1967), table 10, p. 64 ff.; W.D. Rubinstein in Collins and Robbins (eds), *British Culture*, pp. 81–5.

26. Ibid., p. 82.

27. Lyndall Urwick, 'Promotion in Industry', *Public Administration*, 5 (April 1927), 185.

28. Liberal Industrial Enquiry, *Britain's Industrial Future* (London, Benn, 1928), p. 127.

29. G. Anderson, *Victorian Clerks* (Manchester, Manchester University Press, 1976), p. 12.

30. G.H. Williams, *Careers for our Sons* (London, Adam and Charles Black, 1914), pp. 428–9.

31. Evidence of Mr F. Hyde, *Royal Commission on the Civil Service 1929–31*, q. 21, 602, 23 Feb. 1931.

32. Duncan Cross, *Choosing a Career* (London, Cassell, 1908), pp. 7, 239.

33. Letter from 'Cantab', *The Times*, 15 February 1914, p. 19.
34. *RCCS*, Evidence of Sir Frank Ree, 25 April 1913, q. 35, 196; q. 35, 197.
35. See *Rolls of Directors and Principal Officers*, PRO RAIL 410/1268 in conjunction with *Gratuities on Retirement*, PRO RAIL 410/1869.
36. M.R. Bonavia, *Railway Policy between the Wars* (Manchester, Manchester University Press, 1981), n. 46, p. 41.
37. Ibid., n. 45, p. 40.
38. Tim Dale, *Harrods, the Store and the Legend* (London, Pan, 1981).
39. Liberal Industrial Enquiry, *Britain's Industrial Future*, p. 90.
40. Anon., 'What is the Secret of Lower Costs and Higher Wages', *System*, April 1926.
41. Shirley Keeble, 'University Education and Business Management' (unpublished PhD thesis, University of London, 1984), p. 174.
42. Cathy Courtney and Paul Thompson, *City Lives* (London, Methuen, 1996), p. xxii.
43. See the exchange under the title 'The Restless Civil Service', *World's Work*, February 1914.
44. For insurance, see the evidence of Mr Robert Lewis, *RCCS*, 11 April 1913. For accountancy, see the statement of Pixley in 1897 that articled clerks now came from the same class of schools as recruits at Woolwich, Sandhurst and the Inns of Court. Quoted in Edgar Jones, *Accountancy and the British Economy* (London, Batsford, 1981), p. 137.
45. Quail, 'Proprietors and Managers', ch. 2.
46. Chandler, *Scale and Scope*.
47. Quail, 'Proprietors and Managers', ch. 3.
48. Compare the role of engineers in the USA. See n. 17.
49. Lord Claud Hamilton, *The Times*, 14 Feb. 1914. See also Keeble, *Ability to Manage*, p. 56.
50. Quail, 'Proprietors and Managers', ch. 3.
51. Evidence of Mr E. Middleton, *RCCS*, 11 Apr. 1913; Mr Barrow Cadbury, *RCCS*, 18 Apr. 1913; Mr Robert Lewis, *RCCS*, 11 Apr. 1913; Sir Frank Ree, *RCCS*, 25 Apr. 1913.
52. Anon., 'The Grading of Clerical Staff', *Business Organisation and Management*, 1, 6 (March 1920).
53. Harold Perkin, *The Rise of Professional Society* (London, Routledge, 1989), p. 259.
54. There does not appear to be any definitive research on overcrowding in the professions before the First World War. W.J. Reader in his *Professional Men* tends to dismiss the idea but does not treat the matter in depth. But see R.V. Jackson in *Economic History Review*, second series, XL, 4 (1987), 561–70 who shows that the earnings of engineers and surveyors fell, presumably as a result of market forces, by 50 per cent between 1871 and 1911 and suggests that the earnings of solicitors and doctors also fell. It is suggested by M. Webster Jenkinson in his *Costing for Small Manufacturers* (London, Gee and Co., 1907), p. 55 that accountancy was also overcrowded. Part of the problem was the pupillage system which encouraged professionals to treat trainees as a source of income and over-recruit.
55. See e.g. Williams, *Careers for Our Sons* and Cross, *Choosing a Career*.
56. 'The Armament Business and Civil Servants', *Economist*, 4 Jan. 1913 gives a list of these men and the salaries they left behind. The '£10,000 a year' man seems to have been a phrase coined by Lloyd George in 1913 (quoted in *Electrical*

*Review*, 73 (1 Aug. 1913), 162) and kept alive by people like Lord Ashfield: see a speech in 1922 quoted in *Business Organisation and Management*, 6, 2 (May 1922) ('Notes of the Month').

57. Williams, *Careers for Our Sons*, append. 'Business for Public School and University Men'.

58. Letter from J. Gardner, *The Times*, 18 Feb. 1914, p. 8.

59. Anon., 'The Public School Man in Business', *World's Work*, 22 (Oct. 1913), 490.

60. 'Restless Civil Service', p. 241.

61. R.P. Scott in *Fortnightly Review*, 67 (1900), 313. Quoted in Linda M. Simpson, 'Education, Imperialism and National Efficiency in England 1895–1905' (unpublished PhD thesis, University of Glasgow, 1979), p. 231.

62. Some blamed the boys and their parents. See the letters to *The Times* by A.H. Gilkes, headmaster of Dulwich College, 4 Jan. 1912, p. 8 and 11 January 1912, p. 10. Others blamed the stultifying syllabus based on the classics. See the series of letters in *The Times* in January and February 1912 on 'why the average [public] schoolboy fails'.

63. 'The Public School Man in Business', p. 456.

64. Ibid., p. 457.

65. Cross, *Choosing a Career*, p. 240.

66. See the letters from Gilkes cited in n. 62. Also 'Restless Civil Service', pp. 237, 240–1.

67. Evidence of Sir Frank Ree, *RCCS*, 25 Apr. 1913, q. 35, 199.

68. "Home Born Colonial", 'English Public School Boys in Colonial Life', *World's Work*, 39, 231 (February 1922).

69. 'Speech by Mr Bryce', *The Times*, 3 Jan. 1914, p. 3.

70. Evidence of Mr Robert Lewis, *RCCS*, 11 Apr. 1913, q. 33, 847.

71. 'Public School Man in Business', p. 460.

72. T.R. Gourvish, 'A British Business Elite: the Chief Executive Managers of the Railway Industry, 1850–1922', *Business History Review*, XLVII, 3 (1975), 295.

73. Ibid. The company involved was the Manchester, Sheffield and Lincolnshire Railway later to become part of the Great Central. The timing is interesting, 1854 being the year of the Northcote Trevelyan Report which *inter alia* proposed civil service recruitment by competitive examination.

74. Quoted in D. Lockwood, *The Blackcoated Worker* (London, George Allen & Unwin, 1958), p. 24, n. 1.

75. Document headed 'Probationers' in PRO RAIL 410/1928. A scheme to recruit graduates set up at the same time was later abandoned.

76. Evidence of Sir Frank Ree, *RCCS*, q. 35, 254.

77. Ibid, qq. 35, 258–35, 260.

78. Quoted in Keeble, 'University Education and Business Management', p. 33.

79. Anon. memo, probably Dickens to Mond, 1927? 1929? at ICHO/CFD/1203(ii), ICI Archives. A truncated version of this was sent to the Cambridge University Appointments Board by Mond (Keeble, *Ability to Manage*, p. 81) but two different dates are given by Keeble in the text and footnote (p. 91, n. 45).

80. Evidence of Sir Frank Ree, *RCCS*, q. 35, 256.

81. Sir Albert H Stanley, 'How to Find and Train the £10,000 a Year Man', *System* (January 1920); see also n. 41.

82. R. Jones and O. Marriott, *Anatomy of a Merger* (London, Cape, 1970), p. 86.

83. Hugo Hirst, 'System or Man', *System* (November 1923).

84. Keeble, *Ability to Manage*, ch. 6.

85. Ibid., p. 141.

86. Ibid., *passim*.
87. Particularly the London Underground and ICI schemes.
88. A. Hollis Vickers, 'Letter from a Railway Clerk', *Business Organisation and Management*, 3, 6 (Mar. 1921).
89. 'Is it not a recognised way for an ambitious young man, to make his mark, to pass an outside examination or take a degree?'
    'No.'
    Evidence of Sir Frank Ree, *RCCS*, 25 Apr. 1913.
90. Anon., *£300 a Year Business Positions* (London, 1912), pp. 23–39.
91. Helen Mercer, *Constructing a Competitive Order* (Cambridge, Cambridge University Press, 1995).
92. D.C. Coleman, 'Gentlemen and Players', *Economic History Review*, second series, XXVI (1973), 92–116.
93. Courtney and Thompson, *City Lives*, *passim*; Paul Thompson, 'The Pyrrhic Victory of Gentlemanly Capitalism: The Financial Elite of the City of London, 1945–90', pts 1 and 2, *Journal of Contemporary History*, 32, 3 and 4 (1997).
94. A 'temporary civil servant' (Keynes?) quoted by the editor in A. Dunsire (ed.), *The Making of an Administrator* (Manchester, Manchester University Press, 1956), p. xiii.

## CHAPTER 11

1. 'Wealth, Elites and the Class Structure of Modern Britain', originally *Past and Present* (1977), repr. in W.D. Rubinstein, *Elites and the Wealthy in Modern British History* (Brighton, Harvester Press, 1987).
2. Peter Cain and Anthony Hopkins, *British Imperialism: Crisis and Deconstruction, 1914–1990* (London, Longman, 1993), p. 312.
3. W.D. Rubinstein, *Men of Property: The Very Wealthy in Britain Since the Industrial Revolution* (London, Croom Helm, 1981), p. 48. No comparable figures are available prior to 1911 when Lloyd George's 'super tax' on gross incomes of £5,000 or more made it possible to ascertain the number of very high income earners for the first time.
4. These figures are even more noteworthy than they seem when it is realized that all of the trends in these statistics should go to make for their diminution rather than their growth. Average lifespans rose meaning that fewer wealth-holders died each year. The increase in direct taxation should have diminished the net total fortunes of rich persons during their lifetimes while, in particular, the rise in the level of death duties should have led to considerably more estate duty avoidance (by *inter vivos* gifts, etc.) and the growth of a sophisticated estate duty avoidance 'industry', presumably situated in London. In so far as any of these factors (especially the last) was important, the actual number of top wealth-holders was even greater during the interwar period than the published figures indicate.
5. That appeasement had an economic motive in terms of the continuing viability of the British neo-Orthodox economic and financial system has been interestingly argued by Scott Newton in *Profits of Peace: The Political Economy of Anglo-German Appeasement* (Oxford, Clarendon Press, 1996). This work, however, in my opinion does not go far enough, failing to depict how successfully things were going for most individual members of Britain's affluent

élite. Only when it became clear that a revision of the Versailles Treaty in order to produce an enlarged, but finite, German-speaking Reich was not Hitler's goal – the rational face of appeasement – but merely the first slice of the salami, following the incorporation of Bohemia and Moravia into the Reich in March 1939 did the British Establishment reluctantly but firmly conclude that Hitler had to be stopped regardless of cost.

6. F.M.L. Thompson, *English Landed Society in the Nineteenth Century* (London, Routledge, 1963), pp. 327–45.

7. David Cannadine, *The Decline and Fall of the British Aristocracy* (New Haven, Conn., Yale University Press, 1990).

8. Among the twenty-one cabinet ministers in the National Government formed by Stanley Baldwin in June 1935, six came from the bona fide landed aristocracy – Lords Londonderry, Halifax, and Zetland, Lord Eustace Percy, Oliver Stanley and William Ormsby-Gore. Sir Philip Cunliffe-Lister (né Lloyd-Graeme) emerged from the landed gentry but inherited an industrial fortune, as did Sir Bolton Eyres-Monsell at one or two generations remove. The father of Walter Elliott was a Glasgow businessman who became a prominent agriculturalist. Two – Ramsay MacDonald and J.H. Thomas – were, of course, of working-class origins. The father of Ernest Brown, the Liberal National Minister for Labour, was a boat proprietor and Baptist preacher in Torquay who left £833, the father of Sir Kingsley Wood was the minister of Wesley's Chapel in London, who left £284, and the father of Sir John Simon a Congregationalist minister in Bath who left £516. The remaining seven cabinet ministers emerged from the middle classes, especially the upper middle classes of top businessmen (like Walter Runciman, Baldwin, and Chamberlain). There are, of course, other ways to ascertain social origins, such as secondary education, which give different results.

9. See the useful essays on British power in the interwar period in the *International History Review*, XIII, 4 (November 1991), esp. John R. Ferris, '"The Greatest Power on Earth": Great Britain in the 1920s', and B.J.C. McKercher, '"Our Most Dangerous Enemy": Britain Pre-eminent in the 1930s'.

10. John Rickard, 'Loyalties' in John Arnold, Peter Spearritt, and David Walker (eds), *Out of Empire: The British Dominion of Australia* (Melbourne, Mandarin, 1993), p. 48. Leaders of the other dominions voiced very similar sentiments, for example Richard B. Bennett, the Canadian Prime Minister, who closed his final speech at the 1931 Ottawa economic conference by stating how proud he and his fellow Canadians were to be 'British subjects'. At the conference, Bennett had been a notably difficult negotiator with Britain. On this subject generally, see John Mackenzie, *Propaganda and Empire: The Manipulation of British Public Opinion, 1880–1960* (Manchester, Manchester University Press, 1984), although, as with all such works which postulate the 'manipulation' of 'public opinion' by a small élite, the assumption that 'public opinion' would otherwise adopt a different stance is contentious. One might equally assume that nationalism required less 'manipulation' to manifest itself than any other twentieth-century instinct. Note, too, the tendentious tacit assumption that pro-Empire sentiment is 'manipulation', without questioning whether, say, the activities of the Labour Party or the trade unions to engender support for themselves also constitutes 'manipulation'.

11. On British cultural life in the interwar period, see the following works, which stress the central importance of Oxbridge as the matrix of a hugely

disproportionate percentage of leading cultural figures in this period: Valentine Cunningham, *British Writers of the Thirties* (Oxford, Oxford University Press, 1988), esp. pp. 106–54; and *idem*, 'Literary Culture' in Brian Harrison (ed.), *The History of the University of Oxford, Volume VIII, The Twentieth Century* (Oxford, Clarendon Press, 1994), pp. 413–50; Samuel Hynes, *The Auden Generation: Literature and Politics in England in the 1930s* (London, Bodley Head, 1976); and Frank Gloversmith (ed.), *Class, Culture, and Social Change: A New View of the 1930s* (Brighton, Harvester Press, 1980).

12. E.H.H. Green, *The Crisis of Conservatism: The Politics, Economics and Ideology of the British Conservative Party, 1880–1914* (London, Routledge, 1995). It should perhaps be noted that other historians have held a much more sanguine view of the fortunes of the Conservative Party just before the First World War, for instance John Ramsden, *The Age of Balfour and Baldwin, 1902–1940* (London, Longman, 1978), pp. 85–6 and Michael Kinnear, *The British Voter: An Atlas and Survey Since 1885* (London, Batsford, 1968), pp. 70–2. Kinnear argues on the basis of by-election and redistribution data that the Conservatives might well have won a 1915 general election had it not been postponed by the war. One point to bear in mind here is that the Irish Home Rule Bill of 1912, due to come into effect in September 1914, removed forty-eight southern Irish seats from the Westminster Parliament. Ibid., p. 70.

13. Surprisingly, few studies have appreciated the significance of this point. For a social history of Britain which understands (accurately) that the First World War did not mark an invariable and total break, see José Harris, *Private Lives, Public Spirit: Britain 1870–1914* (Harmondsworth, Penguin, 1993), pp. 252–3. See also Harold Perkin, *The Rise of Professional Society: England Since 1880* (London, Routledge, 1989), and Keith Middlemas, *Politics in Industrial Society: The Experience of the British System Since 1911* (London, A. Deutsch, 1979).

14. One indication of the marginality *vis-à-vis* the 'Establishment' of the British Union of Fascists which deserves to be better known is the fact that from the time of his violent Olympia rally in June 1934 until 1968, Mosley was banned from broadcasting on the BBC due to repeated pressuring of the 'independent' network by the government and Foreign Office, although Mosley and his party were perfectly legal until the war and Mosley was universally regarded as one of the best public speakers in Britain. W.J. West, *Truth Betrayed* (London, Duckworth, 1987), pp. 15–21.

15. Between 1916 and 1922, however, the leaders of both the Conservative and Liberal Parties were Dissenters, the first and only time this occurred; no one knew (or cared), although even twenty years before this would have attracted wide comment. For a particularly illuminating account of the Churches in this period, see Adrian Hastings's remarkable *A History of English Christianity, 1920–1990* (London, SCM Press, 1991). Virtually all of the symbolic and collective mourning memorials to the fallen of the First World War were non-denominational, e.g. the Cenotaph. In any previous war they would have been Anglican.

16. *Making of a Ruling Class*, p. 60. Other relevant studies include John Scott and M.D. Hughes, *The Anatomy of Scottish Capital* (London, Croom Helm, 1980), and P.J. Waller, *Democracy and Sectarianism: A Political and Social History of Liverpool, 1868–1939* (Liverpool, Liverpool University Press, 1981).

17. Peter Jones, 'Politics' in David Nash and David Reeder (eds), *Leicester in the Twentieth Century* (Leicester, Leicester University Press, 1993), pp. 92–3.
18. Ibid., pp. 94–8.
19. Ibid., pp. 96–7.
20. All figures from David and Gareth Butler, *British Political Facts, 1900–1994* (London, Macmillan, 1994), pp. 213–19. To be sure, comparisons with earlier elections are fraught with difficulties because of the large numbers of uncontested seats and the Irish vote. As well, of course, some of the National Government's vote came to National Liberal and National Labour candidates rather than to Conservatives.
21. Ibid., p. 246. The remaining percentage were 'don't knows'. It is not clear whether the 'Opposition' percentage is meant to include both Labour and Liberal support; if so – and presumably it does – the figures are even more striking. In all of its editions, *British Political Facts* has inverted the December 1939 and February 1940 findings. See George H. Gallup (ed.), *The Gallup International Public Opinion Polls: Great Britain, 1937–1975, Volume One: 1937–1964* (Westport, Conn., Greenwood Press, 1977), pp. 26, 30.
22. T.E.B. Howarth, *Cambridge Between Two Wars* (London, Collins, 1978), p. 156.
23. Brian Harrison, 'Politics' in Harrison (ed.), *History of the University of Oxford, Volume VIII*, p. 392.
24. Ibid., p. 158.
25. It has been argued that the makers of newsreels had close links with the Conservative Party and deliberately manipulated the newsreel filming of Attlee to make him appear in the worst possible light, while aiding Baldwin in every way. See John Ramsden, 'Baldwin and Film' in Nicholas Pronay and D.W. Spring (eds), *Propaganda, Politics, and Film* (London, Macmillan, 1982). This may be readily seen in a widely distributed video '1935 – A Year To Remember', consisting of extracts from British Pathé newsreels for that year, and part of a recent series covering most of the years of the century. This video, which is part of a series currently on sale in WH Smith and many other retail outlets, contains newsreel scenes of both Attlee and Baldwin speaking to the public, filmed by Pathé, either in each man's office or at Pathé studios, as part of its coverage of the 1935 general election campaign. While Baldwin is statesmanlike, Attlee was photographed cross-eyed and frankly seems to resemble a madman.

## CHAPTER 12

1. D. Read, *The English Provinces: A Study in Influence 1760–1960* (London, Edward Arnold, 1964).
2. W.D. Rubinstein, 'Wealth, Elites and the Class Structure of Modern Britain', *Past and Present*, 76 (1977), 99–126; *idem, Men of Property: The Very Wealthy since the Industrial Revolution* (London, Croom Helm, 1981); M.J. Wiener, *English Culture and the Decline of the Industrial Spirit 1850–1980* (Cambridge, Cambridge University Press, 1981); J.A. Garrard, *Leadership and Power in Victorian Industrial Towns 1830–1880* (Manchester, Manchester University Press, 1983); F.M.L. Thompson, 'Social Control in

Victorian Britain', *Economic History Review*, second series, 34 (1981), 189–208.

3.  C.H. Lee, 'The Service Sector, Regional Specialization and Economic Growth in the Victorian Economy', *Journal of Historical Geography*, 10 (1984), 139–55; G. Ingham, *Capitalism Divided? The City and Industry in British Social Development* (London, Macmillan, 1984); P.J. Cain and A.G. Hopkins, 'Gentlemanly Capitalism and British Expansion Overseas II: New Imperialism 1850–1945', *Economic History Review*, second series, 40 (1987), 1–26.

4.  H.J. Dyos, 'Greater and Greater London: Notes on Metropolis and Provinces in the Nineteenth and Twentieth Centuries' in J.S. Bromley and E.H. Kossman (eds.), *Britain and the Netherlands: Volume IV: Metropolis, Dominion and Province* (The Hague, Martinus Nijhoff, 1971), pp. 89–112.

5.  On the economic trends, see: J. Stevenson, *British Society 1914–1945* (London, Penguin, 1984), pp. 107–8, 114–15.

6.  Dyos, 'Greater and Greater London', p. 91.

7.  This argument is developed in R.H. Trainor, *Black Country Elites: The Exercise of Authority in an Industrialized Area 1830–1900* (Oxford, Clarendon Press, 1993), esp. chs 2 and 8 and in *idem* 'The Elite' in W.H. Fraser and I. Maver (eds), *Glasgow Volume II: 1830 to 1912* (Manchester, Manchester University Press, 1996), pp. 227–64. For other works questioning, to a greater or lesser extent, the weakness of nineteenth-century industrialists and the divided nature of the Victorian middle class see, for example: H. Berghoff, 'British Businessmen as Wealth-Holders 1870–1914', *Business History*, 23 (1991), 222–40; M.J. Daunton, 'Gentlemanly Capitalism and British Industry 1820–1914', *Past and Present*, 122 (1989), 119–58; M. Dintenfass, *The Decline of Industrial Britain 1870–1980* (London, Routledge, 1992); S. Gunn, 'The "Failure" of the Victorian Middle Class: A Critique' in J. Wolff and J. Seed (eds), *The Culture of Capital: Art, Power and the Nineteenth-century Middle Class* (Manchester, Manchester University Press, 1988), pp. 17–43; A.C. Howe, *The Cotton Masters 1830–1860* (Oxford, Clarendon Press, 1984); T. Koditschek, *Class Formation and Urban Industrial Society: Bradford 1750–1850* (Cambridge, Cambridge University Press, 1990); R.J. Morris, *Class, Sect and Party: The Making of the British Middle Class: Leeds, 1820–50* (Manchester, Manchester University Press, 1990); D. Nicholls, 'Fractions of Capital: The Aristocracy, the City and Industry in the Development of Modern British Capitalism', *Social History*, 13 (1988), 71–83. For reassertions of the 'weakness and division' school, see, for instance, F.M.L. Thompson, 'Town and City' *idem* (ed.) *Cambridge Social History of Britain, 1750–1950* (3 vols, Cambridge, Cambridge University Press, 1990), I, pp. 65–73; R. Pearson, 'Thrift or Dissipation? The Business of Life Assurance in the Early Nineteenth Century', *Economic History Review*, second series, 43 (1990), 236–54. For aspects of both approaches, see Garrard, 'Urban Elites, 1850–1914: The Rule and Decline of a New Squirearchy', *Albion*, 27 (1995), 583–621.

8.  Compare the emphasis on a split between professionals and others in M. Savage et al., *Property, Bureaucracy and Culture: Middle-class Formation in Contemporary Britain* (London, Routledge, 1992), pp. 44–5 and *passim*.

9.  Trainor, *Black Country Elites*, ch. 2, and 'Urban Elites in Victorian Britain', *Urban History Yearbook* (1985), 1–17.

10. Trainor, *Black Country Elites*, pp. 377–84; A.J. McIvor, *Organised Capital: Employers' Associations and Industrial Relations in Northern England 1880–1939* (Cambridge, Cambridge University Press, 1996).

11. Cf. Read, *English Provinces*, sections I–IV.

12. This is the emphasis of B. Robson, 'Coming Full Circle: London versus the rest 1890–1980' in G. Gordon (ed.), *Regional Cities in the UK 1890–1980* (London, Harper & Row, 1986), pp. 217–21. For other indications of a continuing lack of integration between London and the provinces, see: Berghoff, 'Wealth-Holders', p. 226; Rubinstein, '"Stinking Rich": A Response', *Social History*, 16 (1991), 359–65. For an analysis of the social variety within the London middle class, see H. McLeod, *Class and Religion in the Late Victorian City* (London, Croom Helm, 1974).

13. Cf. K.G. Robbins, *Nineteenth-century Britain: Integration and Diversity* (Oxford, Oxford University Press, 1988); and compare F. Sheppard, 'London and the Nation in the Nineteenth Century', *Transactions of the Royal Historical Society*, fifth series, 35 (1986), 51–74.

14. Cf. P.J. Waller, *Town, City, and Nation 1850–1914* (Oxford, Oxford University Press, 1983), pp. 22–3, 65–6.

15. This is the general thrust of Robson, 'Coming full circle', pp. 217–32.

16. For a sustained discussion of comparative occupational information, see Trainor, 'The Middle Class', in M.J. Daunton (ed.), *Cambridge Urban History of Britain: Volume 3: 1840–1950* (Cambridge, Cambridge University Press, forthcoming).

17. J.B. Priestley, *English Journey: being a rambling but truthful account of what one man saw and heard and felt and thought during a journey through England during the autumn of the year 1933* (London, Mandarin, 1994, first published 1934); P. Vaughan, *Something in Linoleum: A Thirties Education* (London, Sinclair-Stevenson, 1994) and its sequel *Exciting Times in the Accounts Department* (London, Sinclair-Stevenson, 1995). For background on Priestley, see: J. Braine, *J.B. Priestley* (London, Weidenfeld and Nicolson, 1978); J. Atkins, *J.B. Priestley: The Last of the Sages* (London, John Calder, 1981); C. Waters, 'J.B. Priestley 1894–1984: Englishness and the politics of nostalgia' in S. Pedersen and P. Mandler (eds), *After the Victorians: Private Conscience and Public Duty in Modern Britain: Essays in Memory of John Clive* (London, Routledge, 1994), pp. 208–26.

18. This archive is now housed in the ESRC Qualidata Centre at the University of Essex.

19. For the differential regional impact of interwar economic trends on incomes, see W.D. Rubinstein, *Wealth and Inequality in Britain* (London, Faber & Faber, 1986), p. 73 and A.A. Jackson, *The Middle Classes 1900–1950* (Nairn, David St John Thomas, 1991), p. 16; for similar trends regarding wealth, see Stevenson, *British Society*, pp. 337–8; for the accelerating financial and demographic biases in favour of London, see Robson, 'Coming Full Circle', pp. 220, 222.

20. Vaughan, *Exciting Times*, chs 4–6.

21. *English Journey*, pp. 367, 380–1. For the general argument, see, for example, Robson, 'Coming Full Circle', pp. 227–8 and *passim*; Read, *English Provinces*, pp. 237–43; J.K. Walton, 'The North-west', *Cambridge Social History*, I, pp. 410–11; Stevenson, *British Society*, p. 314.

22. Family Life and Work Experience before 1918 Archive, ESRC Qualidata Centre: QDA/FLWE/24, Adams, p. 36; QD1/FLWE/33, Dr Bernard Thornley, p. 55; QD1/FLWE/282, John Clough, p. 40.

23. For a qualification of this generalization, especially for the 1920s, see B.M. Doyle, 'Urban Liberalism and the "Lost Generation": Politics and Middle Class Culture in Norwich, 1900–1935', *Historical Journal*, 38 (1995), 617–34.

24. For the limitations of such movement before 1914, see Trainor, 'The Gentrification of Victorian and Edwardian Industrialists', in A.L. Beier et al. (eds), *The First Modern Society: Essays in English History in Honour of Lawrence Stone* (Cambridge, Cambridge University Press, 1989), pp. 167–97; for the acceleration of the interwar years, see Jackson, *Middle Classes*, pp. 239–40.

25. *English Journey*, p. 359.

26. Ibid., p. 196.

27. Ibid., p. 359.

28. Ibid., pp. 28, 120.

29. Ibid., pp. 160–1. On the press, for example, see Read, *English Provinces*, pp. 247–51.

30. *Something in Linoleum*, chs 13–16.

31. As Read pointed out in the early 1960s, 'London as the headquarters of the pressure groups, of the national newspapers, of the B.B.C., and of Government and Civil Service is effectively as remote from individual Londoners as from individual Bradfordians or Mancunians'; 'Life in the sprawling suburbs of the capital is as near to desert aridity as life in the provinces.' (*English Provinces*, pp. 268, 286).

32. Ibid., pp. 97, 102, 106.

33. R. Cobb, *Still Life* and *A Classical Education* (London, Hogarth, 1992; first published 1983 and 1985 respectively).

34. *Something in Linoleum*, p. 78.

35. Essex Oral History Archive, QD1/FLWE/MUC/2 C707/473/1–4.

36. J.F.C. Harrison, *Scholarship Boy: A Personal History of the Mid-Twentieth Century* (London, Rivers Oram Press, 1995), p. 54. For the significant extent to which the provinces shared in the growth of privately owned suburban houses, see Jackson, *Middle Classes*, p. 30 and A. O'Carroll, 'Tenements to Bungalows: Class and the Growth of Home Ownership before "World War II"', *Urban History*, 24 (1997), 221–41; on the functioning of the grammar school system, see G. Sutherland, 'Education', *Cambridge Social History*, III, 162–3.

37. *English Journey*, pp. 365, 114.

38. E.L. Delafield, *The Diary of a Provincial Lady* (London, Virago, 1984, first published 1930). For the increasing ease of transport to London and the larger cities more generally, see Jackson, *Middle Classes*, pp. 239–40.

39. For the complex economic pattern of the interwar period, see Stevenson, *British Society*, p. 108 and J. Stevenson and C. Cook, *Britain in the Depression 1929–39* (2nd edn, London, Longman, 1994), chs 2 and 3.

40. *English Journey*, p. 32.

41. Ibid., p. 26.

42. For the semi-detached prosperity of Leicester in the 1930s, see Harrison, *Scholarship Boy*, p. 58.

43. *English Journey*, p. 158.

44. Ibid., pp. 302, 314, 312.

45. Ibid., p. 126.

46. Trainor, 'Urban Elites', p. 12; B. Keith-Lucas and P.G. Richards, *A History of Local Government in the Twentieth Century* (London, George Allen & Unwin, 1978), pp. 99–100, 111, 115; D.N. Cannadine, 'The Transformation of Civic

Ritual in Modern Britain: The Colchester Oyster Feast', *Past and Present*, 94 (1982), 123 n.63, 125–6, 126 n.76; B.M. Doyle, 'The structure of élite power in the early twentieth-century city: Norwich, 1900–35', *Urban History*, 24 (1997), 179–99.

47. Essex Oral History Archive, QD1/FLWE/282, John Clough, p. 54.

48. Essex Oral History Archive, QD1/FLWE/33, Dr Bernard Thornley.

49. Essex Oral History Archive, QD1/FLWE/MUC/2 C707/473/1–4; *Exciting Times*, p. 104. For the general importance of the provincial middle class in twentieth-century pressure groups increasingly headquartered in London, see Read, *English Provinces*, pp. 209–10 and section V, p. 223 and *passim*.

50. M. Pegg, *Broadcasting and Society 1918–1939* (London, Croom Helm, 1983), pp. 147, 159–61, 218–20, 223.

51. Jackson, *Middle Classes*, p. 98; ibid., pp. 294–7 and J. Cox, *The English Churches in a Secular Society: Lambeth, 1870–1930* (Oxford, 1982) for declining middle-class religious observance.

52. Cf. R. Weight, 'State, Intelligentsia and the Promotion of National Culture in Britain, 1939–45', *Historical Research*, 69 (1996), 83–101, which emphasizes social rather than geographical unity.

53. Cf. Read, *English Provinces*, section V.

54. Cf. Savage, *Property, Bureaucracy and Culture*, ch. 3.

55. Cf. P.L. Garside, 'London and the Home Counties' in Thompson, *Cambridge Social History*, pp. 471–539.

56. M.W. Dupree (ed.), *Lancashire and Whitehall: The Diaries of Sir Raymond Streat 1931–1957* (2 vols, Manchester, Manchester University Press, 1987).

57. E. Gordon and R. Trainor, 'Employers and Policymaking: Scotland and Northern Ireland, c. 1880–1939' in S.J. Connolly et al. (eds), *Conflict, Identity and Economic Development: Ireland and Scotland, 1600–1939* (Preston, Carnegie Publishing, 1995), pp. 254–67; Trainor, 'The Elite', pp. 251–2. Cf. N. Morgan and R. Trainor, 'The Dominant Classes' in W.H. Fraser and R.J. Morris (eds), *People and Society in Scotland: Volume II: 1830–1914* (Edinburgh, John Donald, 1990), pp. 103–37.

58. Vaughan, *Exciting Times*, p. 78. Cf. I. Bradley, *The English Middle Classes are Alive and Kicking* (London, Collins, 1982), pp. 119–25.

59. For an emphasis on the impact of post-1945 political centralization, see Robson, 'Coming Full Circle', pp. 224–5.

## CHAPTER 13

1. I would like to thank the participants in the conference on the history of the British middle class at Manchester Metropolitan University, and especially David Nicholls, John Quail and Bernhard Rieger, for their constructive responses to the original version of this paper. I would also like to thank Sylvia Schafer of the University of Wisconsin-Milwaukee for the invaluable suggestions she made as I revised it.

2. The literature spawned by each approach is now of considerable proportions. The best route into the social history of middle-class economic life is through the exchanges of W.D. Rubinstein and his critics. The essential shots in these campaigns include W.D. Rubinstein, *Men of Property: The Very Wealthy in*

*Britain Since the Industrial Revolution* (London, Croom Helm, 1981), and *idem, Elites and the Wealthy in Modern British History: Essays in Social and Economic History* (New York, St Martin's Press, 1987); Hartmut Berghoff, 'British Businessmen as Wealth-Holders, 1870–1914: A Closer Look', *Business History*, 33 (April 1991), 222–40 and his debate with Rubinstein in *Business History*, 34 (April 1992), 69–85; M.J. Daunton, '"Gentlemanly Capitalism" and British Industry 1820–1914', *Past and Present*, 122 (February 1989), 119–58 and his debate with Rubinstein in *Past and Present*, 132 (August 1991), 150–87; R. Pahl, 'New Rich, Old Rich, Stinking Rich?', *Social History*, 15 (May 1990), 229–39 and his debate with Rubinstein in *Social History*, 16 (October 1991), 359–65 and 17 (January 1992), 99; and F.M.L. Thompson, 'Life After Death: How Successful Nineteenth-century Businessmen Disposed of Their Fortunes', *Economic History Review*, second series, XLIII (February 1990), 40–61 and his debate with Rubinstein in *Economic History Review*, XLV (May 1992), 350–75. On the social history of middle-class cultural life one ought to begin with R.J. Morris, *Class, Sect and Party: The Making of the British Middle Class, Leeds 1820–1850* (New York, Manchester University Press, 1990) and Leonore Davidoff and Catherine Hall, *Family Fortunes: Men and Women of the English Middle Class, 1780–1850* (Chicago, University of Chicago Press, 1987).

3. The *Colliery Guardian* profiled 155 such 'Men of Note' in a series that ran from 1923 to 1929. The majority of the individuals the paper honoured had distinguished themselves as colliery owners, coal-company directors, mining engineers and mine managers, and coal merchants, but two-sevenths of the figures on its who's who list were government officials, educators, scientists and trade union leaders, none of whom were connected with the profit-seeking getting and selling of coal – an occupational distribution that in itself tells a good deal about the culture of this particular sector of the industrial middle class. This column and the élite it constructed are the subject of my 'The Voice of Industry and the Ethos of Decline' in *British Industrial Decline*, ed. Michael Dintenfass and Jean-Pierre Dormois (London and New York, Routledge, forthcoming) and a book-length study to be entitled *For Coal and Country*.

4. *Transactions of the Institution of Mining Engineers*, 115 (1955–6), 558.

5. Sir Richard A.S. Redmayne, *Men, Mines, and Memories* (London, Eyre & Spottiswoode Ltd, 1942), p. vii.

6. Ibid., p. 23.

7. Ibid., pp. 72, 248.

8. Ibid., p. 284.

9. Ibid., pp. 301–2.

10. Ibid., p. 285.

11. Ibid., pp. 292 and 297.

12. Ibid., p. 287. Leslie Hannah has written that 'if anyone deserves the title of the British Edison, it is surely Charles Merz, who, more than any of the British pioneers, shared Edison's capacity to view the engineer's duty as that of creating an economic and *integrated* system. It was Merz's unique combination of commercial vision, engineering skill and controlled business optimism which guaranteed that the crucial decisions in the [Newcastle upon Tyne Electric Supply] company's history paid off' and that made the firm's network 'the biggest integrated power system in Europe' before the First World War. See Leslie Hannah, *Electricity Before*

*Nationalisation: A Study of the Development of the Electricity Supply Industry in Britain to 1948* (London, Macmillan, 1979), p. 33 (emphasis in the original).

13. Redmayne, *Men*, p. 302.
14. Ibid., p. 310.
15. *Transactions*, 103 (1943–4), 264.
16. *Transactions*, 103 (1943–4), 263 (Wynne), 104 (1944–5), 172 (Clive), and 75 (1927–8), 60 (Smith). Hay's memoir of Clive was written with Basil Pickering and Holland's obituary of Smith with W.F. Clark. Neither of these co-authors appeared in the *Colliery Guardian*'s 'Men of Note' series.
17. *Transactions*, 91 (1935–6), 419.
18. *Transactions*, 104 (1944–5), 173 (Clive) and 114 (1954–5), 179 (Walker).
19. *Transactions*, 75 (1927–8), 60 (Smith), 104 (1944–5), 2 (Thornton) and 172 (Clive), and 103 (1943–4), 264 (Wynne).
20. *Transactions*, 101 (1941–2), 43–5.
21. *Transactions*, 75 (1927–8), 60 (Smith) and 101 (1941–2), 44–5 (Cadman).
22. *Transactions*, 104 (1944–5), 2 (Thornton) and 172 (Clive) and 115 (1955–6), 558 (Redmayne).
23. *Transactions*, 114 (1954–5), 179 (Walker) and 75 (1927–8), 61 (Smith).
24. *Transactions*, 104 (1944–5), 172 (Clive) and 115 (1955–6), 558 (Redmayne).
25. Dintenfass, 'Voice of Industry' and *For Coal and Country*.
26. For the several intellectual traditions that articulated the civic ideal in Britain, see Stefan Collini, *Public Moralists: Political Thought and Intellectual Life in Britain 1850–1930* (Oxford, Clarendon Press, 1991), pp. 67–74, 79–80, 86, 100–1, 186–7; Kenneth Fielden, 'Samuel Smiles and Self-Help', *Journal of British Studies*, XII (December 1968), 155–76; Jose Harris, 'Political Thought and the Welfare State 1870–1940: An Intellectual Framework for British Social Policy', *Past and Present*, 135 (May 1992), 116–41; Craig Jenks, 'T.H. Green, the Oxford Philosophy of Duty and the English Middle Class', *British Journal of Sociology*, XXVIII (December 1971), 481–97; Morris, *Class, Sect and Party*, p. 330; and Frank M. Turner, *The Greek Heritage in Victorian Britain* (New Haven, Yale University Press, 1981), pp. 358–68.
27. There is now something of a consensus, albeit a barely recognized one, in the social-historical literature about the integrative effects of the civic imperative in nineteenth-century Britain. The studies that tell this story include Brian Harrison, *Peaceable Kingdom: Stability and Change in Modern Britain* (Oxford, Clarendon Press, 1982), pp. 229–31, 240 (and p. 241 where the phrase 'the participatory values [of] the middle classes' appears); H.L. Malchow, *Gentleman Capitalists: The Social and Political World of the Victorian Businessman* (Stanford, CA, Stanford University Press, 1992), pp. 353, 379–80; Morris, *Class, Sect and Party*, pp. 325, 329; and Richard H. Trainor, *Black Country Elites: The Experience of Authority in an Industrial Area 1830–1900* (Oxford, Clarendon Press, 1993), pp. 359–61, 383–4. That the triumph of a 'professional ideal of public service, a sense that service to the community should come before the pursuit of profit', has been the distinguishing mark of British history in the twentieth century is the central theme of Harold Perkin, *The Rise of Professional Society: England since 1880* (London and New York, Routledge, 1989). The passage I quote can be found on p. 374.

## CHAPTER 14

This article is based on the 'City Lives' project at the National Life Story Collection, which I carried out jointly with Cathy Courtney as Project Officer, and on our joint book from the project, *City Lives* (London, Methuen, 1996). We owe particular debts for advice and support to Sir Nicholas Goodison and Sir Kenneth Kleinwort; to the many sponsors of the project within the City, including in particular the Esmee Fairbairn Trust; to the other interviewers, who included Professor Kathleen Burk; to the 78 interviewees on whom this analysis is based and to all those 150 City men and women who generously gave their time for their stories to be recorded and deposited in the British Library National Sound Archive. A full list of both sponsors and interviewees is printed in *City Lives*. For a longer discussion of the issues considered in this essay, see my two-part article, 'The Pyrrhic Victory of Gentlemanly Capitalism', *Journal of Contemporary History* (1997).

1.  David Kynaston, *The City of London: The Golden Years, 1890–1914* (London, Chatto & Windus, 1995); Youssef Cassis, *City Bankers, 1890–1914* (Cambridge University Press, 1994); Michael Lisle-Williams, 'Beyond the Market: the Survival of Family Capitalism in the English Merchant Banks', *British Journal of Sociology*, 35 (1984), 241–71, 333–62; Anthony Sampson, *The Anatomy of Britain* (London, Hodder & Stoughton, 1962) and *The Essential Anatomy of Britain: Democracy in Crisis* (London, Hodder & Stoughton, 1992).

2.  Kathleen Burk, *Morgan Grenfell 1838–1988: the Biography of a Merchant Bank* (Oxford, Oxford University Press, 1989); Richard Roberts, *Schroders: Merchants and Bankers* (London, Macmillan, 1992); David Kynaston *Cazenove and Co: a History* (London, Batsford 1991); David Kynaston and Richard Roberts (eds), *The Bank of England 1694–1994* (Oxford, Oxford University Press, 1995); Elizabeth Hennessy, *A Domestic History of the Bank of England 1930–1960* (Cambridge, Cambridge University Press, 1992).

3.  Martin Wiener, *English Culture and the Decline of the Industrial Spirit* (Cambridge, Cambridge University Press, 1981); P.J. Cain and Anthony Hopkins, *British Imperialism: Crisis and Deconstruction* (London, Longman, 1993); Will Hutton, *The State We're In* (London, Jonathan Cape, 1995); Paul Thompson, 'The Pyrrhic Victory of Gentlemanly Capitalism: the Financial Elite of the City of London, 1945–90', *Journal of Contemporary History*, 32 (1997), 283–304, 427–40.

4.  W.D. Rubinstein, *Capitalism, Culture and Decline in Britain, 1775–1990* (London, Routledge, 1993), p. 39.

5.  Russell Taylor, *Going for Broke: Confessions of a Merchant Banker* (New York and London, Simon & Schuster, 1993); Michael Lewis, *Liar's Poker: Two Cities, True Greed* (London, Hodder & Stoughton, 1989); Nick Leeson, *Rogue Trader: His Own Amazing Story* (London, Little, Brown, 1996). Only one great traditional merchant family bank now survives, Rothschilds.

6.  Cathy Courtney and Paul Thompson, *City Lives* (London, Methuen, 1996).

7.  Caryl Churchill, *Serious Money* (London, Methuen, 1987), p. 12.

8.  J. Attali, *A Man of Influence: Sir Siegmund Warburg, 1902–82* (London,

Weidenfeld and Nicolson, 1986); *City Lives*, Interview 98; Taylor, *Going for Broke*, p. 55.

9. *City Lives*, Interviews 35, 98.

10. John Fidler, *The British Business Elite: Its Attitudes to Class, Status and Power* (London, Routledge, 1981), p. 84.

11. Fidler, *The British Business Elite*, p. 84; David J. Hall, 'The European Business Elite', *European Business*, 23 (19), 23–9.

12. *City Lives*, Interviews 66 and 67.

13. Interview 65.

14. Interview 7.

15. Interviews 112, 9, 87, 116.

16. Interviews X, 15, 98.

17. Interviews 64, 87.

18. Interview 51.

19. Interview 3.

20. Jeremy Paxman, *Friends in High Places: Who Runs Britain?* (London, Michael Joseph, 1992), p. 275.

21. *City Lives*, Interviews 61, 26.

22. Interviews X, 12.

23. Interview 26.

24. Interviews 109, 63, 35, 44.

25. Interview 24.

26. Interview 43.

27. Interviews 18, 44.

28. Interview 46.

29. Interview 54.

30. Kynaston describes the Stock Exchange a century earlier as 'a club with a high proportion of overgrown schoolboys', and its members' customary larking, including newspaper-burning: *The Golden Years*, pp. 4, 23, 78–9, 104–5, 157–8, and plate 5. In the 1880s the Wool Exchange was also notably rough, 'a menagerie': p. 17.

31. *City Lives*, Interview 31.

32. Interview 27.

33. Interviews 54, 123.

34. Interview 21.

35. Kynaston, *City of London*, 1, p. 16.

36. Interview X.

37. Sampson, *Anatomy*, p. 353.

38. Kynaston, *Cazenove and Co*, pp. 242–3, 274–5.

39. Interview 51.

40. Interview Z.

41. Interview C409/007.

42. Interview 45.

43. Interview 46.

44. Interview 125.

45. The eurodollar market was created through the establishment of London as an 'offshore' base for meeting the growing financial needs of the European Community's new institutions. This proved the first crucial postwar move in recovering London's innovative role in international finance. New York was at this time also highly regulated. Some of the younger bankers therefore launched a market in eurodollars and eurobonds in London but in dollars and

therefore outside both systems. Although Warburgs had already started in Italy, the London market was initiated from 1957 by Hambros with the connivance of, but unregulated by, the Bank of England. Kathleen Burk, 'Witness Seminar of the Early Development of the Eurobond', *Contemporary European History*, 1 (1992), 65–88 – although this witness seminar focused on the 1960s and did not consider the role of Hambros; Taylor, *Going for Broke*, p. 64.

# BIBLIOGRAPHY OF KEY
# TEXTS

The following is a compilation of further reading and key texts recommended by the several contributors to this volume. It is not intended to be a comprehensive bibliography of the history of the modern middle class.

Abel, Richard, *The Legal Profession in England and Wales* (Oxford, Basil Blackwell, 1988)

Abercrombie, Nicholas, Hill, Stephen and Turner, Bryan S. (eds) *Dominant Ideologies* (London, Unwin Hyman, 1990)

Adelman, Paul *Victorian Radicalism: The Middle-class Experience, 1830–1914* (London, Longman, 1984)

Albers, Jan '"Papist traitors" and "Presbyterian rogues": religious identities in eighteenth-century Lancashire' in John Walsh, Colin Haydon and Stephen Taylor (eds) *The Church of England* c. *1689–c. 1833. From Toleration to Tractarianism* (Cambridge, Cambridge University Press, 1993)

Barry, J. 'The Making of the Middle Class?', *Past and Present*, 145 (1994)

—— and Brooks, Christopher (eds) *The Middling Sort of People: Culture, Society and Politics in England, 1550–1800* (London, Macmillan, 1994)

Becattini, G. 'The Marshallian Industrial District as a Socio-economic Notion' in Pyke, F., Becattini, G., and Sengenburger, W. (eds) *Industrial Districts and Inter-Firm Cooperation in Italy* (Geneva, International Institute for Labour Studies, 1990)

Behagg, C. *Politics and Production in the Early Nineteenth Century* (London, Routledge, 1990)

Belchem, John (ed.) *Popular Politics, Riot and Labour: Essays in Liverpool History 1790–1940* (Liverpool, Liverpool University Press, 1992)

Beresford, M.W. 'East End, West End: the Face of Leeds During Urbanization, 1684–1842', *Publications of the Thoresby Society*, LX and LXI, nos 131 and 132 (Leeds, 1985–6)

Best, Geoffrey *Mid-Victorian Britain 1851–1875* (London, Weidenfeld and Nicolson, 1971)

Biagini, Eugenio F. and Reid, Alastair J. (eds) *Currents of Radicalism: Popular Radicalism, Organized Labour and Party Politics in Britain, 1850–1914* (Cambridge, Cambridge University Press, 1991)

Black, Jeremy *The English Press in the Eighteenth Century* (London, Croom Helm, 1987)

Breuilly, John *Labour and Liberalism in Nineteenth-century Europe. Essays in Comparative History* (2nd edn, Manchester, Manchester University Press, 1994)

Brewer, John *Party Ideology and Popular Politics at the Accession of George III* (Cambridge, Cambridge University Press, 1976)

—— *The Sinews of Power. War, Money and the English State, 1688–1783* (London, Unwin Hyman, 1989)

Briggs, A. *The Collected Essays of Asa Briggs. Vol. 1: Words, Numbers, Places, People* (Brighton, Harvester Press, 1985)

Bush, M.L. (ed.) *Social Orders and Social Classes in Europe Since 1500. Studies in Social Stratification* (Harlow, Longman, 1992)

Bythell, D. *The Sweated Trades: Outwork in Nineteenth-century Britain* (Newton Abbot, Batsford, 1978)

Cain, P.J. and Hopkins, A.G. *British Imperialism. Vol. 1: Innovation and Expansion 1688–1914; vol. 2: Crisis and Deconstruction, 1914–1990* (London, Longman, 1993)

Cassis, Youssef *City Bankers, 1890–1914* (Cambridge, Cambridge University Press, 1994)

Caunce, S. 'Complexity, Community Structure, and Competitive Advantage Within the Yorkshire Woollen Industry, *c.* 1700–1850', *Business History*, 39 (1997), 26–43

Chandler, A.D. *Scale and Scope* (Cambridge, Mass., Belknap Harvard, 1990)

Chaytor, M. 'Household and Kinship: Ryton in the Late 16th and Early 17th Centuries', *Past and Present*, 10 (1980), 25–60

Clarke, Peter *Hope and Glory: Britain 1900–1990* (London, Allen Lane, 1996)

Coleman, D.C. 'Gentlemen and Players', *Economic History Review*, second series, XXVI (1973), 92–6

Colley, Linda *Britons. Forging the Nation 1707–1837* (New Haven and London, Yale University Press, 1992)

Collini, Stefan *Public Moralists: Political Thought and Intellectual Life in Britain 1850–1930* (Oxford, Clarendon Press, 1991)

Collins, B. and Robbins, K. (eds) *British Culture and Economic Decline* (London, Weidenfeld and Nicolson, 1990)

Cook, Chris *The Age of Alignment: Electoral Politics in Britain, 1922–1929* (London, Macmillan, 1975)

Corfield, Penelope J.(ed.) *Language, History and Class* (Oxford, Oxford University Press, 1991)

—— *Power and the Professions in Britain, 1780–1850* (London, Routledge, 1995)

Courtney, Cathy and Thompson, Paul *City Lives* (London, Methuen, 1996)

Cranfield, G.A. *The Development of the Provincial Newspaper, 1700–1760* (Oxford, Clarendon Press, 1962)

Crossick, Geoffrey (ed.) *The Lower Middle Class in Britain 1870–1914* (London, Croom Helm, 1977)

—— and Haupt, H.-G. *The Petite Bourgeoisie in Europe 1780–1914* (London, Routledge, 1995)

Crouzet, François *L'Economie Britannique et le Blocus Continental (1806–1813)* (Paris, Presses Universitaire de France, 1958), vol. II.

Curry, Patrick 'Towards a post-Marxist social history: Thompson, Clark and beyond' in Wilson, Adrian (ed.) *Rethinking Social History: English Society 1570–1920 and its Interpretation* (Manchester, Manchester University Press, 1993)

Daunton, Martin J. '"Gentlemanly Capitalism" and British Industry, 1820–1914', *Past and Present*, 122 (1989), 119–58

—— *Progress and Poverty: An Economic and Social History of Britain 1700–1850* (Oxford, Oxford University Press, 1995)

Davidoff, Leonore and Hall, Catherine *Family Fortunes. Men and Women of the English Middle Class, 1780–1850* (London, Hutchinson, 1987)

Dickenson, M.J. 'The West Riding Worsted and Woollen Industries, 1679–1770: An Analysis of Probate Inventories and Insurance Policies' (unpublished PhD thesis, University of Nottingham, 1974)

Dickinson, H.T. *Liberty and Property: Political Ideology in Eighteenth-century Britain* (2nd edn, London, Methuen, 1979)

Dinwiddy, J.R. *Radicalism and Reform in Britain, 1780–1850* (London, Hambledon Press, 1992)

Dirks, Nicholas B., Eley, Geoff and Ortner, Sherry B. (eds) *Culture/Power/History: A Reader in Contemporary Social Theory* (Princeton, Princeton University Press, 1994)

Doyle, B.M. 'The Structure of Elite Power in the Early Twentieth-century City: Norwich, 1900–35', *Urban History*, 24 (1997), 179–99

Dozier, Robert R. *For King, Constitution, and Country. The English Loyalists and the French Revolution* (Lexington, KY, University Press of Kentucky, 1983)

Dyos, H.J. 'Greater and Greater London: Notes on Metropolis and Provinces in the Nineteenth and Twentieth Centuries' in J.S. Bromley and E.H. Kossman (eds) *Britain and the Netherlands. Volume IV: Metropolis, Dominion and Province* (The Hague, Martinus Nijhoff, 1971)

Earle, P. *The Making of the English Middle Class: Business, Society and Family Life in London, 1660–1730* (London, Methuen, 1989)

Eastwood, David 'Patriotism and the English State in the 1790s' in Mark Philp, (ed.), *The French Revolution and British Popular Politics* (Cambridge, Cambridge University Press, 1991)

Elliott, Phillip *The Sociology of the Professions* (London, Macmillan, 1972)

Erickson, A.L. *Women and Property in Early Modern England* (London, Routledge, 1993)

Farnie, D.A. *The English Cotton Industry and the World Market 1815–1896* (Oxford, Clarendon Press, 1979)

Ferdinand, Christine *Benjamin Collins and the Provincial Newspaper Trade in the Eighteenth Century* (Oxford, Oxford University Press, 1997)

Fidler, John *The British Business Elite: Its Attitudes to Class, Status and Power* (London, Routledge, 1981)

Finn, Margot *After Chartism: Class and Nation in English Radical Politics, 1848–1874* (Cambridge, Cambridge University Press, 1993)

Foster, John *Class Struggle and the Industrial Revolution. Early Industrial Capitalism in Three English Towns* (London, Weidenfeld and Nicolson, 1974)

Foucault, Michel *Discipline and Punish. The Birth of the Prison* (New York, Pantheon Books, 1977)

—— *The History of Sexuality. Vol. 1: An Introduction* (New York, Vintage Books, 1990)

Fraser, D. *Urban Politics in Victorian Towns: The Structure of Politics in Victorian Cities* (Leicester, Leicester University Press, 1976)

—— and Sutcliffe, A. (eds) *The Pursuit of Urban History* (London, Edward Arnold, 1983)

Garrard, John *Leadership and Power in Victorian Towns, 1830–1880* (Manchester, Manchester University Press, 1983)

—— *The Great Salford Gas Scandal of 1887* (Altrincham, British Gas North Western, 1988)

Gellner, Ernest *Nations and Nationalism* (Oxford, Basil Blackwell, 1983)

Giddens, Anthony *A Contemporary Critique of Historical Materialism. Vol. 1: Power, Property and the State* (Berkeley and Los Angeles, University of California Press, 1981); *Vol. 2: The Nation State and Violence* (Cambridge, Polity Press, 1987)

Goldman, L. 'The Social Science Association, 1857–86: A Context for Mid-Victorian Liberalism', *English Historical Review*, 101 (1986), 95–134

Goodwin, Albert *The Friends of Liberty: The English Democratic Movement in the Age of the French Revolution* (London, Hutchinson, 1979)

Goody, Jack, Thirsk, Joan and Thompson, E.P. (eds) *Family and Inheritance. Rural Society in Western Europe, 1200–1800* (Cambridge, Cambridge University Press, 1976)

Greenleaf, W.H. *The British Political Tradition. Vol. 2: The Ideological Heritage* (London, Methuen, 1983)

Gregory, D. *Regional Transformation and Industrial Revolution: A Geography of the Yorkshire Woollen Industry* (London, Macmillan, 1982)

Gunn, S. 'The Failure of the Victorian Middle Class: A Critique' in J. Woolf and J. Seed (eds) *The Culture of Capital: Art, Power and the Nineteenth-century Middle Class* (Manchester, Manchester University Press, 1988)

—— 'The Manchester Middle Class, 1850–80' (unpublished Ph.D. thesis, University of Manchester, 1992)

—— 'The Ministry, the Middle Class and the "Civilizing Mission" in Manchester, 1850–80', *Social History*, 21 (1996), 22–36

Harris, Bob *Politics and the Rise of the Press: Britain and France 1620–1800* (London, Routledge, 1996)

Harris, Michael *London Newspapers in the Age of Walpole: A Study in the Origins of the Modern English Press* (London and Toronto, Associated University Presses, 1987)

Harris, O. 'Households and Their Boundaries', *Past and Present*, 13 (1982), 143–52

Harrison, Brian *Peaceable Kingdom. Stability and Change in Modern Britain* (Oxford, Clarendon Press, 1982)

Heaton, H. *The Yorkshire Woollen and Worsted Industries* (2nd edn, Oxford, Oxford University Press, 1965)

Holcombe, Lee *Wives and Property. Reform of the Married Women's Property Law in Nineteenth-century England* (Oxford, Martin Robertson, 1983)

Holmes, Geoffrey and Szechi, Daniel *The Age of Oligarchy. Pre-industrial Britain 1722–1783* (London, Longman, 1993)

Hudson, P. 'Proto-industrialisation: The Case of the West Riding', *Past and Present*, 12 (1981), 34–61

—— *The Genesis of Industrial Capital: A Study of the West Riding Wool Textile Industry*, c. *1725–1850* (Cambridge, Cambridge University Press, 1986)

Hutton, Will, *The State We're In* (London, Cape, 1995)

Ignatieff, Michael 'Total Institutions and Working Classes: A Review Essay', *History Workshop*, 15 (Spring, 1983)

Jackson, A. *The Middle Classes 1900–1950* (London, David St John Thomas, 1991)

Jenkins, T.A. *The Liberal Ascendancy, 1830–1886* (New York, St Martin's Press, 1994)

Joyce, Patrick (ed.) *Class* (Oxford, Oxford University Press, 1995)

Keeble, S.P. *The Ability to Manage* (Manchester, Manchester University Press, 1992)

Kidd, A.J. and Nicholls, D. *Gender, Civic Culture and Consumerism: Middle-class Identity in Britain, 1800–1940* (Manchester, Manchester University Press, 1999)

Kirk, Harry *Portrait of a Profession: A History of the Solicitor's Profession* (London, Oyez, 1976)

Kocka, Jürgen 'The Middle Classes in Europe', *Journal of Modern History*, 67, 4 (1995), 783–806

Koditschek, Theodore *Class Formation and Urban Society. Bradford, 1750–1850* (Cambridge, Cambridge University Press, 1990)

Kynaston, David *The City of London: The Golden Years, 1890–1914* (London, Chatto & Windus, 1995)

Lane, J. *Apprenticeship in England, 1600–1914* (London, University College London Press, 1996)

Lane, Tony *Liverpool: Gateway of Empire* (London, Lawrence and Wishart, 1987)

Lisle-Williams, Michael 'Beyond the Market: The Survival of Family Capitalism in the English Merchant Banks', *British Journal of Sociology*, 35 (1984), 241–71, 333–62

McCord, Norman *The Anti-Corn Law League 1838–1846* (London, George Allen & Unwin, 1958)

Malchow, H.L. *Gentleman Capitalists: The Social and Political World of the Victorian Businessman* (Stanford, CA, Stanford University Press, 1992)

Mandler, Peter *Aristocratic Government in the Age of Reform. Whigs and Liberals, 1830–1852* (Oxford, Clarendon Press, 1990)

Mann, Michael *The Sources of Social Power. Vol. 2: The Rise of Classes and Nation-States, 1760–1914* (Cambridge, Cambridge University Press, 1993)

Medick, H. 'The Proto-Industrial Family Economy: The Structural Function of Household and Family During the Transition from Peasant Society to Industrial Capitalism', *Social History*, 3 (1976), 292–315

Messinger, Gary S. *Manchester in the Victorian Age. The Half-Known City* (Manchester, Manchester University Press, 1985)

Millerson, Geoffrey *The Qualifying Associations: A Study in Professionalisation* (London, Routledge & Kegan Paul, 1964)

Money, John *Experience and Identity: Birmingham and the West Midlands, 1760–1800* (Manchester, Manchester University Press, 1977)

Morris, R.J. (ed.) *Class, Power and Social Structure in British Nineteenth-century Towns* (Leicester, Leicester University Press, 1986)

—— *Class, Sect and Party. The Making of the British Middle Class, Leeds 1820–1850* (Manchester, Manchester University Press, 1990)

Nenadic, S. 'Record Linkage and the Exploration of Nineteenth-century Social Groups: A Methodological Perspective on the Glasgow Middle Class in 1861', *Urban History Yearbook*, 14 (1987)

—— 'Businessmen, the Urban Middle Class and the "Dominance" of Manufacturers in Nineteenth-century Britain', *Economic History Review*, second series, 44 (1991)

Newman, Gerald *The Rise of English Nationalism: A Cultural History 1740–1830* (New York, St Martin's Press, 1987)

Nicholls, David, 'The English Middle Class and the Ideological Significance of Radicalism, 1760–1886', *Journal of British Studies*, 24 (1985), 415–33

O'Brien, Patrick and Quinault, Roland (eds) *The Industrial Revolution and British Society* (Cambridge, Cambridge University Press, 1993)

Offer, Avner *Property and Politics 1870–1914* (Cambridge, Cambridge University Press, 1981)

O'Gorman, Frank 'Pitt and the "Tory" Reaction to the French Revolution 1789–1815' in Dickinson, H.T. (ed.) *Britain and the French Revolution, 1789–1815* (London, Macmillan, 1989)

Parrott, Vivienne, 'Pettyfogging to Respectability: A History of the Profession of Solicitor in the Manchester Area 1800–1914' (unpublished PhD thesis, University of Salford, 1992)

Paxman, Jeremy *Friends in High Places: Who Runs Britain?* (London, Michael Joseph, 1992)

Perkin, Harold *The Origins of Modern British Society 1780–1880* (London, Routledge, 1969)

—— *The Rise of Professional Society: England since 1880* (London, Routledge, 1989)

Pickstone, J.V. *Medicine and Industrial Society: A History of Hospital Development in Manchester and Its Region, 1752–1946* (Manchester, Manchester University Press, 1985)

Poovey, M. *Making a Social Body: British Cultural Formation, 1830–1864* (Chicago, Chicago University Press, 1995)

Prest, John *Liberty and Locality. Parliament, Permissive Legislation, and Ratepayers' Democracies in the Nineteenth Century* (Oxford, Clarendon Press, 1990)

Price, Richard 'Historiography, Narrative, and the Nineteenth Century', *Journal of British Studies*, 35 (1996), 220–56

Pugh, Martin *The Making of Modern British Politics, 1867–1939* (Oxford, Basil Blackwell, 1982)

Quail, J.M. 'Proprietors and Managers: Structure and Technique in Large British Enterprise, 1890–1939' (unpublished PhD thesis, University of Leeds, 1996)

Ramsden, John *The Age of Balfour and Baldwin, 1902–1940* (London, Longman, 1978)

Randall, A. *Before the Luddites: Custom, Community and Machinery in the Woollen Industry, 1776–1809* (Cambridge, Cambridge University Press, 1991)

Read, D. *The English Provinces c. 1760–1960: A Study in Influence* (London, Edward Arnold, 1964)

Reader, W.J. *Professional Men: The Rise of the Professional Classes in Nineteenth-century England* (London, Weidenfeld and Nicolson, 1966)

Royal Commission on Historical Monuments of England *Rural Houses of West Yorkshire* (London, HMSO, 1986)

Rubinstein, W.D. *Men of Property: The Very Wealthy in Britain since the Industrial Revolution* (London, Croom Helm, 1981)

—— *Elites and the Wealthy in Modern British History* (Brighton, Harvester Press, 1987)

—— *Capitalism, Culture and Decline in Britain, 1750–1990* (London, Routledge, 1993)

Rule, John *Albion's People. English Society, 1714–1815* (London, Longman, 1992)

Sabel, C. and Zeitlin, J. 'Historical Alternatives to Mass Production: Politics, Markets and Technology in Nineteenth-century Industrialization', *Past and Present*, 108 (1985), 133–76

Sack, James J. *From Jacobite to Conservative. Reaction and Orthodoxy in Britain, c. 1760–1832* (Cambridge, Cambridge University Press, 1993)

Sampson, Anthony *The Anatomy of Britain* (London, Hodder & Stoughton, 1962)

—— *The Essential Anatomy of Britain: Democracy in Crisis* (London, Hodder & Stoughton, 1992)

Samuel, R. 'Workshop of the World: Steam Power and Hand Technology in Mid-Victorian Britain', *History Workshop*, 3 (1977), 6–72

Savage, M., Barlow, J., Dickens, P. and Fielding, T. *Property, Bureaucracy and Culture. Middle-class Formation in Contemporary Britain* (London, Routledge, 1992)

Saville, John *1848. The British State and the Chartist Movement* (Cambridge, Cambridge University Press, 1987)

—— *The Consolidation of the Capitalist State, 1800–1850* (London, Pluto Press, 1994)

Seed, John 'Capital and Class Formation in Early Industrial England', *Social History*, 18, 1 (1993), 17–30

Seldon, Anthony (ed.) *How Tory Governments Fall: the Tory Party in Power since 1783* (London, Fontana, 1996)

Smail, J. *The Origins of Middle Class Culture: Halifax, Yorkshire, 1660–1780* (Ithaca, Cornell University Press, 1985)

Stearns, Peter 'The Middle Class: Towards a Precise Definition', *Comparative Studies in Society and History*, 21 (1979), 377–96

Stedman Jones, Gareth *Languages of Class. Studies in English Working Class History 1832–1982* (Cambridge, Cambridge University Press, 1983)

Stevenson, J. *Britain 1914–1939: A Social History* (London, Penguin, 1984)

Stone, Lawrence (ed.) *An Imperial State at War* (London, Routledge, 1994)

Sykes, Robert 'Physical-Force Chartism: The Cotton District and the Chartist Crisis of 1839', *International Review of Social History*, XXX, 2 (1985), 207–36

Taylor, Miles *The Decline of British Radicalism, 1847–1860* (Oxford, Oxford University Press, 1995)

—— 'Rethinking the Chartists: Searching for Synthesis in the Historiography of Chartism', *Historical Journal*, 39, 2 (1996), 479–95

Taylor, Peter *Popular Politics in Early Industrial Britain: Bolton 1825–1850* (Keele, Ryburn Publishing, 1995)

Thompson, E.P. *The Making of the English Working Class* (rev. edn, Harmondsworth, Pelican, 1980)

Thompson, Paul 'The Pyrrhic Victory of Gentlemanly Capitalism: The Financial Elite of the City of London 1945–90', *Journal of Contemporary History*, 32 (1997), 283–304, 427–40

Tilly, Charles *Coercion, Capital, and European States, AD 990–1990* (Oxford, Basil Blackwell, 1990)

Trainor, Richard H. 'Urban Elites in Victorian Britain', *Urban History Yearbook* (1985), 1–17

—— *Black Country Elites: The Exercise of Authority in an Industrialised Area 1830–1900* (Oxford, Clarendon Press, 1993)

Turner, M.J. *Reform and Respectability: The Making of a Middle-class Liberalism in Early Nineteenth-century Manchester* (Manchester, Chetham Society, vol. 40, 1995)

Wahrman, Dror *Imagining the Middle Class: The Political Representation of Class in Britain* (Cambridge, Cambridge University Press, 1995)

Waller, P.J. *Democracy and Sectarianism: A Political and Social History of Liverpool, 1868–1939* (Liverpool, Liverpool University Press, 1981)

Weatherill, Lorna *Consumer Behaviour and Material Culture in Britain, 1660–1760* (London, Methuen, 1988)

Webb, S. and B. *Statutory Authorities for Special Purposes* (London, Longman, Green and Co., 1922)

Wiener, Martin J. *English Culture and the Decline of the Industrial Spirit, 1850–1980* (Cambridge, Cambridge University Press, 1981)

Wilson, Adrian, 'A Critical Portrait of Social History' in *idem* (ed.) *Rethinking Social History: English Society 1570–1920 and its Interpretation* (Manchester, Manchester University Press, 1993)

Wilson, Kathleen *The Sense of the People: People, Culture and Imperialism in England, 1715–1785* (Cambridge, Cambridge University Press, 1995)

Wilson, R.G. *Gentlemen Merchants: The Merchant Community in Leeds* (Manchester, Manchester University Press, 1971)

Winstanley, Michael 'Oldham Radicalism and the Origins of Popular Liberalism, 1830–52', *Historical Journal*, 36 (1993), 619–44

Wolff, Janet and Seed, John (eds) *The Culture of Capital: Art, Power and the Nineteenth-century Middle Class* (Manchester, Manchester University Press, 1988)

Wright, T. *The Autobiography of Thomas Wright of Birkenshaw, in the County of York, 1736–1797* (ed. T. Wright, John Russell Smith, 1864)

Wrightson, K. 'Household and Kinship in Sixteenth-century England', *Past and Present*, 12 (1981), 151–8

Yeo, E. Janes *The Contest for Social Science: Relations and Representations of Gender and Class* (London, Rivers Oram Press, 1996)

# INDEX